Study Guide

Essentials of Criminal Justice

EIGHTH EDITION

Larry Siegel
University of Massachusetts, Lowell

John L. Worrall
University of Texas at Dallas

Prepared by

Todd Scott
Schoolcraft Community College

WADSWORTH
CENGAGE Learning·

Australia · Brazil · Japan · Korea · Mexico · Singapore · Spain · United Kingdom · United States

For product information and technology assistance, contact us at **Cengage Learning Customer & Sales Support, 1-800-354-9706**

For permission to use material from this text or product, submit all requests online at **www.cengage.com/permissions** Further permissions questions can be emailed to **permissionrequest@cengage.com**

ISBN-13: 978-1-111-84183-6
ISBN-10: 1-111-84183-7

Wadsworth
20 Davis Drive
Belmont, CA 94002-3098
USA

Cengage Learning is a leading provider of customized learning solutions with office locations around the globe, including Singapore, the United Kingdom, Australia, Mexico, Brazil, and Japan. Locate your local office at: **www.cengage.com/global**

Cengage Learning products are represented in Canada by Nelson Education, Ltd.

To learn more about Wadsworth, visit **www.cengage.com/wadsworth**

Purchase any of our products at your local college store or at our preferred online store **www.cengagebrain.com**

Printed in the United States of America
1 2 3 4 5   17 16 15 14 13

Table of Contents

CHAPTER 1
Crime and Criminal Justice

LEARNING OBJECTIVES

After studying this chapter, students will:

1. Discuss the formation of the criminal justice system in America
2. Be able to define the concept of a criminal justice system
3. Be familiar with the basic component agencies of criminal justice
4. Comprehend the size and scope of the contemporary justice system
5. Trace the formal criminal justice process
6. Know what is meant by the term "criminal justice assembly line"
7. Characterize the "informal criminal justice system"
8. Describe the "wedding cake" model of justice
9. Be familiar with the various perspectives on justice
10. Understand the ethical issues involved in criminal justice

KEY TERMS AND CONCEPTS

criminal justice system (p. 6) The law enforcement, court, and correctional agencies that work together to effect the apprehension, prosecution, and control of criminal offenders. They are charged with maintaining order, enforcing the law, identifying transgressors, bringing the guilty to justice, and treating criminal behavior.

criminal justice process (p. 6) The process that takes an offender through a series of decision points, beginning with arrest and concluding with reentry into society.

Law Enforcement Assistance Administration (LEAA) (p. 7) Funded by the federal government's Safe Streets Act, this agency provided technical assistance and hundreds of millions of dollars in aid to local and state justice agencies between 1968 and 1982.

social control (p. 7) The process of external regulation of individual and/or group behavior. Social control can be informal and applied through sanctions (or rewards) employed by families, neighbors, peers, and so on. There is also formal social control, which is applied by the justice system through the legal process.

in-presence requirement (p. 10) The condition that in order to make an arrest for a misdemeanor, the arresting officer must have personally witnessed the crime being committed.

1

nolle prosequi (p. 10) The term used when a prosecutor decides to drop a case after a complaint has been formally made. Reasons for nolle prosequi include evidence sufficiency, crime seriousness, case pressure, political issues, as well as personal factors such as a prosecutor's own specific interests and biases.

grand jury (p. 10) A type of jury, responsible for investigating alleged crimes, examining evidence, and issuing indictments.

true bill of indictment (p. 10) A written statement charging a defendant with the commission of a crime, drawn up by a prosecuting attorney and considered by a grand jury. If the grand jury finds sufficient evidence to support the indictment, it will issue a "true bill of indictment."

information (p. 10) Charging document filed by the prosecution that forms the basis of the preliminary hearing.

probable cause hearing (p. 10) Term used in some jurisdictions for a preliminary hearing to show cause to bring a case to trial.

courtroom work group (p. 14) Made up of the prosecutor, defense attorney, judge, and other court personnel, this group helps streamline the process of justice through the extensive use of deal making and plea negotiation.

crime control perspective (p. 16) A model of criminal justice that emphasizes the control of dangerous offenders and the protection of society. Its advocates call for harsh punishments as a deterrent to crime.

rehabilitation perspective (p. 17) A model of criminal justice that views its primary purpose as helping to care for people who cannot manage themselves. Crime is an expression of frustration and anger created by social inequality that can be controlled by giving people the means to improve their lifestyle and helping them overcome any personal and or psychological problems caused by their life circumstances.

due process perspective (p. 18) Due process is the basic constitutional principle based on the concept of the privacy of the individual and the complementary concept of limitation on governmental power; a safeguard against arbitrary and unfair state procedures in judicial or administrative proceedings. Embodied in the due process concept are the basic rights of a defendant in criminal proceedings and the requisites for a fair trial. See Glossary for further details.

nonintervention perspective (p. 18) A justice philosophy that emphasizes the least intrusive treatment possible. Among its central policies are decarceration, diversion, and decriminalization. In other words, less is better.

decriminalization (p. 19) Reducing the penalty for a criminal act but not actually legalizing it.

2

legalization (p. 19) The removal of all criminal penalties from a previously outlawed act.

victimless crime (p. 19) An act that is in violation of society's moral code and therefore has been outlawed—for example, drug abuse, gambling, and prostitution. These acts are linked together because, although they have no external victim, they are considered harmful to the social fabric.

deinstitutionalization (p. 19) The movement to remove as many offenders as possible from secure confinement and treat them in the community.

pretrial diversion (p. 19) A program that provides non-punitive, community-based alternatives to more intrusive forms of punishment such as jail or prison.

widening the net of justice (p. 19) The charge that programs designed to divert offenders from the justice system actually enmesh them further in the process by substituting more intrusive treatment programs for less intrusive punishment-oriented outcomes.

equal justice perspective (p. 20) A view of justice that holds that all people should be treated equally before the law. Equality may be best achieved through the control of individual discretion in the justice process.

truth-in-sentencing laws (p. 20) A sentencing scheme requiring that offenders serve at least 85 percent of their original sentence before being eligible for parole or other forms of early release.

restorative justice perspective (p. 20) A view of criminal justice that advocates peaceful solutions and mediation rather than coercive punishments.

CHAPTER OUTLINE

I. **INTRODUCTION**
   1. Criminal justice is the system of law enforcement, adjudication, and correction that is directly involved in the apprehension, prosecution, and control of those who violate the criminal law and consequently charged with criminal offenses
      a. These agencies are responsible for:
         i. Protecting the public
         ii. Maintaining order
         iii. Enforcing the law
         iv. Identifying transgressors
         v. Bringing the guilty to justice
         vi. Treating criminal behavior
   2. Those who study criminal justice describe, analyze, and explain the behavior of criminal justice agencies authorized by law and statute to dispense justice:
      a. Police departments
      b. Courts

3

    c. Correctional agencies

3. Many people form opinions about criminal justice from the media which often leads to false impressions and unrealized expectations

II.   DEVELOPING THE CRIMINAL JUSTICE SYSTEM

1. During the 19th century America experienced a surge in violent behavior.

2. Responding to public outcry over rising crime rates in the United States and abroad, the first criminal justice agencies began to appear.

3. Formal criminal justice agencies developed the same time criminal gangs developed.

4. In 1829 the London Metropolitan Police, the first police agency, was established

5. First police agencies created in the U.S. were Boston (1838), New York (1844), and Philadelphia (1854).

6. The penitentiary, or prison, was created to provide nonphysical correctional treatment for convicted offenders

    a. These were considered "liberal" innovations

7. In 1919 the Chicago Crime Commission was created, it wasn't until this time that the work of the criminal justice system began to be recognized

    a. It still exists today

8. In 1931 President Herbert Hover appointed the National Commission of Law Observance and Enforcement commonly known as the Wickersham Commission

    a. Commission made a detailed analysis of the U.S. justice system and helped usher in the era of treatment and rehabilitation

A. The Modern Era of Justice

1. Can be traced to a series of research projects, beginning in the 1950s under the sponsorship of the American Bar Foundation

2. Identified many criminal justice procedures hidden from the public

    a. These procedures and their interrelationship were examined:

        i. Investigation

        ii. Arrest

        iii. Prosecution

        iv. Plea negotiations

3. Discretion by criminal justice professionals identified

4. For the first time, the term *Criminal Justice System* began to be used:

    a. A view that justice agencies could be connected in an intricate yet often unobserved network of decision making processes

B. Federal Involvement in Criminal Justice

1. In 1967 *The Challenge of Crime in a Free Society* was published by the President's Commission on Law Enforcement and Administration of Justice

    a. This was a group of practitioners, educators, and attorneys responsible for creating a comprehensive view of the criminal justice process and recommending reforms

2. In 1968 Congress passed Safe Streets and Crime Control Act which provided federal funds for state and local crime control and to restructure the justice system
3. Safe Streets and Crime Control Act funded the National Institute of Law Enforcement and Criminal Justice, renamed the National Institute of Justice (NIJ) in 1979
4. Also funded the Law Enforcement Assistance Administration (LEAA) which granted hundreds of millions of dollars in aid to local and state justice agencies – ended in 1982
5. Federal government continues to fund innovation through the NIJ and the Bureau of Justice Assistance (BJA)

III. **THE CONTEMPORARY CRIMINAL JUSTICE SYSTEM**
1. The criminal justice system is society's instrument of social control
   a. The task of the agencies of justice to prevent or deter outlawed behavior by apprehending, adjudicating, and sanctioning lawbreakers
2. Society maintains other forms of social control:
   a. Parenting and school discipline
      i. Designed to deal with moral not legal misbehavior
3. Only the criminal justice system maintains the power to control crime and punish those who violate the law
4. Contemporary criminal justice agencies are political entities whose structure and function are lodged within the separate branches of government:
   a. Legislative
   b. Judicial
   c. Executive
      i. Can be divided into three main components:
         a) Law enforcement – investigate crimes and apprehend suspects
         b) Court agencies – charges are brought, indictments submitted, trials conducted, and sentences formulated
         c) Correctional agencies – monitor, treat, and rehabilitate convicted offenders
5. Because of its varied and complex mission, the contemporary criminal justice system in the United States is monumental in size.
6. The cost of law enforcement, court agencies, and correctional agencies has increased significantly during the past 25 years.
7. Per capita expenditure for criminal justice functions is now more than 720 dollars each year for every American.
   a. Employs more than 2.4 million people
      i. 18,000 local law enforcement agencies employ 1,000,000 people
         a) 12,000 local
         b) 3,000 county sheriffs' offices
         c) 49 state police departments – all states except Hawaii
      ii. 2000 other specialized law enforcement agencies
         a) More than 700,000 are full-time sworn law enforcement officers and the remainder are civilian employees

5

        b)   600,000 are in local agencies
        c)   330,000 work in county sheriffs' offices
        d)   90,000 work for state police

  b. There are also:
    i. Nearly 17,000 courts
    ii. More than 8,000 prosecution agencies
    iii. About 6,000 correctional institutions
    iv. More than 3500 probation and parole departments

  c. Population
    i. Fourteen million individuals arrested each year
    ii. More than 2 million for serious felonies
    iii. One million convicted of felony charges in state and federal courts
    iv. One and a half million juveniles handled by juvenile courts

  d. Corrections
    i. More than 7 million people under some form of correctional supervision
    ii. Two million in jails and prisons
    iii. Five million in community supervision while on probation or parole
    iv. More people are likely to be convicted than in the past and serve more of sentence in jails or prisons
    v. Costs about 70 billion per year, about $30,000 per inmate.

IV. THE FORMAL CRIMINAL JUSTICE PROCESS

1. Criminal justice is a series of decision points from arrest to reentry into society
2. Decisions are a matter of individual discretion based on:
  a. Legal factors, considered legitimate influences:
    i. Charge seriousness
    ii. Available evidence
    iii. Suspect's prior record
  b. Extralegal factors involving the suspect:
    i. Race
    ii. Class
    iii. Gender
    iv. Age
3. Most cases are handled informally, and quickly
4. Concept of formal justice implies every defendant is given access to full range of legal rights under law
5. The formal criminal justice process includes the following:
  a. Initial contact, most likely as a result of police action:
    i. Suspect behavior
    ii. Victim initiated
    iii. Informant initiated
    iv. Initiated by response to a request by mayor or other political figure
    v. Confessions

b. Investigation – purpose of investigation is to gather sufficient evidence to identify a suspect and support a legal arrest, investigations can take minutes to years

c. Arrest is considered legal when the following conditions exist:
   i. Police officer has probable cause (sufficient evidence) to believe a crime has been or is being committed and the suspect is the person who committed it
   ii. The officer deprives the individual of freedom
   iii. Suspect submits to arrest, and lose his liberty
      a) Officer not required to use the word "arrest" or similar term, or bring subject to the station
      b) To make an arrest in a misdemeanor, the officer must have witnessed the crime personally, known as the in-presence requirement
   iv. Warrant issued by magistrate

d. Custody
   i. After arrest police may wish to search for evidence, interrogate the suspect, or encourage a confession
   ii. Witnesses may be brought to view suspect in lineup or one-on-one confrontation
   iii. Supreme Court has granted suspects in police custody protection from the unconstitutional abuse of police power such as:
      a) Illegal searches
      b) Intimidating interrogations

e. Charging factors (prosecutor)
   i. Evidence sufficiency
   ii. Seriousness of offense
   iii. Case pressure
   iv. Political issues
   v. Prosecutor's personal factors
      a) Interests
      b) Biases
   vi. No prosecution – *Nolle Prosequi*

f. Preliminary hearing/grand jury (prosecutor/courts)
   i. Government must prove probable cause to believe that a crime occurred and the suspect committed it
   ii. Grand jury (1/2 states and federal government use this)
      a) Closed hearing
      b) Sufficient evidence, grand jury issues true bill of indictment, which specifies the exact charges on which the accused must stand trial

g. Probable cause hearing (states that don't use grand jury system)
   i. Prosecution files a charging document, often called an information before a lower trial court
   ii. Open hearing
   iii. Defendant and defendant's attorney may appear and dispute the prosecutor's charges

7

      iv. Defendant will be called to stand trial if judge or magistrate finds the evidence factual and sufficient

h. Arraignment (courts)
    i. Formally charging defendant
    ii. Defendant notified of Constitutional rights
    iii. Plea entered, not guilty or guilty
    iv. Trial date set
    v. Bail issues considered

i. Bail/detention (courts/corrections)
    i. Bail – money posted to assure later appearance in court, allowing defendant to remain in the community prior to trial
    ii. Fail to show for trial– forfeit bail money
    iii. Those who cannot afford bail are held in custody
    iv. If defendant is stable member of the community and have committed non-violent crime they may be released on their own recognizance (promise to court) to show up for trial without bail

j. Plea bargaining (prosecution/courts) – Deal to drop or reduce charges for guilty plea – 90 percent of all cases are pled, rather than a criminal trial

k. Trial/adjudication (courts)
    i. Bench – judge decides
    ii. Jury – jury decides. If jury cannot reach a decision (deadlocked) the case is left unresolved, prosecution can decide if issue should be retried
    iii. Guilt must be beyond a reasonable doubt

l. Sentencing/disposition – if suspect is found guilty he will return to court for sentencing. Possible dispositions include:
    i. Fine
    ii. Probation
    iii. Community-based correction
    iv. Incarceration
    v. Death (in rare cases)

m. Appeal/post conviction remedies (courts)
    i. Defense can ask the trial judge to set aside the jury's verdict because the jury has made a mistake of law for example:
      a) Misinterpreting the judge's instructions
      b) Convicting on a charge not supported by the evidence
    ii. Appeal – Appellate courts review such issues as:
      a) Evidence properly used
      b) Judge conducted the trial in an approved fashion
      c) Jury properly selected
      d) Attorneys in the case acted appropriately
    iii. If court rules appeal has merit can order a new trial or release

n. Correctional treatment (corrections) – after conviction offender is placed under the jurisdiction of state or federal correctional authorities. Offender may serve:
    i. Probationary term
    ii. Placed in community correctional facility

           iii. Serve term in county jail, or state or federal prison

           iv. During this stage offender may be asked to participate in rehabilitation programs

      o. Release – most inmates do not serve full term due to parole, pardon, or good behavior

           i. Offenders sentenced to community supervision simply finish their term and resume their lives in the community

      p. Post release

           i. After termination of correctional treatment offenders may be asked to spend time in a community correction center which acts as a bridge between a secure treatment facility and freedom

B. The Criminal Justice Assembly Line
1. Developed by Herbert Packer
2. Criminal justice system is a "conveyer belt" of cases moving through the fifteen decision points in the formal criminal justice process
    a. At the investigatory stage police must decide whether to pursue the case or terminate involvement because of insufficient evidence to identify a suspect, case is too trivial, or victim does not want to press charges
    b. At bail stage decision must be made to set a high bail, reasonable bail, or release the defendant on own recognizance
3. Each decision point is critical to:
    a. Defendant
    b. Justice system
    c. Society
4. About 30 percent of people arrested on felony charges are eventually convicted in court, almost 1/3 convicted are sentenced to probation
5. For every 1000 crimes, about 20 people are sent to prison
6. The justice process can be viewed as a funnel that holds many cases at its mouth and relatively few at its end

V. **THE INFORMAL CRIMINAL JUSTICE SYSTEM**
1. The "ideal" criminal justice system
2. Cases settled using a more informal process based on cooperation and informal agreements between major actors in the justice process
3. Law enforcement and court officers are allowed tremendous discretion in their decision to:
    a. Make an arrest
    b. Bring formal charges
    c. Handle a case informally
    d. Substitute charges
4. Most criminal cases are cooperative ventures in which all parties work together to work out a deal, this is the courtroom work group
5. Courtroom workgroup consists of:
    a. Prosecutor
    b. Defense attorney
    c. Judge

  d. Other court personnel
   i. Helps streamline the process of justice through deal making and plea negotiation
   ii. Upward of 80 percent of all felony cases and over 90 percent of misdemeanors are settled without trial

A. The "Wedding Cake" Model of Justice – four layer cake metaphor developed by justice historian Samuel Walker. Layers include:
 1. Level I:
  a. Celebrated cases
  b. Receive full array of the criminal justice procedures, defense attorney, expert witnesses, jury trials, elaborate appeals
  c. Public is given the impression that most criminals are sober, intelligent, and most victims are members of the upper classes, a patently false impression
 2. Level II:
  a. Serious felonies – full attention of criminal justice system, Seriousness of offense places them in level II, these include:
   i. Rapes, robberies, burglaries
    a) Committed by experienced, repeat offenders
    b) Amount stolen in a burglary or larceny is significant
    c) Violent acts are committed by a stranger who uses a weapon
    d) Robberies involve large amounts of money taken by a weapon-wielding criminal
   ii. Receive full jury trial, and if convicted offenders can look forward to a prison sentence
 3. Level III:
  a. Less serious felonies:
   i. Committed by young or first time offenders
   ii. Involve people who knew each other or were otherwise related
  b. Typically adjudicated by dismissal, plea, charge reductions, or most typically a probationary sentence
 4. Level IV:
  a. Consist of millions of misdemeanors – most common, include:
   i. Disorderly conduct
   ii. Shoplifting
   iii. Public drunkenness
   iv. Minor assault
  b. Cases handled in assembly-line fashion
  c. Punishment is typically a fine or probation
 5. Model is useful because it helps us realize that public opinion about criminal justice is often formed on the basis of what happened in an atypical case

VI. **PERSPECTIVES ON JUSTICE**
 1. Criminal justice is far from a unified field
 2. Practitioners, academics, and commentators alike have expressed irreconcilable differences concerning its goals, purpose, and direction

3. No single view, perspective, or philosophy dominates the field
A. Crime Control Perspective
People who hold this view believe that the proper role of criminal justice system is to prevent crime through the judicious use of criminal sanctions to those who choose to violate the law. Key positions of this perspective are:
  1. Purpose of the justice system is to deter crime through application of punishment
  2. The more efficient the system, the greater its effectiveness
  3. The justice system is not equipped to treat people, but rather, to investigate crimes, apprehend suspects, and punish the guilty
B. Rehabilitation Perspective: Assumptions:
  1. Advocates of this perspective view crime as an expression of frustration and anger created by social inequality and justice system as a means of caring for and treating people who have been the victims of this inequality
  2. Crime can be controlled by giving people the means to improve their lifestyle and helping them overcome problems caused by their circumstances
  3. Assumes that people are at mercy of the following factors:
     a. Social
     b. Economic
     c. Interpersonal conditions and interactions
  4. Criminals are victims of:
     a. Racism
     b. Poverty
     c. Strain
     d. Blocked opportunities
     e. Alienation
     f. Family disruption
     g. Other social problems
  5. Advocates believe that government programs can reduce crime on two levels:
     a. Societal (macro)
        i. Prevent crimes before they occur
        ii. If legitimate opportunities increase, crime rates decline
        iii. Goal may be achieved at the neighborhood level by increasing economic opportunities through:
           a) Job training
           b) Family counseling
           c) Educational services
           d) Crisis intervention
     b. Individual (micro) — aimed at known offenders who have already violated the law. Best method to reduce crime and recidivism is through:
        i. Intensive one-on-one counseling
        ii. Pro-social changes in attitudes
        iii. Improved cognitive thinking patterns
     c. Key provisions of this model are:
        i. In the long run, it is better to treat than punish
        ii. Criminals are society's victims

11

        iii. Helping others is part of the American culture

        iv. Convicted criminals can be successfully treated within the confines of the justice system

C. Due Process Perspective

1. According to this perspective the justice system should be dedicated to providing fair and equitable treatment to those accused of crime by providing:
    a. Impartial hearings
    b. Competent legal counsel
    c. Evenhanded treatment
    d. Reasonable sanctions to ensure that no one suffers from racial, religious, or ethnic discrimination and their basic Constitutional rights are respected
2. Advocates point out that the criminal justice system is an adversarial process that pits the suspect against the state
3. If concern for justice and fairness did not exist, defendants could easily be overwhelmed; miscarriages of justice are common
4. Key positions of this perspective are:
    a. Every person deserves their full array of constitutional rights and privileges
    b. Preserving the democratic ideals of American society takes precedence over the need to punish the guilty
    c. Because of potential errors, decisions made within the justice system must be carefully scrutinized
    d. Steps must be taken to treat all defendants fairly regardless of their race, religion or socio-economic status

D. Nonintervention Perspective

1. Advocates believe criminal justice agencies should limit involvement with criminal defendants
2. Any intervention by the justice system is harmful and will have long-term negative effects
3. Labeling individuals as criminals disrupts their personal and family life and harms their self image. They may view themselves as bad, evil, outcasts, troublemakers, or crazy
4. When people are given less stigmatized forms of punishment, such as probation, they are less likely to become repeat offenders
5. Advocates call for limiting government intervention through:
    a. Decriminalization (reduction of penalties)
    b. Legalization of victimless crimes, such as possession of small amounts of marijuana
    c. Deinstitutionalization – removing nonviolent offenders from correctional system
    d. Pretrial diversion – first offenders, who commit minor crimes, placed in informal community-based treatment
6. Widening net of justice is the stigmatizing of offenders beyond the scope of their actual offense
7. Key elements of this perspective are:
    a. The justice process stigmatizes offenders
    b. Stigma locks people into a criminal way of life

c. Less is better. Decriminalize, divert, and deinstitutionalize whenever possible

E. Equal Justice Perspective
1. Advocates believe the greatest challenge facing the American criminal justice system is its ability to dispense fair and equal justice for all
2. Unequal and inconsistent justice results in:
   a. Disrespect for system
   b. Suspiciousness
   c. Frustration
   d. Increases the likelihood of recidivism
3. Offender's present behavior is punished, not past or future behaviors. Punishment must be equitably administered and based on "just deserts"
4. Reduce discretion in sentencing
5. Truth in sentencing laws – offender serves substantial portion of their sentence behind bars, limiting early release on parole
6. Key elements of the equal justice perspective:
   a. People should receive equal treatment for equal crimes
   b. Decision making in the justice system must be standardized and structured by rules and regulations
   c. Whenever possible, individual discretion must be reduced and controlled
   d. Inconsistent treatment produces disrespect for the system

F. Restorative Justice Perspective
1. Criminal justice system should promote a peaceful and just society; peacemaking should be the aim, not punishment
2. Inspired by religious and philosophical teachings ranging from Quakerism to Zen
3. Advocates view state punishments similar to violent acts by individuals
4. Mutual aid rather than coercive punishment is the key to a harmonious society
5. Resolution of the conflict between criminal and victim should take place in the community in which it originated and not in some far-off prison
6. Victim should be given a chance to voice his story, and offender can directly communicate his need for social reintegration and treatment
7. The goal is to enable the offender to appreciate the damage he has caused, to make amends, and to be reintegrated back into society
8. Most important elements of the restorative justice model are:
   a. Offenders should be reintegrated back into society
   b. Coercive punishments are self-defeating
   c. The justice system must become more humane

G. Perspectives in Perspective
1. During the past decade, crime control and justice models have dominated
2. Rehabilitation, due process, and non-intrusive treatment are still utilized
3. No single view is correct. Each individual must choose the perspective that best fits his or her own ideas and judgment

VII. **ETHICS IN CRIMINAL JUSTICE**
1. Ethics are difficult in criminal justice because moral ambiguity is the norm

     2. Ethics are important in criminal justice considering the power granted to individuals who control the system

     3. Without ethical decision making, constitutional and civil rights violations are possible

     4. The need for an ethical criminal justice system is further enhanced by cyber-age advances in record keeping and data recording

     5. Issues of privacy and confidentiality, which can have enormous economic, social, and political consequences, are now more critical than ever

A. Ethics and Law Enforcement

     1. Particularly important because police have authority to deprive people of liberty and use physical and deadly force

     2. Discretion in who they investigate, how far to investigate, and how much effort to investigate, such as the use of

        a. Undercover operations

        b. Listening devices

        c. Surveillance

     3. Police officers must be responsive to the public's demand for protection while at the same time remaining sensitive to the rights and liberties of those they must deter and control

     4. Police are the interface between the power of the state and citizens it governs

     5. Various national organizations such as the International Association of Chiefs of Police (IACP) produce model codes to guide conduct

B. Ethics and the Courts

     1. The prosecutor must seek justice for all parties in a criminal matter and should not be merely hunting a conviction, this includes

        a. Sharing evidence with the defense

        b. Not utilizing scare tactics or intimidation

        c. Represent public interest

     2. The prosecutor has dual-role:

        a. Represents people by:

           i. Presenting evidence

           ii. Upholding the law

           iii. Obtaining convictions

           iv. Representing the victim

        b. Represents the court by:

           i. Overseeing investigation of crime

           ii. Ensuring constitutional standards are met

           iii. Remedying constitutional violations

C. Defense Attorney

     1. The defense attorney seeks to uncover basic facts and elements of the criminal act

        a. Defense attorney has dual role as a defense advocate and officer of the court

        b. Job is not to decide whether client committed the offense, but to provide a vigorous defense and ensure prosecution meets its burden; proof beyond a reasonable doubt

D. Ethics and Corrections
1. Ethics are also challenged by the discretion afforded to correctional workers and administrators including:
   a. Reporting an inmate for rule violations which might jeopardize his or her parole
   b. Prisoner rights
   c. Abuses of power
      i. Examples include:
         a) Officer who beats an inmate
         b) Staff member who coerces sex from an inmate
      ii. Recent survey reported 8,210 allegations of sexual violence were reported by correctional inmates. About 42 percent were staff on inmates; 11 percent staff sexual harassment of inmates
2. Making ethical decisions is an increasingly important task in a society that is becoming more diverse, pluralistic, and complex every day

CHAPTER SUMMARY

The concept of criminal justice refers to the agencies that dispense justice and the process in which justice is carried out. America has a long history of crime and justice, and crime is not a recent development. America has experienced crime throughout most of its history.

There was little in the way of a formal criminal justice system until the nineteenth century, when the first police agencies were created. The term *criminal justice system* became prominent around 1967, when the President's Commission on Law Enforcement and the Administration of Justice began a nationwide study of the nation's crime problem. Criminal justice is a field that uses knowledge from various disciplines in an attempt to understand what causes people to commit crimes and how to deal with the crime problem.

The criminal justice system is society's instrument of social control. There are three basic component agencies of criminal justice: law enforcement, courts, and corrections. Criminal justice consists of the study of crime and the agencies concerned with its prevention and control. On an ideal level, the criminal justice system functions as a cooperative effort among the primary agencies.

The contemporary criminal justice system in the United States is monumental in size. It now costs federal, state, and local governments about $215 billion per year for civil and criminal justice, up more than 300 percent since 1982. The criminal justice system employs more than 2.4 million people. The system is massive because it must process, treat, and care for millions of people. More than 14 million people are still being arrested each year. There are more than 7 million people in the correctional system.

The formal criminal justice process consists of the actual steps the offender takes from the initial investigation through trial, sentencing, and appeal. The justice process contains fifteen stages, each of which is a *decision point* through which cases flow. Each of these decisions can have a critical effect on the defendant, the justice system, and society.

Some experts believe that the justice system processes cases in a routine, ritualized manner resembling an assembly line. Because justice is often dispensed in a hasty fashion, an innocent person may suffer or a dangerous individual may be released to continue to prey upon society. The system also acts as a "funnel": Most people who commit crime escape detection, and of those who do not, relatively few are bound over for trial, convicted, and eventually sentenced to prison.

In the "wedding cake" model of justice, the criminal justice system works informally to expedite the disposal of cases. Criminal acts that are very serious or notorious may receive the full complement of criminal justice processes, from arrest to trial. However, less serious cases are often settled when a bargain is reached between the prosecution and the defense.

The role of criminal justice can be interpreted in many ways. People who study the field or work in its agencies bring their own ideas and feelings to bear when they try to decide on the right course of action. Therefore, there are a number of different perspectives on criminal justice today. The crime control perspective is oriented toward deterring criminal behavior and incapacitating serious criminal offenders. The rehabilitation model views the justice system as a treatment agency focused on helping offenders, and counseling programs are stressed over punishment and deterrence strategies. The due process perspective sees the justice system as a legal process in which every defendant should receive the full share of legal rights granted under law. The nonintervention model is concerned about stigma and helping defendants avoid a widening net of justice, and advocates of this model call for employing the least intrusive methods possible. The equal justice model is concerned with making the system equitable in that the arrest, sentencing, and correctional process should be structured so that everyone is treated equally. The restorative justice model focuses on finding peaceful and humanitarian solutions to crime.

The justice system must deal with many ethical issues. It is sometimes difficult to determine what is fair and just and balance it with the need to protect the public.

DISCUSSION QUESTIONS

1. Can a single standard of ethics be applied to all criminal justice agencies? Or is the world too complex to legislate morality and ethics?

2. Describe the differences between the formal and informal justice systems. Is it fair to treat some offenders informally?

3. What are the layers of the criminal justice "wedding cake"? Give an example of a crime for each layer.

4. What are the basic elements of each model or perspective on justice? Which best represents your own point of view?

16

5. How would each perspective on criminal justice consider the use of the death penalty as a punishment for first-degree murder?

6. What amendments to the Constitution are the most important for the administration of justice?

MEDIA TOOLS

- The decision points in a flow chart format provide an overview of the criminal justice process from investigation to sentencing. The document provides a great reference to understand the decision making aspects that employees of the criminal justice system make. Provided by the United Nations Office on Drugs and Crime. http://www.unodc.org/documents/justice-and-prison-reform/cjat_eng/Decision_Points.pdf

- Read the transcript interview with Stephen Bright is a defense attorney, professor of law at Yale and Harvard Universities and director of the Southern Center for Human Rights. He describes the "assembly line justice." Provided by Frontline from American Public Television. http://www.pbs.org/wgbh/pages/frontline/shows/plea/interviews/bright.html

- For more information on the restorative justice perspective and examples of the use of the restorative justice model visit Restorative Justice Online at http://www.restorativejustice.org

- Listen to a debate about restorative justice. The audio file is provided by Justice Talking, National Public Radio. Listen at: http://www.justicetalking.org/ShowPage.aspx?ShowID=41

- For a more in-depth discussion on the due process rights of individuals and what due process really means visit the Cornell University Law School's Legal Information Institute at http://topics.law.cornell.edu/wex/due_process

PRACTICE TEST BANK

MULTIPLE CHOICE

1. The first police agency developed in 1829 in the city of
    a. Mesopotamia.
    b. New York.
    c. Boston.
    d. London.

    The first police agency developed in 1829 in the city of London

2. The modern era of criminal justice can be traced to the 1950s with a series of criminal justice research projects sponsored by the
    a. federal government.
    b. National Commission on Law Observance and Enforcement.
    c. President's Crime Commission.
    d. American Bar Foundation.

    The modern era of criminal justice can be traced to the 1950s with a series of a research projects sponsored by the American bar fund.

3. Beginning in the 1960s, millions of dollars in federal funds were granted to agencies to improve the criminal justice system in the U.S. through the federal
    a. Crime Commission.
    b. National Institute of Justice.
    c. Law Enforcement Assistance Administration.
    d. Bureau of Justice Statistics.

    1960's millions of $$ grant to agencies to improve CJ on US. through federal law enforcement assistance administration. assisted w/ $$

4. Which one of the following is society's system of social control?
    a. Pension
    b. Congress
    c. Criminal justice
    d. State government

    Societys system of social control is CJ.

5. The three main components of the criminal justice system are
    a. police, prosecutors, and defense attorneys.
    b. judges, prosecutors, and defense attorneys.
    c. defendants, police, and courts.
    d. law enforcement, courts, and corrections.

    3 main components law enforcement courts corrections

6. In general, for every 1,000 serious crimes, about _____ adults are sent to prison.
    a. 2
    b. 20
    c. 200
    d. 500

    every 1000 serious crimes 20 sent to prison

7. Herbert Packer described the criminal justice system as an "assembly line" whose fifteen stages are best described as
   a. pass/fail points.
   b. point of no return.
   c. decision points.
   d. thinking points.

8. Which branch of the criminal justice system is charged with monitoring, treating, and rehabilitating convicted offenders?
   a. Adjudication
   b. Corrections
   c. Courts
   d. Law enforcement

9. The law dictating that offenders serve a substantial portion of their prison sentence behind bars is known as
   a. standard sentencing.
   b. truthful sentencing.
   c. correct sentencing.
   d. truth in sentencing.

10. Level II of Walker's "Wedding Cake" model of justice include
    a. non-criminal violations.
    b. misdemeanors.
    c. serious felonies.
    d. celebrity crimes, high profile crimes.

11. The justice system should be dedicated to providing fair and equitable treatment to those accused of crime is the view of the
    a. due process perspective.
    b. restorative justice perspective.
    c. crime control perspective.
    d. nonintervention perspective.

12. Which perspective has fostered the rise of reduced sentencing discretion for judges?
    a. Nonintervention
    b. Equal justice
    c. Restorative justice
    d. Rehabilitation

13. Proponents of which perspective fear the harmful effects of stigmas and labels?
    a. Justice
    b. Crime control
    c. Rehabilitation
    d. Nonintervention

14. Which crime models have dominated in the last decade?
    a. Crime control, equal justice
    b. Restorative justice, non-intervention
    c. Rehabilitation, crime control
    d. Restorative justice, equal justice

    Crime control and equal justice have dominated in the last decade.

15. The great majority of criminal cases are settled
    a. through *habeas corpus*.
    b. without trial.
    c. by a sentence of imprisonment.
    d. by jury trial.

    majority cases are settled without trial.

16. At what stage will formal charges be read to a defendant?
    a. indictment
    b. arraignment
    c. arrest
    d. *nolle prosequi*

    Stage formal charges will be read to defendant is arraignment

17. Which perspective focuses on resolving the conflict between the offender and victim and reintegrating the offender back into the community?
    a. Restorative justice
    b. Crime control
    c. Rehabilitation
    d. Justice

    Perspec resolving conflict between offender and victim & offender back into the community is restorative justice.

18. The movement to remove as many offenders as possible from secure confinement into less restrictive environments is known as
    a. decriminalization.
    b. restorative justice.
    c. deinstitutionalization.
    d. nonintervention.

    movement to remove offender to less restrictive environments deinstitutionalization.

19. The operations of the stable, long-term courtroom work group are generally characterized by:
    a. conflict.
    b. adversarial confrontation.
    c. disposition by jury trial.
    d. cooperation.

    The operations of stable, long term courtroom work group are generally characterized by cooperation

20. The argument that criminals are society's victims is consistent with which perspective?
    a. Restorative justice
    b. Crime control
    c. Rehabilitation
    d. Justice

    criminals are societys victims rehabilitation.

21. Considering the formal criminal justice process, which one of the following depicts the correct chronological order?
    a. Correctional treatment, custody, grand jury, charging
    b. Investigation, charging, arraignment, plea bargaining
    c. Initial contact, bail, arrest, release
    d. Post release, appeal, preliminary hearing, detention

22. What is the term used to describe case dismissal by the prosecution?
    a. Habeas corpus
    b. Plea bargain
    c. Arraignment
    d. Nolle prosequi

    term used to describe dismissed case by prosecution is nolle prosequi

23. The viewpoint that efforts to help or treat offenders may actually stigmatize them beyond the scope of their actual offense is known as
    a. legalization.
    b. pretrial diversion.
    c. widening the net of justice.
    d. decriminalization.

    help or treat offenders may actually stigmatize them beyond the scope of their actual offense is widening the net of justice.

24. In 1931, President Hoover appointed the National Commission of Law Observance and Enforcement, which is commonly known today as:
    a. Assembly Commission
    b. Wickersham Commission
    c. Safe Streets Commission
    d. American Bar Commission

    1931 Hoover National commission of law observance and enforcement = Wickersham Commission.

25. Which one of the following individuals is not considered a member of the courtroom workgroup?
    a. Prosecutor
    b. Parole officer
    c. Judge
    d. Defense attorney

    Parole officer is not considered a member of the courtroom workgroup.

26. The most common outcome of level III crimes of the "Wedding Cake" model is
    a. dismissal.
    b. plea bargain.
    c. probation.
    d. reduction in charges.

    common outcome of level III crimes (less serious felony) is probation.

27. What layer of Walker's Wedding Cake Model of Justice contains the most celebrated and famous cases?
    a. level I
    b. level II
    c. level III
    d. level IV

    Most celebrated case is level I

28. Ethical considerations transcend _____ elements of the justice system.
    a. some
    b. all
    c. most
    d. no

    Ethical considerations transcent all elements of the justice system

29. The cannon of legal ethics in most states forbids the prosecutor from pursuing charges where there is no
    a. defense lawyer.
    b. probable cause.
    c. physical evidence.
    d. victim.

    Cannon of legal ethics forbids prosecutor from pursuing charges without probable cause.

30. _____ in criminal justice is an especially important topic today considering the power granted to those who control the justice system.
    a. Ethics
    b. Common sense
    c. Equality
    d. Honesty

    Ethics in cj is very important.

TRUE/FALSE

1. T F Police departments are an American creation.

2. T **F** In the United States, police agencies began to appear during the mid-eighteenth century.

3. T F The modern era of criminal justice began in the 1950s.

4. **T** F The justice system is formal social control.

5. T F The criminal justice system is viewed as having six main components.

6. T F Agents of the justice system have varied and differing perspectives on what justice is all about.

7. T **F** Upward of 80% of all felony cases and over 90% of misdemeanors are settled without trial.

8. **T** F Widening the net is a possible problem with pretrial diversion programs.

9. T F Rehabilitation is the most important value for the due process perspective.

10. T F The "Wedding Cake" model is a model of formal criminal justice.

11.   T   F   Walker's Level I cases are the most representative of the criminal justice system.

12.   T   F   The restorative justice perspective opposes violent punishments.

13.   T   F   Police officers serve as the interface between the power of the state and the citizens it governs.

14.   T   F   Rehabilitation advocates believe that criminals are society's victims.

15.   T   F   Agents of the justice system face ethical dilemmas on a daily basis.

FILL-IN-THE-BLANK

1.   The first American police agency created in 1838 was in the city of _Boston_.

2.   In 1967, President _Johnson_ established the President's Commission on Law Enforcement and Administration of Justice.

3.   The term _system_ is used to describe the interdependence of criminal justice agencies.

4.   One of the problems with some diversion programs is termed _widening_ the net (that they bring people into the system who would otherwise not have such contacts).

5.   The _crime control_ perspective focuses on incapacitation and deterrence.

6.   Determinate sentencing and the abolition of parole are positions of the _equal justice_ perspective.

7.   To get a case dismissed, a prosecutor files a document called a *nolle* _prosequi_.

8.   The criminal justice system is society's instrument of _social_ control.

9.   The prosecutor's charging document is usually called an _information_

10.   The _restorative justice_ perspective includes mediation and conflict resolution programs.

11.   Pretrial programs designed to keep offenders out of the system are called pretrial _diversion_ programs.

12. A community correction center acts as a bridge between a secure treatment center and absolute _freedom_ .

13. The _due_ process perspective focuses on the rule of law and rights of defendants.

14. The prosecutor, defense attorney, judge, and other court personnel make up the _courtroom_ workgroup.

15. The term _decriminalization_ refers to reducing the penalties for crime but not actually legalizing it.

ESSAY

1. List three different perspectives on crime and the main focus of each. Which one do you favor? Explain your position.

2. List and briefly describe the functions of the three main components of the criminal justice system. Which component do you think is the most important? Explain your position.

3. Who are the actors in the criminal justice system that face ethical issues? Describe one issue per actor?

4. List and describe the first 5 steps in the formal criminal justice process.

5. Discuss and label each of the layers of the criminal justice wedding cake. Provide examples of types of crimes that would be prosecuted at each level.

CHAPTER 1 ANSWER KEY

Multiple Choice

1. d [p. 6, LO1]   2. d [p. 7, LO1]   3. c [p. 7, LO1]   4. c [p. 7, LO2]   5. d [p. 8, LO3]

6. b [p. 12, LO3]   7. c [p. 12, LO4]   8. b [p. 8, LO3]   9. d [p. 20, LO9]   10. c [p. 15, LO7]

11. a [p. 18, LO9]   12. b [p. 17, LO9]   13. d [p. 19, LO9]   14. a [p. 21, LO9]   15. b [p. 14, LO7]

16. b [p. 10, LO5]   17. a [p. 20, LO9]   18. c [p. 19, LO9]   19. d [p. 14, LO7]   20. c [p. 17, LO9]

21. b [p. 9-12, LO5]   22. d [p. 12, LO5]   23. c [p. 19, LO9]   24. b [p. 7, LO1]   25. b [p. 14, LO5]

26. c [p. 15, LO7]   27. a [p. 15, LO7]   28. b [p. 21, LO10]   29. b [p. 24, L10]   30. a [p. 22, LO10]

True/False

1. F [p. 6, L01]   2. F [p. 6, LO1]   3. T [p. 7, LO2]   4. T [p. 7, LO3]   5. F [p. 8, LO3]

6. T [p. 21, LO9]   7. F [p. 14, LO7]   8. T [p. 19, LO9]   9. F [p. 18, LO9]   10. F [p. 14, LO8]

11. F [p. 15, LO8]   12. T [p. 20, LO9]   13. T [p. 22, LO10]   14. T [p. 17, LO9]   15. F [p. 22, LO10]

Fill-in-the-Blank

1. Boston [p. 6, LO1]   2. Johnson [p. 7, LO3]   3. system [p. 8, LO3]

4. widening [p. 19, LO9]   5. crime control [p. 17, LO9]   6. equal justice [p. 20, LO9]

7. prosequi [p. 10, LO5]   8. social [p. 22, LO2]   9. information [p. 10, LO5]

10. restorative justice [p. 21, LO9]   11. diversion [p. 19, LO9]   12. freedom [p. 12, LO5]

13. due [p. 18, LO9]   14. courtroom [p. 14, LO7]   15. decriminalization [p. 19, LO9]

Essay

1.   **List three different perspectives on crime and the main focus of each. Which one do you favor? Explain your position.**

- **Crime Control Perspective:** The proper role of the justice system is to prevent crime through the judicious use of criminal sanctions. Because the public is outraged by violent crimes, it demands an efficient justice system that hands out tough sanctions to those who violate the law. If punishment is swift, certain and severe, few would be tempted to break the law. In sum, this perspective views the justice system as protecting the public and controlling criminal elements.

- **Rehabilitation Perspective:** the proper role of the justice system is to help reduce crime on both a societal (macro) and individual (micro) level. Crime is an expression of frustration and anger created by social inequality and the justice system as a means for caring for and treating the victims of this inequality. Government programs can help reduce crime on both levels. People are at the mercy of social, economic, and interpersonal conditions and interactions. Punishment cannot deter these people but proper treatment may prevent their crimes. If legitimate opportunities increase, crime rates decline.

- **Due Process Perspective:** The justice system should be dedicated to providing fair and equitable treatment to those accused of crime. This means providing impartial hearings, competent legal counsel, evenhanded treatment and reasonable sanctions to ensure that no one suffers from racial, religious, or ethnic discrimination and that basic constitutional rights are respected.

- **Nonintervention Perspective:** Justice agencies should limit their involvement with criminal defendants. Ultimate effect of any involvement (whether intervention is designed to treat or punish) is harmful and will have long-term negative effects including stigmatizing offenders. Once involved in the criminal justice system, criminal defendants develop a permanent record that follows them the rest of their lives. In summary, decriminalize, divert and deinstitutionalize whenever possible.

- **Equal Justice Perspective:** The greatest challenge facing the American criminal justice system is its ability to provide fair and equitable treatment to those accused of crime. It is unfair for police to issue one offender a violation while letting another off with a warning for the very same violation or to have two people sentenced differently for committing the same crime. People should be judged on current behavior not past behavior or what they may do in the future. Decisions should be structured and standardized by rules and guidelines. Disparate treatment produces disrespect for the system.

- **Restorative Justice:** Criminal justice should promote a peaceful and just society and the justice system must become more humane. The system should aim for peacemaking, not punishment. Offenders should be reintegrated back into society.

[pp. 16-21, LO9]

2.   **List and briefly describe the functions of the three main components of the criminal justice system. Which component do you think is the most important? Explain your position.**

- **Law Enforcement Agencies:** Responsible for investigating crimes and apprehending suspects.

- **Court Agencies:** Responsible for managing charges and indictments, conducting trials and determining sentences.

- **Correctional Agencies:** Responsible for monitoring, treating and rehabilitating convicted offenders.

[pp. 8-9, LO3]

3.   **Who are the actors in the criminal justice system that face ethical issues? Describe one issue per actor?**

- **Law Enforcement**
  Ethical behavior is particularly important in law enforcement because, quite simply, police officers have the authority to deprive people of their liberty. And, in carrying out their daily activities, they also have the right to use physical and even deadly force. Depriving people of liberty and using force are not the only police behaviors that require ethical consideration. Police officers exercise considerable discretion when they choose whom to investigate, how far the investigation should go, and how much effort is required—for example, undercover work, listening devices, or surveillance. In carrying out their duties, police officers must be responsive to the public's demand for protection, while at the same time remaining sensitive to the rights and liberties of those they must deter and/or control. In this capacity, they serve as the interface between the power of the state and the citizens it governs. This duality creates many ethical dilemmas.

- **Prosecutor**
  Ethical concerns do not stop with an arrest. As an officer of the court and the "people's attorney," the prosecutor must seek justice for all parties in a criminal matter and should not merely be targeting a conviction. To be fair, prosecutors must share evidence with the defense, must not use scare tactics or intimidation, and must represent the public interest. It would be inexcusable and illegal for prosecutors to suppress critical evidence, a practice that might mean the guilty walked free and the innocent were convicted. Prosecutorial ethics become tested when the dual role of prosecutors cause them to experience role conflict. On the one hand, a prosecutor represents the people and has an obligation to present evidence, uphold the law, and obtain convictions as vigorously as possible. In the adversary system, it is the prosecutor who takes the side of victims and on whom they rely for justice.
  But as a fair and impartial officer of the court, the prosecutor must oversee the investigation of crime and make sure that all aspects of the investigation meet constitutional standards. If during the investigation it appears that the police have violated the constitutional rights of suspects—for example, by extracting an illegal confession or conducting an illegal search—then the prosecutor has an ethical obligation to take whatever action is necessary and appropriate to remedy legal or technical errors, even if it means rejecting a case in which the defendant's rights have been violated. Moreover, the canon of legal ethics in most states forbids the prosecutor from pursuing charges when there is no probable cause and mandates that all evidence that might mitigate guilt or reduce the punishment be turned over to the defense.

- **Defense Attorney**
  As an officer of the court the defense attorney seeks to uncover the basic facts and elements of the criminal act. In this dual capacity of being both a defensive advocate and an officer of the court, the attorney is often confronted with conflicting obligations to his client and profession. If the attorney assisted the client in engaging in illegal behavior, the attorney would be subject to charges of unprofessional conduct and even criminal liability.

What is said privately before trial, even at a plea discussion, is never admissible during trial. An attorney would be accused of incompetence if she or he did not try to raise reasonable doubt in every case. The attorney's job is not to decide whether the client committed the offense but to provide a vigorous defense and ensure that the client is not convicted unless the prosecution can prove its case beyond a reasonable doubt. And it is impossible to make the prosecution meet its burden without aggressively challenging the evidence, even if the defender believes the client committed the crime. However, if a client attempted to take the stand and lie about his involvement in the crime, then the attorney would be required to tell the judge.

- **Corrections**
  Ethics is also challenged by the discretion afforded to correctional workers and administrators. Discretion is involved when a correctional officer decides whether to report an inmate for disorderly conduct, which might jeopardize his or her parole. Correctional officers have significant coercive power over offenders. They are under a legal and professional obligation not to use unnecessary force or take advantage of inmate powerlessness. Examples of abuse would be an officer who beats an inmate, or a staff member who coerces sex from an inmate. The possibility that these abuses of power will be perpetrated exists because of the powerlessness of the offender relative to the correctional professional.

[pp. 21-25, LO10]

4. **List and describe the first 5 steps in the formal criminal justice process.**

    1. *Initial contact.* In most instances, an offender's initial contact with the criminal justice system takes place as a result of a police action:
        - Patrol officers observe a person acting suspiciously, conclude the suspect is under the influence of drugs, and take her into custody.
        - Police officers are contacted by a victim who reports a robbery; they respond by going to the scene of the crime and apprehend a suspect.
        - An informer tells police about some ongoing criminal activity in order to receive favorable treatment.
        - Responding to a request by the mayor or other political figure, the local department may initiate an investigation into an ongoing criminal enterprise such as gambling, prostitution, or drug trafficking.
        - A person walks into the police station and confesses to committing a crime—for example, killing his wife after an altercation.

    2. *Investigation.* The purpose of the criminal investigation is to gather sufficient evidence to identify a suspect and support a legal arrest. An investigation can take only a few minutes, as in the case where a police officer sees a crime in progress and can apprehend the suspect quickly. Or it can take many years and involve hundreds of law enforcement agents.

3. *Arrest.* An arrest is considered legal when all of the following conditions exist: (1) the police officer believes there is sufficient evidence, referred to as *probable cause*, that a crime is being or has been committed and the suspect is the person who committed it; (2) the officer deprives the individual of freedom; and (3) the suspect believes that he is now in the custody of the police and has lost his liberty.

4. *Custody.* After an arrest and while the suspect is being detained, the police may wish to search for evidence, conduct an interrogation, or even encourage a confession. Witnesses may be brought to view the suspect in a lineup or in a one-on-one confrontation.

5. *Charging.* If the arresting officers or their superiors believe that sufficient evidence exists to charge a person with a crime, the case will be turned over to the prosecutor's office. The prosecutor's decision to charge the suspect with a specific criminal act involves many factors, including evidence sufficiency, crime seriousness, case pressure, and political issues, as well as personal factors such as a prosecutor's own specific interests and biases.

[pp. 9-12, LO5]

5. **Discuss and label each of the layers of the criminal justice wedding cake. Provide examples of types of crimes that would be prosecuted at each level.**

- **Level or Layer I:** Comprised of celebrated cases and includes full level criminal justice service (e.g., competent defense attorneys, expert witnesses, jury trials, and elaborate appeals). This layer includes celebrity cases that garner attention from the media. The public is given the impression that most criminals are sober, intelligent people and most victims are members of the upper classes, a false impression.

- **Level or Layer II:** Comprised of serious felony cases—rapes, robberies and burglaries. Police, prosecutors and judges all agree that these are serious cases, worthy of the full attention of the justice system. The seriousness of the crime (e.g., repeat offenders, violence, weapon used, and high value) places it in level II.

- **Level or Layer III:** Comprised of felonies but these crimes are either less serious or committed by young or first time-time offenders or involve people who knew each other or were otherwise related. Level III cases may be dealt with by outright dismissal, a plea bargain, reduction of charges or probationary sentence.

- **Level or Layer IV:** Comprised of misdemeanors most often handled exclusively by lower courts in an assembly line fashion. Few defendants insist on exercising their Constitutional rights because the delay would cost them valuable time or money. Punishment is often a fine or probation.

[pp. 14-15, LO8]

Test on 10/2

CHAPTER 2
The Nature of Crime and Victimization

LEARNING OBJECTIVES

After studying this chapter, students will:

1. Be able to discuss how crime is defined
2. Be familiar with the methods used to measure crime
3. Discuss the strengths and weaknesses of crime measures
4. Recognize the trends in the crime rate
5. Comment on the factors that influence crime rates
6. Be familiar with international crime trends and how the United States compares to other nations
7. Know the various crime patterns
8. Understand the concept of the criminal career
9. Be able to discuss the characteristics of crime victims
10. Distinguish among the various views of crime causation

KEY TERMS AND CONCEPTS

consensus view of crime (p. 29) The belief that the majority of citizens in a society share common ideals and work toward a common good, and that crimes are acts that are outlawed because they conflict with the rules of the majority and are harmful to society.

View promote the consensus of various citizens

conflict view of crime (or critical view of crime) (p. 29) The belief that the law is controlled by the rich and powerful who shape its content to ensure their continued economic domination of society. The criminal justice system is an instrument of social and economic repression.

interactionist view of crime (p. 30) Criminal law reflects the values of people who use their social and political power to shape the legal system.

moral entrepreneurs (p. 30) People who wage moral crusades to control criminal law so that it reflects their own personal values.

crime (p. 30) A violation of societal rules of behavior as interpreted and expressed by a criminal legal code created by people holding social and political power. Individuals who violate these rules are subject to sanctions by state authority, social stigma, and loss of status.

Uniform Crime Report (UCR) (p. 30) The FBI's yearly publication of where, when, and how much serious crime occurred in the prior year.

official crime statistics (p. 30) Compiled by the FBI in its Uniform Crime Reports, these are a tally of serious crimes reported to police agencies each year.

part I crimes (p. 30) The eight crimes that, because of their seriousness and frequency, the FBI reports the incidence of in the annual Uniform Crime Report. Index crimes include murder, rape, assault, robbery, burglary, arson, larceny, and motor vehicle theft.

part II crimes (p. 30) All other crimes except the eight Part I crimes. The FBI records all arrests made for Part II crimes, including race, gender, and age information.

National Crime Victimization Survey (NCVS) (p. 32) The ongoing victimization study conducted jointly by the Justice Department and the U.S. Census Bureau that surveys victims about their experiences with law violation.

self-report survey (p. 33) A research approach that requires subjects to reveal their own participation in delinquent or criminal acts.

racial threat hypothesis (p. 40) The view that the percentage of minorities in the population shapes the level of police activity.

relative deprivation (p. 40) The view that extreme social and economic differences among people living in the same community exacerbate criminal activity.

broken windows hypothesis (p. 40) The view that deteriorated communities attract criminal activity.

chronic offender (p. 41) A delinquent offender who is arrested five or more times before he or she is eighteen and who stands a good chance of becoming an adult criminal; these offenders are responsible for more than half of all serious crimes.

rational choice theory (p. 45) People will engage in delinquent and criminal behavior after weighing the consequences and benefits of their actions. Delinquent behavior is a rational choice made by a motivated offender who perceives the chances of gain as outweighing any perceived punishment or loss.

biosocial theory (p. 45) Human behavior is a function of the interaction of biochemical, neurological, and genetic factors with environmental stimuli.

psychoanalytic view (p. 46) Criminals are driven by unconscious thought patterns, developed in early childhood, that control behaviors over the life course.

bipolar disorder (p. 46) A psychological condition marked by mood swings between periods of wild elation and deep depression.

social learning theory (p. 47) Behavior patterns are modeled and learned in interactions with others.

antisocial (sociopathic, psychopathic) personality (p. 48) Individuals who are always in trouble and do not learn from either experience or punishment. They are loners who engage in frequent callous and hedonistic behaviors, are emotionally immature, and lack responsibility, judgment, and empathy.

social structure theory (p. 48) A person's position in the social structure controls his or her behavior. Those in the lowest socioeconomic tier are more likely to succumb to crime-promoting elements in their environment, whereas those in the highest tier enjoy social and economic advantages that insulate them from crime-producing forces.

culture of poverty (p. 48) The crushing lifestyle of slum areas produces a culture of poverty, passed from one generation to the next, marked by apathy, cynicism, feelings of helplessness, and mistrust of social institutions, such as schools, government agencies, and the police.

subculture (p. 49) A substratum of society that maintains a unique set of values and beliefs.

cultural transmission (p. 49) The passing of cultural values from one generation to the next.

social process theory (p. 49) An individual's behavior is shaped by interactions with key social institutions—family, school, peer group, and the like.

social conflict theory (p. 50) Human behavior is shaped by interpersonal conflict, and those who maintain social power use it to further their own interests.

developmental theory (p. 50) Social interactions that are developed over the life course shape behavior. Some interactions (such as involvement with deviant peers) encourage law violations, whereas others (such as marriage and military service) may help people desist from crime.

CHAPTER OUTLINE

I. **INTRODUCTION**
    1. Accurate crime data measurement is important. Without it, it is impossible to assess the effectiveness of crime control policy
    2. It is difficult to prevent crime and/or treat criminals unless we understand criminal motivation

II. **HOW IS CRIME DEFINED?**
    1. Justice system centers around crime and its control
    2. Three views of how and why some behaviors become illegal and considered crimes while others remain noncriminal

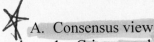

A. Consensus view
   1. Crimes are behaviors that are essentially harmful to a majority of citizens and have been controlled or prohibited by the existing criminal law
   2. Criminal law is a set of rules, codified by state authorities, which express the norms, goals, and values of the vast majority of society
   3. Criminal law also represents the consensus of public opinion and that there is general agreement about which behaviors society needs to control and which should be beyond state regulation
   4. Criminal law has a social control function, controlling behaviors that are inherently destructive and dangerous to maintain the social fabric and ensure peaceful functioning of society

B. Conflict View
   1. Content of criminal law shaped and controlled by the ongoing struggle between the rich and the poor, and the haves and have-nots
   2. Criminal law is created and enforced by the ruling class or the rich controlling the poor
   3. The law is an instrument that enables the wealthy to maintain their position of power and control the behavior of those who oppose their ideas and values
   4. Laws defining property crimes, such as larceny and burglary created to protect the wealth of the affluent

C. Interactionist View
   1. Criminal law is structured to reflect the preferences and opinions of people who hold social power and use their influence to shape the legal process
      a. These moral entrepreneurs wage moral crusades to control behaviors they view as immoral or wrong, or legalize behaviors they consider harmless
   2. Many crimes are not inherently evil or immoral, but are illegal because they conflict with social norms
   3. All views of crime generally agree:
      a. Criminal law defines crime
      b. Definition of crime is constantly changing and evolving
      c. Social forces mold the definition of crimes
      d. Criminal law has a social control function
   4. Definition of crime:
      a. Crime is a violation of social rules of conduct, interpreted and expressed by a written criminal code, created by people holding social and political power. Its content may be influenced by prevailing public sentiments, historically developed moral beliefs, and the need to protect public safety. Individuals who violate these rules may be subject to sanctions administered by state authority, which include social stigma and loss of status, freedom, and on occasion, their lives

III. **HOW IS CRIME MEASURED?**
   1. Important for criminal justice scholars to measure nature, extent, and trends in crime rate
   2. Three principal types of crime data:
      a. Official data

Focus on pinning the UCR down.

    b. Victim data

    c. Self-report data

A. Official Crime Data: The Uniform Crime Report (UCR)

    1. Compiled by the FBI; best known and most widely cited source of criminal records

    2. Published annually in *Crime in the United States*, serves as the nation's official crime statistic

    3. Compiled from reports from over 17,000 police agencies

    4. Analysis involves part I crimes:

        a. Criminal homicide

            i. Includes murder, nonnegligent manslaughter, and manslaughter by negligence

        b. Forcible rape

        c. Robbery

        d. Aggravated assault

        e. Burglary

        f. Larceny/theft

        g. Motor vehicle theft

        h. Arson

    5. FBI compiles the number of known offenses by:

        a. City

        b. County

        c. Standard metropolitan statistical area

        d. Geographical divisions of the U.S.

    6. UCR also calculates the number and characteristics of people who have been arrested for part I and part II crimes

    7. Part II crimes examples:

        a. Prostitution

        b. Drug trafficking

    8. UCR uses three methods to express crime data:

        a. Number of crimes reported to the police and arrests; expressed as raw figures

        b. Crime rates per 100,000 people

            i. Calculated:

                a) Number of reported crimes x 100,000 ÷ the total U.S. Population = rate per 100,000

        c. Changes in raw number and rate over time

B. How Accurate is the UCR?

    1. Many serious crimes are not reported to the police, why?

        a. Victims consider the crime trivial or unimportant and therefore choose not to call police

        b. Victim does not trust the police or has little confidence in the police and their ability to solve the crime

        c. Useless to report without insurance

        d. Victim fears reprisal from an offender's friends or family

        e. Victim is involved in illegal activity

2. Because of this, less than half of all criminal incidents are reported to the police
3. Reporting practices of police are not always standardized, affecting the validity of UCR statistics
4. Some departments define crimes loosely, or make systematic errors in UCR reporting
5. Hierarchy rule: In a multiple offense incident, only the most serious crime is reported
6. Although problematic, UCR is still widely used sources of criminal statistics
7. Because it is collected using a careful and systematic fashion, it is considered a highly reliable indicator of crime patterns and trends

C. The National Crime Victimization Survey (NCVS)
1. Federally sponsored
2. Utilizes large, carefully drawn sample of citizens who are asked about their experiences with criminal activity during the past year
3. NCVS enables crime experts to estimate the total number of criminal incidents that occur each year, including those that are never reported to police
4. Conducted through:
   a. Sample of housing units selected using a complex, multistage sampling technique
   b. Victimization rates are based on data collected during the calendar year
   c. Interviews almost 75,000 people in more than 40,000 households biannually
      i. So that is 150,000 interviews a year
      ii. Households stay in sample for three years
5. Those contacted are asked to report on frequency, characteristics, and consequences of their victimization for such crimes as:
   a. Rape
   b. Sexual assault
   c. Robbery
   d. Assault
   e. Theft
   f. Household burglary
   g. Motor vehicle theft
6. Considered relatively unbiased, valid estimate of victimization
7. Also has potential methodological problems:
   a. Victims may overreport due to their misinterpretation of events
   b. Victims may underreport because they are embarrassed about reporting crime to interviewers, afraid of getting in trouble, or simply forget an incident
   c. There may be an inability to record the personal criminal activity of those interviewed, such as drug use or gambling; murder is not included
   d. Sampling errors may produce a group of respondents that does not represent the nation as a whole
   e. An inadequate question format may invalidate responses

f. For some crimes, number of people reporting victimization is quite small, so that even slight year to year changes can produce significant results.

D. Self-Report Surveys

1. Asks subjects to describe their past and current criminal activities, including if they have ever been involved in:
   a. Substance abuse
   b. Theft
   c. Violence
   d. How often they engage in these activities
   e. What specific kinds of drugs they took
   f. Whether they acted alone or in groups
2. Anonymously administered to large groups of subjects in hopes individuals will answer accurately
3. Used to try to get at the "dark figure of crime," which are those crimes missed by statistics
4. Self report surveys used to determine extent of youth crime, prison inmate criminal histories, and drug users
   a. Monitoring the Future study conducted by the Institute of Survey Research at the University of Michigan, uses nationwide sample of approximately 50,000; has been collected annually for more than three decades.

E. Are Self-Reports Valid?

1. Problems
   a. Those that participate may:
      i. Exaggerate their criminal acts
      ii. Forget some of their criminal acts
      iii. Be confused about what is being asked
   b. Because of a mix of offenses in the crime index, comparisons between groups can be misleading
   c. High rate offenders or persistent substance abusers may be underrepresented or underreported
   d. Unlikely that most serious chronic offenders in the teenage population are the most willing to cooperate with university-based criminologists administering self-report tests
2. Using known group as comparison may reduce problems of validity
   a. There is evidence that kids known to be active delinquents self-report more crime than those who are not involved in criminality
   b. Research shows that when kids are asked if they have ever been arrested or sent to court their responses accurately reflect their true life experiences

F. Compatibility of Crime Data Sources

1. Despite differences
   a. UCR:
      i. Carefully tallied and contains data on the number of murders and people arrested
      ii. Omits the many crimes that victims choose not to report to police
      iii. Subject to the reporting caprices of police agencies

b. NCVS:
  i. Contains unreported crimes and characteristics of victims
  ii. Limited samples
  iii. Relies on personal recollections that may be inaccurate
  iv. Does not include data on important crime patterns, including murder and drug abuse
c. Self-reports:
  i. Can provide personal characteristics of offenders such as attitudes, values, beliefs, and psychological profiles
  ii. Relies on honesty of offenders and drug abusers, who are not known for their accuracy and integrity
2. Data seem more compatible than first believed
3. Crime patterns and trends recorded are often similar
4. All 3 similar in describing characteristics of criminals, and where and when crime occurs

IV. **CRIME TRENDS**
  1. Studies indicate that a gradual increase in crime rate, especially violent crime occurred from 1830-1860
  2. Following Civil War, rate increased significantly for about 15 years
  3. From 1880-World War I, number of reported crimes decreased
  4. Crime rate steadily declined until about 1930
  5. Crime rates increased gradually following 1930s until the 1960s, when growth rate became much greater
  6. By 1991, police recorded about 14.5 million crime
    a. Since then, the number of crimes has been in decline
  7. In 2009 about 10.5 million crimes reported
    a. NCVS recorded about 4 million violent crimes, and 16 million property crimes, and 133,000 personal thefts
      i. This number has dropped by half since 1991
  8. Victimization rate in 1991: more than 50 incidents per 1,000 population
    a. Today, less than 20 per 1,000 population
    b. 1991: More than 300 incidents of property crime per 1,000 population, today less than 150
  9. Violent crimes reported to police and violent victimizations reported to NCVS have been in decline for almost 2 decades.
A. Trends in Self-Reporting
  1. Use of drugs and alcohol increased in the 1970s, leveled off in the 1980s, increased until mid-1990s, and have been in decline ever since.
  2. In 2010, about 38% of 12th graders reporting using drugs in the past year, compared to 41% in 2000.
  3. MTF key findings:
    a. Marijuana use continues to increase
    b. Ecstasy following a recent decline appears to making a comeback
    c. Occasions of heavy drinking alcohol continues long-term decline among teens

V. **WHAT THE FUTURE HOLDS**
1. Risky to speculate about the future of crime trends because current conditions can change rapidly
2. Technological developments on the Internet have created new classes of crime that are not recorded by any of the traditional methods of crime measurement

VI. **CRIME PATTERNS**
1. By studying crime data, experts can determine if there are stable patterns in the crime rate
A. Ecological Patterns
1. Rural and suburban areas have much lower crime rates than large metropolitan centers, suggesting that urban problems – overcrowding, poverty, social inequality, narcotic use, and racial conflict are related to crime rates
2. Crime rates highest in summer months because people are less likely to be home, schools are closed, and young people have greater opportunity for criminal activity
3. West and South regions of U.S. have higher crime rates than Midwest and New England
B. Gender Patterns
1. Males have higher rates than females
   a. Arrest ratio male to female is 3 to 1 (3 male offenders to 1 female offender)
   b. For serious violent crimes, ratio is 4 to 1
   c. Female crime rates rose more rapidly between 1970-1995
      i. New female criminal, anti-social behaviors were similar to males
      ii. Gender role differences at home, school, and workplace narrowed
   d. Gender differences possibly explained through:
      i. Males are stronger and better able to commit violent crimes
      ii. Hormonal differences make males more aggressive
      iii. Girls are socialized to be less aggressive
      iv. Girls have better verbal skills and use them to diffuse conflict
      v. Males granted greater personal freedom and have more opportunities to commit crime
C. Racial Patterns
1. Minority group members are disproportionately involved in criminal activity
2. According to UCR, African Americans are 14 percent of the population but account for 39 percent of part I crime arrests and 30 percent of property crime arrests
3. Number of competing views on this issue:
   a. Systemic Racism
      i. Police more likely to arrest racial minorities because of discriminatory patterns
      ii. Racial threat hypothesis:
         a) As the percentage of minorities in the population increases, so too does the amount of social control that police direct at minority group members

Put on more activities in vactionland during the summer months that the community will attend rather than causing trouble.

inform my police that arrest minorities is causing a decrease in tourism, only arrest people who commit a crime

38

       b. Institutional Racism
         i. Racism infects educational, government and corporate institutions creating differential opportunity and powerlessness in the minority community
         ii. High rate of crime by African Americans is an expression of anger and frustration at an unfair social order
       c. Structural Racism
         i. African American families forced to reside in some of nation's poorest communities
    4. Most experts argue that when and if interracial economic, social, and educations difference converge, so will crime rates

D. Social Class Patterns
    1. Crime rates are highest in deprived, inner-city areas
    2. Level of poverty and social disorganization in an area can predict crime rate
    3. Why lower-class neighborhoods more crime prone:
       a. Produce high levels of stress and strain
       b. Family life is disrupted, and law-violating youth groups and gangs thrive
       c. Neighborhoods lack the ability to exert social control over residents
       d. Social differences are magnified when deteriorated areas are in close proximity to affluent neighborhoods, cause of a feeling of relative deprivation
       e. Experience of poverty, dilapidate housing, poor schools, broken families, drugs, and street gangs. Deteriorating neighborhoods attract law violators

E. Age Patterns
    1. Young people are disproportionately involved in criminal activity
    2. Peak age for property crime is 16 years, and 18 years for violence
    3. Males 65 and over are predominately arrested for alcohol-related offenses, while elderly females are arrested for shoplifting
    4. Elderly crime rate has been stable for 20 years
    5. Crime surge in 1980s due to amount of young people
    6. Age-crime relationship explained through:
       a. Youth culture favors risk taking, short run hedonism
       b. Adolescents are psychologically immature and unlikely to appreciate wrongfulness or destructive consequences
       c. Limited financial resources result in youths resorting to theft and drug dealing for income
       d. Young people have the energy, strength, and physical skills needed to commit crime
       e. Adolescents are aware that juvenile justice system is not as punitive as adult system

F. Career Patterns: The Chronic Offender
    1. Some people who begin committing crime at an early age and maintain a high rate of criminal violations throughout their lifetime are chronic offenders
    2. Responsible for a significant part of all serious crime behavior
    3. Conventional criminals usually have one-time, minor offense, while chronic offenders persist in serious crime

Give prisoners more attention and keep them doing community service work

39

4. Chronic offender has serious and persistent brushes with the law, building a career in crime, behavior is excessively violent and destructive

5. Research in chronic offenders: Marvin Wolfgang and associates – 1972 study *Delinquency in a Birth Cohort* followed criminal careers of 9,945 boys born in Philadelphia in 1945 until they reached 18 in 1963, they found:

   a. Two-thirds never had contact with police

   b. One-third had at least one contact

   c. Of repeat offenders, small group (627) arrested five times or more. These were chronic offenders:

      i. This group responsible for 51.9 percent of total arrests

      ii. Committed 71 percent of homicides, 73 percent of rapes, 82 percent of robberies, and 69 percent of aggravated assaults

      iii. Arrest and punishment did little. The stricter the sanction, the more likely they were to engage in repeated criminal behavior

6. Key findings about chronic offenders:

   a. Young persistent offenders grow up to become adult repeat offenders

   b. Chronic delinquents who commit the most serious violent acts have greatest chance of later becoming adult offenders

   c. Youth offenders who persist are more likely to abuse alcohol, get into trouble while in military service, become economically dependent, have lower aspirations, get divorced or separated, and have a weak employment record

7. Get-tough laws seen as a way to stop them, led to increased prison population and lower crime rates

G. Victim Patterns

1. About 21 million victimizations occur each year. Attributes:

   ★ a. Gender

      i. Men more likely than women to be victims of robbery, aggravated assault, and to a lesser extent, theft

      ii. Men more likely to be victimized by stranger

      iii. Women more likely to be victimized by husband, boyfriend, family member, or acquaintance

      iv. In 2/3 of sexual assaults, victim knows the attacker

   ★ b. Age

      i. Young people victimized more than older persons

      ii. Risk diminishes rapidly after 25 years of age

      iii. Those over the age of 65 (14 percent of population) account for 1 percent of violent victimizations

      iv. Those between the ages of 12 and19 (14 percent of population) account for more than 30 percent of victimizations

      v. Factors:

        a) Adolescents stay out late, go to public places, and hang out in places where crime is most likely to occur

        b) Teens spend great deal of time in presence of the adolescent peers, group that is most likely to commit crime

    c. Income

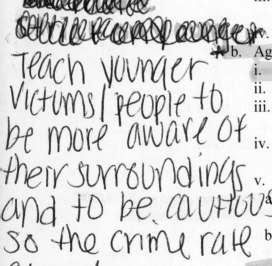

Teach younger victims/people to be more aware of their surroundings and to be cautious so the crime rate goes down.

      i.   Least affluent most likely to be victims of violent crime regardless of gender, race, or age

d. Marital Status

      i.   Single people are victimized more often, probably as a result of age, gender, and lifestyle

         a)   Unmarried people tend to be younger, young people have the highest victim risk

         b)   Widows, most likely older women, suffer much lower victimization rates because they interact with older people and are more likely to stay home

e. Race

      i.   African Americans are victims of violent crime at a higher rate than other groups

     ii. Crimes against African Americans are more serious than those against whites

         a)   Higher rates of aggravated assault

         b)   Whites more often victim of simple assault

         c)   African Americans are three times more likely to be robbery victims

         d)   Young African American males at higher risk of homicide:

              a. Murder rate 4 or 5 times higher than African American females

              b. Five to eight times higher than young white males

              c. Sixteen to twenty-two times higher than young white females

    iii. Young African American males tend to live in largest U.S. cities, in areas beset by alcohol and drug abuse, poverty, racial discrimination, and violence

f. Ecological Factors - Patterns in victim rate

      i.   Most occur in large urban areas

     ii. Most occur in evening hours (6pm to 6am), more serious after 6pm, less serious before 6pm

    iii. Most common areas are open, public areas, especially violent crimes such as rape, robbery, and aggravated assault

    iv. One of the most dangerous places is a public school building; about 10 percent of all U.S. youths are crime victims while on school grounds

     v. Overwhelming number of incidents involve a solo victim

    vi. Most perpetrators of assault not armed

         a)   Use of guns and knives about equal, no particular pattern

g. Victim-Offender Relationships -- Characteristics involving rape, assault, robbery:

      i.   50 percent of all violent crimes are committed by strangers

     ii. Women are more likely to be victimized by acquaintances

    iii. Offender is alone and over the age of twenty

    iv. 25 percent of victims say offender was young— 12 to 20 years of age

     v. Whites are offenders in majority of single offender rapes and assaults

    vi. Multiple offender robberies are more likely to be committed by African Americans

✱h. Repeat Victimization
    i. Research indicates those who are prior victims have higher chance of repeat victimization
    ii. Includes household victimization
    iii. Most likely to occur in high crime areas
        a) During a four year period in Ohio, 40 percent of all trauma patients in an urban medical center were repeat victims
    iv. Not fighting back, not reporting crime, and repurchasing stolen goods may encourage repeat victimization

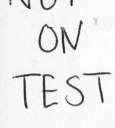

NOT ON TEST

VII. **CAUSES OF CRIME AND VICTIMIZATION**
1. Knowing why an individual commits a crime is important. Critical if programs are going to be devised to deter or prevent crime
2. Criminologist study crime data to:
    a. Identify the factors and motivations that predict crime
    b. Assess the most effective responses to crime
A. Choice Theory
1. Rational choice theory:
    a. Crime is a matter of rational decision making and personal choice
    b. Crime is attractive because it holds the promise of great rewards without corresponding effort
2. People of free will can choose between conventional or criminal behavior
3. Most people have potential to violate law because crime promises rewards and requires little effort
4. Before deciding to act, motivated offenders balance the risks and rewards of crime. Factors they consider:
    a. Personal factors: need for money, excitement, experience, or revenge
    b. Situational factors: how well target is protected, risk of apprehension, chance of hurting bystanders
    c. Legal factors: efficiency of police, threat of legal punishment, effect of prior criminal record
5. People will avoid anti-social behavior if they believe:
    a. Severity of punishment will outweigh potential gain
    b. There is a substantial likelihood they will be caught
    c. Punishment will be swift and timely
6. Punishments are primary deterrence to crime
7. Motivated people, after thoughtful consideration will commit crime if they believe that it will provide immediate benefits without the threat of long-term risks
    a. Benefits include:
        i. Monetary gains
        ii. Psychic rewards such as excitement and increased social status among peers
8. Veteran criminals may not fear some future punishment because they know apprehension risk is low

B. Biosocial theory – crime has a biological basis. Elements of the environment interact with biological factors to control and influence behaviors
  1. Sociobiological theories divided into three broad areas:
    a. Biochemical Factors
      i. Biochemical abnormality may lead to anti-social behaviors. These may include:
        a) Vitamin and mineral deficiencies
        b) Hormone imbalance
        c) Environmental contaminants
      ii. May begin before birth or later in life
        a) Maternal alcohol abuse and or smoking during gestation has long been linked to prenatal damage and subsequent antisocial behavior in adolescence
        b) Adolescents exposed to harmful chemicals and poor diet may be prone to antisocial behavior.
    b. Neurological Factors
      i. Some people may engage in anti-social behaviors because some neurological impairment reduces impulse control and self-control
      ii. Sometimes manifested as attention deficit/hyperactive disorder (ADHD) which has been linked to antisocial behavior

        a) About 3 percent of all U.S. children, primarily boys, are believed to have this disorder
        b) Results in poor school performance, bullying, stubbornness, and a lack of discipline
    c. Genetic Factors
      i. Violent behavior is possibly inherited and a function of a person's genetics
      ii. Adopted childhood studies
      iii. Twin studies
C. Psychological Theory
  1. Psychodynamic Theory
    a. Some people encounter problems during their early development that cause an imbalance in their personality
    b. Psychotics cannot restrain their impulsive behavior
    c. Schizophrenia – condition marked by incoherent thought processes, lack of insight, hallucinations, and feelings of persecution
    d. Bipolar disorder – moods alternate between periods of wild elation and deep depression
    e. Crime is a manifestation of feelings of oppression and the inability to develop the proper psychological defenses and rationales to keep these feelings under control
    f. Research findings are conflicting, mentally ill who are violent or criminal typically manifest other problems such as drug abuse and alcoholism
  2. Social Learning Theory
    a. Criminal behavior is learned through interactions with others, may be through experience from:

        i. Home life – children model their behavior after the violent acts of adults

        ii. Media – studies have shown that youths exposed to aggressive, antisocial behavior on television and in movies are likely to copy violent behavior

        iii. Attributes that makes some people especially prone to effects of media violence

3. Cognitive Theory

    a. Law violators may lack the ability to perform cognitive functions in a normal and orderly fashion

    b. Crime is viewed as an appropriate means to satisfy their immediate needs

4. Personality Theory

    a. Antisocial personality (previously sociopathic or psychopathic) personality

        i. Dangerous, aggressive individuals who act in a callous manner

        ii. Neither learn from their mistakes nor are deterred by punishment

        iii. From an early life, they have home lives filled with frustrations, bitterness, and quarreling

        iv. Exhibit low levels of guilt and anxiety and persistently violate the rights of others

        v. High intelligence enhances the destructive potential

        vi. Between 10 and 30 percent of all prison inmates can be classified as psychopaths or sociopaths

D. Social Structure Theory

1. Social structure theory

    a. Contrast in rich versus poor in America

    b. Culture of poverty:

        i. Marked by apathy, cynicism, helplessness, and distrust

        ii. Passed from one generation to the next

        iii. Members become part of the truly disadvantaged who suffer social and physical incivilities:

            a) Rowdy youth

            b) Trash and litter

            c) Graffiti

            d) Abandoned storefronts

            e) Burned-out buildings

            f) Littered lots

            g) Strangers

            h) Drunks

            i) Vagabonds

            j) Loiterers

            k) Prostitutes

            l) Noise

            m) Congestion

            n) Angry words

            o) Dirt and stench

   iv. Forced to endure substandard housing and schools in deteriorated inner-city, socially disorganized neighborhoods, and cut off from conventional society, the urban poor face a constant assault on their self-image and sense of worth

   v. A socially disorganized area is one in which institutions of social control, such as family, commercial establishments, and schools have broken down and can no longer carry out their functions

2. Strain Theory
   a. Most people in the United States desire wealth, material possessions, power, prestige, and other comforts
      i. Members of the lower class are unable to achieve symbols of success (wealth, material possessions) through conventional means; consequently they feel anger, frustration, and resentment
      ii. They can either accept their condition or choose an alternative method to achieve symbols such as theft, violence, or drug trafficking

3. Cultural Deviance Theory
   a. Combination of both strain and social disorganization
      i. Because of strain and social isolation a unique lower class culture has developed in disorganized poverty- ridden neighborhoods
      ii. Independent subcultures maintain a unique set of values and beliefs that are in conflict with conventional social norms
      iii. Criminal behavior is an expression of conformity to lower-class subcultural values, which stress toughness, independence, and standing up to authority
      iv. Cultural transmission is the process of handing down subcultural values from one generation to the next

E. Social Process Theory
   1. People commit crime as a result of the experiences they have while they are being socialized by various organizations, institutions, and processes of society
   2. People are most strongly influenced toward criminal behavior by:
      a. Poor family relationships
      b. Destructive peer-group relations
      c. Educational failure
      d. Labeling by agents of the justice system
   3. Social process theory has several branches:
      a. Social learning theory — People learn the techniques and attitudes of crime from close and intimate relationships with criminal peers; crime is a learned behavior
      b. Social control theory — Crime occurs when the forces that bind people to society are weakened or broken
      c. Social reaction (labeling) theory — People become criminals when significant members of society label them as such and they accept those labels as a personal identity

F. Social Conflict Theory
   1. Views the economic and political forces operating in society as the fundamental causes of criminality

      a. Criminal law and criminal justice systems are viewed as vehicles for controlling the poor members of society

      b. Crimes are defined in a way that meets the needs of the ruling classes

      c. Those in power control the content and direction of the law and legal system

G. Developmental Theory

    1. As toddlers, people begin relationships and behaviors that will determine their adult life course

    2. Disruptions in life's major transitions can be destructive and ultimately can promote criminality:

      a. Adolescents engaging in precocious sex

      b. Failing to graduate on time

      c. Teenage childbirth

      d. School yard bullying

    3. The propensity to commit crimes is neither stable nor constant; it is a developmental process

      a. Positive life experiences may help some criminals desist from crime for a while, whereas negative ones may cause them to resume criminal activities

CHAPTER SUMMARY

There are three views on how behaviors become crimes: consensus, conflict, and interactionist. The consensus view holds that criminal behavior is defined by laws that reflect the values and morals of a majority of citizens. The conflict view states that criminal behavior is defined in such a way that economically powerful groups can retain their control over society. The interactionist view portrays criminal behavior as a relativistic, constantly changing concept that reflects society's current moral values.

We get our information on crime from a number of sources, including surveys, records, interviews, and observations. One of the most important sources is the Uniform Crime Report (UCR) compiled by the FBI. This national survey compiles criminal acts reported to local police. The acts are called Part I crimes (murder, rape, burglary, robbery, assault, larceny-theft, and motor vehicle theft). The federal government also sponsors the National Crime Victimization Survey (NCVS), which asks people about their experiences with crime. A third form of information is self-report surveys, which ask offenders themselves to give information about their criminal behaviors. The validity of the UCR has been suspect because many people fail to report crime to police because of fear, apathy, or lack of respect for law enforcement. Many crime victims also do not report criminal incidents to the police because they believe that nothing can be done or that they should not get involved. Self-reports depend on the accuracy of respondents, many of whom are involved in drugs or delinquent. The crime patterns found in all three data sources may be more similar than some critics believe.

Crime rates were high in the 1930s, declined afterward, and then began a rapid increase in the 1960s. Crime rates have been in a downward trend for about a decade. Changes in the crime rate have been attributed to social factors, including the age structure of society. Crime rate increases have been tied to drug epidemics. The effect of the economy is less certain. Crime trends have been linked to the legalization of abortion and the amount of gangs. Crime rates were traditionally higher in the United States than abroad. In recent years, crime rates have been climbing overseas while declining in the United States. Crime rates may be spiraling upward in nations undergoing rapid changes in their social and economic makeup.

Crime occurs more often in large cities during the summer and at night. Some geographic areas (the South and West) have higher crime rates than others (the Midwest and New England). Arrest data indicates that males, minorities, the poor, and the young have relatively high rates of criminality. About 20 percent of all reported crimes are solved by police. However, a positive relationship exists between the seriousness of crimes and the probability of a successful clearance; that is, murders and rapes are solved much more often than car thefts or larcenies. Victims of crime tend to be poor, young, male, and members of a minority group.

One of the most important findings in the crime statistics is the existence of the chronic offender. Repeat, career criminals are responsible for a significant amount of all law violations. Career criminals begin their careers early in life and, instead of aging out of crime, persist into adulthood. About 20 million U.S. citizens are victims of crime each year. Like crime, victimization has stable patterns and trends. Violent crime victims tend to be young, poor, single males living in large cities. Females are more likely than males to be victimized by someone they know. Adolescents maintain a high risk of being physically and sexually victimized.

Diverse schools of criminological theory approach the understanding of the cause of crime and its consequences. Some theories focus on the individual, whereas others view social factors as the most important element in producing crime. Developmental theories integrate variables at the social, individual, and societal levels.

DISCUSSION QUESTIONS

1. Why are crime rates higher in the summer than during other seasons?

2. What factors account for crime rate trends?

3. What factors that are present in poverty-stricken urban areas produce high crime rates?

4. It seems logical that biological and psychological factors might explain why some people commit crime. How would a biologist or a psychologist explain the fact that crime rates are higher in the West than in the Midwest? Or that there is more crime in the summer than in the winter?

5. Considering the patterns that victimization takes, what steps should you take to avoid becoming a crime victim?

MEDIA TOOLS

- The FBI maintains an extensive website concerning the UCR. You may want to explore this site for use in this course and for use in future courses. Be sure to read about the proper use of UCR statistics and the report, Crime in the United States where you can view your local statistics. The site is available at: http://www.fbi.gov/about-us/cjis/ucr/ucr

- Information regarding the National Crime Victimization Survey (NCVS) is housed within the Bureau of Justice Statistics. Explore this site to learn more information regarding the NCVS. You can view the actual questionnaire used to gather the data and a great description on the methodology used to collect the data. The site is available at: http://bjs.ojp.usdoj.gov/index.cfm?ty=dcdetail&iid=245

- Another helpful resource to investigate how crime is measure is a comprehensive overview of the self-report survey Monitoring the Future. Visit the site to learn about how the survey is conducted, and review its most recent findings. This information can be found at http://monitoringthefuture.org

- You can find further explanations of all of the crime theories covered in this chapter at: http://www.crimetheory.com/

- Review a local report of chronic offenders prepared by the Mecklenburg County North Carolina Sheriff's Office in collaboration with University of North Carolina at Charlotte. Review the findings; are they consistent with what you have read in the chapter? The report, provided by the City of Charlotte and County of Mecklenburg, can be found at: http://charmeck.org/mecklenburg/county/MCSO/InmateInformation/Research/final0407.pdf

PRACTICE TEST BANK

MULTIPLE CHOICE

1. According to the consensus view of crime, the criminal law reflects
   a. the outcome of social conflicts.
   b. the beliefs of most people in society.
   c. historical accidents.
   d. our biological and genetic heritage.

2. The conflict view of crime assumes that the law reflects
   a. the interests of the powerful.
   b. consensus in society about what is wrong.
   c. conflicts between countries.
   d. natural law.

3. Which of the following is not a principal type of crime data?
   a. Official
   b. Victim
   c. Observation
   d. Self-report

4. Data on the number of victimizations in the U.S. are collected in the
   a. American Survey of Victims.
   b. Federal Crime Victimization Project
   c. Uniform Crime Reports.
   d. National Crime Victimization Survey.

5. The best known and most widely cited source of crime statistics is the
   a. Uniform Crime Report.
   b. National Self-Report Survey.
   c. National Prisoner Report.
   d. American Crime Survey.

6. When the crime rate is computed, for instance, the UCR indicates that the murder rate was 5.0 in 2009, it means about 5 people in every _____ were murdered.
   a. 10
   b. 100
   c. 1,000
   d. 100,000

49

7. People who wage moral crusades to control criminal law so that it reflects their own personal values are called
   a. moralists.
   b. moral entrepreneurs.
   c. moral crusaders.
   d. conflict theorists.

8. Research shows that the three major types/sources of crime data
   a. show similar patterns and trends.
   b. are wildly inconsistent.
   c. are totally incompatible.
   d. are useless for research purposes.

9. Many serious crimes are not reported to the police, which of the following is not a reason a victim would fail to report a serious crime?
   a. Distrust of the police
   b. Fear reprisal from offender
   c. Victim has "dirty hands"
   d. Victim was lazy

10. According to the hierarchy rule in reporting crime, if an armed bank robber commits a robbery, assaults a patron as he flees, steals a car to get away, and damages property during a police chase, which crime would be reported to the UCR?
    a. Assault
    b. Bank robbery
    c. Fleeing and eluding police
    d. Damage to property

11. Which country currently has the highest homicide rates?
    a. United States
    b. Colombia
    c. Denmark
    d. Brazil

12. Higher crime rates are generally found in
    a. small towns.
    b. rural areas.
    c. urban areas.
    d. suburbs.

13. In general, crime rates are higher in
    a. New England and the Midwest.
    b. West and South.
    c. Midwest and South.
    d. West and New England.

14. Which source of crime data collection asks subjects to describe their past and current criminal activities?
    a. UCR
    b. **Self-report survey**
    c. NCVS
    d. Arrest report survey

15. Elderly females are most likely to be arrested for which crime?
    a. Public drunkenness
    b. Drunk driving
    c. **Shoplifting**
    d. Writing bad checks

16. Which of the following groups are associated with high rates of victimization?
    a. Senior citizens and females
    b. **Teens and African Americans**
    c. Females and Asian Americans
    d. Males and Asian Americans

17. Which theory of crime assumes that persons have free will?   *Not on test*
    a. Sociobiological
    b. Psychological
    c. Social structure
    d. **Choice**

18. Social structure theories frequently point to _____ as the main cause of crime.
    a. socialization   *Not on test*
    b. **poverty**
    c. developmental problems
    d. the media

19. Social process theories tend to focus on _____ as the explanation for crime.
    a. **socialization**   *Not on test*
    b. neurological abnormality
    c. social strain
    d. early childhood trauma

20. Which of the listed crime data sources does not include data on important crime patterns, including murder and drug abuse?
    a. UCR
    b. Self-report
    c. **NCVS**
    d. NIBRS

51

21. According to the racial threat hypothesis, as the percentage of minorities in the population increases, so too does the amount of social control by police is an example of what type of theorized racism?
    a. Institutional
    b. Structural
    c. Educational
    d. Systemic

    NO on test

22. Data from the _____ is published in an annual volume and serves as the nation's official crime statistic.
    a. UCR
    b. self-report data
    c. UCC
    d. victim data

23. Which of the following describes relative deprivation?
    a. Residents experiencing stress and strain resort to crime to relieve these feelings
    b. Gangs thrive in a climate where adult supervision has been undermined
    c. Crime rates are high in deteriorated areas where the disadvantaged live in close proximity to the affluent
    d. Deteriorating neighborhoods attract law violators

24. According to this theory crime is a matter of rational decision making.
    a. Biosocial
    b. Choice
    c. Biochemical
    d. Neurological

    Not on test

25. According to this theory, crime is learned through interactions with others.
    a. Psychodynamic
    b. Cognitive
    c. Social learning
    d. Social process

    Not on test

26. Which crime measurement method is able to identify the "dark figure of crime?"
    a. UCR
    b. Self-report survey
    c. NIBRS
    d. NCVS

27. This culture is marked by apathy, cynicism, helplessness, and distrust.
    a. Poverty
    b. Violence
    c. Strain
    d. Deviance

Traci

28. According to this theory, the economic and political forces operating in society are the fundamental causes of criminality. *Not on test*
    a. Social reaction
    b. Social conflict
    c. Social process
    d. Social deviance

29. Which subculture values stress toughness, independence, and standing up to authority?
    a. Violent
    b. Lower-class
    c. Criminal
    d. Middle-class

30. Which group is disproportionally arrested when compared to their percentage of the population?
    a. Young
    b. Elderly
    c. Females
    d. Males

TRUE/FALSE

1. T **F** Psychoanalytic theory assumes that people learn to become criminals. *Not on test*

2. **T** F Biosocial theories focus on biochemical, neurological, and genetic factors. *Not on test*

3. **T** F The UCR is considered a highly reliable indicator of crime patterns and trends.

4. **T** F According to strain theory, people who adopt the goals of society but lack legitimate means to attain them, may seek alternatives, such as crime. *Not on test*

5. T **F** Choice theory assumes that criminals are the product of forces beyond their control. *Not on test*

6. **T** F Young people face a greater risk of victimization than older persons.

7. **T** F African Americans have higher rates of victimization than whites.

8. T **F** Males have lower crime rates than females.

9. **T** F Peak age for property crime is 16, and for violence 18.

10. T **F** NCVS data is considered biased.

11. T **F** Conflict theory is based on the work of Sigmund Freud. *Not on test*

12. (T) F   Social control theory assumes people are born bad and must be controlled to be good. **Not on test**

13. (T) F   Social structure theory assumes that a person's position in the social structure influences their behavior. **Not on test.**

A 14. (T) (F)   According to self-report studies, drug and alcohol use has been increasing since the mid 1990s.

15. (T) F   Crime in the U.S. has declined significantly for almost two decades.

FILL-IN-THE-BLANK

1. Men are much more likely than women to be victims of _Robbery_.

2. Criminal law defines _Crimes_.

3. Critics of self-report studies suggest that it is unreasonable to expect people to candidly admit to _illegal_ acts.

4. Marvin Wolfgang and other researchers have recognized the existence of a type of serious, repeat juvenile offender termed the _Chronic_ offender.

5. According to the _developmental_ theory of crime, the propensity to crime varies over a lifetime.

6. Social reaction theory is also known as _labeling_ theory. **Not on test**

7. According to _conflict_ theory, crimes are defined in ways that serve the interests of the ruling classes. **Not on test**

8. According to choice theories of crime, _deterrence_ is the best solution to the crime problem. **Not on test**

9. The _West_ and _South_ usually have significantly higher crime rates than the Midwest and New England.

10. Chronically antisocial persons who do not learn from experience and are incapable of caring for others are called sociopathic or _psychopathic_ personalities

11. The Uniform Crime Report is published by the _FBI_.

12. _Self report_ surveys ask respondents about their own criminal behavior.

13. Overall male and female arrest ratio is about _____3_____ male offenders to 1 female offender.

14. The _NCVS_____ is a federally sponsored survey that uses a large, carefully drawn sample of citizens who are asked about their experiences with criminal activity during the past year.

15. The theory that focuses on the interaction between the environment and biological factors is called biosocial or _sociobiological_ theory. *NOT ON TEST*

ESSAY

1. Define, compare, and contrast the social learning, social control, and social reaction theories of crime and their assumptions about why people are "good" or "bad."

2. Identify two of the four points the various views on crime agree on.

3. Victimization is not distributed equally throughout society. Discuss factors associated with high or low victimization rates.

4. Define, compare, and contrast the crime-measurement approaches taken in 1) the Uniform Crime Report, 2) the National Crime Victimization Survey, and 3) Self-report studies. Briefly discuss some of the weaknesses in each approach.

5. Identify the findings of the ecological and gender patterns related to the crime rate.

CHAPTER 2 ANSWER KEY

Multiple Choice

1. d [p. 29, LO1]   2. a [p. 29, LO1]   3. c [p. 31, LO2]   4. d [p. 32, LO2]   5. a [p. 31, LO2]

6. d [p. 31, LO2]   7. b [p. 30, LO1]   8. a [p. 33, LO3]   9. d [p. 31, LO5]   10. b [p. 32, LO3]

11. b [p. 38, LO6]   12. c [p. 37, LO7]   13. b [p. 37, LO7]   14. b [p. 33, LO2]   15. c [p. 41, LO7]

16. b [p. 42, LO9]   17. d [p. 45, LO10]   18. b [p. 48, LO10]   19. a [p. 49, LO10]   20. c [p. 32, LO3]

21. d [p. 40, LO7]   22. a [p. 31, LO2]   23. c [p. 40, LO7]   24. b [p. 45, LO10]   25. c [p. 47, LO10]

26. b [p. 33, LO2]   27. a [p. 48, LO10]   28. b [p. 50, LO10]   29. b [p. 49, LO10]   30. a [p. 40, LO5]

True/False

1. F [p. 46, LO10]   2. T [p. 45, LO10]   3. T [p. 32, LO2]   4. T [p. 49, LO10]   5. F [p. 45, LO10]

6. T [p. 42, LO9]   7. T [p. 43, LO9]   8. F [p. 42, LO9]   9. T [p. 41, LO7]   10. F [p. 32, LO8]

11. F [p. 29, LO2]   12. T [p. 50, LO10]   13. T [p. 48, LO10]   14. F [p. 34, LO4]   15. T [p. 34, LO4]

Fill-in-the-Blank

1. Robbery/Aggravated assault [p. 42, LO9]   2. Crime [p. 29, LO1]   3. illegal [p. 33, LO3]

4. chronic [p. 41, LO8]   5. developmental [p. 50, LO10]   6. labeling [p. 50, LO10]

7. conflict [pp. 50, LO10]   8. deterrence [p. 45, LO10]   9. West/South [p. 37, LO5]

10. psychopathic [p. 48, LO10]   11. FBI [p. 31, LO2]   12. Self-report [p. 33, LO3]

13. 3 [p. 39, LO5]   14. NCVS [p. 32, LO2]   15. sociobiological [p. 45, LO10]

Essay

1.   **Define, compare, and contrast the social learning, social control, and social reaction theories of crime and their assumptions about why people are "good" or "bad."**

Social Learning Theory: People learn to commit crime from exposure to antisocial behaviors. Criminal behavior depends on the person's experiences with rewards for conventional behaviors and punishments for deviant ones. Being rewarded for deviance leads to crime.

Social Control Theory: A person's bond to society prevents him or her from violating social rules. If the bond weakens, the person is free to commit crime.

Social Reaction Theory: People become criminals when significant members of society label them as such and they accept those labels as a personal identity.

Social learning theory assumes people are born "good" and learn to be "bad"; social control theory assumes people are born "bad" and must be controlled in order to be "good"; social reaction theory assumes that whether "good" or "bad," people are controlled by the reactions of others.

[pp. 49-50, LO10]

2.   Identify two of the four points the various views on crime agree on.

Although these views of crime differ, they generally agree on four points: (1) Criminal law defines crime; (2) the definition of crime is constantly changing and evolving; (3) social forces mold the definition of crimes; and (4) criminal law has a social control function.

[p. 30, LO1]

3.   Victimization is not distributed equally throughout society. Discuss factors associated with high or low victimization rates.

Gender:
- Men more likely to be victims of robbery, aggravated assault, and theft. Females more likely to be the victim of sexual assault. Women are much more likely to be attacked by a relative; about two thirds of all attacks against women are committed by a husband or boyfriend, family member, or acquaintance.

Age:
- Young people face a much greater victimization risk than older persons do. Victim risk diminishes rapidly after age 25. People over age 65 account for 1 percent of violent victimizations; teens aged 12 to 19 account for more than 30 percent of crime victims.

Income:
- The least affluent are the most likely to be victims of violent crimes, this association occurs across all gender, racial, and age groups.

Marital Status:
- Unmarried or never married people are victimized more often than married people or widows and widowers.

Race:
- African Americans experience violent crime victimizations at a higher rate than other groups. African Americans experience higher rates of aggravated assault, whereas whites are more often the victims of simple assault. African Americans are about three times as likely to become robbery victims as whites. Young African American males are also at great risk for homicide victimization. They face a murder risk 4 or 5 times greater than that of young African American females, 5 to 8 times higher than that of young white males, and 16 to 22 times higher than that of young white females.

Ecological Factors:
- Most victimizations occur in large urban areas. Most incidents occur during the evening hours (6:00 P.M. to 6:00 A.M.). More serious crimes take place after 6:00 P.M.; less serious, before 6:00 P.M. The most likely site for a violent crime such as rape, robbery, and aggravated assault— is an open, public area such as a street, park, or field. One of the most dangerous public places is a public school building. About 10 percent of all U.S. youths aged 12 to 19 (approximately 2 million) are crime victims while on school grounds each year.

[pp. 42-44, LO9]

4. Define, compare, and contrast the crime-measurement approaches taken in 1) the Uniform Crime Report, 2) the National Crime Victimization Survey, and 3) Self-report studies. Briefly discuss some of the weaknesses in each approach.

Uniform Crime Report
- Data is collected from records from police departments across the nation, crimes reported to police, and arrests.
- Strengths of the UCR are that it measures homicides and arrests. It is a consistent, national sample.
- Weaknesses of the UCR are that it omits crimes not reported to police, omits most drug usage, and contains reporting errors.

National Crime Victimization Survey
- Data is collected from a large national survey.
- Strengths of the NCVS are that it includes crimes not reported to the police, uses careful sampling techniques, and is a yearly survey.
- Weaknesses of the NCVS are that it relies on victims' memory and honesty, and it omits substance abuse.

Self-Report Surveys
- Data is collected from local surveys.
- Strengths of self-report surveys are that they include nonreported crimes, substance abuse, and offenders' personal information.
- Weaknesses of self-report surveys are that they rely on the honesty of offenders and that they omit offenders who refuse to or who are unable to participate and who may be the most deviant.

[pp. 31-34, LOs 2, 3]

5. Identify the findings of the ecological and gender patterns related to the crime rate.

There are distinct ecological patterns in the crime rate:

- Rural and suburban areas have much lower crime rates than large metropolitan centers, suggesting that urban problems—overcrowding, poverty, social inequality, narcotics use, and racial conflict—are related to crime rates.
- Crime rates are highest in the summer months, probably because people spend so much time outdoors and are less likely to secure their homes, and because schools are closed and young people have greater opportunity for criminal activity.
- Crime rates are also related to the region of the country. The West and South usually have significantly higher rates than the Midwest and New England.

Gender Patterns
UCR arrest data consistently shows that males have a much higher crime rate than females. The UCR arrest statistics indicate that the overall male–female arrest ratio is about 3 male offenders to 1 female offender; for serious violent crimes, the ratio is closer to 4 males to 1 female.
Male–female arrest ratios have been much higher in the past; typically, the violent crime ratio was 8:1 in favor of males
How can gender differences in the crime rates be explained? A number of views have been put forward:

- Males are stronger and better able to commit violent crime.

- Hormonal differences make males more aggressive.
- Girls are socialized to be less aggressive than boys and consequently develop moral values that strongly discourage antisocial behavior.
- Girls have better verbal skills and use them to diffuse conflict.
- Males are granted greater personal freedom and therefore have more opportunities to commit crime. Girls are subject to greater parental control.

When female arrest rates rose more rapidly than male arrests between 1970 and 1995, some experts began to proclaim the emergence of a "new female criminal" whose antisocial behaviors were similar to those of their male counterparts. The thinking was that as gender role differences at home, school, and the workplace narrowed, female participation in traditionally male-oriented forms of criminality such as violent crime and juvenile gang membership would increase. Today, the overall gender ratio in the arrest rate is 3:1 and for violent crime its 4:1.

[pp. 42-43, LO7]

Test on 10/2

CHAPTER 3

Criminal Law:
Substance and Procedure

LEARNING OBJECTIVES

1. Know the similarities and differences between criminal law and civil law
2. Understand the concept of substantive criminal law and its history
3. Discuss the sources of the criminal law
4. Be familiar with the elements of a crime
5. Define the term "strict liability"
6. Be able to discuss excuses and justification defenses for crime
7. Be familiar with the most recent developments in criminal law reform
8. Describe the role of the Bill of Rights in shaping criminal procedure
9. List the elements of due process of law
10. Know about the role the Supreme Court plays in interpreting the Constitution and shaping procedural law

KEY TERMS AND CONCEPTS

substantive criminal law (p. 54) A body of specific rules that declare what conduct is criminal and prescribe the punishment to be imposed for such conduct.

criminal procedure (p. 54) The rules and laws that define the operation of the criminal proceedings. Procedural law describes the methods that must be followed in obtaining warrants, investigating offenses, effecting lawful arrests, conducting trials, introducing evidence, sentencing convicted offenders, and reviewing cases by appellate courts.

civil law (p. 54) All law that is not criminal, including torts (personal wrongs), contract, property, maritime, and commercial law.

tort (p. 54) A personal injury or wrong for which an action for damages may be brought.

public law (p. 54) The branch of law that deals with the state or government and its relationships with individuals or other governments.

lex talionis (Latin for "law as retaliation") (p. 55) From Hammurabi's ancient legal code; the belief that the purpose of the law is to provide retaliation for an offended party and that the punishment should fit the crime.

stare decisis (p. 55) To stand by decided cases. The legal principle by which the decision or holding in an earlier case becomes the standard by which subsequent similar cases are judged.

common law (p. 56) Early English law, developed by judges, that incorporated Anglo-Saxon tribal custom, feudal rules and practices, and the everyday rules of behavior of local villages. Common law became the standardized law of the land in England and eventually formed the basis of the criminal law in the United States.

mala in se (p. 56) A term that refers to acts that society considers inherently evil, such as murder or rape, and that violate the basic principles of Judeo-Christian morality.

mala prohibitum (p. 56) Crimes created by legislative bodies that reflect prevailing moral beliefs and practices.

felony (p. 58) A more serious offense that carries a penalty of incarceration in a state prison, usually for one year or more. Persons convicted of felony offenses lose such rights as the right to vote, hold elective office, or maintain certain licenses.

misdemeanor (p. 58) A minor crime usually punished by less than one year's imprisonment in a local institution, such as a county jail.

actus reus (p. 58) An illegal act. The actus reus can be an affirmative act, such as taking money or shooting someone, or a failure to act, such as failing to take proper precautions while driving a car.

mens rea (p. 58) Guilty mind. The mental element of a crime or the intent to commit a criminal act.

strict liability crime (p. 60) Illegal act whose elements do not contain the need for intent, or mens rea; usually, acts that endanger the public welfare, such as illegal dumping of toxic wastes.

insanity (p. 61) A legal defense that maintains a defendant was incapable of forming criminal intent because he or she suffers from a defect of reason or mental illness.

self-defense (p. 61) A legal defense in which defendants claim that their behavior was legally justified by the necessity to protect their own life and property or that of another victim from potential harm.

entrapment (p. 61) A criminal defense that maintains the police originated the criminal idea or initiated the criminal action.

obitiatry (p. 65) Helping people take their own lives.

stalking (p. 65) The willful, malicious, and repeated following and harassing of another person.

USA Patriot Act (USAPA) (p. 67) A law designed to grant new powers to domestic law enforcement and international intelligence agencies in an effort to fight terrorism.

Bill of Rights (p. 67) The first ten amendments to the Constitution.

exclusionary rule (p. 68) Evidence seized in violation of the Fourth Amendment cannot be used in a court of law.

CHAPTER OUTLINE

I.   **INTRODUCTION**
1. The rule of law governs almost all phases of human enterprise, including crimes, family life, property transfer, and the regulation of interpersonal conflict
2. Can be divided into four categories:
    a. Substantive criminal law:
        i. Branch of law that defines crimes and punishment
        ii. Involves mental and physical elements of crime, crime categories, and criminal defenses
          a) Goals of substantive criminal law:
            1. Enforce social control
            2. Distribute retribution
            3. Express public opinion and morality
            4. Deter criminal behavior
            5. Punish wrongdoing
            6. Maintain social order
            7. Restoration
    b. Procedural law:
        i. Establishes basic rules of practice in government and the criminal justice system
        ii. Elements:
          a) Rules of evidence
          b) Law of arrest
          c) Law of search and seizure
          d) Questions of appeal
          e) Jury selection
          f) Right to counsel
    c. Civil law:
        i. Rules that govern relations between private parties (individuals and organizations)
        ii. Resolves, controls, and shapes personal interactions that may involve:
          a) Contracts
          b) Wills and trusts
          c) Property ownership
          d) Commerce

d. Public or administrative law
  i. The branch of law that deals with the government and its relationships with individuals or other governments
  ii. It governs the administration and regulation of city, county, state, and federal government agencies
  iii. Overlap between branches of law
     a) A victim of a criminal act may sue the perpetrator for damages in a civil tort, even if person is found not guilty in criminal action
     b) Evidence standard in a tort claim is less than standard for a criminal conviction:
     c) Preponderance of the evidence compared to beyond a reasonable doubt
  iv. Governments also sue perpetrators, but most common in white collar crimes such as:
     a) Mail fraud
     b) Wire fraud
     c) Tax-related fraud
     d) Computer fraud
     e) Money laundering violations

II. **HISTORICAL DEVELOPMENT OF THE CRIMINAL LAW**
  1. Roots to U.S. law traced back to:
     a. Babylonian code of Hammurabi (2000 BCE)
        i. Hammurabi's concept of lex talionis (an eye for an eye) still guides proportionality in punishment
     b. Mosaic code of Israelites (1200 BCE)
        i. Better known as the Ten Commandments
           a) Contains prohibitions against theft, violence, and perjury
  2. Early formal legal codes were lost during the Dark Ages (500-1000 CE)
  3. In its place a legal system featuring monetary compensation called wergild, for criminal violations. Guilt determined by:
     a. Compurgation:
        i. Accused person swears oath of innocence backed up by group of 12 to 25 oath helpers who attest to individual's character and innocence
     b. Ordeal:
        i. Divine forces would not allow an innocent person to be harmed
        ii. Trial by combat, allowed accused to challenge his accuser to a duel
  A. Common Law and the Principle of Stare Decisis
  1. Traveling judges trying cases throughout the land, holding court in each county of the domain of William the Conqueror
  2. Judge summoned a number of citizens who would, on their oath, tell of the serious crimes and serious breaches of the peace that occurred since the judge's last visit
  3. Judge then based decision on local customs and rules of conduct, known as Stare Decisis, or "to stand by decided cases"

4. Present English system of law established during reign of Henry II (1154-1189)
5. Judges began to publish decisions, fixed body of legal rules and principles produced, which developed into precedents when the new rules were successfully applied in a number of different cases
6. Unified system evolved into common law of the country that incorporated local custom and practice into a national code
7. Mala in se (inherently evil) crimes joined by mala prohibitum (acts prohibited by law) which reflected existing social and economic conditions
8. Before American Revolution, colonies were subject to the common law
9. After independence, state legislatures standardized common-law crimes such as:
   a. Murder
   b. Burglary
   c. Arson
   d. Rape
10. Whenever common law proved inadequate to deal with changing social and moral issues, the states and Congress supplemented it with legislative statutes
   a. Recently statutes prohibiting such offenses as identity theft and pirating of videotapes have recently been passed to control human behavior.

III. **SOURCES OF THE CRIMINAL LAW**
   1. Contemporary American legal system codified by state and federal legislatures and is constantly evolving
   2. Content of law may be influenced by judicial decision making, potentially making some criminal offenses unenforceable, or it may expand the scope of the law
   A. Constitutional limits
      1. All criminal law must conform to rules and dictates of U.S. Constitution
      2. Substantive due process:
         a. Constitution forbids any criminal law that violates a person's right to be treated equally and fairly
      3. Laws that are too vague, criminalize a person's status, or that are overly cruel and/or capricious are prohibited by the Constitution
      4. Constitution also forbids bills of attainder:
         a. Legislative acts that inflict punishment with a judicial trial
      5. Ex post facto laws are also forbidden. Ex post facto laws are:
         a. A law that makes an action previously non-criminal, criminal and punishes offenders that committed the act prior to the law
         b. A law that makes a crime more serious after the fact than it was when first committed
         c. A law that inflicts a greater punishment than was available when the crime was committed
         d. A law which makes it easier to convict an offender than it was when the crime was committed

6. No issue has inspired more debate in the constitution than the Second Amendment's instruction:
    a. A will regulated militia, being necessary to the security of a free state, the right of the people to keep and bear arms, shall not be infringed

B. Crimes and Classifications
    1. Each state and the federal government have developed their own body of criminal law that grades offenses, sets levels of punishment, and classifies crimes into categories Crimes are generally grouped into three categories:
        a. Felonies – most serious crimes, punishable by imprisonment:
            i. Criminal homicide
            ii. Robbery
            iii. Rape
            iv. Burglary
            v. Larceny
        b. Misdemeanors – less serious, punished by jail terms:
            i. Petty larceny
            ii. Assault and battery
            iii. Unlawful possession of marijuana
        c. Violations or infractions – violations of city or town ordinances, often traffic violations, or public intoxication, punishable by a fine. Some states consider these civil matters, others consider them criminal
    2. Felony – Misdemeanor classification
        a. Felonies
            i. Police may arrest using either arrest warrant or probable cause
            ii. If convicted:
                a) Person may be barred from certain employment or some professions such as law and medicine
                b) Status as an alien in the U.S. may be affected
                c) Might be denied the right to hold public office, vote, or serve on a jury
        b. Misdemeanors:
            i. Can only be taken into custody with an arrest warrant or if police officer observed the infraction (in-presence requirement). There are exceptions depending on the jurisdiction and offense

IV. **THE LEGAL DEFINITION OF A CRIME**
    1. For the prosecutor to prove a crime occurred and the defendant committed it, the prosecutor must prove that the defendant:
        a. Engaged in a guilty act (actus reus)
        b. Acted in an intentional and purposeful manner (mens rea – guilty mind)
            i. Concept originated in common law
            ii. Thought of committing a crime alone does not constitute a crime
    A. Actus Reus
        1. Voluntary and deliberate illegal act such as:
            a. Taking someone's money
            b. Burning a building
            c. Shooting someone

65

2. Accident or involuntary act not considered criminal, unless negligence or disregard for rights of others involved
3. Occasions when failure to act or omission to act can be considered criminal:
   a. Failure to perform a legally required duty that is based on relationship or status can include:
      i. Parent, child, or spousal relationship
   b. Imposition by statute:
      i. Some states require action, for instance to stop and help at an accident scene
   c. Contractual relationship:
      i. Lifeguard, swimmer
      ii. Doctor, patient
      iii. Babysitter or au pair, child
         a) Duty to act is a legal and not moral duty
         b) Obligation arises from relationship between the parties or from explicit legal requirements

B. Mens Rea
   1. Crime must be committed with deliberate purpose or criminal intent
   2. Can be interpreted through person's actions
   3. Intent can be derived from recklessness or negligence, for example:
      a. Drunk driver may not have intended to kill a specific victim, yet negligent behavior creates a condition that a reasonable person can assume may lead to injury
C. The relationship of Mens Rea and Actus Reus:
   1. Law requires a connection between mens rea and actus reas; offender's conduct as proximate cause of criminal act
D. Criminal harm
   1. Thought alone is not a crime
   2. An act is required to prove actor's willingness to cause harm
   3. Asportation – possession of another's property by taking it illegally
      a. Value of property not important, value to victim is important
E. Strict liability
   1. Also known as public safety
   2. Mens rea is not essential in certain offenses
   3. Person can be responsible for violation of a crime independent of intent to commit the offense
   4. Generally includes:
      a. Narcotic control laws
      b. Traffic laws
      c. Health and safety regulations
      d. Sanitation laws
      e. Other regulatory statutes
   5. No state of mind required when strict liability statute is violated

V.   **CRIMINAL DEFENSES**
1. When actors accused of a crime raise a defense, they must refute one or more of the elements of a crime. They deny either through actus reus or mens rea
A. Excuse Defenses – Excuses refer to situations where defendants admit physical act of crime but deny responsibility because they lacked free will. They had no control over their actions. Examples:
  1. Ignorance or Mistake:
    a. Actions were either a mistake, or the person was unaware that the behavior was a crime
    b. As a general rule, ignorance of the law is no excuse
      i. According to legal scholar William Blackstone:
        a) Ignorance of the law, which everyone is bound to know, excuses no man
    c. Accused cannot present a legitimate defense by unawareness or misinterpretation of the law, or believe the law unconstitutional
    d. Mistake of fact may be a valid defense:
      i. Honest mistake
      ii. Government failed to make enactment of a new law public
      iii. Accused relied on false statement of law by an official
  2. Insanity:
    a. State of mind negates one's criminal responsibility
    b. Successful insanity defense results in a verdict of "not guilty by reason of insanity"
    c. Insanity is a legal category
      i. Does not mean that everyone who suffers from a form of mental illness can be excused from legal responsibility
    d. Defendant's state of mind at the time the crime was committed made it impossible for them to have the necessary mens rea to satisfy the legal definition of crime
    e. Usually left to psychiatric testimony to prove person understood wrongfulness of actions
    f. Jury must weigh evidence in light of test for sanity currently used in the jurisdiction
    g. Tests vary throughout the U.S., include:
      i. M'Naghten rule
      ii. Irresistible impulse
      iii. Durham rule
      iv. Insanity Defense Reform Act
      v. Substantial capacity test
  3. Intoxication:
    a. Generally not considered a defense unless defendant becomes involuntary intoxicated through duress or mistake
    b. Involuntary intoxication may also lessen the degree of the crime
  4. Age:
    a. Child generally not criminally responsible for actions committed at an age that precludes a full realization of the gravity of certain types of behavior

67

         i.   Generally a conclusive presumption of incapacity for a child under 7

         ii. Reliable presumption for ages 7 to 14

         iii. No presumption over 14

    b. Maximum age of criminal responsibility for children ranges from 14-18, minimum age may be set by statute at age 7 or under age 14

B. Justification Defenses – Defendant does not deny they committed the crime but claims they had a valid reason for doing so. Examples:

   1. Consent:

      a. Person may be innocent if the victim consented to the act in question

      b. Consent is an essential element of these crimes, valid where it can be proven existed when act committed

      c. Consent not an option in some crimes; e.g. statutory rape

   2. Self-Defense:

      a. Defendant must have acted under reasonable belief that he was in danger of death or great harm with no means of escape

      b. Must only use such force as reasonably necessary to prevent personal harm

      c. Danger must have been immediate

      d. Defendant in some instances must have sought alternative means of avoiding danger such as escape, retreat, or assistance from others. Includes battered-wife or battered-child syndromes

   3. Stand Your Ground:

      a. Most self-defense statutes require a duty to retreat before reacting to a threat with physical violence

         i. Exception is one's own home

           a) According to the "castle exception", a person is not obligated to retreat within his or her residence before fighting back.

           b) Florida has stand your ground law which allows people to use force in a wide variety of circumstances and eliminate or curtail the need to retreat, even if they are not in their own home but in a public place

   4. Entrapment:

      a. Criminal activity justified because law enforcement used traps, decoys, or deception to induce criminal activity

         i. Generally legitimate for law enforcement to set traps for criminals by getting information about crimes from informers, undercover agents, and codefendants

         ii. Police allowed to use ordinary opportunities for defendants to commit crime

      b. Entrapment occurs when law enforcement instigates the crime, implants criminal ideas, or coerces individuals into bringing about crime

         i. *Sherman v. United States*:

           a) Supreme Court found the function of law enforcement is to prevent crime and to apprehend criminals, not to implant a criminal design originating with officials of the government in the mind of an innocent person

5. Duress:
   a. Defendant must show they were forced into committing the crime in order to prevent death or serious harm of self or others
   b. Generally duress is no defense for an intentional killing
6. Necessity:
   a. Defendant could not behave in any other fashion considering the circumstances or conditions at the time the crime occurred

VI. **REFORMING THE CRIMINAL LAW**
   1. In some instances what was formally legal is now a crime, in other instances what was considered illegal is now legal
   2. Until recently, sexual relations between consenting same-sex adults was punished as a serious felony under sodomy statutes.
      a. *Lawrence v. Texas* (2003)
         i. Supreme Court declared that laws banning sodomy are unconstitutional if they restrict adults' private sexual behavior and impose on their personal dignity.
   A. Creating New Crimes — New laws have been created to conform to emerging social issues:
   1. Physician-Assisted Suicide – Doctors helping people end their life (obitiatry)
      a. Michigan created statutory ban on assisted suicide, reflecting what lawmakers believed to be prevailing public opinion
      b. Forty four states now disallow assisted suicide either by statute or common law
   2. Stalking – Willful, malicious, and repeated following and harassing of another person
      a. More than 25 states have enacted statutes prohibiting this behavior
      b. Often enacted to protect women from ex-boyfriend and husbands, also used to protect celebrities
   3. Community Notification Laws – Registration of convicted sex offenders
      a. On May 17, 1996 President Clinton signed Megan's Law, contains two components:
         i. Sex offender registration – requires the states to register individuals convicted of sex crimes against children.
         ii. Community notification – compels the states to make private and personal information on registered sex offenders available to the public.
   4. Controlling Technology
      a. Many new criminal behaviors have spawned a new generation of criminal acts.
      b. There has been an on-going effort by state legislatures to change their criminal codes to penalize many of these acts
      c. Acts include:
         i. Vishing
         ii. Smishing
         iii. Theft of access numbers
         iv. Software piracy

       v. Bulk e-mail messages designed to trick consumers into revealing bank account passwords

5. Protecting the Environment – Designed to protect the nation's environmental well-being Environmental Protection Agency successfully prosecuted significant violations of environmental laws including:
   a. Data fraud cases
   b. Indiscriminate hazardous waste dumping that resulted in serious injury or death
   c. Industrywide ocean dumping by cruise ships
   d. Oil spills that caused significant damage to:
      i. Waterways
      ii. Wetlands
      iii. Beaches
   e. Illegal handling of hazardous substances such as pesticides and asbestos that exposed children, the poor, and other especially vulnerable groups to potentially serious illness

6. Legalizing Marijuana
   a. About 16 states have legalized the use of marijuana for medical purposes and some including California allow dispensaries to fill prescriptions
   b. While providing medical marijuana has strong public support, the federal government still criminalizes any use of marijuana
   c. *Gonzales v. Raich*
      i. Supreme Court ruled that the federal government can prosecute medical marijuana patients, even in states with compassionate use laws

7. Fighting Terrorism
   a. Soon after September 11, 2001, U.S. government enacted several laws focused on preventing further acts of violence against the U.S.
   b. Congress passed the USA Patriot Act (USAPA) on October 26, 2001:
      i. Creates new laws
      ii. Makes changes to over 15 different existing statutes
      iii. Aim is to give sweeping new powers to domestic law enforcement and international intelligence agencies in an effort to fight terrorism
      iv. Expands all four traditional tools of surveillance:
         a) Wiretaps
         b) Search warrants
         c) Pen/trap orders (installing devices that record phone calls)
         d) Subpoenas
      v. Expanded the Foreign Intelligence Surveillance Act (FISA)
      vi. Gave the FBI greater power to check an monitor phone, Internet, and computer records
      vii. Expands the definition of terrorism and enables the government to more closely monitor individuals suspected of harboring and giving material support to terrorists
      viii. Increases the authority of the U.S. attorney general to detain and deport noncitizens with little or no judicial review

ix. Attorney general and secretary of state given the authority to designate domestic groups as terrorist organizations and to deport any noncitizen who is a member

VII. **CONSTITUTIONAL CRIMINAL PROCEDURE**
1. Law of criminal procedure consists of the rules and procedures that govern the pretrial processing of criminal suspects and the conduct of criminal trials
2. Main source of procedural law is Bill of Rights:
   a. First ten amendments are known as the Bill of Rights. Purpose was to prevent the government from usurping the personal freedoms of citizens
      i. Added December 15, 1791
      ii. Of Primary concern are the Fourth, Fifth, Sixth, and Eighth Amendments
         a) These limit and control the manner in which the federal government operates the criminal justice system
3. Due process clause of Fourteenth Amendment applies these limits to the state and local level:
   a. Fourth Amendment:
      i. Bars illegal searches and seizures
         a) Exclusionary rule:
            1. Evidence seized in violation of the Fourth Amendment cannot be used in a court of law
   b. Fifth Amendment:
      i. Limits the admissibility of confessions that have been obtained unfairly
      ii. *Miranda v. Arizona* (1966):
         a) Supreme Court held that a person accused of a crime has the right to refuse to answer questions when in police custody
      iii. Guarantees defendants the right to a grand jury
      iv. Protection from double jeopardy, being tried twice for the same crime
      v. Due process clause guarantees right to fundamental fairness and the expectation of fair trials, hearings, and procedural safeguards
   c. Sixth Amendment:
      i. Right to a speedy and public trial by impartial jury
      ii. Right to be informed of the nature of charges
      iii. Right to confront any prosecution witnesses
      iv. Right to be represented by an attorney at:
         a) Pretrial custody
         b) Identification and lineup procedures
         c) Preliminary hearing
         d) Submission of guilty plea
         e) Trial
         f) Sentencing
         g) Postconviction appeal
   d. Eighth Amendment:
      i. No excessive bail:
         a) An amount far greater than that imposed on similar defendants who are accused of committing similar crimes

71

      ii. Forbids cruel and unusual punishment:
        a)   Prohibits actions regarded as unacceptable by a civilized society, including corporal punishment and torture
           1. Capital punishment is legal unless employed in a random, haphazard fashion or if especially cruel ways of execution used
           2. *Baze and Bowling v. Rees* (2008) – Supreme Court held use of lethal injection not cruel unless there is a substantial risk of serious harm that the drugs will not work effectively
    e. Fourteenth Amendment applies the protection of the Bill of Rights to the states
      i. No state shall deprive any person of life, liberty, or property, without due process of law

VIII. DUE PROCESS OF LAW

    1. Found in Fifth and Fourteenth Amendments: been used to evaluate the constitutionality of legal statutes and to set standards and guidelines for fair procedures in the criminal justice system
    2. Can be divided into two categories:
    a. Substantive:
      i. Citizens' right to be protected from criminal laws that may be biased, discriminatory, and otherwise unfair
        a)   These laws may be vague or apply unfairly to one group over another
      ii. Concern that Patriot Act authority is not limited to true terrorism but that investigations cover a much broader range of activity involving reasonable political dissent
      iii. Significant controversy over the long-term detention of suspected terrorists without trial at the Guantanamo camp in Cuba
        a)   Boumediene v. Bush – Supreme Court held that Guantanamo prisoners had a right to habeas corpus protection under the Constitution
        b)   On January 7, 2011, President Obama signed the 2011 Defense Authorization Bill which contains provisions preventing prisoners at Guantanamo from being transferred to the mainland or to other foreign countries
    b. Procedural:
      i. Ensures no person will be deprived of life, liberty, or property without proper and legal criminal process
      ii. Specific due process procedures:
        a)   Freedom from illegal searches and interrogations
        b)   Prompt notice of charges and a formal hearing
        c)   The right to counsel or some other representation
        d)   The opportunity to respond to charges
        e)   The opportunity to confront and cross-examine witnesses and accusers
        f)   The privilege to be free from self-incrimination

g) The opportunity to present one's own witnesses
h) A decision made on the basis of substantial evidence and facts produced at the hearing
i) A written statement of the reasons for the decision
j) An appellate review procedure

B. Interpreting the Constitution
1. Supreme Court decides cases based on:
   a. Facts of the case
   b. Federal and state constitutional and statutory provisions
   c. Previous court decisions
   d. Judicial philosophy
   e. Ideas and principles that society considers important at a given time and in a given place
2. The judicial interpretation of the Constitution is not fixed but rather reflects what society deems fair and just at a particular time and place
3. The degree of loss suffered by the individual (victim or offender) balanced against the state's interest also determines how many Constitutional requirements are ordinarily applied
4. When Supreme Court justices are conservative they are less likely to create new rights and privileges and more likely to restrict civil liberties

CHAPTER SUMMARY

The law can generally be divided into three broad categories: (a) substantive criminal law— the branch of the law that defines crimes and their punishment (b) procedural criminal law— those laws which set out the basic rules of practice in the criminal justice system, and (c) civil law— the set of rules governing relations between private parties.

The roots of the criminal codes can be traced back to such early legal charters as the Babylonian Code of Hammurabi, the Mosaic Code of the Israelites, and the Roman Twelve Tables. The present English system of law came into existence during the reign of Henry II, when royal judges began to publish their decisions in local cases. This system evolved into a common law of the country that incorporated local custom and practice into a national code. Crimes that were mala in se, inherently evil and depraved, were the cornerstone of the common law. They were joined by new mala prohibitum crimes which reflected existing social and economic conditions.

All criminal law in the U.S. must conform to the rules of the Constitution. Criminal laws have been interpreted as violating constitutional principles if they are overbroad or too vague. Each state and the federal government have developed criminal laws that define and grade offenses, set levels of punishment, and classify crimes. Crimes are generally grouped into felonies, misdemeanors, and violations.

Almost all common law crimes contain both mental and physical elements. The prosecutor must show that the accused engaged in the guilty act (actus reus or guilty act) and that the act was intentional and purposeful (mens rea or guilty mind). Actus reus is a voluntary and deliberate illegal act. There are occasions when the failure or omission to act can be considered a crime; these include failure to perform a legally required duty that is based on relationship or status, imposition by statute, and contractual relationships.

For an act to constitute a crime, it must be done with criminal intent. To constitute a crime a connection must be made between the mens rea and actus reas. Certain statutory offenses exist in which mens rea is not essential. These offenses are strict liability crimes.

There are two types of defenses, excuse and justification. Excuse defenses include: ignorance or mistake, insanity, intoxication and age. The justification defenses are: consent, self-defense, stand your ground, entrapment, duress, and necessity.

States may take action to decriminalize or legalize some crimes because the general public simply ignores the laws. New crimes have been created to control stalking, environmental damage, cyber crime, and terrorism. Others have been decriminalized or legalized, such as sodomy. In some cases, such as distributing medical marijuana, states may legalize acts that are still banned by Federal law.

The main source of the procedural law is the body of the Constitution and the first ten amendments—the Bill of Rights—added to the Constitution on December 15, 1791. Of primary concern are the Fourth, Fifth, Sixth, and Eighth Amendments, which limit and control the manner in which the federal government operates the justice system. The concept of due process is found in both the Fifth and Fourteenth Amendments. Due process has been used to evaluate the constitutionality of legal statutes and to set standards and guidelines for fair procedures in the criminal justice system.

The law of criminal procedure consists of the rules and procedures that govern the pretrial processing of criminal suspects and the conduct of criminal trials. It is the job of the Supreme Court to interpret the Constitution and set limits on governmental behavior, for example, limiting the ability of the police in their searching, questioning and punishing those suspected of crime.

DISCUSSION QUESTIONS

1. What are the specific aims and purposes of the criminal law? To what extent does the criminal law control behavior?

2. What kinds of activities should be labeled criminal in contemporary society? Why?

3. What is a criminal act? What is a criminal state of mind? When are individuals liable for their actions?

4. Discuss the various kinds of crime classifications. To what extent or degree are they distinguishable?

5. Numerous states are revising their penal codes. Which major categories of substantive crimes do you think should be revised?

6. Entrapment is a defense when the defendant was entrapped into committing the crime. To what extent should law enforcement personnel induce the commission of an offense?

7. What legal principles can be used to justify self-defense? Given that the law seeks to prevent crime, not promote crime it, are such principles sound?

8. What are the minimum standards of criminal procedure required in the criminal justice system?

MEDIA TOOLS

- Investigate the insanity defense further by reviewing An Overview of Insanity on Trail. This site includes frequently asked questions, notorious insanity cases, from Daniel M'Naughten to John Hinkley: A brief history of the insanity defense, state insanity defense laws, and In Congress: Mental health courts.
  http://www.pbs.org/wgbh/pages/frontline/shows/crime/trial/
  Site provided by the Public Broadcasting Service, Frontline.

- View a Fox News video discussing the Florida "Stand Your Ground" law. Controversial 'Stand Your Ground' Law Put to Test. When should use of deadly force be allowed? Jan 16, 2011. Video provided by Fox News, find the video at:
  http://video.foxnews.com/v/4499131/controversial-stand-your-ground-law-put-to-test

- Watch a 60 Minutes interview with Dr. Jack Kevorkian regarding his controversial practice of helping others commit suicide. Video shows Dr. Kevorkian assisting an individual with suicide. Video provided by CBS News. Video can be found at:
  http://www.cbsnews.com/video/watch/?id=7368313n

- Interpreting the original meaning of the constitution is a topic of continual conflict within the law. See University of Missouri - Kansas City School of Law Professor Douglas Linder's website regarding: Theories of Constitutional Interpretation The issue: What are appropriate sources of authority to guide interpretation of the Constitution and what relative weight should be assigned to the various appropriate sources? This site provides interesting information regarding the interpretation of the Constitution by various individuals. Are you an originalist or non-originalist? Find out at:
  http://law2.umkc.edu/faculty/projects/ftrials/conlaw/interp.html

RA14

PRACTICE TEST BANK

MULTIPLE CHOICE

1. The substantive criminal law
    a.   defines the steps necessary to get a conviction.
    b.   is the same as tort law.
    c.   defines crimes and defenses and their punishment.
    d.   is a part of the civil law.

2. Which of the following is not one of the categories of the rule of law?
    a.   Substantive criminal law
    b.   Administrative law
    c.   Civic law
    d.   Procedural law

3. The legal principle that new cases are to be decided in a manner consistent with prior cases is called
    a.   common law.
    b.   stare decisis.
    c.   male in se.
    d.   *Carriers* case.

4. What type of law is described as the judge-made law that was originally based on the customs of the people?
    a.   Administrative
    b.   Constitutional
    c.   Statutory
    d.   Common

5. New York City passes a statute that makes it illegal for suspicious persons to loiter near public buildings. This statute is probably unconstitutional because
    a.   it is vague and gives too much discretion to the police.
    b.   loitering is protected by freedom of speech.
    c.   only the state of New York can pass loitering statutes.
    d.   the Eighth Amendment gives people a right to loiter near public buildings.

6. Which branch of law defines crimes and their punishment?
    a.   Substantive
    b.   Civil
    c.   Procedural
    d.   Administrative

76

7. Regardless of its source, all criminal law in the United States must conform to the rules and dictates of the
   a. Declaration of Independence.
   b. Articles of Confederation.
   c. U.S. Constitution.
   d. Federal Statutes.

8. Which branch of law sets out the basic rules of practice in the government, including the criminal justice system?
   a. Procedural
   b. Civil
   c. Public
   d. Substantive

9. In most jurisdictions, a felony can be distinguished from a misdemeanor in that felony sentences are
   a. less severe.
   b. served in jail.
   c. served in prison.
   d. not appealable.

10. The actus reus constitutes what element of a crime?
    a. Mental
    b. Act
    c. Punishment
    d. Concurrence

11. The mens rea constitutes what element of a crime?
    a. Mental
    b. Harm
    c. Causation
    d. Circumstantial

12. What type of illegal act does not require the elements of intent and mens rea?
    a. Strictly punitive
    b. Liberal accord
    c. Causative action
    d. Strict liability

13. Which of the following in not considered a mala in se crime?
    a. Arson
    b. Burglary
    c. Embezzlement
    d. Murder

14. Petty larceny would be considered a
    a. felony.
    b. misdemeanor.
    c. violation.
    d. infraction.

15. How many Amendments to the U.S. Constitution are contained in the Bill of Rights?
    a. 5
    b. 7
    c. 10
    d. 13

16. As originally ratified, the Bill of Rights limited the power of
    a. both state and federal governments.
    b. only federal government.
    c. only state government.
    d. private citizens.

17. Which Amendment provides for protection against unreasonable searches and seizures by the government?
    a. Fourth
    b. Fifth
    c. Sixth
    d. Eighth

18. Which Amendment provides the right to an attorney, right to a jury trial, and the right to confront witnesses?
    a. Fifth
    b. Sixth
    c. Eighth
    d. Fourteenth

19. In which Amendment is the ban on cruel and unusual punishments found?
    a. Sixth
    b. Seventh
    c. Eighth
    d. Ninth

20. The concept of due process is found in two Amendments; the Fifth Amendment and the
    a. Fourth.
    b. Sixth.
    c. Eighth.
    d. Fourteenth.

21. In some cases, a crime victim may forgo criminal action and choose to file a
    a. tort claim.
    b. strict liability claim.
    c. criminal claim.
    d. social claim.

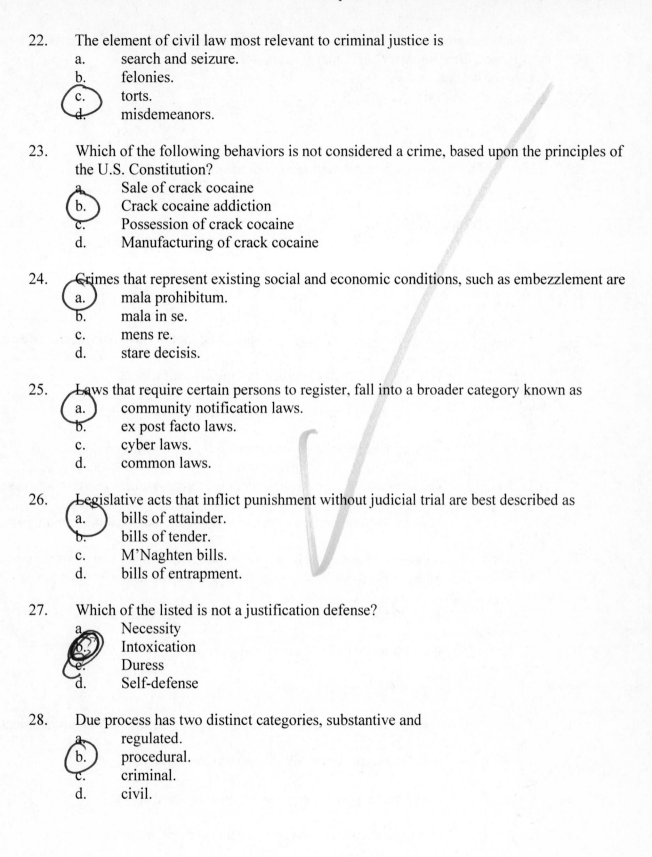

22.   The element of civil law most relevant to criminal justice is
       a.   search and seizure.
       b.   felonies.
       c.   torts.
       d.   misdemeanors.

23.   Which of the following behaviors is not considered a crime, based upon the principles of
       the U.S. Constitution?
       a.   Sale of crack cocaine
       b.   Crack cocaine addiction
       c.   Possession of crack cocaine
       d.   Manufacturing of crack cocaine

24.   Crimes that represent existing social and economic conditions, such as embezzlement are
       a.   mala prohibitum.
       b.   mala in se.
       c.   mens re.
       d.   stare decisis.

25.   Laws that require certain persons to register, fall into a broader category known as
       a.   community notification laws.
       b.   ex post facto laws.
       c.   cyber laws.
       d.   common laws.

26.   Legislative acts that inflict punishment without judicial trial are best described as
       a.   bills of attainder.
       b.   bills of tender.
       c.   M'Naghten bills.
       d.   bills of entrapment.

27.   Which of the listed is not a justification defense?
       a.   Necessity
       b.   Intoxication
       c.   Duress
       d.   Self-defense

28.   Due process has two distinct categories, substantive and
       a.   regulated.
       b.   procedural.
       c.   criminal.
       d.   civil.

29.   Which due process refers to a citizen's right to be protected from criminal laws that may be biased, discriminatory, and otherwise unfair?
        a.   Substantive
        b.   Procedural
        c.   Civil
        d.   Regulated

30.   Which of the following is not a traditional tool of surveillance?
        a.   Wiretap
        b.   Subpoena
        c.   Fixed-wing aircraft
        d.   Search warrant

TRUE/FALSE

1.   T   **F**   A private citizen is under no legal obligation to save a drowning person.

2.   **T**   F   The U.S. Constitution is the supreme law of the land.

3.   **T**   F   Bail is meant to ensure a trial appearance.

4.   T   **F**   A strict liability crime is one that has no actus reus component.

5.   T   **F**   The substantive criminal law specifies the procedures in a criminal case.

6.   T   **F**   Mala in se crimes reflects the existing social and economic conditions.

7.   **T**   F   A defense of necessity must show that the defendant could not have behaved in any other way considering the circumstances of the crime.

8.   T   **F**   Mala prohibitum crimes are those that are inherently evil.

9.   T   **F**   Thought alone can be considered a crime.

10.   **T**   F   Capital punishment is legal.

11.   T   **F**   The Fourteenth Amendment limits the power of the federal government.

12.   **T**   F   Judicial interpretation of the Constitution is fixed.

13.   **T**   F   Felonies are more serious crimes than misdemeanors.

14.   **T**   F   Entrapment involves government inducement, traps, and decoys.

15.   T   **F**   Ignorance of the law is generally a defense to crime.

FILL-IN-THE-BLANK

1.   The ban on excessive bail and fines is found in the __eighth__ Amendment.

2.   The protection from being tried twice for the same crime is found in the __fifth__ Amendment.

3.   The Latin term "mala in __se__" means inherently wrong or evil.

4.   __Civil__ law is used to resolve, control, and shape personal interactions such as contracts, wills, property ownership, and commerce.

5.   The most serious crimes punishable by imprisonment are known as __felonies__

6.   Under common law, there is generally a conclusive presumption of incapacity for a child under the age of __7__.

7.   Regardless of its source, all criminal law in the United States must conform to the rules and dictates of the __constution__.

8.   An ex post __facto__ law is basically a retroactive criminal statute.

9.   In some crimes, omission or failure to act can be the __actus__ reus.

10.   Recklessness and negligence are examples of the __mens__ rea element of a crime.

11.   A mistake can be a defense if __criminal intent__ is absent.

12.   Generally, __ignorance__ of the law is no excuse.

13.   Certain statutory offenses exist in which mens rea is not essential. These offenses fall into a category known as public safety or __strict liability__ crimes.

14.   The famous __Miranda__ warnings were designed to protect the privilege against self-incrimination.

15.   Under the __exclusionary__ rule, evidence seized in violation of the Fourth Amendment cannot be used in a court of law.

ESSAY

1. Discuss four amendments found in the Bill of Rights.

2. Identify and explain three of the four categories of the rule of law.

3. Define and discuss four criminal defenses. Provide examples.

4. Identify and describe three recent developments in criminal law.

5. What are the differences between felonies, misdemeanors, and violations?

CHAPTER 3 ANSWER KEY

Multiple Choice

1. c [p. 53, LO2]   2. c [p. 54, LO1]   3. b [p. 55, LO2]   4. d [p. 56, LO2]   5. a [p. 56, LO3]

6. a [p. 56, LO1]   7. c [p. 56, LO3]   8. a [p. 54, LO1]   9. c [p. 58, LO3]   10. b [p. 58, LO4]

11. a [p. 60, LO4]   12. d [p. 60, LO5]   13. c [p. 56, LO3]   14. b [p. 58, LO4]   15. c [p. 67, LO8]

16. b [p. 67, LO8]   17. a [p. 67, LO8]   18. b [p. 68, LO8]   19. c [p. 68, LO8]   20. d [p. 68, LO8]

21. a [p. 54, LO1]   22. c [p. 54, LO1]   23. b [p. 57, LO4]   24. a [p. 56, LO2]   25. a [p. 65, LO8]

26. a [p. 57, LO9]   27. b [pp. 63-65, LO6]   28. b [p. 69, LO9]   29. a [p. 69, LO9]   30. c [p. 67, LO10]

True/False

1. F [p. 60, LO5]   2. T [p. 56, LO2]   3. T [p. 68, LO8]   4. F [p. 60, LO5]   5. F [p. 54, LO2]

6. F [p. 56, LO2]   7. T [pp. 64-65, LO6]   8. F [p. 56, LO2]   9. F [p. 60, LO4]   10. T [p. 68, LO8]

11. F [p. 68, LO10]   12. [p. 70, LO10]   13. T [p. 58, LO3]   14. T [p. 64, LO6]   15. F [p. 61, LO6]

Fill-in-the-Blank

1. Eighth [p. 68, LO7]   2. Fifth [p. 68, LO7]   3. se [p. 56, LO2]

4. Civil [p. 54, LO1]   5. felonies [p. 58, LO4]   6. 7 [p. 62, LO6]

7. Constitution [p. 56, LO3]   8. Facto [p. 57, LO3]   9. actus [p. 58, LO4]

10. mens [p. 60, LO4]   11. criminal intent [p. 61, LO4]   12. ignorance [p. 61, LO6]

13. strict liability [p. 60, LO5]   14. Miranda [p. 68, LO7]   15. exclusionary [p. 68, LO10]

Essay

1. Discuss four amendments found in the Bill of Rights.

The Fourth Amendment prohibits unreasonable search and seizure. It bans illegal search and seizure by prohibiting police officers from stopping, questioning or searching an individual without legal justification. The Fourth Amendment protects people not places. Evidence seized in violation of the Fourth amendment cannot be used in a court of law as the exclusionary rule attaches.

The Fifth Amendment limits the admissibility of confessions that have been obtained fairly. It guarantees a defendant a right to a grand jury and protection from being tried twice (i.e., double jeopardy). Its due process clause guarantees defendants the right to fundamental fairness (e.g., fair trials and proceedings).

The Sixth Amendment guarantees the defendant the right to a speedy and public trial by impartial jury of peers. It also contains the right for a defendant to be represented by legal counsel at various stages of the criminal justice process and requires the defendant be informed as to the nature of the charges and the right to confront prosecution witnesses.

The Eighth Amendment prohibits excessive bail, excessive fines, cruel and unusual punishment from be inflicted. It does not guarantee bail, it prohibits excessive bail. Punishments must be acceptable by civilized society.

[pp. 67-68, LO8]

2. Identify and explain three of the four categories of the rule of law.

- Substantive criminal law. The branch of the law that defines crimes and their punishment. It involves such issues as the mental and physical elements of crime, crime categories, and criminal defenses.
- Procedural law. Those laws that set out the basic rules of practice in the government, including the criminal justice system. Some elements of the law of criminal procedure are the rules of evidence, the law of arrest, the law of search and seizure, questions of appeal, jury selection, and the right to counsel.
- Civil law. The set of rules governing relations between private parties, including both individuals and organizations (such as business enterprises and/or corporations). Civil law is used to resolve, control, and shape such personal interactions as contracts, wills and trusts, property ownership, and commerce. The element of civil law most relevant to criminal justice is torts, or the law of personal injuries
- Public or administrative law. The branch of law that deals with the government and its relationships with individuals or other governments is known as public law. It governs the administration and regulation of city, county, state, and federal government agencies.

[pp. 53-55, LO1]

3. Define and discuss four criminal defenses. Provide examples.

Excuse defenses are often seen when a person admits the physical act of the crime but claim they are not responsible for it because they lack free will. In other words they had no control over their actions therefore they should be "excused" from criminal responsibility.

Under the general category of "excuse defenses" are the following subcategories:

- Ignorance or Mistake: The defendant's actions were either a mistake or the defendant was unaware that the behavior was a crime. As a general rule ignorance of the law is no excuse. An example of a mistake defense could include a scenario where a person mistakenly takes the wrong coat (similar looking coat) from the coat rack. If the defendant can convince the jury/ judge it was a mistake and there was no intent to deprive the person of their property, a mistake defense applies.

- Insanity: The person's state of mind negates their criminal responsibility. The defendant was incapable of forming the necessary mens rea (guilty intent) to commit the crime. The defendant's state of mind negates criminal responsibility.

84

- Intoxication: Although this is not generally accepted a defense it can be considered where intoxication occurred under duress or mistake. A defendant who was tricked or duped into consuming intoxicants (beverage or food was contaminated and subsequently consumed) may be able to raise involuntary intoxication as a defense for criminal activity.

- Age: The person's age makes them incapable of forming the mens rea (guilty intent) to commit a crime. A presumption of incapacity attaches to children under seven. An age defense may apply to a scenario where a child under seven picks up a loaded firearm and shoots it wounding or killing another person. The child does not realize the gravity of his / her behavior.

[pp. 61-65, LO6]

4. Identify and describe three recent developments in criminal law.

Physician-Assisted Suicide Doctors helping people to end their life became the subject of a national debate when Dr. Jack Kevorkian began practicing what he calls obitiatry, helping people take their lives. In an attempt to stop Kevorkian, Michigan passed a statutory ban on assisted suicide, reflecting what lawmakers believed to be prevailing public opinion; Kevorkian was convicted and imprisoned.

Stalking More than 25 states have enacted **stalking** statutes, which prohibit and punish acts described typically as "the willful, malicious, and repeated following and harassing of another person." Stalking laws were originally formulated to protect women terrorized by former husbands and boyfriends, although celebrities often are plagued by stalkers as well. In celebrity cases, these laws often apply to stalkers who are strangers or casual acquaintances of their victims.

Community Notification Laws These laws require the registration of people convicted of sex-related crimes; they were enacted in response to concern about sexual predators moving into neighborhoods. One of the best-known such statutes, New Jersey's "Megan's Law," was named after seven-year-old Megan Kanka of Hamilton Township, New Jersey, who was killed in 1994. Charged with the crime was a convicted sex offender who (unknown to the Kankas) lived across the street. On May 17, 1996, President Clinton signed Megan's Law, which contained two components:
- Sex offender registration. Requires the states to register individuals convicted of sex crimes against children.
- Community notification. Compels the states to make private and personal information on registered sex offenders available to the public.

Controlling Technology. The chapter discussed two new internet crimes, Vishing and Smishing. These cyber crimes are not unique and their effect on the criminal law has been profound. Such technologies as automatic teller machines and cellular phones have already spawned a new generation of criminal acts involving theft of access numbers and software piracy. For example, identity theft has become a national problem, and as a result, there has been an on-going effort by state legislatures to change their criminal codes to penalize sending out bulk e-mail messages designed to trick consumers into revealing bank account passwords, Social Security numbers, and other personal information, as a felony offense.

Protecting the Environment. In response to the concerns of environmentalists, the federal government has passed numerous acts designed to protect the nation's well-being. The Environmental Protection Agency has successfully prosecuted significant violations of these and other new laws, including data fraud cases (e.g., private laboratories submitting false environmental data to state and federal environmental agencies); indiscriminate hazardous waste dumping that resulted in serious injuries and death; industrywide ocean dumping by cruise ships; oil spills that caused significant damage to waterways, wetlands, and beaches; and illegal handling of hazardous substances such as pesticides and asbestos that exposed children, the poor, and other especially vulnerable groups to potentially serious illness.

Legalizing Marijuana. About 16 states have legalized the use of marijuana for medical purposes and some including California allow dispensaries to fill prescriptions.

For example, New Jersey Senate Bill 119, signed into law on January 18, 2010, protects "patients who use marijuana to alleviate suffering from debilitating medical conditions, as well as their physicians, primary caregivers, and those who are authorized to produce marijuana for medical purposes" from "arrest, prosecution, property forfeiture, and criminal and other penalties."

While providing medical marijuana has strong public support, the federal government still criminalizes any use of marijuana, and federal agents can arrest users even if they have prescriptions from doctors in states where medical marijuana is legal (though Federal guidelines "suggest" to local prosecutors that they concentrate their efforts on abusers and not patients in need). In *Gonzales v. Raich* the Supreme Court ruled that that the federal government can prosecute medical marijuana patients, even in states with compassionate use laws.

Fighting Terrorism. Soon after the September 11 terrorist attacks, the U.S. government enacted several laws focused on preventing further acts of violence against the United States and creating greater flexibility in the fight to control terrorist activity. Most important, Congress passed the USA Patriot Act (USAPA) on October 26, 2001. The bill is over 342 pages long, creates new laws, and makes changes to over 15 different existing statutes. Its aim is to give sweeping new powers to domestic law enforcement and international intelligence agencies in an effort to fight terrorism, to expand the definition of terrorist activities, and to alter sanctions for violent terrorism. USAPA expands all four traditional tools of surveillance—wiretaps, search warrants, pen/trap orders (installing devices that record phone calls), and subpoenas. The Foreign Intelligence Surveillance Act (FISA) that governs domestic operations by intelligence agencies is also expanded. USAPA gives the FBI greater power to check and monitor phone, Internet, and computer records without first having to demonstrate that they were being used by a suspect or the target of a court order. The act also expands the definition of "terrorism" and enables the government to monitor more closely those people suspected of "harboring" and giving "material support" to terrorists. It increases the authority of the U.S. attorney general to detain and deport noncitizens with little or no judicial review. The attorney general may certify that he has "reasonable grounds to believe" that a noncitizen endangers national security and is therefore eligible for deportation. The attorney general and secretary of state are also given the authority to designate domestic groups as terrorist organizations and to deport any noncitizen who is a member of such an organization.

[pp. 65-67, LO7]

5. What are the differences between felonies, misdemeanors, and violations?

Distinguishing between a felony and a misdemeanor is difficult and put simply; a felony is a serious offense, and a misdemeanor is a less serious one. A person who has been convicted of a felony may be barred from certain fields of employment or some professions, such as law and medicine. A felony offender's status as an alien in the United States might also be affected, or the offender might be denied the right to hold public office, vote, or serve on a jury. These and other civil liabilities exist only when a person is convicted of a felony offense, not of a misdemeanor. The felony/misdemeanor classification has a direct effect on the way an offender is treated within the justice system. Felonies allow police officers to arrest based upon probable cause or upon issuance of a warrant. Felonies are punishable by imprisonment and are more serious than misdemeanors and other violations. Misdemeanors are less serious and generally punishable by combination of fine and or jail sentence.

Misdemeanors generally require a police officer to observe the crime (e.g., in-presence requirement). There are exceptions to this requirement based upon jurisdiction and type of crime. A misdemeanor is a minor crime usually punished by less than one year's imprisonment in a local institution, such as a county jail.

Violations are generally violate local (e.g., municipal) ordinances or traffic codes. Some violations may be civil and others criminal.

[pp. 57-58, LO3]

CHAPTER 4
Police in Society:
History and Organization

After studying this chapter, students will:

1. Describe how law enforcement developed in feudal England
2. Summarize characteristics of the first law enforcement agencies
3. Discuss the development of law enforcement in the United States
4. Analyze the problems of early police agencies
5. Discuss how reformers attempted to create professional police agencies
6. Describe the major changes in law enforcement between 1970 and today
7. Be familiar with the major federal law enforcement agencies
8. Summarize the differences among state, county, and local law enforcement
9. Explain the role of technology in police work

KEY TERMS AND CONCEPTS

tithing (p.) In medieval England, a group of ten families who collectively dealt with minor disturbances and breaches of the peace.

hue and cry (p.) A call for assistance in medieval England. The policy of self-help used in villages demanded that everyone respond if a citizen raised a hue and cry to get their aid.

hundred (p.) In medieval England, a group of 100 families responsible for maintaining order and trying minor offenses.

constable (p.) In medieval England, an appointed official who administered and supervised the legal affairs of a small community.

shire reeve (p.) In medieval England, the senior law enforcement figure in a county; the forerunner of today's sheriff.

sheriff (p.) The chief law enforcement officer in a county.

watch system (p.) During the Middle Ages in England, men were organized in church parishes to guard at night against disturbances and breaches of the peace under the direction of the local constable.

justice of the peace (p.) Established in 1326 England, the office was created to help the shire reeve in controlling the county; it later took on judicial functions.

vigilantes (p.) Groups of citizens who tracked down wanted criminals in the Old West.

Bureau of Alcohol, Tobacco, Firearms, and Explosives (ATF) (p.) Federal agency with jurisdiction over the illegal sale, importation, and criminal misuse of firearms and explosives and the distribution of untaxed liquor and cigarettes.

U.S. Marshals Service (p.) Federal agency whose jurisdiction includes protecting federal officials, transporting criminal defendants, and tracking down fugitives.

Drug Enforcement Administration (DEA) (p.) The federal agency that enforces federal drug control laws.

Federal Bureau of Investigation (FBI) (p.) The arm of the U.S. Justice Department that investigates violations of federal law, seeks to protect America from terrorist attacks, gathers crime statistics, runs a comprehensive crime laboratory, and helps train local law enforcement officers.

Department of Homeland Security (DHS) (p.) Federal agency responsible for preventing terrorist attacks within the United States, reducing America's vulnerability to terrorism, and minimizing the damage and assisting in recovery from attacks that do occur.

Customs and Border Protection (CBP) (p.) Federal agency responsible for the control and protection of America's borders and ports of entry. Its first priority is keeping terrorists and their weapons out of the United States.

Secret Service (p.) Federal agency responsible for the executive protection and investigation of counterfeiting and various forms of financial fraud.

DNA profiling (p.) The identification of criminal suspects by matching DNA samples taken from their person with specimens found at the crime scene.

augmented reality (AR) technology (p.) Wearable components that supply computer-generated virtual information.

ABIS (Automated Biometric Identification System) (p.) Facial recognition system designed to sift through millions of images to find duplicates before issuing an ID or clearing a passport.

CHAPTER OUTLINE

I. **INTRODUCTION**
    1. Police are the gatekeepers of the criminal justice process. They:
        a. initiate contact with law violators

       b. decide whether to arrest them formally

       c. settle the issue in an informal way

       d. can take no action at all

2. The strategic position of law enforcement officers, their visibility and contact with the public, and their use of weapons and arrest power kept them in the forefront of public thought for most of the twentieth century.

II.   THE HISTORY OF POLICE

1. Origins of police traced to early English society
2. Before Norman Conquest in 1066 C.E., no regular English police force existed
3. Pledge system — Everyone is responsible for aiding and protecting neighbors
   a. Tithings — Groups of ten families entrusted with policing their own minor problems
4. Hue and cry — Citizens call out when trouble occurred
5. Hundred
   a. Ten tithings
      i. Supervised by constable, who was considered the first real police officer, dealt with more serious breaches of the law
6. Shires, which resembled the counties of today were controlled by shire reeve
   a. Shire reeve
      i. Supervise territory or shire
      ii. Forerunner of today's sheriff
7. Watch system created in the thirteenth century to help protect property in England's larger cities and towns. Watchmen patrolled at night and protected town against:
   a. Robberies
   b. Fires
   c. Disturbances
8. Watchmen reported to constable, who became the primary metropolitan law enforcement agent
   a. In larger cities, the watchmen were organized within church parishes and were usually members of the parish they protected
9. Office of justice of the peace created in 1326
   a. Assisted shire reeve in controlling the county
   b. These justices took on judicial functions in addition to their primary role as peacekeepers
   c. Local constable became the operational assistant of the justice of the peace, they:
      i. Supervised night watchmen
      ii. Investigated offenses
      iii. Served summonses
      iv. Executed warrants
      v. Secured prisoners
   d. This system helped delineate the relationship between police and the judiciary, this has continued for more than 670 years

A. Private Police and Thief Takers

1. Raising crime rates in eighteenth century encouraged new form of private, monied police, the thief takers. They profited legally and criminally from a lack of formal police departments
   a. Universally corrupt
      i. Received stolen property
      ii. Theft
      iii. Intimidation
      iv. Perjury
      v. Blackmail
      vi. Made more income by:
         a) Accepting hush money
         b) Giving perjured evidence
         c) Swearing false oaths
         d) Operating extortion rackets
   b. Court bailiffs were the most passionately detested thief taker
   c. Use of violence notorious
      i. Jack Wild most notorious thief taker
2. Henry Fielding
   a. Sought to clean up thief-taking system
   b. Appointed city magistrate in 1748
   c. Operated own group of monied police
      i. Bow street runners in London
      ii. Agents carefully instructed on their legitimate powers and duties
      iii. Marked improvement over earlier police models because they actually had an administrative structure that improved record keeping and investigative procedures

B. Creating Public Police
1. 1829: Sir Robert Peel, England's home secretary
   a. Lobbied an "Act for Improving the Police in and near the Metropolis"
   b. Established the first organized police force in London
      i. Comprised of over 1000 men
      ii. Structured along military lines
      iii. Known as Bobbies after Peel
      iv. Wore a distinctive uniform and led by two magistrates
      v. Ultimate responsibility for the police fell to the home secretary and consequently the Parliament
      vi. Bobbies:
         a) Many corrupt
         b) Unsuccessful at stopping crime
         c) Influenced by wealthy
         d) One-third dismissed each year because of corruption

C. Law Enforcement in Colonial America
1. Paralleled British model
2. In the colonies, county sheriff became most important law enforcer, in addition to keeping the peace and fighting crime, they also:
   a. Collected taxes

      b. Supervised elections

      c. Other legal business

  3. Sheriff was paid on a per arrest system

  4. Tax collecting duties were more lucrative than crime fighting, so law enforcement was not one of their primary concerns

  5. In cities, town marshal was chief law enforcement aided, often unwillingly by:

      a. Constables

      b. Night watchmen

      c. Police justices

      d. City council members

  6. Local governments had little power of administration, and enforcement of criminal law was largely an individual or community responsibility

  7. In southern rural areas, slave patrols used to capture escaped slaves, they were an early, if loathsome, form of law enforcement

  8. Western territories encouraged practice of rewarding capture of felons. If there was trouble in town, the vigilance committee formed a posse

      a. These vigilantes were called on to eradicate problems such as theft of livestock through force or intimidation

D. Early Police Agencies

  1. Modern police departments were born out of mob violence

  2. Boston created first formal police department in 1838

  3. New York police department was created in 1844

  4. Philadelphia police department was created in 1854

  5. These new police agencies replaced the night-watch system and relegated constables and sheriffs to serving court orders and running jails

  6. Besides police duties, many departments also maintained public health or swept streets

  7. Politics dominated agencies determining the recruitment of new officers and promotion of supervisors

  8. Agencies were corrupt, brutal, and inefficient

  9. In the late nineteenth century, police work paid well

      a. Factory worker – $450/year

      b. Police officer – $900/year

  10. Conflict between police and the public was born in the difficulty that untrained, unprofessional officers had in patrolling the streets of cities and controlling labor disputes

  11. Police were not crime fighters as we know them today. Their role was to maintain order, and power went unchecked

  12. Average officer had:

      a. Little training

      b. No law education

      c. Minimum supervision

      d. Ability to exercise unlimited discretion

  13. Primary function of police was to:

      a. Serve as the enforcement arm of the reigning political power

      b. Protecting private property

       c. Keep control of the ever-rising numbers of foreign immigrants

14. Uniforms introduced in New York in 1853
15. Communications became the first technological breakthrough
    a. 1850s — Telegraph between headquarters and area precincts
    b. 1867 – First telegraph boxes installed
16. Transportation
    a. 1897 – Bicycles at Detroit Police Department
    b. 1913 – Motorcycle used by departments in eastern part of the nation
    c. 1910 – First police car, Akron OH
    d. 1912 – Police wagon becomes popular in Cincinnati
17. Still not respected

III. **POLICING IN THE TWENTIETH CENTURY**
  A. The Emergence of Professionalism
    1. Creation of police administrative boards to reduce local officials' control over the police: Most failed because private citizens appointed to them lacked expertise in intricacies of police work
    2. Another reform was the takeover of some agencies by state legislators
      a. Cities regained control of their police forces in the first decades of the twentieth century
    3. 1919 Boston Police Strike heightened interest in police reform
      a. Police officers were dissatisfied with their status in society
      b. Boston police association and the Boston Social Club voted to become unionized with the American Federation of Labor
      c. On strike September 9, 1919
      d. Resulted in looting and rioting
      e. All striking officers were fired
      f. Governor Calvin Coolidge mobilized state militia to take over the city
      g. This incident ended police unionism for decades and solidified power in the hands of reactionary, autocratic police administrators
    4. In Depression, reform became less of an issue than economic revival
    5. 1893 – International Association of Chiefs of Police, a professional society, was formed. Called for civil service and removing political influence
    6. Most famous reformer:
      a. August Vollmer
        i. Chief in Berkeley California
        ii. Instituted university training for young officers and helped develop the School of Criminology at the University of California at Berkeley
      b. Protégé O.W. Wilson — Applied modern management and administrative techniques to policing
      c. Police professionalism was equated with an incorruptible, tough, highly trained, rule-oriented department along militaristic lines
    7. Most respected department – Los Angeles: Incorruptible crime fighters
  B. The 1960s and Beyond
    1. Turmoil and crisis hallmarks of policing in the 1960s
    2. Supreme Court decisions control police operations and procedures

3. Police were now required to obey strict legal guidelines when:
   a. Questioning suspects
   b. Conducting searches
   c. Wiretapping
4. Civil rights of suspects are significantly expanded
5. Civil unrest between police and public, especially African Americans – Riots (1964-68)
   a. New York
   b. Detroit
   c. Los Angeles
6. Anti-Vietnam demonstrations
7. Police ill equipped and poorly trained to deal with these social problems
8. Rapidly growing crime rate
   a. Violent and property crimes increased dramatically
9. The 1970s witnessed many structural changes in police agencies
10. Local fears and distrust, combined with conservative federal policies, encouraged police departments to control what was perceived as an emerging minority group "threat"
11. Law Enforcement Assistance Administration (LEAA) allocates significant funds to police agencies
    a. Helped officers further college education
    b. Technological innovations involving computers transformed the way police kept records, investigated crimes, and communicated
    c. State training academies improved the way police learned to deal with:
       i. Job stress
       ii. Community conflict
       iii. Interpersonal relations
12. More women and minorities recruited into police work
13. Affirmative action programs helped alter the ethnic, racial, and gender composition of U.S. policing
14. Policing in the 1980s
    a. Police role changed significantly
    b. Emergence of community policing concept
    c. Police unions which began to grow in the 1960s continued to grow to make significant impact on operations
       i. In many instances, unions eroded the power of the police chief to make unquestioned policy and personnel decisions
    d. Police departments also beset by problems that impeded their effectiveness
       i. State and local budgets were cut back during Regan administration
       ii. Federal support for innovative police programs were severely curtailed with the demise of the LEAA
    e. Police community relations continued to be a major problem
       i. Riots and incidents of urban conflict occurred in some of the nation's largest cities
       ii. Questions concerning police role, especially in inner-city neighborhoods

      a)   Rodney King incident on March 3, 1991 helped change the face of American policing

      b)   Prompted an era of reform

  f. Interest renewed in reviving an earlier style of police work featuring:
    i. Foot patrols
    ii. Increased citizen contact

  g. Police experts decreed that the nation's police forces should be rated not on their crime-fighting ability but on their:
    i. Courteousness
    ii. Deportment
    iii. Helpfulness

  h. Police departments began to embrace new forms of policing that stressed:
    i. Cooperation with the community
    ii. Problem solving

15. Most notable achievements of police departments in the 1990s:
  a. Rise in intellectual caliber
  b. Use of advanced management techniques and the application of empirical data
  c. Standards of conduct rose
  d. More diverse workforce in terms of race and gender
  e. Work of police became intellectually more demanding, requiring an array of new knowledge concerning:
    i. Technology
    ii. Forensic analysis
    iii. Crime
  f. Accepted civilian review of police discipline

IV. POLICING AND LAW ENFORCEMENT TODAY

1. Ongoing effort to make police more user friendly by
  a. Decentralization
  b. More responsive to community needs
2. Law enforcement agencies are also adapting to the changing nature of crime. They must be prepared to handle:
  a. Terrorism
  b. Internet fraud schemes
  c. Identify theft
  d. Rape
  e. Robbery
  f. Burglary
3. Law enforcement duties are distributed across local, county, state, and federal jurisdictions
4. There are currently:
  a. Approximately 700,000 sworn law enforcement officers in the U.S.
  b. Employed in almost 20,000 different agencies
5. There is no real hierarchy, each branch has its own sphere of operations, though overlap may exist

A. Federal Law Enforcement Agencies — Each federal agency created to enforce specific laws and cope with particular situations, no single agency has unlimited jurisdiction
   1. Have no particular rank order or hierarchy of command or responsibility
   2. Dozens of federal law enforcement agencies exist both inside and outside the cabinet-level departments. Focus of this chapter is on:
      a. U.S. Justice Department
      b. Department of Homeland Security
B. U.S. Justice Department Agencies:
   1. Federal Bureau of Investigations
      a. Investigative agency with jurisdiction over all matters in which the United States is or may be an interested party
      b. Limits its jurisdiction to federal laws, including all federal statutes not specifically assigned to other agencies
      c. Have Approximately 30,000 employees, including 12,000 special agents and 17,000 support personnel who perform operations involving:
         i. Professional
         ii. Administrative
         iii. Technical
         iv. Clerical
         v. Craft
         vi. Trade
         vii. Maintenance
      d. Since 9/11 number one priority is protecting the United States from a terrorist attack
      e. Now charged with coordinating intelligence collection with the:
         i. Border Patrol
         ii. Secret Service
         iii. CIA
      f. Other activities are:
         i. Gathering crime statistics
         ii. Running a comprehensive crime laboratory
         iii. Training local law enforcement officers
   2. Drug Enforcement Administration
      a. Assist local and state authorities in investigating illegal drug use and carrying out independent surveillance and enforcement activities to control importation of narcotics
      b. Undercover DEA agents infiltrate drug rings and simulate buying narcotics to arrest drug dealers
   3. Bureau of Alcohol, Tobacco, Firearms, and Explosives
      a. Helps control sales of untaxed liquor and cigarettes
      b. Through Gun Control Act of 1968 and Organized Crime Control Act of 1970:
         i. Jurisdiction over illegal sales, importation, and criminal misuse of firearms and explosives
   4. U.S. Marshals Service

       a. Nation's oldest and most versatile federal law enforcement agency

       b. More than 3,000 Deputy Marshals and Criminal Investigators perform a number of functions including:

          i. Judicial security

          ii. Fugitive investigations

          iii. Witness protection

          iv. Prisoner transportation

          v. Prisoner services

             a) Houses nearly 60,000 federal detainees each day

          vi. Administering the U.S. Justice Department's Asset Forfeiture Program

C. Homeland Security Agencies

       a. On November 19, 2002, Congress passed legislation authorizing the creation of the Department of Homeland Security and assigned it the mission of:

          i. Providing intelligence analysis

          ii. Infrastructure protection

          iii. Strengthening the borders

          iv. Improving the use of science and technology to counter weapons of mass destruction

          v. Creating a comprehensive response and recovery division

   1. Customs and Border Protection

       a. Combined the agencies of:

          i. U.S. Border Patrol

          ii. U.S. Customs Service (portions)

          iii. Immigration and Naturalization Service

          iv. Animal and Plant Health Inspection Service

       b. Employs more than 40,000 personnel

       c. Responsible for protection of America's borders and ports of entry

       d. Most visible agency is Border Patrol

          i. 10,000 agents combine to form one of the largest uniformed law enforcement agencies in the U.S.

   2. The Secret Service

       a. Two main functions:

          i. Protection of national leaders:

             a) President

             b) Vice-president

             c) President-elect

             d) Vice-president elect

             e) Immediate families of above individuals

             f) Former presidents and their families

             g) Visiting heads of state

       b. Established in 1865, tasked with investigating the counterfeiting of U.S. currency

       c. Since 1984, investigative activities have been expanded to include:

          i. Investigation of financial institution fraud

          ii. Computer and telecommunication fraud

       iii. False identification documents

D. State Law Enforcement Agencies

1. Created in response to citizen demands for effective and efficient law enforcement, bereft of corruption, and not being tied to local politics
   a. First agency was the Texas Rangers, created in 1835
   b. 1865 – Massachusetts State Constables
   c. 1901 – Arizona Rangers
2. First truly modern state police agencies:
   a. 1903 – Connecticut
   b. 1905 – Pennsylvania
3. Today, about 23 state police agencies have the same general police powers as municipal police and are territorially limited only by state boundaries
   a. Provide investigative services to smaller communities
   b. Remaining state police agencies primarily responsible for highway patrol and traffic law enforcement
   c. Some state police are prohibited from becoming involved in strikes or other labor disputes, unless violence erupts
4. 90,000 state police employees – 60,000 officers, 30,000 civilians
5. Carry out a variety of functions beside law enforcement and highway safety, including training academies, providing emergency medical services, and crime laboratories
6. State police also provide:
   a. Bomb-site analysis
   b. Homicide investigations
7. State Law Enforcement and the War on Terror
   a. A number of states have beefed up their intelligence-gathering capabilities and aimed them directly at homeland security

E. County Law Enforcement Agencies

1. From the time of westward expansion in the United States until municipal departments were developed, the sheriff was often the sole legal authority over vast territories
2. Today sheriffs' offices contain 330,000 full-time employees including 175,000 sworn personnel
3. Employment has risen an average of about 4% per year since 1990
4. Duties vary widely depending on size but may include:
   a. General Law enforcement, routine patrol
   b. Responding to calls for service
   c. Investigating crimes
5. Other standard tasks include:
   a. Serving civil process
   b. Court security
   c. Operating county jail
6. May also serve as:
   a. Coroners
   b. Tax collectors
   c. Overseers of highways and bridges

  d. Custodians of county treasury
  e. Animal, fire, emergency medical services
  f. Executioners in the past
  7. Typically, jurisdiction are restricted to unincorporated areas of a county, unless a city or town requests its help
  8. As a rule, agencies serving large populations (over 1 million) are devoted to maintaining county correctional facilities, whereas those in smaller population areas are focused on law enforcement
F. Metropolitan Law Enforcement Agencies
  1. Form the majority of the nation's authorized law enforcement personnel
  2. Range in size from 1 officer to 40,000 officers and 10,000 civilian employees (New York City)
  3. 13,000 local police departments have an estimated 600,000 full-time employees, including 460,000 sworn personnel
  4. Majority of departments have fewer than 50 officers and serve a population under 25,000
    a. Nearly ¾ of all local police departments serve populations of under 10,000 people
    b. Approximately 650 agencies employ just one sworn officer
  5. Responsibility is immense, officers often forced to make split-second decisions on life-and-death matters
  6. Must be sensitive to the needs of a racially and ethnically diverse citizenry
  7. Perform multiple roles including:
    a. Investigating crimes
    b. Identifying suspects
    c. Making arrests
  8. Smaller agencies can have trouble carrying out many of the same functions as their big-city counterparts.
    a. Hundreds of small police agencies in each state often provide duplicate services
      i. One approach is to combine smaller agencies into "superagencies"
      ii. Another approach is to link smaller agencies via computerized information sharing and resource management networks
G. Private Policing
  1. Private security has become multibillion dollar industry with
    a. 10,000 firms
    b. 1.5 million employees
  2. Today, people employed in private policing outnumber public police by almost 3:1
  3. Example is Wackenhut Corporation, U.S. based division of Group 4 Securicor, world's 2nd largest provider of security services
    a. Clients include Fortune 500 companies
    b. Primary contractor to NASA and the Army
    c. Assists U.S. government to:
      i. Protect nuclear reactors
      ii. Guard the Trans-Alaska Pipeline Systems

        iii. Maintain security in secret government laboratories and facilities

  4. Questions arise regarding Fourth Amendment issues and private security forces performing public duties

V. TECHNOLOGY AND LAW ENFORCEMENT

1. Policing is relying more and more frequently on modern technology to increase effectiveness, and police are becoming more sophisticated in their use of computer software
   a. Criminal investigation will be enhanced by the application of sophisticated electronic gadgetry:
      i. Computers
      ii. Cell phones
      iii. Digital communication devices
2. Crime Mapping
   a. There are now geographic hot spots where a majority of predatory crimes are concentrated
   b. Computer maps allow police agencies to identify location, time, and linkage among criminal events to concentrate police forces
   c. Simplest maps display crime locations and concentrations, while complex maps can be used to chart trends
   d. Makes use of new computer technology, can assist police in detecting crime patterns and pathologies of related problems
3. License Plate Recognition Technology
   a. Employs camera and computer technology to identify letters and numbers of license plates to compare with records in state and federal databases
   b. Cameras placed on police cars
   c. Initially designed for parking lots, access control, or for paying tolls
   d. Expanded into the realms of border control, identification of stolen vehicles, and traffic fine enforcement
4. Digitizing Criminal Identification
   a. Police agencies using computerized imaging systems for criminal identification
   b. Used to help witnesses create a composite picture of a perpetrator
   c. Creation of photo line-ups
   d. Mug shots can be re-created in three-dimensions
5. Automated Fingerprint Identification Systems
   a. Using mathematical models, it can classify fingerprints and identify up to 250 characteristics (minutiae) of a print
   b. Uses high-speed computer chips to plot each point of minutiae and count number of ridge lines between that point and its four nearest neighbors
   c. Improves the speed and accuracy of fingerprint identification
6. DNA profiling
   a. Allows suspects to be identified on the basis of the genetic material found in
      i. Hair
      ii. Blood

   iii. Other bodily tissues and fluids
  7. DNA segments in rape cases taken from:
   a. Victim
   b. Suspect
   c. Blood and/or semen found on victim
   d. DNA match indicates a four-billion-to-one likelihood that suspect is the offender
 A. Fusion Centers
  1. An effective and efficient mechanism to exchange information and intelligence, maximize resources, streamline operations, and improve the ability to fight crime and terrorism by analyzing data from a variety of sources
  2. Typically set up for the purpose of sharing information and intelligence within specific jurisdictions and across levels of government
   a. Often emphasize terrorism prevention and crime fighting with extensive use of technology
   b. Frequently resemble a department's technological "nerve center"
   c. Usually housed in a central location and information shared with decision-makers
  3. Four main goals:
   a. Support for a range of law enforcement activities, including anti-crime operations and terrorism prevention
   b. Help for major incident operations and support for units charged with interdiction and criminal investigations
   c. Provide the means for community input, often through "tip lines"
   d. Assistance to law enforcement executives so they can make informed decision about departmental priorities
  4. Premised on a model of collaboration
  5. Likely that more will be developed

CHAPTER SUMMARY

The origin of U.S. police agencies can be traced to early English society. Before the Norman Conquest, every person was responsible for aiding neighbors and protecting the settlement. This was known as the pledge system. People were grouped in collectives of 10 families, or tithings, and were entrusted with policing their own minor problems. When trouble occurred, citizens were expected to make a hue and cry. Ten tithings were grouped into a "hundred," whose affairs were supervised by a constable appointed by the local nobleman. The constable, considered the first real police officer, dealt with more serious breaches of the law. Shires, which resembled the counties of today, were controlled by the shire reeve.

Early thief takers were private police who apprehended criminals for reward payments. The first organized police force was founded by Sir Robert Peel in London. Law enforcement in colonial America paralleled the British model. In the colonies, the county sheriff became the most important law enforcement agent. The modern police department was born out of urban mob violence that wracked the nation's cities in the nineteenth century. The first true U.S. police departments were formed in Boston, New York, and Philadelphia in the early nineteenth century. The police were viewed as being dominated by political bosses who controlled their hiring practices and policies. In the nineteenth century, big-city police were still not respected by the public, unsuccessful in their role as crime stoppers, and uninvolved in progressive activities.

Reform movements begun in the 1920s culminated in the concept of professionalism. Police professionalism was interpreted to mean tough, rule-oriented police work featuring advanced technology and hardware. The view that these measures would quickly reduce crime proved incorrect. Civic leaders in a number of jurisdictions created police administrative boards to reduce local officials' control over the police. Another reform movement was the takeover of some metropolitan police agencies by state legislators. In 1893 the International Association of Chiefs of Police (IACP), a professional society, was formed.

The police experienced turmoil in the 1960s and 1970s, which led to reforms such as the hiring of women and minorities. Questions about the effectiveness of law enforcement have led to the development of community policing. Police departments began to embrace new forms of policing that stressed cooperation with the community and problem solving. An ongoing effort was made to make departments more diverse. Standards of police conduct climbed.

There are several major law enforcement agencies. On the federal level, the FBI is the largest federal agency. Other agencies include the Drug Enforcement Administration and the U.S. Marshals Service. Most states maintain state police agencies, which investigate crimes and patrol the roadways. County-level law enforcement is provided by sheriffs' departments, who run jails and patrol rural areas. Local police agencies engage in patrol, investigative, and traffic functions, as well as many support activities.

Most police departments have begun to rely on advanced computer-based technology to identify suspects and collate evidence. Computer mapping programs translate addresses into map coordinates and allow departments to identify problem areas for particular crimes, such as drug dealing. Automated fingerprint systems and computerized identification systems have become widespread.

DISCUSSION QUESTIONS

1. List the problems faced by today's police departments that were also present during the early days of policing.
2. Distinguish between the duties of the state police, sheriffs' departments, and local police departments.
3. Do you believe that the general public has greater respect for the police today than in the past? If so, why? If not, why not?
4. What are some of the technological advances that should help the police solve more crimes? What are the dangers of these advances?
5. Discuss the trends that will influence policing during the coming decade. What other social factors may affect police?

MEDIA TOOLS

The website of the London Metropolitan Police contains an extensive history of the London Metropolitan Police, history of British policing, and famous cases including such notorious criminals as Jack the Ripper. History of the Metropolitan Police found at: http://www.met.police.uk/history/definition.htm

Read an extensive history, including photos of the Boston Police Strike of 1919. Site provided by Massachusetts Foundation for the Humanities. Site can be found at: http://www.massmoments.org/moment.cfm?mid=237

Explore the website of the International Association of Chiefs of Police. Spend some time reviewing the training, publications, and technology tabs. Site can be found at: http://theiacp.org

View the potential uses of DNA. This handbook provided by INTERPOL, the international police organization. The handbook includes scenarios that point the advantages of sharing DNA databases. The handbook can be found at: http://www.interpol.int/Public/ICPO/Publications/HandbookPublic2009.pdf

Visit the site of the American Civil Liberties Union in regard to the perceived negative aspects of fusion centers. See the site at: http://www.aclu.org/technology-and-liberty/whats-wrong-fusion-centers-executive-summary

PRACTICE TEST BANK

MULTIPLE CHOICE

1. Law enforcement in colonial America was based on the system of
   a. France.
   b. Canada.
   c. Australia.
   d. Britain.

2. In the rural south, these individuals had the responsibility of recapturing slaves?
   a. Vigilantes
   b. Slave patrols
   c. Constables
   d. Shire Reeves

3. In what century did professionalism emerge in policing?
   a. Eighteenth
   b. Nineteenth
   c. Twentieth
   d. Twenty first

4. Which of the listed federal agencies has unlimited jurisdiction?
   a. No federal agency has unlimited jurisdiction
   b. FBI
   c. DEA
   d. CBP

5. In the thirteenth century, which system of night patrol was created in England's largest cities and towns?
   a. Pledge system
   b. Watch system
   c. Reeve system
   d. Constable system

6. What type of private police agent was created in the 1700s to deal with rising crime?
   a. Watchmen
   b. Pledge men
   c. Thief takers
   d. Committees of vigilance

7. Arguably, the first professional police agency was the London Municipal Police, founded in 1829 by Sir
   a. Walter Raleigh.
   b. Edmund Hillary.
   c. James Noel.
   d. Robert Peel.

8. What type of groups (law enforcement groups) were formed by citizens as an attempt to offset weak law enforcement protection?
   a. Vigilante groups
   b. Constable groups
   c. Pledge groups
   d. Wergild groups

9. The first formal police department in the U.S. was created in 1838 in
   a. New York.
   b. Philadelphia.
   c. Boston.
   d. Atlanta.

10. During the 1800s, in general, American police agencies came to be regarded as
    a. models of efficiency and professionalism.
    b. politically independent and well-trained.
    c. proactive and well-disciplined.
    d. corrupt and incompetent.

11. The most famous police reformer at the turn of the twentieth century was
    a. Rodney King.
    b. August Vollmer.
    c. Robert Peel.
    d. Abner Louima.

12. The Texas Rangers were originally created to patrol
    a. the great plains.
    b. un-traveled mountain terrain.
    c. the Mexican border.
    d. unincorporated U.S. Territory.

13. Who pioneered the use of advanced training for officers and was instrumental in applying modern management and administrative techniques to policing?
    a. Whitworth
    b. Collingswood
    c. Wilson
    d. Vollmer

14. In the 1960s and 1970s, which federal program's funds provided educational opportunities and equipment for police departments?
    a. HUD
    b. FBI
    c. IACP
    d. LEAA

15. During the 1960s, the Supreme Court issued decisions that controlled police operations involving
    a. questioning suspects.
    b. wiretapping.
    c. conducting searches.
    d. all of the above.

16. Which federal agency's jurisdiction includes protecting federal officials, transporting criminal defendants, and tracking down fugitives?
    a. FBI
    b. DEA
    c. U.S. Marshals
    d. Secret Service

17. Today, most law enforcement personnel in the U.S. are employed at the
    a. county level.
    b. federal level.
    c. state level.
    d. municipal/local level.

18. The first truly modern state police agencies were formed by
    a. Delaware and Vermont.
    b. Michigan and Ohio.
    c. Connecticut and Pennsylvania.
    d. New York and Massachusetts.

19. Which of the following agency's typical tasks include serving civil process, providing court security, and operating county jails?
    a. State police
    b. County sheriff
    c. U.S. marshal
    d. City police

20. The majority of municipal police agencies have less than
    a. 5 officers.
    b. 50 officers.
    c. 25 officers.
    d. 10 officers.

21. A geographic area where a majority of predatory crimes are concentrated is known as a
    a. sun spot.
    b. hot spot.
    c. crime concentrate.
    d. hot zone.

22. In which city/town did the first police car make its debut in 1910?
    a. Akron, Ohio
    b. Detroit, Michigan
    c. Philadelphia, Pennsylvania
    d. Cincinnati, Ohio

23. Which technique allows suspects to be identified on the basis of the genetic material found in hair, blood, and other bodily tissues and fluids?
    a. DNA profiling
    b. LPR technology
    c. AFIS
    d. Fusion

24. Uniforms were introduced in 1853 in
    a. Boston.
    b. New York.
    c. Detroit.
    d. Cincinnati.

25. Police reform became a heightened interest in 1919 due in large part to
    a. vigilantism.
    b. the police inability to unionize.
    c. the Boston police strike.
    d. the Great Depression.

26. August Vollmer was the Chief of Police in Berkeley, CA where he developed the
    a. School of Justice.
    b. School of Policing.
    c. School of Crime.
    d. School of Criminology.

27. Which centers resemble a police department's technological nerve center and are usually housed in a central location where information is collected and shared with decision makers?
    a. Dispatch
    b. Emergency operation
    c. Fusion
    d. Fulton

28. Which technological device has expanded into the realms of border control, identification of stolen vehicles, and traffic-fine enforcement?
    a. DNA
    b. Automated Fingerprint Identification System
    c. License Plate Recognition
    d. Fusion Centers

29. The ATF helps control legal sales of:
    a. guns.
    b. cigarettes.
    c. liquor.
    d. all of the above.

30. Criminal investigation will be enhanced by the application of all of the listed sophisticated electronic gadgetry except
    a. computers.
    b. cell phones.
    c. digital communication devices.
    d. video game players.

TRUE/FALSE

1. T   F   AFIS stands for automated fingerprint identification system(s).

2. T   F   The sheriff is generally the chief law enforcement officer for a county.

3. T   F   There are more federal law enforcement officers than state and city agencies combined.

4. T   F   The Bureau of Alcohol, Tobacco, and Firearms is a federal agency.

5. T   F   The Rodney King case prompted an era of police reform.

6. T   F   Purely private search activities violate Fourth Amendment prohibitions.

7. T   F   The "hundred" was a group of 100 constables.

8. T   F   In Medieval England, the tithing was money contributed to the night watch.

9. T   F   IACP is an acronym for International Association of Chiefs of Police.

10. T   F   The first police department in the U.S. was established in Boston.

11. T **F** Early American police forces were well trained, disciplined, and professional.

12. T **F** The DEA is the nation's oldest federal law enforcement agency.

13. **T** F Criminal investigation is being enhanced by the application of sophisticated technology.

14. T **F** In the 1980s, police forces were ill equipped and poorly trained to deal with social problems.

15. T F In the late nineteenth century, police work paid less than most other blue collar jobs.

FILL-IN-THE-BLANK

1. In Medieval England, a group of ten families who policed themselves was called a _tithing_.

2. The identification procedure involving genetic patterns is called _DNA_ profiling.

3. In Medieval England, if someone was victimized, they were expected to raise a hue and _cry_.

4. In the 1970s the end of the _Vietnam_ war significantly reduced tensions between students and police.

5. In the 1990s police began to use advanced management techniques and applied _empirical_ _____ data to their decision making.

6. On November 19, 2002, Congress passed legislation authorizing the creation of the _Dept._ _Homeland Security_.

7. The office in Medieval England that evolved into the office of sheriff was the shire _reeve_.

8. Unlike municipal police departments _state_ police were legislatively created to deal with the growing incidence of crime in nonurban areas.

9. In the 1990s the _Rodney King_ case prompted an era of reform.

10. A group of private citizens who enforce the law on their own are known as _vigilantes_.

11. _Crime maps_ offer police administrators' graphic representations of where crimes are occurring in their jurisdiction.

12. August _Vollmer_ was a famous police chief who advocated police reform.

13. _fusion_ centers often emphasize terrorism prevention and crime fighting with extensive use of technology.

14. One of the first state police agencies was the Texas _Rangers_, created in 1835.

15. The lead federal agency in enforcing drug laws is the _DEA_.

ESSAY

1. Identify 3 federal law enforcement agencies and discuss their duties.

2. Discuss three technological / scientific advances that are utilized by police today.

3. Summarize the differences among state, county, and local law enforcement.

4. Explain why policing in the 1990s began on a sour note and ended with an air of optimism.

5. Discuss some of the developments, problems, challenges, and changes in policing from the 1970s to the present time.

CHAPTER 4 ANSWER KEY

Multiple Choice

1. d [p. 77, LO3]   2. b [p. 77, LO3]   3. c [p. 79, LO6]   4. a [p. 83, LO7]   5. b [p. 76, LO1]

6. c [p. 76, LO2]   7. d [p. 76, LO2]   8. a [p. 77, LO3]   9. c [p. 77, LO3]   10. d [p. 78, LO4]

11. b [p. 79, LO6]   12. c [p. 85, LO8]   13. c [p. 79, LO5]   14. d [p. 81, LO6]   15. d [p. 80, LO6]

16. c [p. 83, LO7]   17. d [p. 87, LO8]   18. c [p. 85, LO8, 3]   19. b [p. 86, LO8]   20. b [p. 87, LO8]

21. b [p. 89, LO9]   22. a [p. 78, LO3]   23. b [p. 91, LO9]   24. b [p. 78, LO3]   25. c [p. 79, LO3,4]

26. d [p. 79, LO5]   27. c [p. 91, LO9]   28. c [p. 90, LO9]   29. d [p. 83, LO7]   30. d [p. 89, LO 9]

True/False

1. T [p. 91, LO9]   2. T [p. 76, LO8]   3. F [p. 82, LO8]   4. T [p. 83, LO7]   5. T [p. 81, LO6]

6. F [p. 89, LO8]   7. F [p. 75, LO1]   8. F [p. 75, LO1]   9. T [p. 79, LO5]   10. T [p. 77, LO3]

11. F [p. 77, LO4]   12. F [p. 83, LO7]   13. T [p. 89, LO9]   14. F [p. 80, LO6]   15. F [p. 77, LO5]

Fill-in-the-Blank

1. tithing [p. 75, LO1]   2. DNA [p. 91, LO9]   3. cry [p. 75, LO1]

4. Vietnam [p. 80, LO6]   5. empirical [p. 81, LO6]   6. Department of Homeland Security (DHS)
[p. 83, LO7]

7. reeve [p. 75, LO1]   8. state [p. 85, LO8]   9. Rodney King [p. 81, LO6]

10. vigilantes [p. 77, LO3]   11. Crime maps [p. 89, LO9]   12. Vollmer [p. 79, LO5]

13. Fusion [p. 91, LO9]   14. Rangers [p. 85, LO8]   15. DEA [p. 83, LO7]

Essay

1.   **Identify 3 federal law enforcement agencies and discuss their duties.**

Federal Bureau of Investigation (FBI) The Federal Bureau of Investigation is an investigative agency with jurisdiction over all matters in which the United States is or may be an interested party. Its jurisdiction is limited, however, to federal laws, including all federal statutes not specifically assigned to other agencies. Since 9/11, the FBI has announced a reformulation of its priorities, making protecting the United States from terrorist attack its number one commitment. It is now charged with coordinating intelligence collection with the Border Patrol, the Secret Service, and the CIA. Among the agency's other activities are gathering crime statistics, running a comprehensive crime laboratory, and training local law enforcement officers.

111

Drug Enforcement Administration (DEA) DEA agents assist local and state authorities in investigating illegal drug use and carrying out independent surveillance and enforcement activities to control the importation of narcotics. For example, DEA agents work with foreign governments in cooperative efforts aimed at destroying opium and marijuana crops at their source—hard-to-find fields tucked away in the interiors of Latin America, Asia, Europe, and Africa. Undercover DEA agents infiltrate drug rings and simulate buying narcotics to arrest drug dealers.

Bureau of Alcohol, Tobacco, Firearms, and Explosives (ATF) The ATF helps control sales of untaxed liquor and cigarettes and, through the Gun Control Act of 1968 and the Organized Crime Control Act of 1970, has jurisdiction over the illegal sale, importation, and criminal misuse of firearms and explosives.

U.S. Marshals Service The U.S. Marshals Service is America's oldest federal law enforcement agency and one of the most versatile. Deputy marshals and criminal investigators perform a number of functions, including judicial security, fugitive investigations, witness protection, prisoner transportation, prisoner services, and administration of the U.S. Justice Department's Asset Forfeiture Program.

Customs and Border Protection (CBP) After 9/11, the U.S. Border Patrol, portions of the U.S. Customs Service, the Immigration and Naturalization Service, and the Animal and Plant Health Inspection Service were combined into one office of Customs and Border Protection. The agency is primarily responsible for protection of America's borders and ports of entry. The largest and most visible element of CBP is the Border Patrol.

Secret Service The U.S. Secret Service performs two main functions. The more visible of these is protection of national leaders, notably the president but also the vice president, the president-elect, the vice president-elect, the immediate families of these individuals, former presidents and their families, visiting heads of state, and other officials. The Secret Service was first established as a law enforcement entity in 1865 and was tasked with investigating the counterfeiting of U.S. currency. Since 1984, Secret Service investigative activities have been expanded to include the investigation of financial institution fraud, computer and telecommunications fraud, false identification documents, and other criminal activities.

[pp. 82-89, LO7]

2. **Discuss three technological / scientific advances that are utilized by police today.**

Modern technology has increased the effectiveness and efficiency of law enforcement. Today Crime Mapping assists officers in identifying "hot spots." These "hot spots' provide guidance to law enforcement managers when deciding how or where to deploy precious resources. Crime mapping allows patterns to be detected and analyzed. More complex maps can even recognize trends in criminal activity. Multiple layers of information can be intertwined for analysis.

License plate recognition technology employs cameras and computer equipment software to "read" vehicle license plates and compare the information against state and federal databases. The technology is portable and is designed to be installed in an officer's police cruiser. The equipment is capable of reading a large volume of plates at a time. The information gleaned can assist in identifying wanted persons, stolen vehicles and unlicensed drivers.

DNA testing has lead to DNA profiling where criminal suspects are identified through matching DNA samples of a suspect with those found as evidence at a crime scene. The identification is made based upon the unique genetic material found in blood, hair, saliva or bodily tissues. There are two methods for conducting matching.

Many state and local law enforcement agencies have formed so-called fusion centers. According to the National Fusion Center Guidelines, a fusion center is "an effective and efficient mechanism to exchange information and intelligence, maximize resources, streamline operations, and improve the ability to fight crime and terrorism by analyzing data from a variety of sources." Fusion centers are typically set up for the purpose of sharing information and intelligence within specific jurisdictions and across levels of government. They often emphasize terrorism prevention and crime fighting with extensive use of technology. They frequently resemble a department's technological "nerve center" and are usually housed in a central location where information is collected and then shared with decision-makers. There are four main goals for fusion centers:

* Support for a range of law enforcement activities, including anti-crime operations and terrorism prevention.
* Help for major incident operations and support for units charged with interdiction and criminal investigations
* Provide the means for community input, often through "tip lines."
* Assistance to law enforcement executives so they can make informed decision about departmental priorities.

[pp. 89-91, LO9]

3.   Summarize the differences among state, county, and local law enforcement.

Most states maintain state police agencies, who investigate crimes and patrol the roadways. County-level law enforcement is provided by sheriffs' departments, who run jails and patrol rural areas. Local police agencies engage in patrol, investigative, and traffic functions, as well as many support activities.

[p. 85-88, LO8]

4.   Explain why policing in the 1990s began on a sour note and ended with an air of optimism.

In March of 1991 Rodney King, a black motorist, fled police. When police finally caught up with Mr. King they delivered in excess of 50 baton blows and 6 kicks to his person. Mr. King suffered significant injuries including brain damage and kidney damage. The event was captured on video tape and went on to be played around the world. The officers were eventually charged and acquitted by an all-white jury. The public outrage from the incident sparked six days of rioting on the streets of Los Angeles.

The King case came to serve as platform for reform. Police departments came to be evaluated not on their crime fighting ability but on how they were perceived by the public. Courtesy, demeanor and professionalism were in demand. Interest revived for patrols and other community centered police actions. The ideal police officer candidate changed as higher education requirements became the standard. Police management techniques grew and advanced as managers were pressed to raise conduct standards and treat the public more fairly. The nature of police work became more intellectually challenging and the use of technology gave educated personnel additional tools to fight crime and capture criminals.

[p. 81, LO6]

5.   Discuss some of the developments, problems, challenges, and changes in policing from the 1970s to the present time.

The 1970s witnessed many structural changes in police agencies themselves. The end of the Vietnam War significantly reduced tensions between students and police. The relationship between police and minorities was still rocky, however. Local fears and distrust, combined with conservative federal policies, encouraged police departments to control what was perceived as an emerging minority group "threat." As the 1980s began, the police role seemed to be changing significantly. A number of experts acknowledged that the police were not simply crime fighters and called for police to develop a greater awareness of community issues, which resulted in the emergence of the community policing concept. The 1990s gave way to community orientated policing where problem resolution took center stage. Police agencies transformed their business model evolving from a reactive to proactive police approach to managing crime. Police personnel also became more educated as higher standards were imposed. Entry level personnel were more effectively screened and police academies offered formal training and instruction. Policing went from being a "job" to becoming a "profession" where education and technological skills are desirous. The 1990s also brought the community and its unique problems into the spotlight. Police agencies were expected to be problem solvers not problem managers. The idea of the police being community partners shaped police operations around the country. Contemporary law enforcement agencies are still undergoing transformation. There has been an ongoing effort to make police "user friendly" by decentralizing police departments and making them responsive to community needs. Police and law enforcement agencies are also adapting to the changing nature of crime: They must be prepared to handle terrorism, Internet fraud schemes, and identity theft, as well as rape, robbery, and burglary.

[pp. 80-81, LO6]

CHAPTER 5
The Police:
Role and Function

After studying this chapter, students will:

1. Understand the organization of police departments
2. Articulate the complexities of the police role
3. Explain the limitations of patrol and methods for improving it
4. Summarize the investigation function
5. Explain what forensics is and what forensics experts do for police agencies
6. Understand the concept of community policing
7. Discuss the concept of problem-oriented policing
8. Be familiar with the various police support functions

KEY TERMS AND CONCEPTS

police chief (p. 95) The top administrator of the police department, who sets policy and has general control over departmental policies and practices. The chief is typically a political rather than a civil service appointee and serves at the pleasure of the mayor.

time-in-rank system (p. 95) For police officers to advance in rank, they must spend an appropriate amount of time, usually years, in the preceding rank—for example, to become a captain, an officer must first spend time as a lieutenant.

order maintenance (peacekeeping) (p. 97) The order-maintenance aspect of the police role involves peacekeeping, maintaining order and authority without the need for formal arrest, "handling the situation," and keeping things under control by using threats, persuasion, and understanding.

proactive policing (p. 98) A police department policy emphasizing stopping crimes before they occur rather than reacting to crimes that have already occurred.

deterrent effect (p. 98) Stopping or reducing crime by convincing would-be criminals that they stand a significant risk of being apprehended and punished for their crimes.

directed patrol (p. 98) A patrol strategy that involves concentrating police resources in areas where certain crimes are a significant problem.

broken windows model (p. 99) The term used to describe the role of the police as maintainers of community order and safety.

CompStat (p. 100) A program originated by the New York City police that used carefully collected and analyzed crime data to shape policy and evaluate police effectiveness.

sting operation (p. 103) An undercover police operation in which police pose as criminals to trap law violators.

vice squad (p. 103) Police officers assigned to enforce morality-based laws, such as those on prostitution, gambling, and pornography.

forensic science (p. 105) The use of scientific techniques to investigate questions of interest to the justice system and solve crimes.

community-oriented policing (p. 108) Programs and strategies designed to bring police and the public closer together and create a more cooperative working environment between them.

foot patrol (p. 109) Police patrols that take officers out of cars and put them on a walking beat in order to strengthen ties with the community.

neighborhood-oriented policing (NOP) (p. 110) Community policing efforts aimed at individual neighborhoods.

problem-oriented policing (p. 112) A style of police operations that stresses proactive problem solving, rather than reactive crime fighting.

hot spots of crime (p. 112) Places from which a significant portion of all police calls originate. These hot spots include taverns and housing projects.

internal affairs (p. 113) The branch of the police department that investigates charges of corruption or misconduct on the part of police officers.

CHAPTER OUTLINE

I. **THE POLICE ORGANIZATION**
1. Most municipal police agencies are independent agencies within the executive branch of government, operating without specific administrative control from any higher governmental authority
2. Often cooperate and participate in mutually beneficial enterprises such as:
   a. Joint task force with state and federal law enforcement agencies
3. Police agencies are functionally independent organizations with unique set of:
   i. Rules
   ii. Policies
   iii. Procedures

           iv. Norms

           v. Budgets

    4. Most police departments are arranged in a hierarchical manner, with each element having its own chain of command

    5. Size of agency determines structure and organization

    6. Regardless of size, head of organization is the police chief who:

      a. Sets policy

      b. Has general administrative control over department's various operating branches

A. Pros and Cons of Police Organization

    1. Administrators must rise through ranks in most organizations because of civil service

    2. To get promoted, officers must pass a battery of:

      a. Tests

      b. Profiles

      c. Interviews

    3. Time in rank system -Must hold certain amount of time in one rank before one can be promoted to the next higher rank

      a. Pros

        i. Promotes stability and fairness

        ii. Limits favoritism

      b. Cons

        i. Restricts administrative flexibility

    4. Police executives most likely to choose elements that confer legitimacy on existing organizations, and on implementing them in ways that minimize disruption, rather than embrace new and truly innovative changes

II. **THE POLICE ROLE**

    1. A police officer's crime-fighting efforts are only a small part of overall activities

    2. Significant portion of officers' time spent handling:

      a. Minor disturbances

      b. Service calls

      c. Administrative duties

    3. Recent survey found almost 44 million persons had at least one contact with police in that year

      a. More than half were for traffic related matters

      b. Thirty percent reported problems or asked for assistance; for example, responding to neighbor complaint

      c. Police role varied and complex

    4. Police make about 14 million arrests, or 20 per officer. Of these, 2 million are for serious Part I crimes, which equals 3 per officer

    5. Average officer:

      a. Fewer than 2 arrests per month

      b. Less than one felony arrest every four months

    6. Figures should be interpreted with caution because:

     a. Not all are assigned to uniform patrol
     b. One-third of all sworn officers are in special units such as:
       i. Communications
       ii. Antiterrorism
       iii. Administration
       iv. Personnel
7. Though police handle thousands of calls each year, relatively few result in an arrest for a serious crime
8. Police officers function in a variety of roles ranging from:
     a. Dispensers of emergency medical care to
     b. Keepers of the peace on school grounds

III. **THE PATROL FUNCTION**
1. Uniform patrol officers are backbone of policing
     a. Account for two-thirds of a department
2. Major purposes of patrol are to:
     a. Deter crime by maintaining a visible police presence
     b. Maintain order within a patrol area
     c. Respond quickly to law violations or other emergencies
     d. Identify and apprehend law violators
     e. Aid individuals and care for those who cannot help themselves
     f. Facilitate movement of people and traffic
     g. Create feeling of security in the community

A. Patrol Activities
1. Great bulk of patrol efforts are devoted to order maintenance, or peacekeeping:
     a. Maintaining order and civility in their assigned jurisdiction
     b. Order maintenance occupies border between criminal and noncriminal behavior
2. Primary role of police is "handling the situation"
     a. May be accomplished by enforcing the law or by:
       i. Use of threats
       ii. Coercion
       iii. Sympathy
       iv. Understanding
3. The real police role may be as a community problem solver
4. Police practice selective enforcement:
     a. Concentrating on some crimes but handling the majority in an informal manner

B. Does Patrol Deter Crime?
1. Primary goal of police patrol has been to deter criminal behavior
2. Research efforts have not supported deterrence capability
3. 1970s – Kansas City study:
     a. Variations in patrol activity had little effect on crime patterns
     b. Presence of absence of patrol officers did not seem to affect:
       i. Residential or business burglaries
       ii. Motor vehicle thefts

    iii. Larceny involving auto accessories
    iv. Robberies
    v. Vandalism
   c. Did not influence citizens' attitudes of police, their satisfaction with police, or fear of crime
  4. Recent studies indicate that police presence may actually reduce crime levels and that adding police may bring crime levels down
 C. Improving Patrol
  1. Police departments have initiated a number of programs and policies to try to improve patrol effectiveness:
   a. Proactive Policing and Directed Patrol:
    i. The use of proactive, aggressive law enforcement style may help reduce crime rates
    ii. Jurisdictions that encourage patrol officer to stop motor vehicles to issue citations and to aggressively arrest and detain suspicious persons experience lower crime rates
    iii. Jurisdictions that more actively enforce minor regulations such as disorderly conduct and traffic laws, more likely to experience lower felony rates
    iv. Proactive patrol efforts may help improve response time and increase the number of patrol cars that respond to crime
    v. May have deterrent effect:
     a) Increases community perception that police arrest many criminals and that most violators get caught
     b) Results in conviction of more criminals
    vi. Because aggressive police arrest more suspects, there are fewer left on the street to commit crime:
     a) Fewer criminals produce lower crime rates
    vii. Targeting Crimes – Targeting specific crimes can be successful, for example, the Kansas City Gun Experiment
    viii. Aggressive patrol tactics have been a critical success
     a) Some fear that aggressive policing will result in antagonism between proactive cops and the general public
     b) Recent research indicates that precinct level efforts to ensure officers are respectful to citizens helped lower the number of complaints and improved community relations
   b. Making Arrests
    i. Some studies show that contact with police may cause some offenders to not repeat criminal behavior, especially first offenders
    ii. Possible that news of increased and aggressive police arrest activity is rapidly diffused through the population and has an immediate impact on crime rates
    iii. As the number of arrests per capita increases, crime rates decrease
   c. Rapid Response
    i. Research indicates that rapid response had virtually no effect on crime
    ii. People tend to be slow when it comes to reporting crime

    d. Broken Windows Policing
       i. 1982 paper by George Kelling and James Q. Wilson made three points:
          a) Neighborhood disorder creates fear
            1. Urban areas filled with street people, youth gangs, prostitutes, and mentally disturbed are likely to maintain high degree of crime
          b) Neighborhood give out crime-promoting signals
            1. Neighborhood filled with deteriorated housing, broken windows, and untended disorderly behavior gives out crime-promoting signals
          c) Police need citizen cooperation
            1. If police reduce fear and successfully combat crime, they must have cooperation, support, and assistance of citizens
      ii. Community preservation, public safety, and order maintenance should become the primary focus of patrol
      iii. Research indicates that areas that followed this model had substantial reductions in crime, disorder, and calls for service
    e. Using Technology – Most well-known use of technology is CompStat
       i. Begun in New York City as a means of directing police effort in a more productive fashion
      ii. Required precinct commanders to demonstrate their intimate knowledge of crime trends and develop strategies to address them effectively
      iii. CompStat proved successful and was credited with being a part of crime drop in New York City

IV. **THE INVESTIGATION FUNCTION**
    1. Modern criminal investigator most likely an experienced civil servant who is:
      a. Trained in investigatory techniques
      b. Knowledgeable about legal rules of evidence and procedure
      c. Somewhat cautious about the legal and administrative consequences of actions
    2. Investigative services division organized in variety of ways; for example, the New York Police Department:
      a. Local squad detectives work closely with patrol officers to provide an immediate investigative response to crimes and incidents
      b. Maintains specialized borough squads to give aid to local squads:
        i. Homicide
       ii. Robbery
      iii. Special victims
  A. How Do Detectives Detect?
    1. Police detectives rely heavily on interviews and forensic evidence to create or manufacture a narrative of the crime
    2. Typically take a three prong approach:
      a. Specific focus – interview witnesses, gather evidence, record events, collect facts at crime scene

      b. General coverage
        i. Canvass neighborhood, make observations
        ii. Interview family, friends, and associates
        iii. Contact coworkers or employers for information
        iv. Construct victim/suspect timelines
      c. Informative – use modern technology to collect records of cell phone use, computer hard drives, diaries, notes, and documents
    3. Detective work is an art as well as a science based on experience and knowledge of human behavior gained on the job

B. Sting Operations
    1. Organized groups of officers working in plain clothes who deceive criminals into openly committing illegal acts or conspiring to engage in criminal activity; for example, vice squads for public moral crimes such as prostitution or gambling
    2. Covert police activities have often been criticized as violating the personal rights of citizens while forcing officers into demeaning roles
    3. Often comes close to entrapment

C. Evaluating Investigations
    1. Rand Corporation Study:
      a. Great deal of detectives' time spent on unproductive work
      b. Investigative expertise did little to solve cases
      c. Half of all detectives could be replaced without negatively influencing crime clearance rates
    2. Detectives do make a valuable contribution to police work because of their skilled interrogation and case processing techniques
    3. Detective work may be more productive if detectives were allowed more time on each case especially in homicide investigations to:
      a. Carefully collect physical evidence at the scene
      b. Identify witnesses
      c. Check departmental records
      d. Use informants
    4. Majority of cases solved when perpetrator is identified at the scene by patrol officers:
      a. If a crime reported in progress – 33 percent chance of arrest
      b. One minute later – 10 percent chance of arrest
      c. Fifteen or more minutes – 5 percent chance of arrest
    5. As time between crime and arrest grows, chances of a conviction are reduced because the ability to recover evidence is lost
    6. Reason for detective ineffectiveness is that they lack sufficient resources
    7. Research shows:
      a. Unsolved cases:
        i. About 50 percent of burglary cases screened out by supervisors, of those assigned 75 percent dropped after the first day. 75 percent of robbery cases also dropped after 1 day of investigation
      b. Length of investigation:

121

    i. Majority of cases investigated for no more than four hours over 3 days Average of 11 days between crime and suspension of investigation

  c. Sources of information:

    i. Most critical information for determining case outcome is name and description of suspect and related crime information

    ii. Victims are most often the source of information

  d. Effectiveness:

    i. Preliminary investigations by patrol officer critical, when identity of suspect is not known immediately, detectives make an arrest in less than 10 percent of all cases

D. Improving Investigation with Technology:

 1. Information technology has revolutionized police work in many areas:

  a. Communication

  b. Criminal identification

  c. Record storage

 2. CopLink:

  a. Integrates information from different jurisdictions into a single database that detectives can access

 3. DNA profiling:

  a. Most important investigative technology since the adoption of fingerprint comparison

E. Improving Investigations with Forensic Science

 1. Forensic means "pertaining to the law"

 2. Forensic scientists perform comprehensive chemical and physical analyses on evidence

 3. Most forensic scientists (criminalists) focus on criminal cases; others are involved in civil cases such as handwriting analysis

 4. Forensic specialists can examine blood and other body fluids and tissues for the presence of:

  a. Alcohol

  b. Drugs

  c. Poisons

 5. Forensic scientists analyze trace physical evidence such as:

  a. Blood spatters

  b. Paint

  c. Soil

  d. Glass

 6. Forensic scientists also provide testimony in a court of law when the case is brought to trial

 7. While some criminalists are generalists many focus on a particular area:

  a. Toxicology

  b. Blood pattern analysis

  c. Crime scene investigation

  d. Impression evidence

  e. Trace evidence

  f. Questioned documents

V.   **COMMUNITY POLICING**
1.   For several decades police agencies have been trying to gain the cooperation and respect of the communities they serve.
2.   First involved improving relationships with the public involved programs with the general title of police-community relations (PCR)
     a.   Designed to make citizens:
          i.   More aware of police activities
          ii.   Alert them to methods of self-protection
          iii. Improve general attitudes toward policing
3.   Some experts believed the core police role must be altered if community involvement is to be won and maintained
4.   Led to the development of community policing:
     a.   A set of programs and strategies designed to bring police and the public closer together to create a more cooperative working environment between them
A.   Implementing Community Policing
1.   Community policing concept implemented through a number of innovative demonstration projects:
     a.   Foot patrol – take officers out of patrol cars and onto walk beats; experiments in Michigan and New Jersey
     b.   Although foot patrol did not reduce crime rate, residents perceived greater safety and were less afraid of crime
2.   Federal government has encouraged the growth of community policing by providing billions of dollars to hire and train officers through the Office of Community Oriented Policing Services (COPS) program
     a.   Has given local police departments more than 10 billion in aid
3.   Recent surveys indicate there has been a significant increase in community policing activities
4.   Community-oriented policing (COP) programs have been implemented in large cities, suburban areas, and rural communities
B.   Changing the Police Role
1.   Community policing also emphasizes sharing power with local groups and individuals
2.   Key element of community policing philosophy is that citizens must actively participate with police to fight crime
     a.   Participation is essential because community climate is influenced by the informal social control created by a concerned citizenry coupled with effective policing
3.   Changes associated with community policing initiatives
     a.   Neighborhood orientation:
          i.   Neighborhood-oriented policing (NOP):
               a)   Problem solving is best done at the neighborhood level where issues originate, not at a far-off central headquarters
               b)   Police decision making must be flexible and adaptive
     b.   Changing management styles:
          i.   Redesign of police administration and management

123

      ii. Vertical organization changed

        a)   Patrol officer becomes manager of beat and key decision maker

    c. Changing recruitment and training:

      i. Future officers must develop community-organizing and problem-solving skills

C. Challenges of Community Policing — If community policing strategies are to be successful, they need to react effectively to significant administrative problems such as:

  1. Defining Community:

    a. Community policing works best in stable, affluent areas

    b. Challenge of community is to reach out to all people in all neighborhoods, including young people and minorities, who may previously have been left out of the proces

  2. Defining Roles:

    a. Police administrators must also establish the exact role of community police agents

  3. Changing Supervisor Attitudes:

    a. Some supervisors are wary of community policing because it supports a decentralized command structure. Supervisors who learn to actively embrace community policing concepts are the ones best able to encourage patrol officers to follow suit

  4. Reorienting Police Values:

    a. Changing traditional crime control orientation to more community policing orientation

    b. Unlikely that community policing activities can be successful unless police line officers form a commitment to the values of community policing

  5. Revise Training:

    a. Training must focus less on ability to make arrests or issue citations and more on ability to solve problems, prevent crime effectively, and deal with neighborhood diversity and cultural values

  6. Reorient Recruitment:

    a. Midlevel managers, who are receptive to and can implement community-change strategies, must be recruited and trained

    b. Selection of recruits must be guided by a desire to find individuals with the skills and attitudes that support community policing

D. Community Policing Effectiveness

  1. There is empirical evidence that some community policing efforts can reduce disorder and impact the crime rate

  2. Most successful programs give officers time to meet with local residents to talk about crime in the neighborhood and to use personal initiative to solve problems

  3. Where used, citizens seem to like community policing initiatives, those who volunteer and get involved report higher confidence in the police force and its ability to create a secure environment

  4. Conversely, there is no clear cut evidence that community policing is highly successful at reducing crime across the board

5. Researchers have found that it is difficult to change the traditional values and attitudes of police officers involved in the programs

E. Problem-Oriented Policing

1. Require police agencies to identify particular long-term community problems and develop solutions to eliminate problems such as:
   a. Street-level drug dealers
   b. Prostitution rings
   c. Gang hangouts

2. Departments must rely on local residents and private resources in order to be problem solvers
   a. Police managers must learn to:
      i. Develop community resources
      ii. Design cost-efficient and effective solutions to problems
      iii. Become advocates as well as agents of reform

3. Police resources concentrate on "hot spots"
   a. A significant portion of all police calls that radiate from a relatively few locations such as:
      i. Bars
      ii. Malls
      iii. Bus depots
      iv. Hotels
      v. Certain apartment buildings
   b. Concentrating police resources on these areas could reduce crime

4. Problem oriented strategies are being developed that focus on specific criminal problems or areas
   a. Success rates should be interpreted with caution – displacing crime to other areas because of police concentration
   b. Evidence shows that merely saturating an area with police may not deter crime, but focusing efforts on a particular problem may have a crime-reducing effect

VI. **SUPPORT FUNCTIONS**

1. Not all members of a police department engage in "real police work" Some members involved in a number of support functions:
   a. Personnel services
      i. Recruit new police officers
      ii. Create exams and handle promotions and transfers
   b. Internal affairs
      i. Policing the police
      ii. Process citizen complaints of police corruption
      iii. Investigate possible unnecessary use of force by police officers
      iv. Probe police participation in actual criminal activity such as:
         a) Burglaries
         b) Narcotics violations
         c) Assist in disciplinary action

125

          v. Rigorous self-scrutiny is the only way police departments can earn the respect of citizens

           a) Police departments often institute citizen oversight over police practices and put in place civilian review boards that have the power to listen to complaints and conduct investigations

   c. Budgeting

     i. Administering payroll

     ii. Purchasing equipment and services

     iii. Planning for future budget expenditures

     iv. Auditing department financial records

   d. Communication

     i. Disseminate information on wanted offenders, stolen merchandise

     ii. Dispatch patrol units

   e. Training

     i. Police academy

       a) May be run exclusively for larger departments or may be part of a regional training center

       b) Over 90 percent of all police departments require preservice training, including almost all departments in larger cities (population over 100,000)

     ii. Average officer receives more than 500 hours of preservice training

       a) Includes 400 hours in the classroom and rest in field training

       b) Large city officers receive over 1000 hours of combined classroom and field training

       c) Topics include:

         1. Law and civil rights

         2. Firearms handling

         3. Emergency medical care

         4. Restraint techniques

     iii. On the job training covers:

       a) Weapons skills

       b) First aid

       c) Crowd control

       d) Community relations

     iv. Some agencies use roll call training or allow police officers time off to attend annual training sessions to sharpen skills or learn new policing techniques

     v. Police Departments provide:

       a) Emergency aid to the ill

       b) Counsel youngsters

       c) Speak to school and community agencies on safety and drug abuse

       d) Other services designed to improve citizen-police interactions

     vi. Larger police departments maintain specialized units that:

       a) Advise citizens on effective home security techniques

       b) Identification campaigns – engraving valuables

       c) Teaching young people about avoiding drug use

        d)   Forensic laboratories:
           1. Identifying substances
           2. Classifying fingerprints
    f. Planning and research
      i. Increasing police efficiency and strategies to test program effectiveness
      ii. Monitor technological developments and institute programs to adapt them to police services

CHAPTER SUMMARY

Most municipal police departments in the United States are independent agencies within the executive branch of government. Most local police departments are organized in a hierarchical manner, administrators must rise through the ranks to get to command positions.

A police officer's crime-fighting efforts are limited; studies of police work indicate that a significant portion of an officer's time is spent handling minor disturbances, service calls, and administrative duties. Police officers function in a variety of roles from dispensers of emergency medical care to keepers of the peace. Uniformed patrol officers are the backbone of the police department. The major purposes of patrol are to deter crime, maintain public order, respond quickly to law violations, identify and apprehend law violators, aid individuals, care for those who cannot help themselves, facilitate the movement of traffic and people, and create a feeling of security in the community.

Research efforts designed to measure the effectiveness of patrol have not supported its deterrence capability. The findings of the 1970s in Kansas City, Missouri study suggested that the presence of police patrol could do little to deter crime. Police departments that use a proactive style may help reduce crime rates. The most well-known program, CompStat, was begun in New York City as a means of directing police efforts.

Detectives investigate the causes of crime and attempt to identify the individuals responsible for committing the offense. Police detectives rely heavily on interviews and forensic evidence to create a narrative of the crime. Contemporary detectives typically use a three-pronged approach: specific focus, general coverage, and informative. Police detectives make a valuable contribution to police work through their skilled interrogation and case-processing techniques. A majority of cases are solved when the perpetrator is identified at the scene.

Investigations have improved along with advances in forensic science. Forensic analyses involve a variety of sciences, mathematical principles, and problem-solving methods, including use of complex instruments and chemical, physical, and microscopic examining techniques. While some forensic scientists are generalists, others specialize in a particular scientific area, such as toxicology, blood pattern analysis, crime scene investigation, impression evidence, trace evidence, and questioned documents.

"Fixing Broken Windows," by Kelling and Wilson advocated a new approach to improving police relations in the community. They made three points: neighborhood disorder creates fear,

127

neighborhoods give out crime-promoting signals, and police need citizen cooperation. A deteriorated neighborhood, whose residents are fearful, pessimistic, and despondent, is a magnet for crime.

Community preservation, public safety, and order maintenance should become the primary focus of patrol. The community policing concept was originally implemented through a number of innovative demonstration projects. There is empirical evidence that some community policing efforts can reduce disorder and impact the crime rate. Other changes linked to community policing initiatives in departments include neighborhood orientation, changing management styles, and changing recruitment and training.

Problem-oriented policing strategies require police agencies to identify particular long-term community problems and to develop strategies to eliminate them. Problem-oriented policing models are supported by the evidence that a great deal of urban crime is concentrated in a few hot spots.

A great deal of police resources are actually devoted to support and administrative functions. Many police departments maintain their own personnel service, internal affairs, budgeting, communication, and training bureaus.

DISCUSSION QUESTIONS

1. Should the primary police role be law enforcement or community service? Explain.
2. Should a police chief be permitted to promote an officer with special skills to a supervisory position, or should all officers be forced to spend "time in rank"? Explain your answer.
3. Do the advantages of proactive policing outweigh the disadvantages? Explain.
4. Explain the concept of broken windows policing. Why might it be successful?
5. What are the problems facing investigators and forensics experts these days?
6. Can the police and the community ever form a partnership to fight crime? Why or why not? Does the community policing model remind you of early forms of policing? Explain.

MEDIA TOOLS

The organization of police departments and the factors that influence or should influence the police organization is a rarely addressed topic. One of the foremost authorities in police research is Steven D. Mastrofski. Mastrofski authored a paper for the National Institute of Justice policing Research Workshop: Planning for the future. Although the paper is 41 pages long, you can review the sections that interest you most. Mastrofski presents some interesting arguments. The paper can be found at: https://www.ncjrs.gov/pdffiles1/nij/grants/218584.pdf

The Community Oriented Policing Services website has great recourses and information for your review. This website is the data house for all things related to community policing. There are many topics presented by book your authors in this site and go into greater detail. This site is a great starting point for any further research that might interest you. The site is provided by the United States Department of Justice. You can visit the website at: http://www.cops.usdoj.gov

Listen to a discussion regarding CompStat provided by New Hampshire Public Radio. The audio portion provides a description of CompStat by policing experts and the implementation of the program by a police agency. The audio portion or a transcript of the discussion can be found at: http://www.nhpr.org/node/10750

Visit the website JUSTNET. This website provided by the National Law Enforcement and Corrections Technology Center has a wide variety of resources dedicated to just about every emerging and existing technology used by police and corrections agency. If you are interested in learning more about any of the technologies presented in this chapter or want to explore the technological innovations, this is the site to visit. You can find the site at: http://www.justnet.org

Learn about DNA forensics and how it works and was developed. Site provided by the U.S. Department of Energy Office of Science, Office of Biological and Environmental Research. The site regarding DNA forensics can be found at: http://www.ornl.gov/sci/techresources/Human_Genome/elsi/forensics.shtml

PRACTICE TEST BANK

MULTIPLE CHOICE

1. In what style or manner are most police agencies organized?
    a. Patriarchal
    b. Bureaucratic
    c. Democratic
    d. Hierarchical

2. Most police agencies employ what type of system for determining an employee's eligibility for promotion?
    a. Time-in-agency
    b. Time-in-task
    c. Time-in-rank
    d. On-the-job-time

3. According to police-citizen contact studies, more than half of the contacts citizens have with police are
    a. traffic-related matters.
    b. calls for assistance.
    c. arrests.
    d. taking reports.

4. This bureau of a police department is the backbone and accounts for about 2/3 of the personnel.
    a. Investigations
    b. Communications
    c. Patrol
    d. Property and evidence

5. The real police role is probably of community
    a. crime fighter.
    b. problem solver.
    c. control agent.
    d. policing specialist.

6. The Kansas City Gun Experiment was
    a. directed at melting down as many guns as possible.
    b. primarily focused on gathering as many gun barrel rifling samples from street guns as possible.
    c. using technology to pinpoint gunfire soon after it occurred by utilizing triangulation methodology.
    d. directed as restricting the carrying of guns in high-risk places at high-risk times.

7. In what method of training police officers do supervisors or outside experts address police officers at the beginning of the workday?
   a. Field training
   b. Roll call
   c. Pre-service
   d. In-service

8. The great bulk of what patrol officers do is
   a. crime fighting.
   b. making arrests.
   c. order maintenance.
   d. apprehending offenders.

9. The Kansas City Patrol experiment found that variations in patrol had
   a. little impact on crime and citizen confidence.
   b. little impact on officer safety and police job satisfaction.
   c. a large impact on officer safety and crime.
   d. a large impact on crime and police job satisfaction.

10. Proactive patrol and policing strategies are designed primarily to
    a. prevent crime.
    b. increase the clearance rate.
    c. increase citizen confidence.
    d. decrease citizen complaints.

11. The first independent detective bureau was created in 1841 by the
    a. Boston Police.
    b. New York State police.
    c. London Metropolitan Police.
    d. Philadelphia Police.

12. Officers responsible for regulating and enforcing prostitution, gambling, and pornography are generally assigned to what type of unit?
    a. Morality squad
    b. Undercover unit
    c. Sting operation
    d. Vice squad

13. Undercover tactics designed to trap criminals are referred to as
    a. entrapment operations.
    b. inducement strategies.
    c. cooptation strategies.
    d. sting operations.

14. Research shows that the time elapsed between crime and report of crime
    a. has no impact on chance of arrest.
    b. has no impact on chance of conviction.
    c. reduces the chance of arrest, but not of conviction.
    d. reduces both the chance of arrest and conviction.

15. When investigators interview witnesses, gather evidence, record events, and collect facts at immediate crime scenes, they are employing what investigative technique?
    a. General coverage
    b. Informative techniques
    c. Sting operations
    d. Specific focus techniques

16. One major trend in policing that has resulted in major changes in police operations is to try to improve relations between police and
    a. other police agencies.
    b. federal law enforcement agencies.
    c. the communities they serve.
    d. high technology laboratories.

17. The broken windows theory focuses on
    a. neighborhood disorder and deterioration.
    b. lack of cooperation between police and citizens.
    c. need for increased patrol efforts.
    d. high technology solutions to crime.

18. Problem-oriented policing is essentially
    a. proactive.
    b. crime-fighting.
    c. technology-oriented.
    d. reactive.

19. One well-known program, Operation Ceasefire, is a problem-oriented policing intervention aimed at reducing youth homicide and youth firearms violence in
    a. New York City.
    b. Richmond.
    c. Chicago.
    d. Boston.

20. The branch of a police agency charged with investigating complaints against officer is called
    a. investigative affairs.
    b. internal affairs.
    c. internal investigations.
    d. personnel investigations.

21. The term forensic means
    a. mathematical principles.
    b. pertaining to the law.
    c. problem solving methods.
    d. physical analysis.

22. Which of the following programs is an example of directed patrol?
    a. Operation Cease Fire
    b. Kansas City Patrol Experiment
    c. Kansas City Gun Experiment
    d. Broken Windows

23. Which of the following would be considered an investigative technique?
    a. Neighborhood canvass
    b. Pre-trial hearing
    c. Walker hearing
    d. Reactive patrol

24. Forensic scientists perform comprehensive tests on evidence, such as chemical and
    a. spiritual tests.
    b. constitutional tests.
    c. physical tests.
    d. metabolic tests.

25. Which of the following is not one of the changes linked to community policing initiatives?
    a. DNA profiling
    b. Neighborhood orientation
    c. Changing management styles
    d. Changing recruitment and training

26. What type of analysis involves the use of complex instruments, chemical, physical, and microscopic examination techniques?
    a. Forensic analysis
    b. Metabolic analysis
    c. Spiritual analysis
    d. Biological analysis

27. Forensic scientists analyze blood spatters, paint, soil, and glass all of which belong to the larger classification of
    a. organic evidence.
    b. trace physical evidence.
    c. toxic material.
    d. carbon neutral material.

28. Which police support bureau functions include designing programs to increase police efficiency and strategies to test program effectiveness?
     a. Planning and research
     b. Budgeting
     c. Communication
     d. Administration and finance

29. What branch of government do police agencies fall within?
     a. Executive
     b. Legislative
     c. Judicial
     d. Municipal

30. Order-maintenance functions (as a patrol duty) include handling criminal behavior and
     a. antisocial behavior.
     b. civil unrest behavior.
     c. noncriminal behavior.
     d. passive behavior.

TRUE/FALSE

1. T   F   Police organizations are run in a democratic fashion.

2. T   F   Most police departments employ a merit rating system to make promotion decisions.

3. T   F   Most of an officer's time is spent in peacekeeping or order- maintenance activities.

4. T   F   Police departments that more actively enforce minor regulations are also more likely to experience lower felony rates.

5. T   F   Proactive policing is aimed at preventing crime.

6. T   F   The broken windows theory is consistent with reactive policing.

7. T   F   All community policing efforts can reduce disorder and impact the crime rate.

8. T   F   Most police officers are employed in the investigation function rather than the patrol function.

9. T   F   In general, the quicker a crime is reported, the greater the probability of arrest.

10. T   F   In general, as the time between the crime and the arrest grows, the probability of getting a conviction decreases.

11. T   F   Detective work may be improved if investigators are able to spend more time on each case.

12. T   F   The DNA database is regarded by many police experts as the most important in investigative technology since the adoption of fingerprint comparison early in the last century.

13. T   F   Aggressive police arrest more suspects, there are fewer criminals left on the streets to commit crime. Fewer criminals produce lower crime rates.

14. T   F   Community policing requires the police role to change from enforcer to community organizer.

15. T   F   The internal affairs division / unit is charged with policing the police.

FILL-IN-THE-BLANK

1. Most local police departments are organized in a _hierarchical_ manner.

2. Regardless of size, at the head of a police organization is the _police chief_

3. The branch of the police department that investigates complaints of officer corruption or officer misconduct is known as the _internal affairs_ division or unit.

4. Most police departments employ a _time-in-rank_ system for determining promotion eligibility.

5. Decentralization of a police agency is an approach used in _Neighborhood_ oriented policing.

6. A patrol strategy where police resources are concentrated to address specific crime problems is called _directed_ patrol.

7. A _deterrent_ effect is one which discourages crimes by the threat of arrest and punishment.

8. An arrest for drunk driving _reduces_ the likelihood of further driving while intoxicated.

9. Areas where crime is concentrated are called _hot_ spots of crime.

10. New York City utilized the __Compstat__ program as means of directing police efforts in a more productive fashion.

11. __Forensic__ scientists analyze trace physical evidence including hair and fibers.

12. A __sting operation__ involves organized groups of detectives or patrol officers working in plain clothes who deceive criminals into openly committing illegal acts.

13. The majority of police officers are involved in the __patrol__ function.

14. The __vice__ squad enforces prostitution and gambling law.

15. __Community__ policing is a set of programs and strategies designed to bring police and the public closer together and create a more cooperative working environment between them.

ESSAY

1. Explain the broken windows model of policing. Provide examples.

2. What changes in traditional police agencies are required to successfully implement community policing?

3. Explain what is meant by "proactive patrol."

4. List five of the seven major purposes of patrol.

5. List and explain at least three support bureaus and their functions.

CHAPTER 5 ANSWER KEY

Multiple Choice

1. d [p. 95, LO1]   2. c [p. 95, LO1]   3. a [p. 96, LO2]   4. c [p. 96, LO3]   5. b [p. 97, LO2]

6. d [p. 98, LO3]   7. b [p. 114, LO8]   8. c [p. 97, LO3]   9. a [p. 98, LO3]   10. a [p. 98, LO3]

11. c [p. 115, LO4]   12. d [p. 103, LO4]   13. d [p. 103, LO4]   14. d [p. 104, LO4]   15. d [p. 101, LO4]

16. c [p. 106, LO6]   17. a [p. 99, LO6]   18. a [p. 112, LO7]   19. d [p. 112, LO7]   20. b [p. 113, LO8]

21. b [p. 106, LO5]   22. c [p. 98, LO3]   23. a [p. 101, LO4]   24. c [p. 106, LO5]   25. a [p. 110, LO6]

26. a [p. 106, LO5]   27. b [p. 106, LO5]   28. a [p. 115, LO8]   29. a [p. 94, LO1]   30. c [p. 97, LO3]

True/False

1. F [p. 95, LO1]   2. F [p. 95, LO1]   3. T [p. 97, LO3]   4. T [p. 98, LO3]   5. T [p. 98, LO3]

6. F [p. 99, LO6]   7. F [p. 112, LO7]   8. F [p. 96, LO3]   9. T [p. 104, LO4]   10. T [p. 104, LO4]

11. T [p. 104, LO4]   12. T [p. 105, LO5]   13. T [p. 98, LO3]   14. T [p. 111, LO6]   15. T [p. 113, LO8]

Fill-in-the-Blank

1. hierarchical [p. 95, LO1]   2. police chief [p. 95, LO1]   3. internal affairs [p. 113, LO8]

4. time-in-rank [p. 95, LO1]   5. neighborhood [p. 111, LO6]   6. directed [p. 98, LO3]

7. deterrent [p. 98, LO3]   8. reduces [p. 99, LO3]   9. hot [p. 112, LO3]

10. CompStat [p. 100, LO3]   11. Forensic [p. 106, LO5]   12. sting operation [p. 103, LO4]

13. patrol [p. 96, LO3]   14. vice [p. 103, LO4]   15. Community [p. 108, LO6]

Essay

1.   **Explain the broken windows model of policing. Provide examples.**

In 1982 George Kelling and James Q. Wilson advocated a new approach to improving police relations in the community. This approach has come to be known as the broken windows model. The model contains three premises; neighborhood disorder creates fear; neighbors give out crime-promoting signals; and police need citizen cooperation. The model suggests that urban areas filled with lawless individuals are the most likely to maintain a high level of crime. A neighborhood with visible disrepair (e.g., broken windows, dilapidated structures) gives out crime-promoting messages. Honest citizens may live in these areas but the areas attract criminals. The neighbors and these neighborhoods become magnets for crime.

If police are to successfully combat crime they must work cooperatively with and receive assistance from the public. The message that needs to be broadcast is that crime and criminals are tolerated here. The model makes proactive policing the tool for preventing crime and criminals from descending upon and decimating an area. Examples of functions under this model include; foot patrols, neighborhood precincts, community workshops focusing on safer neighborhoods and crime prevention.

[pp. 99-100, LO3]

2.   What changes in traditional police agencies are required to successfully implement community policing?

In order to implement community policing agencies must subscribe to the following:

- Decentralize the agency. Address problems at the neighborhood level to allow officers to get involved at the neighborhood level or where the problems exist.
- Change management styles. Administration and management must be reorganized to focus on the needs of the community instead of the needs of the department.
- Change recruitment and training. Recruit and hire people who possess problem solving skills along with the social skills to be neighborhood partners. A community police officer will need to succeed through problem solving instead of making arrests and issuing violations. Training in the traditional manner will no longer be relevant and new approaches will have to be developed so that supervisors and officers learn to embrace the problem solving approach.

[p. 100, LO6]

3.   Explain what is meant by "proactive patrol."

Proactive patrol is an aggressive law enforcement style where uniformed officers are expected to conduct traffic stop investigations and detain and identify suspicious persons. The idea behind the aggressive approach is to be visible and pay attention to minor activities with the notion that it can prevent crime from occurring. Proactive policing is believed to have a deterrent effect because officers are actively engaged in and acutely aware of the activities/problems in their jurisdiction. The proactive approach also suggests that a visible aggressive patrol force acts as a warning to criminals to stay away. Proactive patrol can also include directed patrol, where officers concentrate on an area that has been identified as problematic. By focusing on problematic areas they can drive down crime rates and prevent future crimes.

[pp. 98-101, LO3]

4.   List five of the seven major purposes of patrol.

1.   Deter crime by maintaining a visible police presence
2.   Maintain order within a patrol area
3.   Respond quickly to law violations or other emergencies
4.   Identify and apprehend law violators
5.   Aid individuals and care for those who cannot help themselves
6.   Facilitate movement of people and traffic
7.   Create feeling of security in the community

[pp. 96-97, LO2]

5. **List and explain at least three support bureaus and their functions.**

- Personnel services
  - o Recruit new police officers
  - o Create exams and handle promotions and transfers
- Internal affairs
  - o Policing the police
  - o Process citizen complaints of police corruption
  - o Investigate possible unnecessary use of force by police officers
  - o Probe police participation in actual criminal activity such as:
    - ▪ Burglaries
    - ▪ Narcotics violations
    - ▪ Assist in disciplinary action
- Budgeting
  - o Administering payroll
  - o Purchasing equipment and services
  - o Planning for future budget expenditures
  - o Auditing department financial records
- Communication
  - o Disseminate information on wanted offenders, stolen merchandise
  - o Dispatch patrol units
- Training
  - o Police academy
    - ▪ May be run exclusively for larger departments or may be part of a regional training center
  - o Some agencies use roll call training or allow police officers time off to attend annual training sessions to sharpen skills or learn new policing techniques
- Forensic laboratories:
  - o Identifying substances
  - o Classifying fingerprints
- Planning and research
  - o Increasing police efficiency and strategies to test program effectiveness
  - o Monitor technological developments and institute programs to adapt them to police services

[pp. 113-115, LO8]

CHAPTER 6
Issues in Policing:
Professional, Social, and Legal

LEARNING OBJECTIVES

After studying this chapter, students will:

1. Summarize demographic trends in policing.

2. Explain how minority and female officers act and are treated.

3. Explain police culture and personality

4. Identify distinct policing styles

5. Describe factors that affect police discretion.

6. Discuss four major problems of policing

7. Distinguish between deadly and nondeadly force—and methods for controlling each.

8. Explain the importance of less-lethal weapons.

9. Be familiar with the Supreme Court's involvement with the police through its effort to control search and seizure and interrogation, and through establishment of the exclusionary rule.

KEY TERMS AND CONCEPTS

double marginality (p. 118) The social burden African-American police officers carry by being both minority group members and law enforcement officers.

cynicism (p. 122) The belief that most people's actions are motivated solely by personal needs and selfishness.

blue curtain (p. 122) The secretive, insulated police culture that isolates officers from the rest of society.

discretion (p. 124) The use of personal decision making and choice in carrying out operations in the criminal justice system. For example, police discretion can involve deciding whether to make an arrest; prosecutorial discretion can involve the decision to accept a plea bargain.

emotional intelligence (p. 125) The ability to monitor one's own and others' feelings and emotions, to discriminate among them and to use this information to guide one's thinking and actions.

demeanor (p. 126) The way in which a person outwardly manifests his or her personality.

racial profiling (p. 127) The practice of police targeting minority groups because of a belief that they are more likely to be engaged in criminal activity.

police brutality (p. 130) Usually involves such actions as the use of abusive language, the unnecessary use of force or coercion, threats, prodding with nightsticks, stopping and searching people to harass them, and so on.

corruption (p. 130) Exercising legitimate discretion for improper reasons or using illegal means to achieve approved goals.

Knapp Commission (p. 130) A public body that led an investigation into police corruption in New York and uncovered a widespread network of payoffs and bribes.

meat eaters (p. 131) A term used to describe police officers who actively solicit bribes and vigorously engage in corrupt practices.

grass eaters (p. 131) A term to describe police officers who accept payoffs when everyday duties place them in a position to "look the other way."

deadly force (p. 132) Force that is likely to cause death or serious bodily harm.

suicide by cop (p. 132) A form of suicide in which a person acts in an aggressive manner with police officers in order to induce them to shoot to kill.

nondeadly force (p. 134) Force that is unlikely to cause death or serious bodily harm.

Miranda warning (p. 135) The requirement that police officers inform suspects subjected to custodial interrogation that they have a constitutional right to remain silent, that their statements can later be used against them in court, that they can have an attorney present to help them, and that the state will pay for an attorney if they cannot afford to hire one.

search warrant (p. 137) An order issued by a judge, directing officers to conduct a search of specified premises for specified objects or persons and bring them before the court.

probable cause (p. 137) The evidentiary criterion necessary to sustain an arrest or the issuance of an arrest or search warrant; less than absolute certainty or "beyond a reasonable doubt" but greater than mere suspicion or "hunch."

stop and frisk (p. 138) The situation when police officers who are suspicious of an individual run their hands lightly over the suspect's outer garments to determine whether the person is carrying a concealed weapon. Also called a patdown or threshold inquiry, a stop and frisk is intended to stop short of any activity that could be considered a violation of Fourth Amendment rights.

exclusionary rule (p. 139) The principle that prohibits using evidence illegally obtained in a trial. Based on the Fourth Amendment "right of the people to be secure in their persons, houses, papers, and effects, against unreasonable searches and seizures," the rule is not a bar to prosecution, because legally obtained evidence may be available that may be used in a trial.

good faith exception (p. 140) The principle of law holding that evidence may be used in a criminal trial, even though the search warrant used to obtain it is technically faulty, if the police acted in good faith and to the best of their ability when they sought to obtain it from a judge.

CHAPTER OUTLINE

I. **WHO ARE THE POLICE?**
   1. Composition changing, less than 50 years ago police composed primarily of white males with a high school education who viewed policing as a secure position that brought them respect of family and friends
   2. An increasing number of police officers have at least some college education
   3. Affirmative action programs have slowly helped change the racial and gender composition to reflect community makeup
   A. Demographic makeup
      1. For more than 30 years, U.S. police departments have made a concerted effort to attract women and minorities. Today:
         a. 11 percent of all officers are female
         b. 23 percent are minorities
            i. Reasons for this effort are varied:
               a) Departments intended to field a more balanced force that truly represents the communities they serve
               b) Heterogeneous police force can be instrumental in gaining the confidence of the community to dispel view that departments are generally bigoted or biased
               c) Women and minority police officers possess special qualities that can improve police performance
                  1. Spanish speaking officers
                  2. Asian officers
   B. Minority Police Officers
      1. 1861: First African-American police officer (Washington D.C.)
         a. Chicago, 1872
      2. 1890: Two thousand minority police officers employed in the U.S.
      3. African-American officers have suffered double marginality:
         a. Expected to give members of their own race preferential treatment
         b. Target of institutional racism
      4. African American officers adapted to these pressures in a range of ways:

        a. Denying that African American suspects should be treated differently from whites

        b. Treating African American offender more harshly than white offenders in order to prove their lack of bias

    5. Minority officers now seem as self-assured as white officers

    6. The higher the percentage of black officers on the force, the higher the arrest rate for crimes such as assault

    7. Appear to be experiencing some of the same problems and issues encountered by white officers

        a. Similar rates of job-related stress

    8. Minority officers do report more stress when they consider themselves "tokens" or marginalized within the department

C. Women in Policing

        a. 1910: Alice Stebbins, first woman to hold title of police officer (Los Angeles)

        b. Women endured separate criteria for selection, were given menial tasks and were denied opportunity for advancement

        c. Relief of bias with 1964 Civil Rights Act

        d. Role of women in police work is still restricted by social and administrative barriers

        e. Women comprise 11 percent of officers, up from 7.6 percent in 1987

        f. Women report significantly higher levels of job-related stress than male officers

        g. Research indicates that female officers are highly successful police officers

        h. More likely to receive support from the community and less likely to be charged with improper conduct

        i. Because they have the ability to avoid violent encounters and to deescalate potentially violent arrest situations, they are typically the target of fewer citizen complaints

        j. Future of women in policing grows brighter every year

            i. Females want to remain in policing because:

               a) Good salary

               b) Job security

               c) Challenging and exciting occupation

D. Education Characteristics

    1. About one-third of police agencies require some type of college requirement

        a. More than three times the number than in 1990

    2. Half of police departments in survey preferred criminal justice majors because of:

        a. Enhanced knowledge of the entire criminal justice system and of issues that arise in policing

    3. Benefits of higher educated police officers:

        a. Better communication with the public, especially minority and ethnic groups

        b. Write better and more clearly, and more likely to get promoted

        c. Perform more effectively

d. Generate fewer citizen complaints
e. Show more initiative in performing police tasks
f. Generally act more professionally
g. Less likely to have disciplinary problems
h. Better decision makers
i. Greater self-confidence and assurance

II. **THE POLICE PROFESSION**
   1. Policing has unique characteristics, which separates it from other professions
A. The Police Culture
   1. So-called blue curtain – characterized by:
      a. Cynicism
      b. Clannishness
      c. Secrecy
      d. Insulation from others in society
   2. Joining police subculture means:
      a. Having to stick up for fellow officers against outsiders
      b. Maintaining a tough, mach exterior personality
      c. Distrusting the motives and behavior of outsiders
   3. Code of silence demands officers never turn in their peers even if they engage in corrupt or illegal practices
   4. Written core beliefs of the police culture:
      a. Police are the only real crime fighters
      b. No one else understands the real nature of police work
      c. Loyalty to colleagues counts above everything else
      d. It is impossible to win the war against crime without bending the rules
      e. Members of the public are basically unsupportive and unreasonably demanding
      f. Patrol work is the pits
   5. Recruits join police forces because they want to:
      a. Help people
      b. Fight crime
      c. Have an interesting, exciting, prestigious career
      d. High degree of job security
   6. Recruits are often unprepared for emotional turmoil and conflict that accompany police work, but police culture may help them adjust to the rigors of police work
   7. Subculture encourages members to draw distinction between good and evil
      a. Has developed in response to the insulated, dangerous lifestyle of police officers
   8. May also unify the police and improve the camaraderie and solidarity among fellow officers
B. The Police Personality
   1. Some describe the police personality as:
      a. Dogmatic
      b. Authoritarian

      c. Suspicious
2. Cynicism has been found at all levels of policing, including the chief of police
3. These values and attitudes are thought to be the reason police officers are secretive and isolated from the rest of society
      a. Producing the blue curtain
4. Two opposing viewpoints on the cause of the police personality phenomenon:
      a. Police departments attract recruits who are by nature cynical, authoritarian, and secretive
      b. Socialization and experience on the police force itself cause these character traits to develop
5. Mixed research results on the police personality, or even if one exists
      a. Some studies have concluded that police officers are:
         i. More psychologically healthy than the general population
         ii. Less depressed and anxious
         iii. More social and assertive
6. Police officers have been found to value such personality traits as:
      a. Warmth
      b. Flexibility
      c. Emotion

C. Policing Style
1. Part of socialization as a police officer is developing a working attitude, or style, through which to approach policing
2. Several studies have attempted to define and classify policing styles, these are called typologies
3. Four styles of police work seem to fit the current behavior patterns:
      a. The crime fighter
      b. The social agent
      c. The law enforcer
      d. The watchman

III. **POLICE DISCRETION**
1. Critical aspect of professional responsibility is the personal discretion each officer has in carrying out daily activities
      a. Discretion can involve selective enforcement of the law
      b. Majority of police officers use a high degree of personal discretion in carrying out daily tasks, also known as:
         i. Low-visibility decision making
      c. Unlike members of almost every other criminal justice agency, police are neither regulated in their daily procedures by administrative scrutiny nor subject to judicial review
      d. Emotional intelligence has important implications for the study of police discretion:
         i. The ability to monitor one's own and others' feelings and emotions, to discriminate among them and to use this information to guide one's thinking and actions

    ii. Being in tune with one's emotions, being able to act in an emotionally mature fashion, and managing one's own mental state during difficult encounters can make all the difference

  2. Factors that influence police decision making:

A. Legal Factors

  1. Police discretion is inversely related to the severity of the offense

  2. Police use discretion to separate what they consider nuisance cases from those serious enough to demand police action

B. Environmental Factors

  1. Discretion defined partially by officer's living and working environment

  2. Police officer may work or dwell in a community culture that either tolerates eccentricities and personal freedoms or expects extremely conservative, professional, no-nonsense behavior

C. Departmental Factors

  1. Located in high crime areas

  2. Department directives

D. Peer Factors

  1. Police officers turn to peers for both on-the-job advice and off-the-job companionship

  2. Peers affect decision making on two levels:

    a. Direct:

      i. Other officers dictate acceptable responses to street-level problems by providing or withholding approval in office discussions

    b. Follow behavior models of the most experienced and influential patrol officers

E. Situational Factors

    a. Demeanor (attitude and appearance of the offender)

      i. If offender is surly, talks back, or otherwise challenge officer's authority, formal action likely to be taken

    b. Self-initiated or discovered versus a dispatched run

      i. More discretion involved in self-initiated incidents

F. Extralegal Factors

  1. Research results are mixed as to whether police take age, race, class, or gender into discretionary decision making

  2. Victim characteristics appear to influence police action:

    a. Police more willing to make arrest when victim is older, white, affluent

    b. Neighborhood factors:

      i. Police less likely to take action if victim and offender known each other

  3. Racial profiling:

    a. Research is mixed whether police officers racial profile or not

IV. **PROBLEMS OF POLICING**

A. Stress

  1. Complexity of role, need to exercise prudent discretion, threat of using or being a victim of violence, and isolation from rest of society are stressors on police officers that lead some to:

146

    a. Alcoholism
    b. Depression
    c. Suicide
    d. Marital disputes
    e. Domestic violence
2. Stress may not be constant but at some time, usually the middle years, most officers will feel effects of stress
3. Causes of Stress
    a. Pressure of being on duty 24 hours
    b. Policing is a dangerous profession
    c. Internal conflict with administrative policies
    d. Forced adaptation to community-oriented policing
    e. When they "bring home the job"
    f. Officers who feel alienated from family and friends
    g. Poor training
    h. Substandard equipment
    i. Inadequate pay
    j. Lack of opportunity
    k. Job dissatisfaction
    l. Role conflict
    m. Exposure to brutality
    n. Fears about competence, success, and safety
    o. Feelings that the court system favors the rights of the criminals
    p. Effects of stress can be shocking
        i. High rate of premature death by:
            a) Heart disease
            b) Diabetes
        ii. Disproportionate number of divorces and other marital problems
        iii. Some have higher rates of suicide
        iv. Not open to new ideas such as community policing
4. Combating Stress
    a. Research shows that the more support police officers get in the workplace, the lower their feelings of stress and anxiety
    b. Stress training includes:
        i. Diet information
        ii. Biofeedback
        iii. Relaxation and meditation
        iv. Exercise
    c. Many departments include stress management as part of an overall wellness program designed to promote:
        i. Physical health
        ii. Mental health
        iii. Good nutrition
    d. Stress reduction programs can help officers focus on the positive aspects of police work

147

B. Fatigue
    a. A police officer who is overly tired may be at a higher risk of acting inappropriately or being injured on the job
    b. The problem of tired cops has been overlooked
    c. Controlling Fatigue:
        i. Administrators paying special attention to scheduling such that officers do not work too much overtime
        ii. Adopt policies that place limitations on second jobs

C. Controlling Fatigue
    1. One option is for administrators to make special efforts, during scheduling, to ensure officers do not work too much overtime
    2. Another option is for administrators to adopt policies that place limitations on second jobs

D. Violence and Brutality
    a. Only a small portion of officers are continually involved in use-of-force incidents
    b. Aggressive cops may overreact to stress of police work and feel socially isolated
    c. A few officers are chronic offenders who account for a significant portion of all citizen complaints
        i. Tend to be young and less experienced
  1. Curbing Violence
    a. Specialized training
    b. Early warning systems
        i. Problem officers identified by behavior profiles:
            a) Citizen complaints
            b) Firearm discharge
            c) Use of force reports
            d) Civil litigation
            e) Resisting arrest incidents
            f) High-sped pursuits
            g) Vehicular damage
        ii. Initial intervention consists of review by officer's immediate supervisor
            a) Advises officer of the sanctions if problems continue
        iii. Some cases referred to:
            a) Counseling
            b) Training
            c) Psychologists
        iv. Shown to be successful
    c. Greatest factors in controlling the use of police brutality are the threat of civil judgments against:
        i. Individual officers
        ii. Police chiefs
        iii. Cities and towns

E. Corruption
    a. Since their creation, U.S. police departments have dealt with problems of controlling illegal and unprofessional behavior by officers

    b. In the nineteenth century, officers systematically ignored violations of laws for payoffs related to:
  - i. Drinking
  - ii. Gambling
  - iii. Prostitution

    c. Police officers helped politicians gain office by allowing electoral fraud to flourish

    d. Although most officers are not corrupt, the few dishonest ones bring discredit to the entire profession

1. Varieties of Corruption
   - a. Police deviance involves the misuse of authority by police officers in a manner designed to produce personal gain for themselves or others
   - b. Some argue that the following misconduct is serious corruption and should be considered serious:
     - i. Unnecessary use of force
     - ii. Unreasonable searches
     - iii. Immoral personal life
   - c. These should be considered just as serious as corruption motivated by economic gain
   - d. Knapp Commission, investigating police corruption in New York, classified two types of abusers:
     - i. Meat eaters:
       - a) Those who aggressively misuse police power for personal gain by demanding bribes, threatening legal action, or cooperating with criminals
     - ii. Grass eaters:
       - a) Those who accept payoffs when their everyday duties place them in a position to be solicited by the public
   - e. Police corruption can be divided into four major categories:
     - i. Internal corruption:
       - a) Bending of departmental rules and outright performance of illegal duties
     - ii. Selective enforcement or non-enforcement:
       - a) Abusing or exploiting police discretion
     - iii. Active criminality:
       - a) Police participating in serious criminal behavior
     - iv. Bribery and extortion:
       - a) Exploiting law enforcement roles specifically for money
       - b) Bribery initiated by citizens, extortion initiated by officers

2. Causes of Corruption
   - a. Explanations as to why corruption occurs:
     - i. Police officer position attracts lower class persons who do not have the means to maintain a coveted middle-class lifestyle
     - ii. Police enjoy wide discretion, low visibility, and code of silence
     - iii. It is a function of society's ambivalence toward many forms of vice-related behaviors that police are sworn to control

3. Control of Corruption
    a. Strengthen internal administrative review process
    b. A strong and well-supported internal affairs division linked to lowered corruption rates
    c. Accountability system:
        i. Hold supervisors at each level accountable for illegal behaviors of the officers under them
    d. Create outside review boards or special prosecutors such as:
        i. Mollen Commission in New York
        ii. Christopher Commission in Los Angeles
            a) Often limited by their lack of intimate knowledge of day-to-day operations
            b) Problem of blue curtain
    e. Departmental opposition is most likely when oversight procedures:
        i. Represent outside interference
        ii. Staff lack experience with and understanding of police work
        iii. Are unfair
    f. Many law enforcement administrators have identified positive outcomes from having a review board:
        i. Improved community relations
        ii. Enhancing an agency's ability to police itself
        iii. Improving an agency's policies and procedures

V.   **USE OF FORCE**
    1. Use of force is not a very common event. Surveys found that:
        a. Nineteen percent of U.S. residents age 16 or older had face to face contact with a police officer
        b. More common among males, whites, and younger residents
        c. Nine out of ten felt police acted properly
        d. Estimated two percent of people stopped by police had force used or threatened against them during most recent contact
        e. Blacks and Hispanics experienced police use of force at higher rates than whites
        f. Data also indicated that:
            i. Relatively few contacts with police and the public involve physical force but,
                a) There seem to be race and ethnic differences in the rate at which force is applied
        g. African Americans were less likely than Whites to feel that the police acted properly during a contact, the great majority of all races considered police behavior to be appropriate given the circumstances of the contact
    A. Deadly Force
        1. Deadly force:
            a. Actions of a police officer who shoots and kills a suspect who is fleeing from arrest, assaults a victim, or attacks an officer
        2. Fleeing felon rule, from English common law:

a. Almost every criminal offense was a felony and bore the death penalty

b. The use of deadly force in the course of arresting a felon was considered expedient, saving the state the trouble of conducting a trial

3. Actual number of people killed by police each year is most likely between 250 and 300

a. Some of these may even be precipitated by the target as a form of suicide

i. Suicide by cop

4. At least 6,600 civilian have been killed by the police since 1976

a. True number is probably much higher

B. Controlling Deadly Force

1. 1985: Supreme Court outlawed indiscriminate use of deadly force in *Tennessee v. Garner*.

a. Use of force against apparently unarmed and nondangerous fleeing felons is an illegal seizure under Fourth Amendment

b. Deadly force may not be used unless necessary to prevent escape and officer has probable cause that the suspect poses a significant threat of death or serious injury to others

2. Individual states still control police shooting policy

a. Some have adopted statutory policies that restrict the police use of violence

b. Others have upgraded training in the use of force

i. Officers are taught via lecture, demonstration, computer-based instruction, and training scenarios to assess the suspect's behavior and apply an appropriate and corresponding amount of force

3. Internal review and policymaking by police administrative review boards are used to control police shootings

a. Review board approach is controversial because it can mean that the department recommends that one if its own officers be turned over for criminal prosecution

C. Nondeadly Force

a. Force that is unlikely to cause death or significant bodily harm

i. Nondeadly force can range from the use of handcuffs and suspect compliance techniques to rubber bullets and stun guns

b. Officers resort to nondeadly force in a number of circumstances

i. May begin with verbal commands and then escalate the force used when confronted with a resistant suspect.

c. Researchers have found:

i. Crime in question is strongly linked to the type of nondeadly force used

ii. Officers influenced by past experience

iii. The presence of other officers

iv. Presence and behavior of bystanders

d. Use is still relatively rare

e. Estimated that police use or threaten to use nondeadly force in only 1.7% of all contacts and 20% of all arrests

1. Controlling Nondeadly Force

e. *Graham v. Connor*

    i. Supreme Court ruled that issues related to nondeadly force must be judged from the standpoint of a reasonable officer

D. Less-Lethal Weapons

 1. Most widely used nonlethal weapons
  a. Wood
  b. Rubber
  c. Polyurethane bullets
   i. Shot out of modified 37-mm pistols or 12 gauge shotguns

 2. At short distances officers use:
  a. Pepper spray
  b. Tasers
   i. Deliver electric shocks with long wire tentacles
   ii. Produces intense muscle spasms

 3. Other technologies under development:
  a. Guns that shoot giant nets
  b. Guns that shoot sticky glue
  c. Lights that temporarily blind suspects
  d. Bags filled with lead pellets

 4. Nonlethal weapons may help reduce police use of force

VI. **POLICE AND THE RULE OF LAW**

 1. Police are charged with preventing crime and, when crime does occur, with investigating the case:
  a. Identify the culprit
  b. Make an arrest
  c. All while gathering sufficient evidence to convict the culprit at trial

 2. Police officers need to able to:
  a. Search for evidence
  b. Seize items such as guns and drugs
  c. Question suspects, witnesses, and victims

 3. At trial, they must provide prosecutors with sufficient evidence to prove guilt

 4. Soon after a crime is committed, police must make every effort to gather evidence, obtain confessions, and take witness statements that will stand up in court

 5. The need for police officers to gather evidence can conflict with constitutional rights
   i. Fourth amendment restricts police activities by limiting searches and seizures
   ii. Fifth Amendment prohibits forcing people to incriminate themselves

A. Interrogations and Confessions
  a. Confessions obtained from defendants through coercion, force, trickery, or promises of leniency are inadmissible because their trustworthiness is questionable

 1. The *Miranda* Rule:
  a. 1966: *Miranda v. Arizona*

    i.   Supreme Court created objective standards for questioning by police after a defendant has been taken into custody

    ii. Before questioning, police must inform individuals of Fifth Amendment right

    iii. Accomplished by police issuing suspect Miranda Warning

        a)   Right to remain silent

        b)   Statement can be used in court

        c)   Right to consult an attorney, have the attorney present at the time of the interrogation

        d)   Attorney will be provided, if defendant can't afford an attorney

    iv. Effective waiver of rights

        a)   Waiver made with full knowledge of constitutional rights

        b)   People who cannot understand the Miranda warning because of:

            1. Age

            2. Mental handicap

            3. Language problems

        c)   Cannot be legally questioned without their attorney present

        d)   If they can understand their rights and then waive them, they may be questioned

  b. Miranda is now a police institution

  c. Critics have called Miranda decision incomprehensible and difficult to administer

  d. Many departments now routinely videotape interrogations

B. Search and Seizure

  a. Manner in which police seize evidence governed by search-and-seizure requirements of the Fourth Amendment

    i.   Designed by constitutional framers to protect individuals against unreasonable searches and seizures

  b. Generally, no search or seizure without warrant is legal

  c. Search warrant:

    i.   A court order authorizing and directing the police to search a designated place for evidence of a crime

  d. Procedural process in obtaining a warrant:

    i.   Request warrant from court

    ii. Officer must submit affidavit establishing probable cause

    iii. Affidavit must state place to be searched and property to be seized

  e. Probable cause requirement:

    i.   Presiding judge must conclude from facts that there is probable cause a crime has been committed and person or place to be searched is materially involved in that crime

    ii. Searches must be reasonable under the circumstances of the crime

    iii. Considered unreasonable when it exceeds the scope of police authority or is highly invasive of personal privacy

1. Warrantless Searches

  a. Under certain circumstances a valid search may be conducted without a search warrant

    b. There are six major exceptions
        i. Search incident to a valid arrest:
           a) The reason for this exception is that the arresting officer must have the power to:
              1. Disarm the accused
              2. Protect himself or herself
              3. Preserve the evidence of the crime
              4. Prevent the accused from escaping from custody
           b) Officer only allowed to search defendant and areas in immediate physical surroundings under defendant's control
       ii. Stop and frisk:
           a) *Terry v. Ohio*
           b) Police can perform a stop and frisk when they have reasonable suspicion to believe criminal activity is afoot
           c) Have reason to believe suspect is armed
           d) Frisk:
              1. Pat down the person's outer clothing for the purpose of finding a concealed weapon
      iii. Automobile search:
           a) May be searched without warrant if there is probable cause to believe that the car was involved in a crime
              1. Autos inherently mobile
              2. People should not expect much privacy in their cars
           b) Because traffic stops can be dangerous, Supreme Court has ruled that if a police officer perceives danger, can order the driver and passengers from the car without suspicion and conduct a limited search of their persons
           c) Usually search must be limited to the area under the driver's control or reach
       iv. Consent search:
           a) Consent must be given voluntarily
           b) Police under no obligation to inform individuals of their right to refuse the search
       v. Plain view search:
           a) Object can be freely inspected if it can be seen by the general public
       vi. Exigent circumstances, officer must have probable cause:
           a) Hot pursuit
           b) Danger of escape
           c) Threats to evidence
           d) Threats to others
C. The Exclusionary Rule
    a. All evidence obtained by unreasonable searches and seizures is inadmissible in criminal trials and also excludes use of illegal confessions
    b. Created by 1914 Supreme Court case — *Weeks v. United States*
        i. Evidence obtained by unreasonable search and seizure must be excluded in federal criminal trial

c. Applicable to states in 1961 case — *Mapp v. Ohio*
1. Controversy and Current Status
   a. Because rule often applies to many victimless offenses, the rule is believed to result in excessive court delays and to affect plea-bargaining negotiations negatively
      i. In fact, rule appears to result in relatively few case dismissals
      ii. Prosecutions are lost because of suppression rulings less than 1 percent of the time
   b. Good faith exception
      i. Evidence is admissible in court if the police officers acted in good faith by first obtaining court approval for their search even if the warrant they received was deficient or faulty

CHAPTER SUMMARY

The composition of the nation's police forces is changing. The personnel in most early police departments were white and male. Today, about 11 percent of all officers are female and about 23 percent are minorities. About one third of police departments have some type of college requirement for new recruits. Police experts have found that the experience of becoming a police officer and the nature of the job itself causes most officers to band together in a police subculture, characterized by cynicism, clannishness, secrecy, and insulation from others in society—the blue curtain. Membership in the police culture helps recruits adjust to the rigors of police work and provides the emotional support needed for survival. Four styles fit the behavior patterns of most police agents: crime fighter, social agent, law enforcer, and watchman.

Police officers use a high degree of personal discretion in carrying out daily tasks. The factors that can influence discretion are legal, environmental, departmental, peer, situational, and extralegal. The role ambiguity, social isolation, and threat of danger are the police officer's constant companions. There are three significant problems that are a strain on police officers: job stress, violence, and corruption. Police officers can experience tremendous stress, a factor that leads some to alcoholism, depression, and suicide. Police fatigue is also a problem; overly tired officers may be at a higher risk of acting inappropriately or being injured.

Corruption was pervasive amongst the American police when the early departments were first formed. In the nineteenth century, police officers ignored violations of laws related to drinking, gambling, and prostitution in return for regular payoffs. Police corruption varies. Police corruption is generally divided into four major categories: internal corruption, selective enforcement or non-enforcement, active criminality, and bribery and extortion.

Police officers are empowered to use force and violence in their daily tasks. The term deadly force refers to the actions of a police officer who shoots and kills a suspect who is fleeing from arrest, assaults a victim, or attacks an officer. The following patterns have been related to police shootings: exposure to violence, national crime rates, community threat levels, and administrative policies.

In 1985, the Supreme Court outlawed the indiscriminate use of deadly force in *Tennessee v. Garner*. Nondeadly force is that which is unlikely to cause death or significant bodily harm. Because the police use of force is such a serious issue, ongoing efforts have been made to control its use. Methods used to control police force include adhering to important court decisions and formulating appropriate policies. Less-lethal weapons give police officers an opportunity to subdue certain suspects without the need for lethal force. The TASER is the most popular less-lethal weapon in use today.

In the 1966 case of *Miranda v. Arizona*, the Supreme Court created objective standards for questioning by police after a defendant has been taken into custody. The manner in which police may seize evidence is governed by the search-and-seizure requirements of the Fourth Amendment of the U.S. Constitution. Generally, no search or seizure undertaken without a search warrant is lawful. The six major exceptions are search incident to a valid arrest, stop and frisk, automobile search, consent search, plain view, and exigent circumstances.

The U.S. Supreme Court established the exclusionary rule in 1914. In the case of *Weeks v. United States*, it ruled that evidence obtained by unreasonable search and seizure must be excluded in a federal criminal trial. In the 1961 *Map v. Ohio* case, the Supreme Court made the exclusionary rule applicable to the states. Over time, the Supreme Court has been diminishing the scope of the exclusionary rule.

DISCUSSION QUESTIONS

1. Should male and female officers have the same duties in a police department? Explain your reasoning.
2. How can education enhance the effectiveness of police officers?
3. Do you think that an officer's working the street will eventually produce a cynical personality and distrust for civilians? Explain.
4. Should a police officer who accepts a free meal from a restaurant owner be dismissed from the force? Why or why not?
5. A police officer orders an unarmed person running away from a burglary to stop; the suspect keeps running and is shot and killed by the officer. Has the officer committed murder? Explain.
6. Would you like to live in a society that abolished police discretion and used a full enforcement policy? Why or why not?
7. Should illegally seized evidence be excluded from trial, even though it is conclusive proof of a person's criminal acts? Might there be another way to deal with police violation of the Fourth Amendment—for example, making them pay a fine?
8. Have criminals been given too many rights by the courts? Should courts be more concerned with the rights of victims or the rights of offenders? Have the police been "handcuffed" and prevented from doing their job in the most efficient manner?

MEDIA TOOLS

Contact between the police and the public is a topic that garners a lot of attention. The Bureau of Justice Statistics measures the nature and extent of these contacts by surveying individuals in a nationally representative sample of households. There are many other reports related to this topic. For a comprehensive look at this interesting topic, visit the United States Department of Justice, Office of Justice Programs, Bureau of Justice Statistics website on police-public contacts. The website can be found at: http://bjs.ojp.usdoj.gov/index.cfm?ty=tp&tid=70

Less-Lethal Weapons continues to be a investigated topic in law enforcement. Explore an article and resources that suggest that less-lethal weapons decrease the injuries to police officers and offenders. This article addresses the question of new technologies and if they can further decrease injuries. The article also presents an analysis of information from selected law enforcement agencies. The article is provided by the National Institute of Justice. The article and supporting material can be found at: http://www.nij.gov/journals/267/use-of-force.htm

Miranda v. Arizona is a landmark case in the criminal justice system. Although the case was decided over 45 years ago, it still has profound effects on the way police officers perform their duties. Listen to oral arguments presented to the Supreme Court arguing this case. This provides wonderful insight into the positions presented by both sides. The oral arguments are provided by the Oyez Project. The oral arguments for the Miranda case and other famous Supreme Court cases can be found at: http://www.oyez.org/cases/1960-1969/1965/1965_759

PRACTICE TEST BANK

MULTIPLE CHOICE

1. The double marginality of some African-American police officers means their race causes problems with
   a. their families and white officers.
   b. their supervisors and white politicians.
   c. their white colleagues and other African-Americans.
   d. other African-American officers and whites in the community.

2. The majority of police officers use a high degree of personal discretion in carrying out daily tasks; this is sometimes referred to as
   a. high-visibility decision making.
   b. low-visibility decision making.
   c. policing the blue curtain.
   d. getting things done.

3. The ability to monitor one's own and others' feelings and emotions, to discriminate among them and to use this information to guide one's thinking and actions is the definition of
   a. police intelligence.
   b. emotional intelligence.
   c. discretion.
   d. personality.

4. In general, as compared to male officers, female officers
   a. tend to respond to different types of calls.
   b. are less likely to get convictions in their cases.
   c. are more likely to use force.
   d. are likely to receive harsher punishments.

5. Research suggests that college educated officers (as compared to those without such education)
   a. have less self confidence and job satisfaction.
   b. are better crime fighters and law enforcers.
   c. generate fewer complaints and generally perform better.
   d. have more disciplinary problems and stress.

6. The offender's demeanor is a factor that affects police decision making. The offender's demeanor is a
   a. situational factor.
   b. peer factor.
   c. extralegal factor.
   d. environmental factor.

7. Police officers who actively solicit bribes and vigorously engage in corrupt practices are known as
    a. grass eaters.
    b. bookmakers.
    c. meat eaters.
    d. sharks.

8. One position on cynicism holds that cynicism increases
    a. as officers moved up the ranks.
    b. after being involved in a shooting.
    c. after being disciplined by the department.
    d. with length of service.

9. The style of policing that is most consistent with community policing is the
    a. crime fighter.
    b. social agent.
    c. law enforcer.
    d. watchman.

10. The style of policing that is most frequently portrayed on television and in movies is the
    a. crime fighter.
    b. social agent.
    c. law enforcer.
    d. watchman.

11. All criminal justice officials, including police, have some discretion, which can be defined as
    a. tasks to perform.
    b. personal goals.
    c. a desire to advance.
    d. personal decision making.

12. Which of the following are extralegal factors that may influence police decision-making?
    a. Department regulations
    b. Department policies
    c. U.S. Supreme Court decisions
    d. Age, race, class, and gender of suspects

13. Characteristics of the victim affect police discretion. Victim characteristics are a
    a. legal factor.
    b. environmental factor.
    c. extralegal factor.
    d. Departmental factor.

14. The officers receiving the bulk of complaints tend to be
    a.   young, but experienced.
    b.   older.
    c.   young and less experienced.
    d.   at the middle of their career.

15. A police officer makes a valid arrest of the subject in the subject's home. Incident to that arrest, police may search
    a.   the entire home.
    b.   any area where the suspect could reach.
    c.   only the room in which the suspect is arrested.
    d.   the room in which the suspect is arrested, but not the suspect.

16. To obtain a warrant, the officer must convince a judge or magistrate that the officer's information shows
    a.   reasonable suspicion.
    b.   probable cause.
    c.   proof beyond a reasonable doubt.
    d.   beyond a reasonable certainty.

17. Which one of the listed choices would not be consistent with a behavior profile for problem officers?
    a.   Excessive calls for service
    b.   Citizen complaints
    c.   Incidents of resisting arrest
    d.   High speed pursuits

18. Which of the following is not a recognized situation in which a warrantless search or seizure is authorized?
    a.   Stop and frisk
    b.   Search incident to a valid arrest
    c.   Consent search
    d.   Residential search

19. An officer has a reasonable suspicion that the suspect has stolen money out of a newspaper machine. Which of the following actions is justified?
    a.   Frisk the suspect for the money and weapons
    b.   Conduct a full search of the suspect for the money
    c.   Arrest the suspect for theft
    d.   Temporarily detain the suspect and ask questions regarding the theft

20. A police officer stops a vehicle for speeding. The officer has training in drug detection and detects the odor of marijuana coming from inside the vehicle. May the officer search the vehicle for marijuana?
    a. No, because the officer lacks a warrant
    b. No, because the officer stopped the vehicle for speeding only
    c. Yes, but only if the marijuana offense is felony
    d. Yes, if the officer has probable cause

21. The greatest factor in controlling the use of police brutality is
    a. the threat of civil judgments.
    b. the threat of job loss.
    c. the threat of demotion.
    d. more training.

22. Which of the following is not considered to be a cause of police corruption?
    a. Wide discretion, coupled with low visibility
    b. Corruption is a function of society's ambivalence toward vice-related criminal behavior
    c. The police personality is predisposed to corruption
    d. Policing tends to attract individuals who do not have the financial means to maintain a middle-class lifestyle

23. A police officer approaches a vehicle on a traffic stop and perceives danger and orders the driver and passenger from the vehicle. The police officer can
    a. arrest the driver and search the passengers.
    b. conduct a full search of the vehicle.
    c. conduct a limited search of the driver and passengers as well as the area under the driver's control.
    d. conduct a limited search of the vehicle but a limited search of the driver only.

24. Research reveals that police use of force is
    a. very common.
    b. always excessive.
    c. never excessive.
    d. not very common.

25. Which Supreme Court case ruled that issues related to nondeadly force must be judged from the standpoint of a reasonable officer?
    a. *Miranda v. Arizona*
    b. *Tennessee v. Garner*
    c. *Mapp v. Ohio*
    d. *Graham v. Connor*

26. What term is used to describe the police subculture characterized by police officers feeling insulated from others in society?
    a.   Blue flu
    b.   Blue curtain
    c.   Blue wall
    d.   Blue divide

27. What term best describes victim-precipitated killings by police?
    a.   Pre-mediated suicide
    b.   Mala in se suicide
    c.   Extreme suicide
    d.   Suicide by cop

28. One of the purposes for establishing a firearm discharge review board is to ensure that the discharge was in accordance with law and
    a.   departmental policy.
    b.   administrative rule.
    c.   legal tort.
    d.   judicial review.

29. Which of the following is not a procedural requirement for a police officer to obtain a search warrant?
    a.   Police officer must request the warrant from a court.
    b.   Police officer must submit an affidavit establishing probable cause.
    c.   The police officer must be personally present to respond to questions.
    d.   The affidavit must state the place to be searched and property to be seized.

30. Which concept has important implications for the study of police discretion?
    a.   Emotional intelligence
    b.   Physical stamina
    c.   Spiritual beliefs
    d.   Intelligence quotient

TRUE/FALSE

1.   T   F   Characteristics of victims affect police decision making.

2.   T   F   *Tennessee v. Garner* permits police to use deadly force to stop non-dangerous fleeing suspects.

3.   T   F   If an offender is surly, talks back, or otherwise challenges the officer's authority, formal action by the police officer is unlikely.

4.   T   F   Higher education of police officers is associated with lower levels of self-confidence.

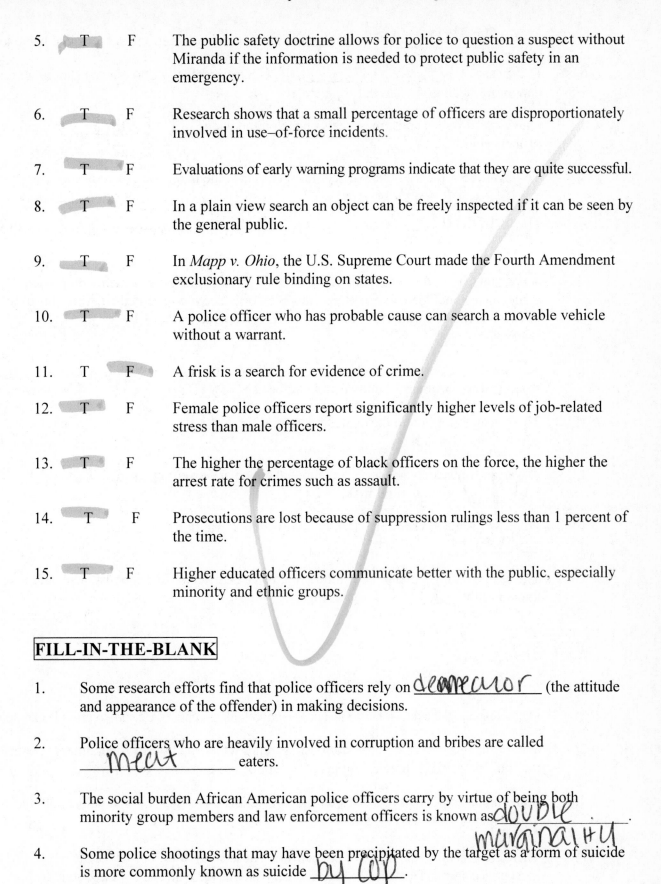

5. T F The public safety doctrine allows for police to question a suspect without Miranda if the information is needed to protect public safety in an emergency.

6. T F Research shows that a small percentage of officers are disproportionately involved in use–of-force incidents.

7. T F Evaluations of early warning programs indicate that they are quite successful.

8. T F In a plain view search an object can be freely inspected if it can be seen by the general public.

9. T F In *Mapp v. Ohio*, the U.S. Supreme Court made the Fourth Amendment exclusionary rule binding on states.

10. T F A police officer who has probable cause can search a movable vehicle without a warrant.

11. T F A frisk is a search for evidence of crime.

12. T F Female police officers report significantly higher levels of job-related stress than male officers.

13. T F The higher the percentage of black officers on the force, the higher the arrest rate for crimes such as assault.

14. T F Prosecutions are lost because of suppression rulings less than 1 percent of the time.

15. T F Higher educated officers communicate better with the public, especially minority and ethnic groups.

FILL-IN-THE-BLANK

1. Some research efforts find that police officers rely on demeanor (the attitude and appearance of the offender) in making decisions.

2. Police officers who are heavily involved in corruption and bribes are called _____ meat _____ eaters.

3. The social burden African American police officers carry by virtue of being both minority group members and law enforcement officers is known as double marginality.

4. Some police shootings that may have been precipitated by the target as a form of suicide is more commonly known as suicide by cop.

5. Active _criminality_ is the participation by police in serious criminal behavior.

6. In the case of _Tennessee v. Garner_, the U.S. Supreme Court outlawed shooting non-dangerous fleeing felons.

7. One view of police corruption casts blame on the wide _discretion_ that police officers enjoy.

8. To obtain a warrant, a police officer must convince the magistrate there is _probable cause_.

9. _nondeadly_ force is force that is unlikely to cause death or significant bodily harm.

10. A warrant cannot be issued unless the presiding magistrate is presented with sufficient evidence to conclude that an offense has been or is being committed and that the suspect is the one who committed the offense, this is referred to as the _probable cause_ requirement.

11. The Supreme Court created objective standards for questioning by police after a defendant has been taken into custody in the case of _Miranda_ v. *Arizona*.

12. There is an exception to the exclusionary rule for _good_ faith on the part of police officers.

13. A warrantless search and seizure technique aimed at preventing crime is _stop_ and frisk.

14. Police officers who are only slightly involved in corruption are termed _grass_ eaters.

15. The secretive, insulated police culture that isolates officers from the rest of society is known as the _blue_ curtain.

ESSAY

1. Identify and describe the benefits of higher education for police officers.

2. Define/explain the exclusionary rule and the good faith exception. Be sure to provide examples.

3. What is the general rule for warrantless searches under the Fourth Amendment? Describe the rule and provide three examples of exceptions to this rule.

4. Some police experts have described six core beliefs as the heart of the police culture today. Identify and explain four.

5. There are generally four styles of police work that seem to fit the current behavior patterns of most police agents. Describe the characteristics associated with each of these styles.

CHAPTER 6 ANSWER KEY

Multiple Choice

1. c [p. ,118 LO2]   2. b [p. 125, LO5]   3. b [p. 125, LO5]   4. d [p. 119, LO2]   5. c [p. 121, LO2]

6. a [p. 126, LO5]   7. c [p. 131, LO6]   8. d [p. 123, LO3]   9. b [p. 124, LO4]   10. a [p. 124, LO4]

11. d [p. 124, LO5]   12. d [p. 126, LO5]   13. c [p. 126, LO5]   14. c [p. 129, LO6]   15. b [p. 138, LO9]

16. b [p. 138, LO9]   17. a [p. 129, LO6]   18. d [p. 138, LO9]   19. d [p. 137, LO9]   20. d [p. 137, LO9]

21. a [p. 130, LO6]   22. c [p. 131, LO6]   23. c [p. 138, LO9]   24. d [p. 132, LO7]   25. d [p. 134, LO7]

26. b [p. 122, LO3]   27. d [p. 132, LO7]   28. a [p. 134, LO7]   29. c [p. 137, LO9]   30. a [p. 125, LO5]

True/False

1. T [p. 126, LO7]   2. F [p. 133, LO7]   3. F [p. 126, LO5]   4. F [p. 121, LO1]   5. T [p. 136, LO9]

6. T [p. 129, LO7]   7. T [p. 129, LO6]   8. T [p. 139, LO9]   9. T [p. 139, LO9]   10. T [p. 138, LO9]

11. F [p. 138, LO9]   12. T [p. 121, LO1]   13. T [p. 118, LO1]   14. T [p. 140, LO9]   15. T [p. 121, LO2]

Fill-in-the-Blank

1. demeanor [p. 126, LO5]   2. meat [p. 131, LO6]   3. double marginality [p. 118, LO1]

4. by cop [p. 132, LO7]   5. criminality [p. 131, LO6]   6. Tennessee v. Garner [p. 133, LO7]

7. discretion [p. 131, LO6]   8. probable cause [p. 138, LO9]   9. Nondeadly [p. 134, LO7]

10. probable cause [p. 137, LO9]   11. *Miranda* [p. 135, LO9]   12. good [p. 140, LO9]

13. stop [p. 138, LO9]   14. grass [p. 131, LO6]   15. blue [p. 122, LO3]

Essay

1.   **Identify and describe the benefits of higher education for police officers.**
   - Better communication with the public, especially minority and ethnic groups.
   - Educated officers write better and more clearly and are more likely to be promoted.
   - Police administrators believe that education enables officers to perform more effectively, generate fewer citizen complaints, show more initiative in performing police tasks, and generally act more professionally.
   - Educated officers are less likely to have disciplinary problems and are viewed as better decision makers.
   - Higher education is also associated with greater self-confidence.

[p. 121, LO1]

2.   **Define/explain the exclusionary rule and the good faith exception. Be sure to provide examples.**

The exclusionary rule provides that all evidence obtained by unreasonable searches and seizures is inadmissible in criminal trials. It also excludes illegal confessions (those obtained under Fifth Amendment prohibitions) from being used. The rule is based on the Fourth Amendment requirement that people have a right to be secure in their persons, houses, papers, and effects, against unreasonable searches and seizures. The rule was the result of the U.S. Supreme Court's ruling in the case *Weeks v. United States* making it applicable to federal criminal cases. In 1961 the U.S. Supreme Court made the rule applicable to the states in its ruling in *Mapp v. Ohio*. The exclusionary rule would apply if an officer, without probable cause, search warrant, consent, or other warrantless exception conducted a search of a person's backpack. The search revealed the defendant to be in possession of an illegal firearm. The firearm may be seized but the firearm is not admissible as evidence in the defendant's criminal trial.

The exclusionary rule intimates that guilty defendants may go free because of police error, intentional or otherwise. Over time the U.S. Supreme Court has diminished the scope of the rule. For example, evidence is admissible in court if the police officers acted in good faith by first obtaining approval for their search, even if the warrant was later determined to be faulty or deficient. This has come to be known as the "good faith exception".

[pp. 139-140, LO9]

3.   **What is the general rule for warrantless searches under the Fourth Amendment? Describe the rule and provide three examples of exceptions to this rule.**

In general warrantless searches are presumed illegal under the Fourth Amendment unless the search is conducted under an allowable exception to the rule. In order to allow police the ability to look for and locate evidence of crime, the court has ruled that under certain circumstances a valid search may be conducted without a search warrant. These circumstances have been identified in a series of exceptions that provide police officers with the ability to conduct warrantless searches.

1.   ***Search incident to a valid arrest.*** A warrantless search is valid if it is made incident to a lawful arrest. The reason for this exception is that the arresting officer must have the power to disarm the accused, protect himself or herself, preserve the evidence of the crime, and prevent the accused from escaping from custody. Because the search is lawful, the officer retains what he or she finds if it is connected with a crime. The officer is permitted to search only the defendant's person and the areas in the defendant's immediate physical surroundings that are under his or her control.

2.   ***Stop and frisk.*** In the landmark *Terry v. Ohio* decision, the Supreme Court held that police officers can perform a stop and frisk when they have reasonable suspicion to believe criminal activity is afoot. For example, say the individual is found lurking behind a closed store. In such a case, the officer has a right to stop and question the individual and, if she or he has reason to believe that the person is carrying a concealed weapon, may frisk the subject—that is, pat down the person's outer clothing for the purpose of finding a concealed weapon. If an illegal weapon is found, then an arrest can be made and a search incident to the arrest performed.

3.   ***Automobile search.*** An automobile may be searched without a warrant if there is probable cause to believe the car was involved in a crime. Because automobiles are inherently mobile, there is a significant chance that evidence will be lost if the search is not conducted

immediately; also, people should not expect as much privacy in their cars as in their homes. Police officers who have legitimately stopped an automobile and who have probable cause to believe that contraband is concealed somewhere inside it may conduct a warrantless search of the vehicle that is as thorough as a magistrate could authorize by warrant. Because traffic stops can be dangerous, the Court has ruled that if a police officer perceives danger during a routine traffic stop, he can order the driver and passengers from the car without suspicion and conduct a limited search of their persons to ensure police officer safety. Police officers can search the car and passengers after a traffic stop, as long as the search is reasonable and related to officer safety. Usually, the search must be limited to the area under the driver's control or reach.

4. *Consent search.* In a consent search, individuals waive their constitutional rights; therefore, neither a warrant nor probable cause need exist. For a consent search to be legal, the consent must be given voluntarily; threat or compulsion invalidates the search. Although it has been held that voluntary consent is required, it has also been maintained that the police are under no obligation to inform individuals of their right to refuse the search.

5. *Plain-view search.* Even when an object is in a house or other areas involving an expectation of privacy, the object can be freely inspected if it can be seen by the general public. If a police officer looks through a fence and sees marijuana growing in a suspect's fields, no search warrant is needed for the property to be seized. The articles are considered to be in plain view, and therefore a search warrant need not be obtained to seize them.

6. *Exigent circumstances.* The Supreme Court has identified a number of exigent, or emergency, circumstances in which a search warrant might normally have been required but, because of some immediate emergency, police officers can search suspects and places without benefit of a warrant. These circumstances include hot pursuit, danger of escape, threats to evidence, and threats to others. In each situation, officers must have probable cause.

[pp. 137-139, LO9]

4. Some police experts have described six core beliefs as the heart of the police culture today. Identify and explain four.

- Police are the only real crime fighters. The public wants the police officer to fight crime; other agencies, both public and private, only play at crime fighting.
- No one else understands the real nature of police work. Lawyers, academics, politicians, and the public in general have little concept of what it means to be a police officer.
- Loyalty to colleagues counts above everything else. Police officers have to stick together, because everyone is out to get the police and make the job more difficult.
- It is impossible to win the war against crime without bending the rules. Courts have awarded criminal defendants too many civil rights.
- Members of the public are basically unsupportive and unreasonably demanding. People are quick to criticize police unless they themselves need police help.
- Patrol work is the pits. Detective work is glamorous and exciting.

[pp. 122-123, LO3]

5. **There are generally four styles of police work that seem to fit the current behavior patterns of most police agents. Describe the characteristics associated with each of these styles.**

Crime Fighter: The most important aspects of police work involve investigating serious crimes and apprehending criminals. Police work is viewed as the only force that can keep "society's dangerous classes" in check. Property crimes, misdemeanors, and traffic enforcement are considered to be less important and serious crime dominates the focus. Managing less important tasks could be handled by other agencies of government. The police officer is best utilized to investigate serious crimes and arrest criminals.

Social Agent: The most important aspects of police work involve a wide range of activities without regard for any connection to law enforcement. A police officer operating as a social agent is concerned with problem solving instead of the more narrowly focused "criminal catching." No work is considered out of bounds; problems blanketing a community automatically and by default become a concern to law enforcement.

Law Enforcer: The most important aspects of police work involve the notion that duty is clearly defined in the law. A police officer operating as a law enforcer believes it should be "played by the book." All crimes (serious and less serious) are fair game. Police officers are perceived as being neither vengeance seekers nor community social workers but as professional law enforcement officers who detect violations, identify, and apprehend criminals to bring them before a court of law.

Watchman: The most important aspects of police work involve a strong emphasis on maintaining public order. It takes priority over the law enforcement or general service functions. Watchmen choose to ignore minor infractions unless social or political order is threatened. Stranded motorists are left to fend for themselves and vice crimes occur under the radar until public order is breached. A police officer who exhibits the watchman style is most often described as passive, more concerned about retirement benefits than crime rates or problem solving.

[p. 124, LO4]

CHAPTER 7
Courts, Prosecution, and the Defense

After studying this chapter, students will:

1.   Describe the varying structures of state court systems
2.   Describe the federal court system
3.   Summarize the selection procedure for and duties of the trial judge
4.   Explain the role of the prosecutor
5.   Describe prosecutorial discretion and summarize its pros and cons
6.   Understand the role of the defense attorney in the justice process
7.   Discuss the different forms of indigent defense
8.   Summarize the pros and cons of private attorneys
9.   Be familiar with the expanding role of technology in the court process

KEY TERMS AND CONCEPTS

state courts of limited jurisdiction (p. 146) Courts that have jurisdiction over misdemeanors and conduct preliminary investigations of felony charges.

court of general jurisdiction (p. 147) State or federal courts that has jurisdiction over felony offenses and more serious civil cases (that is, involving more than a dollar amount set by the legislature).

appellate court (p. 147) A court that reconsiders a case that has already been tried in order to determine whether the measures used complied with accepted rules of criminal procedure and were in line with constitutional doctrines.

court of last resort (p. 147) A court that handles the final appeal on a matter. The U.S. Supreme Court is the official court of last resort for criminal matters.

writ of certiorari (p. 150) An order of superior court requesting that the record of an inferior court (or administrative body) be brought forward for review or inspection.

landmark decision (p. 150) A decision handed down by the U.S. Supreme Court that becomes the law of the land and serves as a precedent for similar legal issues.

jury trial (p. 151) The process of deciding a case by a group of persons selected and sworn in to serve as jurors at a criminal trial, often as a 6- or 12-person jury.

U.S. magistrate judge (p. 154) A federal trial judge who is appointed by a district court judge and who presides over various civil cases with the consent of the parties and over certain misdemeanor cases.

Missouri Plan (p. 154) A way of picking judges through nonpartisan elections as a way to ensure that judges adhere to high standards of judicial performance.

prosecutor (p. 155) Representative of the state (executive branch) in criminal proceedings; advocate for the state's case—the charge—in the adversary trial. Examples include the attorney general of the United States, U.S. attorneys, the attorneys general of the states, district attorneys, and police prosecutors. The prosecutor participates in investigations both before and after arrest, prepares legal documents, participates in obtaining arrest or search warrants, decides whether to charge a suspect and, if so, with which offense. The prosecutor argues the state's case at trial, advises the police, participates in plea negotiations, and makes sentencing recommendations.

public defender (p. 161) An attorney generally employed (at no cost to the accused) by the government to represent poor persons accused of a crime.

adversarial procedure (p. 161) The process of publicly pitting the prosecution and the defense against one another in pursuit of the truth.

Sixth Amendment (p. 161) The U.S. constitutional amendment containing various criminal trial rights, such as the right to public trial, right to trial by jury, and the right to confrontation of witnesses.

indigent (p. 161) Without the means to hire an attorney.

Gideon v. Wainwright (p. 161) The 1963 U.S. Supreme Court case that granted counsel to indigent defendants in felony prosecutions.

assigned counsel (p. 163) A lawyer appointed by the court to represent a defendant in a criminal case because the person is too poor to hire counsel.

contract system (attorney) (p. 163) Providing counsel to indigent offenders by having attorneys under contract to the county handle all (or some) such cases.

CHAPTER OUTLINE

I. **INTRODUCTION**
1. The criminal court is the setting in which many of the most important decisions in the criminal justice system are made such as:
   a. Eyewitness identification
   b. Bail
   c. Trial
   d. Plea negotiations
   e. Sentencing

      2. Court is a complex social agency with many independent but interrelated sub-systems:
- a. Administrator
- b. Prosecutor
- c. Defense attorney
- d. Judge
- e. Probation department

      3. Entire process governed by precise rules of law designed to achieve fairness

      4. The nation's court system is chronically under-budgeted

      5. Plea negotiations and other non-judicial alternatives are far more common than trials

      6. High degree of discretion
- a. Discretion means that two people committing similar crimes will receive highly dissimilar treatment

      7. Each state maintains its own state court organization and structure

      8. Federal court has an independent trial court system

II. **STATE COURTS**

      1. States are free to create as many courts as they wish and name courts what they like and establish specialized courts that handle a single matter such as:
- a. Drug courts
- b. Domestic courts

      2. No two court organizations are exactly alike

A. Courts of Limited Jurisdiction

      1. State courts of limited jurisdiction are limited to minor or less serious civil and criminal cases and are known by a variety of names:
- a. Municipal courts
- b. County courts
- c. District courts
- d. Metropolitan courts

      2. They usually handle:
- a. Misdemeanor criminal infractions
- b. Violations of municipal ordinances
- c. Traffic violations
- d. Civil suits with limited damage amounts, usually less than $1,000

      3. In criminal matters they hear misdemeanors such as:
- a. Shoplifting
- b. Disorderly conduct
- c. Simple assault

      4. Punishments may be limited to:
- a. Fines
- b. Community sentencing
- c. Incarceration in the county jail for up to a year

      5. Also conduct arraignments and preliminary and bail hearings in felony cases

B. Specialized courts:

     a. Of the nation's approximately 13,500 independent courts of limited jurisdiction, most have been accused of providing assembly line justice

     b. Growing phenomenon is to create specialty courts that focus on treatment and care for special needs offenders

1. Drug courts:
   a. Began in Florida to address growing problem of prison overcrowding due to an influx of drug-involved offenders
   b. Created to have primary jurisdiction over cases involving substance abuse and trafficking
   c. Aim is to place nonviolent first offenders into intensive treatment programs rather than jail or prison
   d. Today, more than 2,000 drug courts throughout U.S. and territories
   e. Provide an ideal setting to address drug problems by linking justice system with health services and drug treatment providers
   f. Eases the burden on overtaxed correctional system
2. Mental Health Courts:
   a. Focus on mental health treatment to help people with emotional problems reduce their chances of reoffending
   b. Provide a venue for those dealing with mental issues to avoid the trauma of jail or prison
3. There are now specialized courts for nearly every difficult problem confronting the criminal justice system:
   a. Domestic violence courts
   b. Gang courts
   c. Gun courts
   d. Sex offender courts
   e. Homeless courts
   f. Parole reentry courts
   g. Community courts

C. Courts of General Jurisdiction
   1. 2000 exist
   2. Can be referred to as:
      a. Felony courts
      b. Superior courts
      c. Supreme courts
      d. County courts
      e. Circuit courts
   3. Handle more serious felony cases and higher damage civil cases, usually over $10,000
   4. Hear appeals from limited jurisdiction courts
   5. Typically organized in judicial districts or circuits based on political subdivisions such as a county or group of counties
   6. Handle about 100 million new cases each year, an increase of more than 10 percent in the past decade
      a. Majority are traffic related
      b. 20 million involve some form of criminal conduct

D. Appellate Courts
1. Review violations of constitutional rights
2. Do not try cases, but review procedures of cases to determine if errors were made by judicial authorities
3. Judicial error can include:
   a. Improperly admitted evidence that was illegally seized
   b. Improper charging of jury
   c. Improper questions
4. Court can order new trial or dismiss charge if an error is determined
5. Each state has a court of last resort, or state supreme court:
   a. Reviews issues of law and fact appealed from the trial courts
   b. Some states have two high courts, one for civil and another for criminal
6. Criminal appeals represent a small percentage of the total number of cases processed by nation's appellate courts
7. All states vary in the way they delegate responsibility to a particular court system

III. **FEDERAL COURTS**
1. Established by Article 3, Section 1 of U.S. Constitution — the judicial power of the United States shall be vested in one Supreme Court and in such inferior courts as Congress may, from time to time, ordain and establish
2. Federal courts have jurisdiction over the laws of the U.S. and treaties and cases involving admiralty and maritime jurisdiction as well as over controversies between two or more states and citizens of different states
3. States have jurisdiction over most common law crimes
4. Federal courts have jurisdiction over
   a. Federal criminal statute
   b. Civil suits between citizens and different states
   c. Civil suits between citizens and federal government
5. Three tiered federal court hierarchy:
   a. U.S. district courts
   b. U.S. courts of appeals
   c. U.S. Supreme Court
A. U.S. District Courts
5. Organized by Congress in the Judicial Act of 1789
6. Ninety-four independent courts in operation
7. Have jurisdiction over cases involving violations of federal laws to include:
   a. Civil rights abuses
   b. Interstate transportation of stolen vehicles
   c. Kidnappings
   d. May also hear cases in citizenship and rights of aliens
   e. One state resident sues a resident or business in another state
   f. Federal government is a party in a suit
B. U.S. Court of Appeals
1. Thirteen judicial circuits each with a court of appeal

2. Empowered to review federal and state appellate court cases on substantive and procedural issues involving constitutional rights
3. Do not conduct trials instead they analyze judicial interpretations of the law
4. Steps have been taken to make appealing more difficult

C. The U.S. Supreme Court
   a. Nation's highest appellate body and court of last resort for all cases — state and federal
   b. Nine judges appointed for life by president and with approval by Congress
   c. Has discretion over most cases it will consider and may choose to only hear those that are deemed important, appropriate, and worthy of attention
   d. Chooses about 300 of 5000 case requests each year, only 100 have full opinions
   e. Writ of certiorari — court agrees to hear case, requests transcripts of the case for review
      i. At least four of the nine justices must vote to grant the writ of certiorari
      ii. More than 90% of the cases heard are brought by petition for a writ of certiorari
   f. Has original jurisdiction in a few instances
      i. Those involving disputes between states
   g. Landmark decision — court rules on case, usually by majority decision (five votes), its rule becomes a precedent

1. Supreme Court Procedure
   a. After it decides to hear a case, it reviews written arguments, legal briefs
   b. Attorneys for each side allowed 30 minutes oral argument
   c. Justice then normally meet in a case conference to discuss the case and vote to reach a decision
   d. In cases where decision is split, Chief justice assigns member of majority to write opinion
   e. Another justice writes dissent or minority opinion
   f. Single opinion may be written if case if decision is unanimous
   g. When case is finished, it is submitted to pubic and becomes law of the land

IV. **THE JUDICIARY**
   1. Judge senior officer in court of criminal law. Duties include:
      a. Oversee trial process:
         i. Control appropriateness of conduct
         ii. Settle questions of evidence and procedure
         iii. Guide the questioning of witnesses
      b. Instruct jurors in jury trials:
         i. Instruct jurors on which evidence is proper to examine and which should be ignored
         ii. Instruct jurors on what points of law and evidence they must consider
      c. Finding guilt and sentence in bench trials:
         i. Type of sentence
         ii. Probation conditions if warranted
      d. Controls and influences court agencies:

       i. Probation

      ii. Court clerk

     iii. Police

     iv. District attorney's office

  2. Judges relish using their judicial power as a policymaking tool to influence important social policies such as:

    a. Affirmative action

    b. Privacy

  3. Work together with prosecutors and defense attorneys

  4. Assisted by:

    a. Clerks

    b. Court administrators

    c. Security personnel

    d. Court reporters

A. The Judge and the Justice System

  4. Judicial attitudes can affect:

    a. Police policies

    b. District attorney decisions

    c. Prosecutor decisions

B. Judicial Qualifications and Selection

  1. Qualifications vary between federal and state levels

    a. Federal Level:

      i. Appointed by the president with the advice and consent of the Senate

      ii. U.S. Magistrate Judge is exception:

        a) Federal trial judges appointed by district court judges who preside over various civil cases with the consent of the parties and certain misdemeanor cases

     iii. No formal qualification

     iv. Positions are very prestigious and sought-after

    b. State Level:

      i. Qualifications for the existing 30,000 judgeships vary between states and courts

      ii. Most typically judge must be:

        a) Resident of the state

        b) Licensed to practice law

        c) Member of state bar association

        d) At least 25 years of age

        e) Less than 70 years of age

    c. Many methods are utilized to select judges, including:

      i. Gubernatorial appointment, recommendation by governor with approval by state senate

      ii. Governor's council

     iii. Special confirmation committee

     iv. Executive council elected by state assembly

     v. Elected review board

        vi. Judicial nominating commission that submits names to governor for approval

       vii. Popular election:

          a)   Judges may run as members of the Republican, Democratic, or other party, or without party affiliation

          b)   In some states, judges are elected for 15-year terms other elected for 4-year terms

     d. Missouri Plan for selecting judges (nonpartisan):

        i. Judicial nominating commission selects and nominates potential candidates

        ii. Elected executive branch official makes appointment from list of nominees

       iii. Nonpartisan and noncompetitive elections

  2. Quality of the judiciary is a concern

  3. It has often been charged that many judicial appointments are made to pay off political debts or to reward:

    a. Cronies

    b. Loyal friends

V.   **THE PROSECUTOR**

  1. Depending on the government and jurisdiction, the prosecutor may be known as:

    a. District attorney

    b. County attorney

    c. State's attorney

    d. U.S. attorney

  2. Prosecutor is the people's attorney responsible for representing the public in criminal matters

  3. Chief law enforcement officer in his or her jurisdiction, spans the entire justice system process

  4. General duties include:

    a. Providing advice to law enforcement officers during investigations

    b. In pretrial stage, representing state in plea negotiations, pretrial motions, evidence, and bail hearings

    c. Representing state at hearing, trials, and appeals

    d. Acting as legal advisor to county commissioners and other elected officials

    e. In some instances, identifying dangerous adult and juvenile offenders

    f. Assisting victims, especially domestic violence victims

 A. Types of Prosecutors

  4. Federal system — known as U.S. attorneys

    a. Appointed by president

    b. Represent government in federal district courts

    c. Chief prosecutor is an administrator; assistants normally handle trial work

    d. Professional civil servants with reasonable salaries and job security

  5. State and County — Attorney general and district attorney are the chief prosecutorial officers

a. Typically are administrators; bulk of work handled by:
   i. Full and part-time attorneys
   ii. Police investigators
   iii. Clerical personnel
b. Most attorneys that work for prosecutors at this level are political appointees who earn low salaries, handle many cases, and some maintain private law practices
c. Urban offices are normally specialized to handle:
   i. Felonies
   ii. Misdemeanors
   iii. Trial and appeals
d. In rural offices, they may handle all duties
e. Suffered from bad image in the past, but has improved
   i. Violations of federal laws are being more aggressively investigated by the 94 U.S. Attorneys and nearly 2,000 assistant U.S. attorneys
f. Prosecutor will continue to be one of the most powerful and visible professionals in the justice system
g. About 2400 state court prosecutors' offices employ 79,000 attorneys, investigators, and support staff
h. Most active prosecutors are employed in larger counties with populations over 500,000
i. Survey of federal prosecutors showed:
   i. 80 percent have litigated computer-related crimes
   ii. 69 percent have litigated identity thefts
   iii. 67 percent have litigated transmission of child pornography
   iv. 24 percent participated in state or local homeland security task forces for homeland security
   v. 95 percent relied on state operated forensic laboratories for DNA analysis
   vi. 34 percent also used privately operated DNA labs

B. Prosecutorial Discretion
1. *Nolle prosequi* — charges dropped because conditions are not favorable for a conviction
2. Courts have protected prosecutor's right to exercise discretion over legal case processing
3. Only overturned if a defendant can prove the prosecutor let discrimination guide decision making
4. Prosecutors asked to determine sufficiency of evidence to determine if complaint should be filed; may take place at preliminary hearings or grand juries
5. Prosecutors exercise a great deal of discretion even in the most serious cases
6. Prosecutorial discretion is used to reduce potential trial cases to a minimum

C. Factors Influencing Prosecutorial Discretion
1. Legal Issues:
   a. Characteristics of justice system
   b. Crime

        c. Victim

        d. The criminal and their past history and substance abuse

        e. Victim's injury

        f. Quality of police work

        g. Amount and relevance of the evidence

2. Victim Issues:

        a. Victim's behavior

             i. Some victims reluctant to press charges especially if the offender is a:

                a)   Parent

                b)   Spouse

             ii. Domestic violence cases are often difficult to prosecute

        b. Victim's cooperation

             i. Odds of case prosecution are seven times more likely when victims are considered cooperative

3. Extralegal issues:

        a. Offender's race

        b. Offender's gender

        c. Offender's ethnic background

             i. Studies are mixed on these issues

4. Resource Issues — may be more critical than legal or extralegal issues

        a. Availability of treatment and detention facilities

        b. Size of caseloads

        c. Number of prosecutors available

             i. Prosecutors may be forced to accept plea bargains because it lacks the resources and personnel to bring case to trial

D. The Pros and Cons of Prosecutorial Discretion

        a. Proper exercise of prosecutorial discretion can improve the criminal justice process by preventing the rigid implementation of criminal law

        b. Allows prosecutor to consider alternative decision and humanize the operation of criminal justice system

        c. Too much discretion can lead to abuses that result in the abandonment of law

        d. Prosecutors are political creatures

             i. Must keep their reputations in mind

             ii. Losing too many high-profile cases may jeopardize their chances of reelection

E. Prosecutorial Ethics

        a. Although the prosecutor's primary duty is to enforce law, the fundamental obligation is to seek justice

        b. Unethical prosecutorial behavior is often motivated by the desire to obtain a conviction and by the fact that such behavior is rarely punished by the courts

        c. Some prosecutors may:

             i. Conceal evidence or misrepresent it

             ii. Influence juries by impugning the character of opposing witnesses

            iii. Mentioning tainted evidence

1. Prosecutorial Misconduct
   a. Courts have reviewed prosecutorial misconduct behavior as:
      i. Making disruptive statements in court
      ii. Failure to adhere to sentence recommendations pursuant to a plea bargain
      iii. Making public statements harmful to the state's case that are not constitutionally protected under the First Amendment
      iv. Withholding evidence that might exonerate a defendant
   b. Three cases illustrate controls placed on vindictive prosecutors:
      i. *North Carolina v. Pearce*:
         a) Judge in a retrial cannot impose a sentence more severe than that originally imposed
         b) Prosecutor cannot seek a stricter sentence for a defendant who succeeds in getting first conviction set aside
      ii. *Blackledge v. Perry*:
         a) Imposing a penalty on a defendant who successfully pursued an appeal is a violation of due process and amounts to prosecutorial vindictiveness
      iii. *Bordenkircher v. Hayes*:
         a) Prosecutor may carry out threats of increased charges made during plea negotiations when defendant refused to plead guilty to original charge
   c. Prosecutor's legitimate exercise of discretion must be balanced against the defendant's legal rights

VI. **THE DEFENSE ATTORNEY**
   1. The defense attorney is the counterpart to the prosecuting attorney
   2. When a defendant cannot afford an attorney, the state must provide one
      a. Private counsel or public defender may be assigned by the court
   A. The Role of the Criminal Defense Attorney
      1. An officer of the court
      2. Obligated to uphold the integrity of the legal profession and to observe requirements of the American Bar Association's Code of Professional Responsibility
      3. Prime movers in the adversarial procedure
         a. The prosecution and the defense engage in conflict over the facts of the case at hand
         b. Judge acts as arbiter of the legal rules
         c. Burden is on the state to prove charges beyond a reasonable doubt
         d. Proved to be the most effective method of achieving the truth
      4. Defense must also be aware of their role as officers of the court and is obliged to rely on constitutional ideals of fairplay and professional ethics to provide adequate representation
   B. The Right to Counsel
      1. Sixth Amendment allows for the provision of counsel at trial

2. *Gideon v. Wainwright* (1963) — State courts must provide counsel to indigent defendants in felony prosecutions
3. *Argersinger v. Hamlin* (1972) — Right to attorney extended to all criminal cases in which the penalty includes imprisonment, felony or misdemeanor
4. Most stages of the criminal process involve right to attorney and also includes juvenile court hearings and mental health commitments
5. The Sixth Amendment right to counsel and Fifth and Fourteenth Amendments' guarantee of due process of law have been judicially interpreted together to provide the defendant with counsel by the state in all types of criminal proceedings.
6. Some areas do not require assistance of counsel
   a. Preindictment lineups
   b. Booking procedures
   c. Grand jury investigations
   d. Appeals beyond the first review
   e. Disciplinary proceedings in correctional institutions
   f. Post-release revocation hearings
7. Basically no person can be deprived of freedom or lose a liberty interest without representation by counsel

C. Legal Services for the Indigent
   1. About 3000 state and local agencies are providing indigent legal services in the United States
   2. Recoupment — indigents repay the state for at least part of their legal services
      a. Indigent legal services still cost over $1.5 billion annually
   3. Providing assistance to indigents — three major categories
      a. Public defender systems — Found in larger urban areas with high case flow rates
      b. Assigned counsel systems — Used in less populated areas where case flow is minimal
      c. Contract systems
   4. Other approaches include the use of mixed systems such as representation by:
      a. Public defender
      b. Private bar
      c. Law school clinical programs
      d. Prepaid legal services

D. The Private Bar
   1. Private attorneys who specialize in criminal practice, gain skill from their experience in trial courts
   2. Relatively few represent defendants for large fees in celebrated and widely publicized cases
   3. Very small percentage serves as house lawyers for professional criminals such as:
      a. Narcotic dealers
      b. Gamblers
      c. Prostitutes
      d. Burglars

4. A large number of criminal defendants are represented by lawyers who often accept many cases for small fees
5. A lawyer whose practice involves a substantial proportion of criminal cases is often considered a specialist in the field
6. Research found that having a competent private attorney who puts up a rigorous defense is the single most important factor separating those exonerated in murder cases and those who are executed

E. Does Type of Lawyer Matter?
1. Public v. Private Attorneys — National surveys indicate that state-appointed attorneys do quite well
2. Conviction rates for indigent defendants same as for paying clients in state and federal courts
   a. About 90 percent of federal defendants and 75 percent of defendants in the most populous counties found guilty regardless of the type of attorney
3. Of those found guilty those represented by public attorneys incarcerated at a higher rate than those paying defendants
4. On average, sentence lengths for defendants sent to jail or prison were shorter for those with publicly financed attorneys than those who hired counsel
   a. In federal district court those with public attorneys were given just under five years on average, those with private attorneys, just over five years
   b. In large state courts those with public attorneys sentenced to an average of two and a half years, those with private attorneys, three years

F. The Competence of Defense Attorneys
1. Inadequacy of counsel may occur in a variety of instances:
   a. Attorney refuses to meet regularly with client
   b. Fail to cross-examine key government witnesses
   c. Fail to investigate the case properly
2. In *Strickland v. Washington* (1984), the Supreme Court established a two-prong test for determining effectiveness of counsel
   a. Defendant must show counsel's performance was deficient and serious errors were made to essentially eliminate the presence of counsel guaranteed by the Sixth Amendment
   b. Defendant must also show deficient performance prejudiced the case to an extent that the defendant was deprived of a fair trial
3. For a defense attorney to be considered incompetent, they would have to:
   a. Miss filings
   b. Fail to follow normal trial procedure, and/or fail to use defense tactics that the average attorney would be sure to follow such as:
      i. Using expert witnesses
      ii. Mentioning past behaviors that might mitigate guilt

VII. **COURT ADMINISTRATION**
1. Need for efficient management of the judiciary system
2. Management goals include:
   a. Improving organization and scheduling of cases
   b. Devising methods to allocate court resources efficiently

   c. Administering fines and monies due the court

   d. Preparing budgets

   e. Overseeing personnel

  3. Federal courts have led the way in creating and organizing court administration, such as the 1939 Administrative Office Act

   a. Established the Administrative Office of the United States Courts which was responsible for:

    i. Gathering statistics on the work of the federal courts

    ii. Preparing the judicial budget for approval by the Conference of Senior Circuit Judges

    iii. Also created a judicial council with general supervisory responsibilities for the district and circuit courts

  4. States have experienced slow and uneven growth in the development and application of court management principles

   a. First state to establish an administrative office was North Dakota in 1927

  5. Today, all states employ some form of central administration

 A. Using Technology in Court Management

  5. Rapid retrieval and organization of data are now being used for such functions as:

   a. Maintaining case histories and statistical reporting

   b. Monitoring and scheduling cases

   c. Preparing documents

   d. Indexing cases

   e. Issuing summonses

   f. Notifying witnesses, attorneys, and others of required appearances

   g. Selecting and notifying jurors

   h. Preparing and administering budgets and payrolls

  6. Computer technology is also being applied in the courts in such areas as:

   a. Videotaped testimonies

   b. New court reporting devices

   c. Information systems

   d. Data processing systems to handle court docketing and jury management

  7. Other developing areas:

   a. Communications:

    i. Video connections between police department and court for arraignments

    ii. Video conferencing for judicial conferences and scheduling meetings

    iii. Voice activated cameras to record testimony during trials

   b. Videoconferencing:

    i. 400 courts across the country have videoconferencing capability. Now also being employed for:

     a) Juvenile detention hearings

     b) Expert witness testimony at trial

     c) Oral arguments on appeal

     d) Parole hearings

      ii.   More than 150 courts use two-way live, televised remote link-ups for first appearance and arraignment

  c. Evidence presentation — High-tech courtrooms now equipped to handle:

      i.   Real-time transcription and translation

      ii.   Audio-video preservation of court record

      iii.   Remote witness participation

      iv.   Computer graphics displays

      v.   Television monitors for jurors

      vi.   Computers for counsel and judge

  d. Case Management:

      i.   Older systems limited and could not process complex interrelationships that occur in a court setting

      ii.   Contemporary relational databases now provide the flexibility to handle complex case management

  e. Internet Utilization:

      i.   Utilization makes it easier for judges and court personnel to find important information in a timely fashion

      ii.   Web-based electronic network provides the public with access to court records and other information

  f. Information Sharing — Computer can be used as an ally to help speed the trial process by identifying backlogs and bottlenecks that can be eradicated with intelligent managerial techniques

CHAPTER SUMMARY

The criminal court is where many of the most important decisions in the criminal justice system are made. Eyewitness identification, bail, trial, plea negotiations, and sentencing all involve court-made decisions. The criminal court is a complex social agency with many independent but interrelated subsystems: administrator, prosecutor, defense attorney, judge, and probation department. Plea negotiations and other non-judicial alternatives, such as diversion, are far more common than the formal trial process.

State courts of limited jurisdiction are known by a variety of names—municipal courts, county courts, district courts, and metropolitan courts. There are approximately two thousand courts of general jurisdiction known as felony, superior, supreme, county, or circuit courts. Courts of general jurisdiction handle more serious felony cases and larger civil cases, and review cases on appeal from courts of limited jurisdiction.

Appellate courts do not try cases; they review the procedures of the case to determine if an error was made by lower courts. Each state has at least one court of last resort, usually called a state supreme court, which reviews issues of law and fact appealed from the trial courts.

The federal government has established a three-tiered hierarchy of court jurisdiction that consists of U.S. district courts, U.S. courts of appeals, and the U.S. Supreme Court. The U.S. Supreme Court is the nation's highest appellate body and the court of last resort for all cases tried in the various federal and state courts. When the Supreme Court decides to hear a case, it grants a writ of certiorari.

The judge is the senior officer in a court of criminal law. Many methods are used to select judges, depending on the level of court jurisdiction. The prosecutor may be known as a district attorney, county attorney, state's attorney, or U.S. attorney. The general duties of a prosecutor include providing advice to law enforcement and representing the state in pleas, pre-trials, evidence, and bail hearings. Prosecutors represent the state at hearings, criminal trials, and appeals, and act as legal advisor to elected officials. In the federal system, prosecutors are known as U.S. attorneys and are appointed by the president. On the state and county levels, the attorney general and the district attorney are the chief prosecutorial officers. Today, there are about 2,400 state court prosecutors' offices. The power to institute formal charges against the defendant is the key to the prosecutorial function. Although the prosecutor's primary duty is to enforce criminal law, their fundamental obligation is to seek justice and convict those who are guilty.

The defense attorney is the counterpart of the prosecuting attorney. The accused has a constitutional right to counsel, and when the defendant cannot afford an attorney, the state must provide one. The accused may obtain counsel from the private bar if he can afford to do so; if the defendant is indigent, private counsel or a public defender may be assigned by the court. The defense counsel is an officer of the court. Defense attorneys are viewed as the prime movers in the adversarial procedure, which is where the prosecution and defense engage in conflict over the facts of the case at hand.

The Sixth Amendment allows for provision of counsel at trial. In *Gideon v. Wainwright*, the U.S. Supreme Court ruled that state courts must provide counsel to indigent defendants in felony prosecutions. In *Argersinger v. Hamlin*, the Court extended the obligation to provide counsel to all criminal cases. Programs providing counsel assistance to indigent defendants can be divided into three major categories: public defender systems, assigned counsel systems, and contract systems.

In addition to qualified personnel, there is a need for efficient management of the judiciary system. Management goals include improving organization and scheduling cases, devising methods to allocate court resources efficiently, administering fines and monies, preparing budgets, and overseeing personnel. Other developing areas of court technology include communications, videoconferencing, evidence presentation, and case management.

DISCUSSION QUESTIONS

1. Should attorneys disclose information given them by their clients about participation in an earlier unsolved crime?
2. Should defense attorneys cooperate with a prosecutor if it means their clients will go to jail?
3. Should a prosecutor have absolute discretion over which cases to proceed on and which to drop?
4. Should clients be made aware of an attorney's track record in court?
5. Does the assigned counsel system present an inherent conflict of interest, inasmuch as attorneys are hired and paid by the institution they are to oppose?

6.   Should victims play a role in the application of prosecutorial discretion? Before you answer, consider how that system might harm some defendants and benefit others.

MEDIA TOOLS

The state of Minnesota employs a number of specialty courts that they define as problem-solving courts. The website of the Minnesota Judicial Branch presents several examples and explains the purpose of each problem-solving court. For further research on this interesting topic on how states employ specialty courts visit the Minnesota Judicial Branch Problem-Solving website at: http://www.mncourts.gov/?page=626

The Administrative Office of the U.S. Courts maintains a comprehensive website that provides explanations of all federal courts as well as statistics regarding these courts. There are many interactive resources regarding all aspects of the court process including jury service. This site is worth a visit to enhance your knowledge of the court system. The site can be found at: http://www.uscourts.gov/Home.aspx

Visit the website of the Wayne County Prosecutor's Office in Wayne County Michigan. Make sure to click on the Current Cases Update section. Provides excellent insight into the case load of an urban area prosecutor's office. Document provides defendant's names, next court appearance and description of criminal offense and other pertinent information. Visit the Wayne County Prosecutor's Office website at: http://www.waynecounty.com/prosecutor

Explore how judges are selected and recent controversies regarding the process. The site is part of the Justice for Sale series provided by Frontline the Public Broadcasting System production. Visit the website, How Should Judges be Selected? The site can be found at: http://www.pbs.org/wgbh/pages/frontline/shows/justice/howshould

PRACTICE TEST BANK

MULTIPLE CHOICE

1.   In New York, felony courts are known as:
      a.   supreme courts.
      b.   district courts.
      c.   superior courts.
      d.   court of appeals.

2.   The purpose of appellate courts is to:
      a.   try cases.
      b.   re-try cases.
      c.   hold hearings.
      d.   review cases for errors.

3.   In terms of the meaning in this chapter, two people committing similar crimes may receive highly dissimilar treatment is the definition of
      a.   discrimination.
      b.   discovery.
      c.   discretion.
      d.   diversion.

4.   The trial court in the federal system is the U.S.
      a.   Superior Court.
      b.   Common Pleas Court.
      c.   District Court.
      d.   Circuit Court.

5.   Which plan for selecting judges involves nominating commissions, appointment, and retention elections?
      a.   California
      b.   New York
      c.   Texas
      d.   Missouri

6.   The prosecutor is most responsible to
      a.   get convictions.
      b.   represent the public in criminal matters.
      c.   enforce the law.
      d.   protect public.

7. In the federal system, prosecutors as U.S. Attorneys are responsible for representing the government in federal
   a. district courts.
   b. municipal courts.
   c. superior courts.
   d. Supreme Court.

8. The right to assistance of counsel and an impartial and public jury trial is found in the
   a. Fourth Amendment.
   b. Fifth Amendment.
   c. Sixth Amendment.
   d. Eighth Amendment.

9. Supreme Court decisions must be honored by
   a. supreme courts.
   b. state courts.
   c. district courts.
   d. all of the above

10. In the famous 1963 case, *Gideon v. Wainwright*, the U.S. Supreme Court held that the government must provide attorneys for indigents in
    a. all cases.
    b. misdemeanor cases only.
    c. felony cases only.
    d. only capital felony cases.

11. On average, sentence lengths for defendants sent to jail or prison were shorter for those with
    a. publicly financed attorneys.
    b. Missouri Plan judges.
    c. overzealous prosecutors.
    d. hired counsel.

12. In general, public defender systems tend to be found in
    a. large urban areas.
    b. small urban areas.
    c. suburban areas.
    d. rural areas.

13. Indigent defendants do not have a constitutional right to an attorney at
    a. jury trials.
    b. their first appeal.
    c. juvenile delinquency proceedings.
    d. preindictment lineups.

14. When the Supreme Court decides to hear a case, it grants a writ of
    a. tertiary.
    b. certiorari.
    c. Ferrari.
    d. habeas corpus.

15. Which of the listed is not considered a specialty court?
    a. Drug
    b. Mental health
    c. Sex offender
    d. General jurisdiction

16. The great majority of cases handled in courts of general jurisdiction are
    a. appeals.
    b. civil.
    c. traffic related.
    d. criminal conduct related.

17. The Sixth Amendment right to counsel
    a. is not applicable to the states.
    b. does not apply to pretrial proceedings.
    c. does not apply to first appeal.
    d. does not apply for U.S. Supreme Court proceedings.

18. The U.S. Supreme Court is composed of _____ members.
    a. 5
    b. 7
    c. 9
    d. 11

19. The U.S. district court has original jurisdiction over all of the federal laws except
    a. interstate transportation of stolen vehicles.
    b. civil rights abuses.
    c. misdemeanors.
    d. kidnapping.

20. Felony cases are typically tried in a court of
    a. general jurisdiction.
    b. limited jurisdiction.
    c. concurrent jurisdiction.
    d. exclusive jurisdiction.

21. State courts of limited jurisdiction are limited because they are restricted to hearing
    a. appeals only.
    b. felonies.
    c. only civil cases over $1000.
    d. minor criminal and civil cases.

22. A judge's primary duty is to
    a. decide whether a defendant is guilty or innocent.
    b. oversee the trial process.
    c. charge the jury.
    d. sentence guilty defendants.

23. Which factor affecting prosecutorial discretion addresses the offender's race, gender, and ethnic background?
    a. Victim issues
    b. Resource issues
    c. Extralegal issues
    d. Legal issues

24. Mental health courts are based largely on the organization of the drug courts, but they focus their attention on mental health treatment to help people with emotional problems reduce their chances of
    a. suicide.
    b. reoffending.
    c. mental illness.
    d. drug addiction.

25. Which 1984 Supreme Court case established the two-pronged test for determining effectiveness of counsel?
    a. *Miranda v. Arizona*
    b. *United States v. Armstrong*
    c. *North Carolina v. Pearce*
    d. *Strickland v. Washington*

26. Defendants can file an appeal if they believe the law that they were tried under was in violation of:
    a. constitutional standards.
    b. arrest policy.
    c. writ of certiorari.
    d. pre-trial procedures.

27. How many judicial circuits are there in the United States?
    a. 11
    b. 7
    c. 9
    d. 13

28. All of the listed technologies are currently used in court management except
    a. geospatial mapping.
    b. video conferencing.
    c. remote witness participation.
    d. the Internet.

29. The U.S. Supreme Court is what type of court?
    a. District
    b. Appellate
    c. Superior
    d. Circuit

30. When the Supreme Court rules on a case, its rule becomes a precedent or:
    a. benchmark decision.
    b. demarcation decision.
    c. watermark decision.
    d. landmark decision.

TRUE/FALSE

1. T F The prosecutor is a part of the legislative branch of government.

2. T F Nonjudicial alternatives are less common that the formal trial process.

3. T F Each state has at least five U.S. District Courts.

4. T F The nation's court system is chronically underfunded.

5. T F State judges may run as members of the republican, democratic, or other parties or without party affiliation.

6. T F The Fifth Amendment provides a right to confront adverse witnesses.

7. T F A private attorney appointed to represent an indigent is referred to as assigned counsel.

8. T F Federal circuit courts of appeal retry cases.

9. T F There is no right to an attorney at sentencing.

10. T F *Gideon v. Wainwright* provided a right to attorney in misdemeanor cases.

11. T F More murders get probation than the death penalty.

12. T F The type of state court between the trial court and the court of last resort is the intermediate appellate court.

13. T F A gun court is a court of general jurisdiction.

14. T F The U.S. Supreme Court has attempted to limit the number of appeals by prisoners.

15. T F Each state has at least one court of last resort.

FILL-IN-THE-BLANK

1.   A court whose function is to review cases for errors made by lower courts is called a/n
      _appellate_____ court.

2.   A Supreme Court agrees to hear a case when it grants the writ of
      _certiorari_____.

3.   For a defense attorney to be considered _incompetent_, he or she would have to
      miss filings, fail to follow normal trial procedure, and/or fail to use normal defense
      tactics.

4.   The _Missouri_____ plan for judicial selection involves appointment and
      retention elections.

5.   The judicial power of the United States shall be vested in one _Supreme_ Court.

6.   One form of judicial selection is through popular _election_.

7.   If defendants believe that the procedures used were in violation of their constitutional
      rights, they may ask for a/an _appellate_____ court to review the trial process.

8.   A court that handles the final appeal on a matter is the court of _last resort_.

9.   _federal_____ courts have led the way in creating and organizing court
      administration.

10.   A trial held by a judge without a jury is called a _bench trial_

11.   The _prosecutor_____ is the people's attorney, who is responsible for representing
      the public in criminal matters.

12.   In the federal court system _Jnet_____ is the judiciary's intranet website.

13.   General jurisdiction courts try _felonies_____ rather than misdemeanors.

14.   Courts of limited jurisdiction are accused of providing _assembly_ line justice

15.   A landmark decision on the right to counsel was *Gideon v.* _Wainwright_.

ESSAY

1.   Discuss courts of limited jurisdiction. Provide examples.

2.   Identify and describe the two examples of specialty courts as presented in the chapter.

3. Define, compare, and contrast the obligations of the prosecutor and the defense attorney.

4. Describe, compare, and contrast the three main systems of providing attorneys for indigent criminal defendants.

5. The chapter identified six developing areas of court technology. Identify and describe the uses of three.

CHAPTER 7 ANSWER KEY

Multiple Choice

1. a [p. 145, LO1]   2. d [p. 147, LO2]   3. c [p. 145, LO5]   4. c [p. 149, LO2]   5. d [p. 154, LO4]

6. d [p. 155, LO5]   7. a [p. 156, LO5]   8. c [p. 161, LO7]   9. d [p. 149, LO2]   10. c [p. 161, LO8]

11. a [p. 164, LO8]   12. a [p. 163, LO7]   13. d [p. 162, LO7]   14. b [p. 150, LO2]   15. d [p. 146, LO1]

16. c [p. 147, LO1]   17. d [p. 162, LO7]   18. c [p. 150, LO2]   19. c [p. 149, LO2]   20. a [p. 147, LO1]

21. d [p. 146, LO1]   22. b [p. 151, LO3]   23. c [p. 159, LO5]   24. b [p. 147, LO1]   25. d [p. 164, LO1]

26. a [p. 147, LO6]   27. d [p. 150, LO2]   28. a [p. 166, LO9]   29. b [p. 150, LO2]   30. d [p. 150, LO2]

True/False

1. F [p. 155, LO5]   2. F [p. 145, LO1]   3. F [p. 149, LO1]   4. T [p. 145, LO1]   5. T [p. 154, LO4]

6. F [p. 161, LO7]   7. T [p. 163, LO8]   8. F [p. 150, LO2]   9. F [p. 161, LO7]   10. F [p. 161, LO7]

11. T [p. 145, LO5]   12. T [p. 148, LO1]   13. F [p. 146, LO1]   14. T [p. 150, LO2]   15. T [p. 147, LO1]

Fill-in-the-Blank

1. appellate [p. 147, LO1]   2. certiorari [p. 150, LO2]   3. incompetent [p. 165, LO6]

4. Missouri [p. 154, LO4]   5. Supreme [p. 149, LO2]   6. election [p. 154, LO4]

7. appellate [p. 147, LO7]   8. last resort [p. 147, LO2]   9. Federal [p. 165, LO9]

10. bench trial [p. 151, LO4]   11. prosecutor [p. 155, LO5]   12. J-Net [p. 167, LO9]

13. felonies [p. 147, LO1]   14. assembly [p. 146, LO1]   15. *Wainwright* [p. 161, LO7]

Essay

1.   **Discuss courts of limited jurisdiction. Provide examples.**

Courts of limited jurisdiction are known by a variety of names including municipal courts, county courts, district courts, and metropolitan courts. They are known as courts of limited jurisdiction because they are restricted to hearing minor or less serious criminal and civil cases. Usually these courts handle civil infractions, misdemeanors ordinance violations, civil lawsuits and traffic violations. Their power to sanction is also limited. In criminal cases, punishments may be limited to fines, community service and/or jail incarceration for up to one year. Courts of limited jurisdiction handle trails, arraignments, bail hearings and a range of preliminary hearings for felony cases.

To deal with specific crimes, some courts of limited jurisdiction have specialized to focus on a particular crime such as drug crimes. Courts that handle drug crimes have come to be called drug courts. The state of Florida created drug courts to address prison overcrowding that resulted from a volume of sentenced drug offenders. The aim was to address the special needs of these offenders and assess whether jail or treatment is the best suited sanction. Another specialized court is the mental health court.

[p. 146, LO1]

2.   Identify and describe the two examples of specialty courts as presented in the chapter.

Drug Courts The drug court movement began in Florida to address the growing problem of prison overcrowding due in large part to an influx of drug-involved offenders. Drug courts were created to have primary jurisdiction over cases involving substance abuse and trafficking. The aim is to channel nonviolent first offenders into intensive treatment programs rather than into jail or prison.

Mental Health Courts Based largely on the organization of drug courts, mental health courts focus their attention on mental health treatment to help people with emotional problems reduce their chances of reoffending. By focusing on the need for treatment, along with providing supervision and support from the community, mental health courts provide a venue for those dealing with mental health issues to avoid the trauma of jail or prison, where they will have little if any access to treatment.

[pp. 146-147, LO1]

3.   Define and describe the obligations of the prosecutor and defense attorney.

The prosecutor is the people's representative in criminal proceedings. The prosecutor's primary duty is to enforce the criminal law. The prosecutor advises law enforcement, participates in plea negotiations and makes sentencing recommendations. The prosecutor is responsible for determining what criminal charges should be filed and as such is afforded a great deal of discretion. The prosecutor works closely with law enforcement during an investigation as a guide in building criminal cases. The prosecutor is responsible for managing the criminal case once charges have been filed. This process can involve a large number of court appearances and ultimately trial.

The defense attorney is the prosecutor's counterpart who is responsible to represent the interests of the accused. Defense attorneys may be private or public employees (i.e., public defender). The defense attorney, like the prosecutor is an officer of the court bound by law, ethics, and the Bar Association's code of responsibility. The defense attorney is responsible to provide the best defense possible for his/her client while at the same time upholding the integrity of the legal system.

[pp. 155, 161, LOs 5, 7]

4.   Describe the three main systems of providing attorneys for indigent criminal defendants.

The three main systems for providing indigent criminal defense include: public defenders, assigned counsel, and contract attorneys. Some jurisdictions use a combination of the systems to provide defense services to the indigent.

Public Defender: Public defenders are attorneys who render indigent criminal defense services through public (county, local, or state agency) or private not for profit organizations. Public defenders are most often utilized in large urban areas with high case volumes.

Assigned Counsel: The court of jurisdiction or an administrative body appoints a private attorney from a list of eligible attorneys to represent the indigent accused. The list is comprised of attorneys who are willing to accept indigent defense cases. The fees awarded to counsels are pre-determined based upon the work to be performed. These fees are much lower than those billed to private sector clients.

Contract: Contract attorneys are similar to public defenders but they are employed by a county under an employment contract. Contract attorneys are non-salaried attorneys, bar associations, law firms, or other groups of attorneys who agree to handle indigent case work. They have a funding source that pays the costs associated with the defense including labor.

[p. 163, LO8]

5. **The chapter identified six developing areas of court technology. Identify and describe the uses of three.**

Communications Court jurisdictions are also cooperating with police departments in the installation of communications gear that makes it possible to arraign defendants over closed-circuit television while they are in police custody. Closed-circuit television has been used for judicial conferences and scheduling meetings. Some courts are using voice-activated cameras to record all testimony during trials; these are the sole means of keeping trial records.

Videoconferencing About 400 courts across the country have videoconferencing capability. It is now being employed for juvenile detention hearings, expert witness testimony at trial, oral arguments on appeal, and parole hearings. More than 150 courts use two-way live, televised remote linkups for first appearance and arraignment. In the usual arrangement, defendants appear from a special location in the jail where they can see and hear, and be seen and heard by, the presiding magistrate.

Evidence Presentation High-tech courtrooms are now equipped for real-time transcription and translation, audio-video preservation of the court record, remote witness participation, computer graphics displays, television monitors for jurors, and computers for counsel and judge.

Case Management Case management will soon be upgraded. In the 1970s, municipal courts installed tracking systems, which used databases to manage court data. These older systems were limited and could not process the complex interrelationships that pervade information about persons, cases, time, and financial matters in court cases. Contemporary relational databases now provide the flexibility to handle complex case management.

Internet Utilization The Internet has begun finding its way into the court system. In the federal system, "J-Net" is the judiciary's intranet website. J-Net makes it easier for judges and court personnel to find important information in a timely fashion. The federal court's Administrative Office has begun sending official correspondence by email, which provides instantaneous communication of important information.

Information Sharing Technology has been harnessed to make it easier for courts to share information within and between states. This helps cut down on costs and accelerates the criminal justice process.

[pp. 165-167, LO9]

CHAPTER 8
Pretrial and Trial Procedures

LEARNING OBJECTIVES

After studying this chapter, students will:

1. Summarize the bail process
2. Discuss the main issues associated with bail
3. Differentiate between the two main mechanisms for charging defendants (grand jury indictment and prosecutor's information)
4. Summarize the pleas available to a criminal defendant
5. Explain the issues involved in plea bargaining
6. Describe the plea bargaining process.
7. Explain the purpose of pretrial diversion
8. Describe the goals and purpose of the trial process
9. Explain the legal rights of the accused at trial
10. Summarize the trial process

KEY TERMS AND CONCEPTS

pretrial procedures (p. 171) Critical pretrial processes and decisions, including bail, arraignment, and plea negotiation.

bail (p. 171) The monetary amount for or condition of pretrial release, normally set by a judge at the initial appearance. The purpose of bail is to ensure the return of the accused at subsequent proceedings.

pretrial detention (p. 171) Holding an offender in secure confinement before trial.

release on recognizance (ROR) (p. 173) A nonmonetary condition for the pretrial release of an accused individual; an alternative to monetary bail that is granted after the court determines that the accused has ties in the community, has no prior record of default, and is likely to appear at subsequent proceedings.

Manhattan Bail Project (p. 174) The innovative experiment in bail reform that introduced and successfully tested the concept of release on recognizance.

deposit bail (p. 175) The monetary amount set by a judge at a hearing as a condition of pretrial release; the percentage of the total bond required to be paid by the defendant.

Bail Reform Act of 1984 (p. 175) Federal legislation that provides for both greater emphasis on release on recognizance for non-dangerous offenders and preventive detention for those who present a menace to the community.

preventive detention (p. 175) The practice of holding dangerous suspects before trial without bail.

presentment (p. 176) The report of a grand jury investigation, which usually includes a recommendation of indictment.

indictment (p. 176) The action by a grand jury when it finds that probable cause exists for prosecution of an accused suspect.

no bill (p. 176) The action by a grand jury when it votes not to indict an accused suspect.

information (p. 177) A written accusation submitted to the court by a prosecutor, alleging that a particular individual committed the offense in question.

preliminary hearing (p. 177) A hearing that occurs in lieu of a grand jury hearing, when the prosecutor charges via information. Three issues are decided: whether a crime was committed, whether the court has jurisdiction over the case, and whether there is sufficient probable cause to believe the defendant committed the alleged crime.

plea bargaining (p. 180) Nonjudicial settlement of a case in which the defendant exchanges a guilty plea for some consideration, such as a reduced sentence.

diversion (p. 183) A noncriminal alternative to trial, usually featuring counseling, job training, and educational opportunities.

bench trial (p. 184) The trial of a criminal matter by a judge only. The accused waives any constitutional right to a trial by jury.

adjudication (p. 184) The determination of guilt or innocence; a judgment concerning criminal charges. The majority of offenders charged plead guilty; of the remainder, some cases are adjudicated by a judge and a jury, some are adjudicated by a judge without a jury, and others are dismissed.

confrontation clause (p. 185) A part of the Sixth Amendment that establishes the right of a criminal defendant to see and cross-examine all the witnesses against him or her.

hearsay evidence (p. 185) Testimony that is not firsthand but, rather, relates information told by a second party.

compulsory process (p. 185) Compelling the production of witnesses via a subpoena.

pro se (p. 186) Literally "for oneself"; presenting one's own defense in a criminal trial; self-representation.

proof beyond a reasonable doubt (p. 187) The standard of proof needed to convict in a criminal case. The evidence offered in court does not have to amount to absolute certainty, but it should leave no reasonable doubt that the defendant committed the alleged crime.

preponderance of the evidence (p. 188) The level of proof in civil cases; more than half the evidence supports the allegations of one side.

venire (p. 190) The group called for jury duty from which jury panels are selected.

voir dire (p. 190) The process in which a potential jury panel is questioned by the prosecution and the defense in order to select jurors who are unbiased and objective.

challenge for cause (p. 190) A request that a prospective juror be removed because he or she is biased or has prior knowledge about a case, or for other reasons that demonstrate the individual's inability to render a fair and impartial judgment in a particular case.

peremptory challenge (p. 190) The dismissal of a potential juror by either the prosecution or the defense for unexplained, discretionary reasons.

direct examination (p. 191) The questioning of one's own (prosecution or defense) witness during a trial.

cross-examination (p. 191) The process in which the defense and the prosecution interrogate witnesses for the other side during a trial.

direct verdict (p. 191) The right of a judge to direct a jury to acquit a defendant because the state has not proved the elements of the crime or otherwise has not established guilt according to law.

jury nullification (p. 194) A defense tactic that consists of suggesting that the jury acquit a defendant, despite evidence that he actually violated the law, by maintaining that the law was unjust or not applicable to the case.

appeal (p. 195) A request for an appellate court to examine a lower court's decision in order to determine whether proper procedures were followed.

writ of habeas corpus (p. 195) A judicial order requesting that a person who detains another person produce the body of the prisoner and give reasons for his or her capture and detention. Habeas corpus is a legal device used to request that a judicial body review the reasons for a person's confinement and the conditions of confinement. Habeas corpus is known as "the great writ."

CHAPTER OUTLINE

I. **INTRODUCTION**
   1. Pretrial procedures are important components of the justice process because the vast majority of criminal cases are resolved informally at this stage and never come before the courts.

II. **BAIL**
   1. Cash bond or some other security provided to court to ensure appearance of the defendant at every stage of the criminal justice process, especially trial
   2. Purpose is to obtain release of defendant from custody
   3. Amount set by court, either by percentage or entire amount in cash or security
   4. If defendant fails to appear, bail is forfeited
   5. A defendant who fails to make bail is confined in jail until the court appearance
   A. Right to Bail
      1. Eighth Amendment prohibits excessive bail
      2. Apparent that bail system is discriminatory, as rich can make bail. Indigents are held in jail or pretrial detention in the county jail
      3. Pretrial detention is a financial burden on local and state governments
         a. These factors have given rise to bail reform programs that depend on the defendant's personal promise to appear in court for trial (recognizance)
      4. Defendant has right to be released on reasonable bail
      5. Bail may not:
         a. Be used as a form of punishment
         b. Be used to coerce or threaten a defendant
      6. In *Stack v. Boyle*, the Supreme Court held that bail is a traditional right to freedom before trial that permits unhampered preparation of a defense and prevents defendant from being punished prior to conviction
         a. Bail should be in the amount that is generally set for similar offenses
         b. If crime is bailable, amount should not be:
            i. Frivolous
            ii. Unusual
            iii. Beyond a person's ability to pay
   B. Bail Release Mechanisms
      1. At bail, hearing issues to be considered are:
         a. Crime type
         b. Flight risk
         c. Dangerousness of defendant
      2. In jurisdictions with pretrial release programs program staff often:
         a. Interview arrestees detained at the jail before the first hearing
         b. Verify the background information
         c. Present recommendations to the court at arraignment
      3. Less than half of defendants with an active status (parole or probation) are released compared with two-thirds with no active status
      4. Bail in less serious cases handled through:

       a. Police field citation release
         i. Arresting officer releases arrestee on written promise to appear in court
         ii. Used in misdemeanor charges
         iii. Similar to issuing a traffic ticket
       b. Police station house citation release
         i. Determined at the police station
       c. Police/pretrial jail citation release
         i. Determined after police transfer arrestee to pretrial detention facility for:
           a) Screening
           b) Booking
           c) Admission
       d. Direct release program
         i. Authority releases defendants without direct judicial involvement
       e. Police/court bail schedule
         i. Arrestee posts bail at police station or jail according to amounts specified in a bail schedule
    5. A significant majority of criminal defendants released on bail prior to trial
       a. Two-thirds of felony defendants are released prior to disposition of case
       b. More than half of all violent offenders are released prior to trial
       c. Release rates:
         i. Murder – 8 percent
         ii. Robbery – 42 percent
         iii. Motor vehicle theft – 44 percent
         iv. Burglary – 49 percent
         v. Rape – 55 percent
C. Types of Bail
    1. There are a variety of mechanisms to secure bail, depending on jurisdiction, crime, and defendant
       a. Full cash bail
         i. In some jurisdictions, property can be pledged instead of cash
       b. Deposit bail
         i. Defendant deposits a percentage of the bail amount, typically 10 percent
       c. Surety bail
         i. Defendant pays a percentage of the bond, typically 10 percent to a bonding agent who posts the full bail
           a) Ten percent not returned if defendant appears in court
       d. Conditional bail
         i. Promises to obey some condition such as treatment
       e. Unsecured bail
         i. No immediate requirement of payment
       f. Release on recognizance
         i. Released without bail with promise to return to court
D. Bail Issues

1. Whether defendant can be expected to appear for trial is key issue in determining bail
2. Critics argue bail is one of the most objectionable aspects of criminal justice system because :
   a. It discriminates against the poor
   b. It is costly to government to pay to detain those who cannot make bail
   c. Detainees receive longer sentences than people released on bail
   d. Dehumanizes innocent people who cannot make bail and are therefore jailed in the nation's deteriorated jail system
3. Some research shows bail may be racially or ethnically biased, however variables may include:
   a. Income
   b. Community ties
   c. Family support
   d. Criminal record
4. Bondsmen and Bounty Hunters
   a. When defendants skip bail, bondsmen hire skip tracers, enforcement agents, or bounty hunters to track them down
   b. Each year an estimated 400 full-time bail enforcement agents catch 25,000 fugitives
   c. Although there are professionals, some untrained and/or unprofessional bounty hunters may use brutal tactics that can end in tragedy
5. Pretrial Detention Conditions
   a. Those that can't make bail, end up in pretrial detention in a local county jail
   b. Jail has long been a trouble spot in the criminal justice system
      i. Conditions tend to be poor, and rehabilitation is a low priority
   c. Pretrial detainees are more likely to be convicted and get longer prison sentences than those who commit similar crimes but who were released on bail
   d. Study of case processing in the nation's largest counties found:
      i. 63 percent of all defendants granted bail were convicted
      ii. 78 percent of pretrial detainees were convicted
6. Bail Reform
   a. Indigent defendants languish in pretrial detention and get convicted at higher rates
      i. Factors such as conviction and sentence disparities have given rise to bail reform movement
   b. 1961: Manhattan Bail Project, pioneered by Vera Institute of Justice, was the first bail reform movement
      i. If courts had sufficient background information, it could make reasonably good decisions based on:
         a) Nature of offense
         b) Family ties
         c) Employment record
      ii. Most defendants returned on their own recognizance

        iii. Default rate of less than 0.7 percent
- c. Manhattan Bail Project resulted in the enactment of Federal Bail Reform Act of 1966, which
  - i. Established the presumption of ROR
  - ii. Authorized 10 percent deposit bail
  - iii. Introduced concept of conditional release
  - iv. Stated that release should be under the least restrictive method necessary
- d. Bail Reform Act of 1984
  - i. No defendants shall be kept in pretrial detention because they can't afford bail
  - ii. Formalized restrictive preventive detention provisions
  - iii. Community safety as well as risk of flight must be considered in release detention
  - iv. Criminal justice factors that influence release decision in federal court:
    - a) Seriousness of the charged offense
    - b) The weight of the evidence
    - c) The potential sentence
    - d) Court appearance history
    - e) Prior convictions

7. Preventive Detention
   - a. Certain defendants can be confined before trial without the possibility of bail
   - b. Manifestation of the crime control perspective because it favors the use of incapacitation to control future behavior of suspected criminals
   - c. Bail Reform Act of 1984
     - i. Allows judges to order preventive detention if they determine that no condition or combination of conditions will reasonably assure the appearance of the person and the safety of any other person or community
   - d. A number of states have enacted elements to narrow scope of bail eligibility, which include three main features:
     - i. Exclusion of certain crimes from bail eligibility
     - ii. Definition of bail to include appearance in court and community safety
     - iii. Limitation on right to bail for those previously convicted

8. Pretrial Services
   - a. Hundreds of pretrial bail programs have been established in rural, suburban, and urban jurisdictions
     - i. Typically operated in:
       - a) Probation departments
       - b) Court offices
       - c) Local jails through independent contractors
   - b. Programs provided critical services such as:
     - i. Gathering and verifying information about arrestees including:
       - a) Criminal history
       - b) Current status in the criminal justice system

          c)   Address

          d)   Employment

          e)   Drug and alcohol use history

      ii. Assessing arrestees likelihood of failure

      iii. Monitoring released defendants compliance with conditions

      iv. Provide direct intensive supervision for certain defendants

  c. Court-administered programs make up the greatest percentage of pretrial programs

  d. Some programs aimed at special needs concerning

      i. Mental illness

          a)   About 75% or programs now inquire about mental illness

          b)   About 25% have implemented special supervision procedures

      ii. Domestic violence

          a)   25% of all programs have developed special risk-assessment procedures for defendants charged with domestic violence

          b)   About 33% have implemented special procedures to supervise defendants charged with domestic violence

III.   CHARGING THE DEFENDANT

  1. Process varies depending on whether it occurs via grand jury or preliminary hearing

  A. The Indictment Process and the Grand Jury

    1. Early development of English common law

    2. Magna Carta:

      a. No freeman could be seized and imprisoned unless judged by peers

      b. Grand jury created as a check against arbitrary prosecution by judge

      c. Incorporated into Fifth Amendment

         i. No person shall be held to answer for a capital, or otherwise infamous crime, unless on presentment or indictment of a grand jury

    3. Grand Jury

      a. Has power to act as an independent investigating body

      b. Complies presentment report

         i. Contains information on findings and recommendation of indictment

      c. Secondary role is to act as the community's conscience

      d. Relies on testimony of witnesses

      e. Determines if probable cause exists:

         i. Probable cause results in indictment or true bill:

            a)   No probable cause, no bill

    4. Critiquing the Grand Jury

      a. Usually meets at request of prosecution, hearings closed and secret

      b. Defense attorney, defendant, nor the general public allowed to attend

      c. Process criticized as being a rubber stamp for prosecution

      d. An alternative is to open the grand jury room to the defense and hold the government to same constitutional safeguards required to protect defendants

  B. The Information Process and the Preliminary Hearing

1. Information process is used in about half the states as an alternative to grand jury, it has a similar purpose but different procedures
2. When person charged in this fashion, preliminary hearing is necessary
3. Purpose of grand jury and preliminary hearing are the same
   a. To establish whether probable cause is sufficient to merit a trial, procedures differ however
4. Preliminary hearing
   a. Conducted before a magistrate or lower court judge
   b. Open to the public
   c. Present:
      i. Prosecuting attorney
      ii. Defendant
      iii. Defendant's counsel
   d. Judge decides whether there is sufficient probable cause to believe the defendant committed the alleged crime
      i. If probable cause, the defendant bound over for trial
         a) Usually within 15 days
      ii. If no probable cause, the charges are dismissed
5. Defendants can waive the preliminary hearing, has which advantages for both sides:
   a. Prosecutor avoids revealing evidence to the defense before trial
   b. Defense attorney will waive hearing if:
      i. Defendant has already decided to plead guilty
      ii. It can speed up the criminal justice process
      iii. It can avoid the negative publicity that might result from the hearing
C. Arraignment
   1. Occurs after indictment but before trial
   2. At arraignment, judge informs defendant of charges and availability of counsel
   3. According to Sixth Amendment, the accused has the right to be informed of the nature and cause of the accusation
   4. After charges are read, defendant is asked to enter plea
   5. Trial date set
   6. Upon guilty plea or nolo contendere, a date is set for sentencing
      a. Bail is either set or defendant released on personal recognizance
D. The Plea — Defendant must enter one of three pleas
   1. Guilty
      a. Most defendants plead guilty prior to trial
      b. Guilty plea has several consequences:
         i. Admission of guilt and surrender of an array of constitutional rights including:
            a) Remain silent
            b) Confront witnesses
            c) Trial by jury
            d) Have alleged offense proven beyond a reasonable doubt
      c. Plea cannot be rescinded or withdrawn after sentencing
      d. Judges must follow certain procedures when accepting guilty plea:

       i. Judge must clearly state to defendant constitutional guarantees automatically waived by plea

      ii. Judge must believe facts of case establish a basis for the voluntary plea

     iii. Defendant must be informed of the right to counsel during the pleading process

     iv. In felony cases, judge will insist on presence of defense counsel

      v. Judge must inform defendant of possible sentencing outcomes, including the maximum sentence that can be imposed

  e. In majority of states, a guilty plea may be withdrawn and replaced with not-guilty plea any time prior to sentencing if good cause is shown

2. Not Guilty — Plea entered in one of two ways:

       i. Verbally stated by the defendant or counsel

      ii. Entered for defendant by the court

  a. Once not-guilty plea is recorded, trial date is set

       i. Misdemeanors – trials take place in lower-court system

      ii. Felonies – normally transferred to the superior court

3. Nolo Contendere

  a. No contest — plea in which defendant does not accept or deny responsibility for the charges but agrees to accept punishment

  b. Essentially guilty plea but may not be held against defendant as proof in a subsequent legal matter

  c. Accepted at the discretion of the trial court and must be voluntarily and intelligently made

IV. PLEA BARGAINING

A. Plea Bargaining

1. The exchange of prosecutorial and judicial concessions for pleas of guilty

2. Bargain can be made between prosecutor and defense attorney in one of four ways:

  a. Initial charges reduced

  b. Reduce number of counts or charges

  c. Prosecutor may promise to recommend a lenient sentence

  d. Prosecutor may charge with a more socially acceptable charge

3. Plea bargaining is one of the most common practices in the criminal justice system today and a cornerstone of the informal justice system

4. 90 percent of criminal convictions are a result of negotiated guilty pleas

5. A relatively recent development, taking hold late in the nineteenth century

B. Pros and Cons of Plea Negotiation

1. Proponents argue pleas benefit the state and defendant through:

  a. Overall costs of criminal prosecution reduced

  b. Administrative efficiency of courts improved

  c. Prosecution can devote more time to more serious cases

  d. Defendant avoids possible detention and extended trial and may receive reduced sentence

  e. Resources can be devoted more efficiently to cases that need greater attention

2. Opponents believe plea bargaining should be abolished because:
   a. Encourages defendants to waive right to trial
   b. Allows dangerous offenders to receive lenient sentences
   c. Raises danger that an innocent person be convicted to avoid risk of conviction
   d. Prosecutors given free hand to induce or compel defendants to plea bargain
   e. Possible that an innocent person will admit guilt if they believe system is biased and have little chance of acquittal
   f. Guilty plea culture has developed among defense lawyers

C. Legal Issues in Plea Bargaining — Supreme Court Rulings:
  1. Defendants entitled to effective counsel
  2. Pleas must be voluntary and without pressure
  3. Defendant can still plead guilty to gain lenient sentence while maintaining their innocence
  4. Any promise made by the prosecutor must be kept after defendant admits guilt
  5. Defendants must also keep their side of the bargain to receive the promised offer of leniency
  6. Defendant's due process rights are not violated when the prosecutor threatens to re-indict on a more serious charge if the defendant does not plead guilty
  7. Accepting a guilty plea from a defendant who maintains his or her innocence is valid
  8. Statements made during plea negotiations may be used at trial if:
   a. Defendant admits to crime but then later testifies in court that they are innocent
   b. Defendant is innocent of the charges

D. Plea Bargaining Decision Making
  a. Plea bargaining process is:
   i. Largely informal
   ii. Lacking in guidelines
   iii. Discretionary
  b. Research shows prosecutorial discretion rather than defendant characteristics controls plea negotiations
  c. Plea bargaining is a cost/benefit analysis:
   i. Defendants compare the pain and punishment guaranteed by the bargain
  d. Research suggests that it is much more complicated as it involves characteristics of:
   i. The offender
   ii. The case
   iii. The community
  e. Important in plea bargaining decisions are:
   i. Offense
   ii. Defendant's prior record
   iii. Age
   iv. Type, strength, and admissibility of evidence
   v. Attitude of complainant

        vi. Police attitude in victimless cases
- f. Prosecutor's ego or political factors can factor in
1. The Role of the Defense Counsel
   a. Required to play advisory role in negations
   b. Responsible for ensuring defendant understands the nature of plea
   c. Cannot misrepresent evidence or mislead client
   d. Ethically and constitutionally required to present all plea offers to client, even if defendant considers those unacceptable
2. The Role of the Judge
   a. According to American Bar Association (ABA), judges should not be a party to plea arrangements for the determination of a sentence
   b. According to ABA, judicial participation in plea negotiations:
      i. Creates impression in mind of defendant that they cannot get fair trial
      ii. Lessens the ability of judge to make objective determination of the voluntary nature of the plea
      i. Inconsistent with the theory behind the use of pre-sentence investigation reports
      ii. May induce an innocent defendant to plead guilty because they are afraid to reject the disposition desired by judge
3. The Role of the Victim
   a. Victim is not empowered at pretrial stage of process
   b. Prosecutor should consider impact on victim and victim's families
E. Plea Bargaining Reform
   a. Safeguards developed to ensure innocent individuals do not plead guilty under coercion:
      i. Judge questions defendant about the facts of guilty plea before accepting
      ii. Defense counsel is present and can advise defendant of rights
      iii. Prosecutor and defense attorney openly discuss the plea
      iv. Full and frank information about the defendant and offense made available
      v. Judicial supervision ensures plea bargaining conducted in a fair manner
1. Negotiation Oversight
   a. Some jurisdictions established guidelines providing consistency in pleas
   b. Guidelines may cover:
      i. Over-indictment
      ii. Controlling unprovable indictments
      iii. Reducing felonies to misdemeanors
      iv. Bargaining with defendants
2. Banning Plea Bargaining
   a. Several jurisdictions have banned plea bargaining but have reverted to:
      i. Sentence-related concessions
      ii. Charge-reduction concessions
      iii. Alternative methods for prosecution
   b. Where plea bargaining is limited or abolished:
      i. The number of trials may increase

        ii. Sentence severity may change

        iii. More questions about the right to a speedy trial may arise

        iv. Discretion may also be shifted further up the system

    c. Prosecutors may actually dismiss more cases outright or decide not to prosecute them after initial action has been taken

II.   PRETRIAL DIVERSION

1. Established more than 40 years ago to reduce stigma created by formal trial process
2. Diversion programs suspend criminal proceedings so that accused can participate in community treatment programs
3. Diversion gives the client an opportunity to:
   a. Avoid stigma of criminal record
   b. Continue to work and support family
   c. Continue education goals
   d. Access rehabilitation services such as anger management
   e. Make restitution to the victim or payback community
   f. Reduce costs and alleviate prison crowding
4. Diversion programs take many forms:
   a. Independent agencies
   b. Police internal structure
   c. Prosecutor internal structure
   d. Probation department internal structure
   e. Joint venture between county government and a non-profit organization
5. National evaluations concluded that they are no more successful at avoiding stigma or reducing recidivism
6. May widen the net of justice system:
   a. People diverted into diversion programs are the ones likely to have otherwise been dismissed after a brief hearing with a warning or small fine
7. Diversion programs increase gap rather than limit contact with criminal justice system
8. Recent evaluations indicate that given the proper treatment, some types of offenders (drug) who are offered a place in pretrial program can significantly lower their rates of recidivism

III.   THE TRIAL

1. Criminal trial is an open and public hearing designed to examine the facts of the case brought by the state against the accused
2. Trial is an important and enduring fixture in the criminal justice system
3. It is a symbol of the moral authority of the state
4. Most formal trials heard by a jury, some may waive this right and request a bench trial
   a. Judge alone renders the verdict
   b. Judge may initiate a number of formal or informal dispositions:
      i. Dismiss the case
      ii. Finding the defendant guilty or not-guilty

    iii. Imposing sentence
    iv. Continue the case indefinitely
   c. Judge makes decision based on:
    i. Seriousness of the offense
    ii. Background and previous record of the defendant
    iii. Whether the case can be properly dealt with in the criminal process
   d. Judge may continue the case without a finding
    i. Verdict is withheld without a finding of guilt to induce the accused to improve her behavior in the community

A. Legal Rights during Trial
   a. Underlying every trial are constitutional principles, complex legal procedures, rules of court, and interpretation of statutes, all designed to ensure that the accused will receive a fair trial
 1. The Right to an Impartial Judge
   a. Supreme Court Case of *Tumey v. Ohio* (1927)
    i. Violation of due process when a judge has a direct, personal, substantial pecuniary interest in reaching a conclusion against him in the case
   b. Generally a judge will excuse him or herself if there is a conflict of interest
   c. Judicial codes of ethics provide guidelines
 2. The Right to Be Competent at Trial
   a. In order for a trial to be considered fair, a criminal defendant must be mentally competent to understand the nature and extent of legal proceedings
   b. If a defendant is mentally incompetent, the trial must be postponed until treatment renders the defendant capable of participating in his or her own defense
   d. In *Riggins v. Nevada* (1992) the Supreme Court ruled that forced treatment does not violate a defendant's due process rights if it was medically appropriate and, considering less intrusive alternatives, was essential for the defendant's own safety or the safety of others
 3. The Right to Confront Witnesses
   a. The Sixth Amendment gives criminal defendants the right to confront a witness who testifies against them at trial
    i. Child abuse cases are the exception
   b. The confrontation clause is essential to a fair criminal trial because it restricts and controls the admissibility of hearsay evidence
    i. Witnesses must attest their personal knowledge of a crime and not merely repeat what others have told them
   c. Under the confrontation clause, the accused has the right to confront a witness' assertions and perceptions
 4. The Right to Compulsory Process
   a. Sixth Amendment states the accused shall have compulsory process for obtaining witnesses in his favor
   b. Compulsory process means to compel the production of witnesses via a subpoena

      c.   A subpoena is an order requiring a witness to appear in court

      d.   Supreme Court case of *Washington v. Texas* (1967) decided compulsory process is a fundamental right

5.   The Right to an Impartial Jury

      a.   Right to a jury trial appears in both the Constitution (Article III, Section 2) and the Bill of Rights (Sixth Amendment)

      b.   Defendant has the right to choose a trial by jury or judge

      c.   Substantial portion of defendants, particularly those charged with misdemeanors are tried without jury

      d.   In *Baldwin v. New York* (1970), Supreme Court decided that a defendant has a constitutional right to a jury trial when facing a possible prison sentence of six months or more

         i.   In cases when the possible sentence is six months or less, accused is not entitled to a jury trial unless it is authorized by state statute

6.   The Right to Counsel at Trial

      a.   The defendant has a right to counsel at numerous points in the criminal justice process

      b.   Today, courts must provide counsel to indigent defendants who face the possibility of incarceration

      c.   The Supreme Court ruled that defendants in most states and in the federal system have the right to proceed *pro se* (for themselves)

      d.   This allows defendants to choose between hiring counsel and conducting their own defense

      e.   Defendants almost always cautioned by the court against self-representation

      f.   If defendant becomes disorderly and disruptive, court can terminate their right to represent themselves

7.   The Right to a Speedy Trial

      a.   The tactics employed by defense attorneys, coupled with inefficiencies in the court process, have made delays in criminal cases a serious constitutional issue

      b.   According to the ABA, congestion in the trial process, particularly in urban centers, is one of the major problems in judicial administration

      c.   Delays in the trial process conflict with the Sixth Amendment's guarantee of a right to a speedy trial

8.   The Right to a Public Trial

      a.   The language of the Sixth Amendment refers to a "public trial."

         i.   Underlying this provision is that the trial must be a public activity

         ii. Anyone who wants to see a criminal trial can do so

      b.   In 1966 case of *Sheppard v. Maxwell* courtroom was packed for all nine weeks of the trial

         i.   Supreme Court eventually reversed the defendant's conviction citing a "carnival atmosphere."

         ii. Some judges require cameras excluded from courtroom

            a)   This is why sometimes on sketches only available

      c.   Adverse pretrial publicity can prevent a defendant from getting a fair trial

      d. The release of premature evidence by the prosecutor, extensive and critical reporting by the news media, and vivid and uncalled-for details in indictments can all prejudice a defendant's case

      e. In general, pretrial publicity and reporting cannot be controlled

      f. Judges may bar the press from some pretrial legal proceeding and hearings such as:

          i.   Preliminary hearings

          ii. When police officers make an arrest

          iii. When warrant is being served

      g. If presence will infringe on the defendant's right to a fair trial

      h. Other steps include:

          i.   Changes of venue

            a) Moving trial to another jurisdiction, less press coverage and less contamination of the pool of potential jurors

          ii. Gag orders

            a) Restriction on what the parties or the media can report

9. The Right to Be Convicted by Proof Beyond a Reasonable Doubt

      a. Proof beyond a reasonable doubt is the standard required to convict a criminal defendant at the adjudicatory stage of the criminal process

      b. This requirement dates back to early American history

      c. Many U.S. Supreme Court cases have made this standard and due process a constitutional requirement

      d. The reasonable doubt standard is an essential ingredient in the criminal justice process

      e. Civil law has a standard of "preponderance of the evidence"

B. The Trial Process

      a. The trial of a criminal case is a formal process conducted in a specific and orderly fashion in accordance with rules of criminal law, procedure, and evidence

      b. The modern trial is a technical and complicated affair; it is often misrepresented in TV shows

      c. All jurisdictions conduct criminal trials in a generally similar fashion

1. Jury Selection

      a. In both civil and criminal cases, jurors are selected randomly from licensing or voter registration within the court's jurisdiction

      b. Few states impose qualifications on those called for jury service, though many mandate residency

      c. The initial list of persons chosen is called venire, or jury array

          i.   Provides the state with a group of potentially capable citizens to serve on a jury

      d. The court clerk who handles the administrative affairs on trial randomly selects enough names to fill what he/she believes will be the required number of jurors

      e. After reporting to the courtroom, the prospective jurors are first required to swear that they will truthfully answer all questions asked about their qualifications to serve

    f. Once the twelve prospective jurors are chosen the process of voir dire begins

    g. Voir Dire is a French term that means "to tell the truth"

    h. During Voir Dire, prospective jurors are examined under oath

    i. The prosecutor and defense attorney can remove prospective jurors by challenges known as

        i. Challenge for cause

        ii. Peremptory challenge

          a)   Peremptory challenges are limited in number

        i. The peremptory challenge has been criticized by legal experts who question the fairness and proprietary with which it has been used

        ii. It has been criticized as excluding African Americans from juries

        iii. Race cannot be used as a reason to exclude a juror, even with the peremptory challenge (*Batson v. Kentucky, 1986*)

    j. Increasingly difficult to find impartial jurors in the technological age

2. Opening Statements

    a. Once the jury has been selected and seated and the criminal complaint has been read, the prosecution and defense can make their opening statements

    b. Typically, the prosecutor offers an opening statement followed by the defense counsel

    c. The opening statements give the jury a concise statement of the evidence that is to come

        i. Neither is allowed to make prejudicial remarks or inflammatory statements or to mention irrelevant facts

3. Prosecution's Case

    a. After opening statements, the government begins its case by presenting evidence to the court through its witnesses

    b. Those witnesses that provide testimony do so via direct examination such as:

        i. Police officers

        ii. Victims

        iii. Experts

    c. During direct examination the prosecutor questions the witness to reveal the facts believed pertinent to the government's case

    d. Testimony involves what the witness actually saw, heard, or touched and does not include opinions

    e. Witnesses opinion can be given in certain situations

        i. Expert witnesses

    f. Upon completion of the prosecutor's questioning, the prosecution's witnesses are questioned by the defense under cross examination

        i. The right to cross examine witnesses is an essential part of a trial

    g. If desired, the prosecutor may seek a second direct examination after the defense attorney

    h. The defense attorney may then re-cross examine the witnesses

4. The Criminal Defense

    a. Once the government presents its case, it rests the people's case

    b. The defense attorney (after the people rest) may enter a motion for a directed verdict, a procedural device which asks a judge to order the jury to return a 'not guilty' verdict. The judge must weigh the motion and make a decision

    c. The defense has the option of presenting many, some, or no witnesses on behalf of the defendant

    d. Burden of guilt is on the prosecution

    e. In criminal trial, the defendant is protected by the Fifth Amendment right to be free from self-incrimination

    f. The defense attorney is charged with putting on a vigorous defense in the adversary system of justice

    g. After defense concludes its case, government may present rebuttal evidence:

        i. Involves bringing evidence forward used to refute, counteract, or disprove evidence introduced by the defense

        ii. May not go into new matters or present evidence that further supports the case

    h. Defense may be allowed so-called surrebuttal

        i. Presenting witnesses to respond to rebuttal issues

5. Closing Arguments

    a. Closing arguments are used by attorneys to review the facts of the case in a manner favorable to each of their positions

    b. Both sides are permitted to draw reasonable inferences and relay them to the jury

    c. Normally, the prosecution will make the first closing statement, followed by the defense

6. Instructions to the Jury

    a. The judge will instruct or charge the jury members on the principles of the law that ought to guide and control their decision on the defendant's guilt or innocence

    b. Included in the charge are:

        i. Information about the elements of the alleged offense

        ii. Type of evidence needed to prove each element

        iii. Burden of proof that must be met to obtain a guilty verdict

    c. Although the judge usually provides the instructions, on some occasions they ask each side to submit instructions for consideration

    d. The instructions are important because they may serve as the basis for an appeal

7. Deliberation and Verdict

    a. After instructions, the jury retires to deliberate the verdict

    b. In highly publicized cases, the judge may sequester the jury

    c. A review of the case may take hours or even days

    d. Deliberation is private

    e. If a verdict cannot be reached, the trial may result in a hung jury; after which the prosecutor must bring the defendant to trial again (if desired)

    f. If found not guilty, the defendant is released from custody

  g. If the verdict is guilty, the judge will normally order a pre-sentence investigation before imposing sentence

  h. Jurors are required by law to base their decision on the facts of the case and the judge's legal instructions

  i. In some cases, the defense asks the jury to rule on emotion and personal preference; this is called jury nullification. This has been in practice since 1735

    i. Supporters of nullification argue that it is an important safeguard against government oppression

    ii. Critics say it is an abuse of power

 8. The Sentence

  a. The imposition of criminal justice is the responsibility of the judge

  b. In some jurisdictions, the jury may determine the sentence or make recommendations

  c. Often sentences are formulated based on the probation department's input after a pre-sentence investigation of the defendant

  d. Sentence itself determined by statutory requirements for the particular crime as established by the legislature

  e. Judge ordinarily has a great deal of discretion in reaching a sentence decision

  f. Different sanctions include:

    i. Fines

    ii. Probation

    iii. Imprisonment

    iv. Commitment to a state hospital

 9. Appeals

  a. Once a defendant has been found guilty, they may petition an appellate court to review the procedures used during the trial

  b. Defendants may have two main avenues to challenge such procedures:

    i. Appeals

    ii. Habeas corpus

     a) Both provide the opportunity to appeal to a higher state or federal court on the basis of an error

  c. Extraordinary trial errors such as denial of right to counsel or inability to provide a fair trial can be the basis of an appeal

  d. Harmless errors may not automatically be the basis of an appeal

  e. A postconviction appeal is request for an appellate court to examine a lower court's decision in order to determine whether proper procedures were followed

  f. Appeals do not give the convicted an opportunity to try the case again, only to challenge procedural matters

  g. Direct appeals are guaranteed by law

    i. Most defendants get to appeal at least once if they cannot afford it

  h. Discretionary appeals are decided by appellate court

  i. There is no restriction on the number of discretionary appeals

> j. A writ of habeas corpus is the primary means by which state prisoners have their convictions or sentences reviewed in federal court
>> i. This writ seeks to determine the validity of a detention by asking the court to release the person or give legal reasons for the incarceration

CHAPTER SUMMARY

Prosecutors and defense attorneys often find themselves engaging in fierce and competitive pretrial negotiations. The pretrial stage contains a series of decision points that are critical links in the chain of justice. These include arraignments, grand jury investigations, bail hearings, plea bargaining negotiations, and predisposition treatment efforts.

Bail is a cash bond or some other security provided to ensure the appearance of the defendant at every stage of the process, especially trial. Its purpose is to release a person charged with a crime from custody. The Eighth Amendment of the U.S. Constitution prohibits excessive bail. Bail may not be used as punishment, nor may it be used to coerce a defendant. There are a variety of ways to secure bail: full cash bail, deposit bail, surety bail, conditional bail, unsecured bond, and release on recognizance.

Charging a defendant with a crime occurs via a grand jury or a preliminary hearing. The preliminary hearing is conducted before a magistrate or lower court judge. The prosecution presents its evidence and witnesses to the judge. The judge decides whether there is probable cause to believe the defendant committed the crime. If so, the defendant is bound over for trial.

After an indictment via grand jury or preliminary hearing, an arraignment takes place before the court that will try the case. At arraignment, the judge informs the defendant of the charges and appoints counsel.

After the charges are read, the defendant is asked to enter a plea. A defendant will enter one of three pleas: guilty, not guilty, or nolo contendere. The plea nolo contendere, or no contest, is a plea in which the defendant does not accept or deny responsibility but agrees to accept punishment.

Plea bargaining is one of the most common practices in the criminal justice system and a cornerstone of the informal justice system. Bargains can be made one of four ways: the initial charges reduced, the number of counts reduced, promise of lenient sentence, or a more socially acceptable charge. Offender, case, and community characteristics weigh heavily on the negotiation process. Such factors as the offense, defendant's prior record, age, and the type, strength, and admissibility of evidence are considered in the decision.

Plea bargaining is an inevitable result and essential to the functioning of the criminal justice process. Its merits are still hotly debated. Those opposed to plea bargaining assert it is coercive, encourages unequal exercise of prosecutorial discretion, and complicates sentencing. Others argue that it is unconstitutional and results in cynicism and disrespect. Its proponents contend that it ensures the flow of guilty pleas essential to administration efficiency. It allows the system the flexibility to individualize justice and inspires respect for the system because of its' certain and prompt punishment.

The criminal trial is an open and public hearing designed to examine facts brought by the state against the accused. The trial is the symbol of the administration of objective and impartial justice. Most formal trials are heard by a jury, though some defendants waive their constitutional right and request a bench trial, in which a judge renders a verdict. Principles that guide fair trials are the right to a fair trial, right to be competent at trial, right to confront witnesses, right to a jury trial, right to counsel at trial, right to self-representation, right to a speedy trial, right to a public trial, and the right to be convicted by proof beyond a reasonable doubt.

The modern criminal trial is a complicated, time-consuming, and technical affair. It is a structured adversary proceeding in which the prosecution and defense follow specific procedures and argue the merits of their cases before the judge and jury.

In both civil and criminal cases, jurors are selected randomly from licensing or voter registration lists within each court's jurisdiction. The initial list of persons chosen, which is called venire, or jury array, provides the state with a group of potentially capable citizens able to serve on a jury. The lengthy process of voir dire (from the French for "to tell the truth") starts. A juror who acknowledges any bias for or prejudice against the defendant may be removed by either the prosecution or defense for cause. If the judge accepts the challenge, the juror is removed and replaced with another from the remaining panel. Both the prosecution and the defense are allowed peremptory challenges, which enable the attorneys to excuse jurors for no particular reason or for undisclosed reasons.

Once the jury has been selected and the criminal complaint read, each side makes an opening statement about the case. Once the prosecution has provided all the government's evidence against a defendant, it will inform the court that it rests the people's case. Closing arguments are used by the attorneys to review the facts and evidence of the case in a manner favorable to each of their positions.

In a criminal trial, the judge will instruct, or charge, the jury members on the principles of law to guide and control their decision. Once the charge is given to the jury members, they deliberate on a verdict. If a verdict cannot be reached, the trial may result in a hung jury, after which the prosecutor must bring the defendant to trial again. If the defendant is found not guilty, they are released from the criminal process. If the defendant is convicted, the judge will normally order a pre-sentence investigation by the probation department before imposing a sentence.

The sentence is determined by the statutory requirements for the crime as established by the legislature; in addition, the judge ordinarily has a great deal of discretion in reaching a sentencing decision. The different criminal sanctions available include fines, probation, imprisonment, and even commitment to a state hospital. Once a verdict has been rendered and a defendant found guilty, they may petition an appellate court to review the procedures used during trial.

DISCUSSION QUESTIONS

1. Should those accused of violent acts be subjected to preventive detention instead of bail, even though they have not been convicted of a crime? Is it fair to the victim to have the alleged attacker running around loose?

2. Should criminal defendants be allowed to bargain for a reduced sentence in exchange for a guilty plea? Should the victim always be included in the plea bargaining process?

3. What purpose does a grand jury or preliminary hearing serve in adjudicating felony offenses? Should one of these methods be abandoned, and if so, which one?

4. Do criminal defendants enjoy too many rights at trial? Why or why not?

5. Should people be denied the right to serve as jurors without explanation or cause? In other words, should the peremptory challenge be maintained?

6. "In the adversary system of criminal justice, the burden of proof in a criminal trial to show that the defendant is guilty beyond a reasonable doubt is on the government." Explain the meaning of this statement.

MEDIA TOOLS

As pointed out in this chapter, the Grand Jury is not without criticism. Read an article concerning a criticism of the grand jury process. The author does a wonderful job explaining the origins of the grand jury, the reality of the grand jury, and several proposed reforms. This 1999 article was written by Frederick P. Hafetz and John M. Pellettieri. The article titled, "Time to Reform the Grand Jury." The article is courtesy of The National Association of Criminal Defense Lawyers. The article can be found at:
http://www.nacdl.org/public.nsf/ChampionArticles/19990112?OpenDocument

View a complete investigation into the plea agreement controversy. The Public Broadcasting Service production Frontline has a very interactive website dedicated to plea bargaining. View videos of individual stories and the impact of plea bargaining. This site can be found at:
http://www.pbs.org/wgbh/pages/frontline/shows/plea

Pretrial diversion programs are more complex than it might seem. Individuals selected for pretrial diversion programs must meet, in some cases, a host of eligibility criteria. For instance check out the San Francisco Pretrial Diversion Program. Read about who they are and what they do. Pay particular attention to the eligible criteria; you might be surprised. The San Francisco Pretrial Diversion Program can be found at: http://www.sfpretrial.com/home.html

PRACTICE TEST BANK

MULTIPLE CHOICE

1. If a crime is bailable, the amount set should be
    a. frivolous.
    b. unusual.
    c. beyond a person's ability to pay.
    d. reasonable.

2. Which position has the ABA taken on judicial involvement in plea bargaining?
    a. They have not taken an official position
    b. They are opposed to judicial participation in plea negotiations
    c. They support judicial participation on plea negotiations
    d. They are prohibited by the Constitution from publically expressing an opinion on the matter

3. Which procedure is used in half of the states as an alternative to the grand jury?
    a. Bind-over hearing
    b. Preliminary hearing
    c. Arraignment on the indictment
    d. Initial hearing

4. At the preliminary hearing, what must be established in order to support the continuance of the case?
    a. Reasonable suspicion
    b. Probable cause
    c. Sustainable evidence
    d. Proof beyond a reasonable doubt

5. When an arrested person's release on bail is deferred until after he has been removed from the scene of an arrest and brought to the police station is known as
    a. police field citation release.
    b. police/pretrial citation release.
    c. police station house citation release.
    d. direct release.

6. Bail is money or other security provided by the defendant to secure release and provide assurance that the defendant will
    a. appear at all subsequent proceedings.
    b. not commit any crimes if released.
    c. will cooperate with the prosecution.
    d. will not attempt to intimidate the witnesses.

7.   In lieu of putting up money or other security, a defendant may obtain release on
     a.   recognizance.
     b.   quo warranto.
     c.   corpus delicti.
     d.   referral.

8.   Who is usually responsible for formulating the plea deal and making the offer to the
     defendant?
     a.   Defense Counsel
     b.   Judge
     c.   Victim advocate
     d.   Prosecutor

9.   With regard to bail, what does the Eighth Amendment prohibit?
     a.   Exorbitant bail
     b.   Unfair bail
     c.   Oppressive bail
     d.   Excessive bail

10. At what stage of the criminal trial can a defense attorney enter a motion for a directed
     verdict?
     a.   The criminal defense
     b.   Opening statements
     c.   Voir Dire
     d.   Prosecution's case

11. When a defendant deposits a percentage of the bail amount with the court is known as
     a.   deposit bail.
     b.   surety bail.
     c.   conditional bail.
     d.   unsecured bond.

12. Which of the listed is the term for keeping defendants who are considered dangerous
     behind bars before trial without the possibility of bail?
     a.   Release on recognizance
     b.   Surety
     c.   Pretrial detention
     d.   Preventive detention

13. The two functions of the grand jury are (1) determining whether the accusation of the
     state justifies a trial and (2)
     a.   setting bail.
     b.   holding preliminary hearings.
     c.   acting as an investigative body.
     d.   issuing information.

14. Grand juries are often criticized for being
    a. too independent of the judge and prosecutor.
    b. a rubber stamp for the prosecution.
    c. soft on violent crime.
    d. a cause of delay in the criminal justice system.

15. A noncriminal alternative to trial that usually involves counseling, job training, and educational opportunities is
    a. plea bargaining.
    b. pretrial diversion.
    c. probation.
    d. parole.

16. A report issued by a grand jury following an investigation is known as a
    a. indictment.
    b. true bill.
    c. bill.
    d. presentment.

17. At what stage does the judge inform the defendant of the charges against him and appoints counsel if one has not yet been retained?
    a. Indictment
    b. Information
    c. Arraignment
    d. Preliminary hearing

18. Proponents of plea bargaining contend that plea bargaining benefits both the state and defendant in a number of ways except
    a. it encourages defendants to waive their constitutional right to trial.
    b. the overall costs of criminal prosecution are reduced.
    c. the administrative efficiency of the courts is greatly improved.
    d. the prosecution can devote more time to more serious cases.

19. The trial is considered an important aspect or fixture in the criminal justice system because it is essentially
    a. the moral authority of the state.
    b. the way by which most criminal cases are adjudicated.
    c. required by state constitution.
    d. the only way for a criminal matter to be adjudicated.

20. With regard to plea bargains, victims
    a. have no legal standing to participate or object.
    b. have a due process right to object.
    c. have a due process right to participate.
    d. can sue prosecutors who agree to lenient plea bargains.

21. If a defendant is released on bail but fails to appear in court at the stipulated time, the bail deposit is
    a. forfeited.
    b. increased.
    c. refunded.
    d. donated to charity.

22. The defendant's presence in a courtroom (during trial) is designed to guarantee
    a. that the terms of bail have been complied with.
    b. that he or she will take the stand and testify.
    c. that he or she will have a fair hearing conducted under the rules of procedure.
    d. that he or she can confirm that adequate counsel was provided.

23. What type of evidence is akin to secondhand evidence, it consists of information being relayed by a second party?
    a. Confrontational
    b. Secondary
    c. Hearsay
    d. Direct testimony

24. Most formal trials are heard by a jury, but some defendants can waive a jury trial and request
    a. a verdict in lieu of trial.
    b. a bench trial.
    c. a trial by committee.
    d. an appeal.

25. Essentially, the Constitutional principles, complex legal procedures, and court rules are all designed to ensure that the
    a. defendant physically appears in court.
    b. defendant receives a fair trial.
    c. defendant is able to hear and understand the charges.
    d. defendant is able to hire or obtain an attorney.

26. All of the following are rights afforded to an accused person at trial except the
    a. right to an impartial judge.
    b. right to be competent at trial.
    c. right to confront witnesses.
    d. right to bail.

27. Which term best describes the part of the Sixth Amendment that grants the right of a criminal defendant to see and cross-examine all witnesses against him or her?
    a. Accusation clause
    b. Conformity clause
    c. Confrontation clause
    d. Hearsay clause

28. To stand trial a defendant must be
    a. mentally competent.
    b. physically competent.
    c. literate.
    d. able to speak and understand English.

29. Which process compels the production of witnesses via a subpoena?
    a. Compulsory
    b. Due
    c. Hearsay
    d. Indictment

30. The standard of proof (for conviction) in a criminal trial is
    a. preponderance of the evidence.
    b. beyond a shadow of a doubt.
    c. beyond a reasonable doubt.
    d. probable cause.

TRUE/FALSE

1. T **F** A preliminary hearing is secretive unless the defendant requests a public hearing.

2. **T** F Plea bargaining is a common practice in America.

3. T **F** A *nolo contendere* plea is equivalent to a not guilty plea.

4. T **F** Ordinarily, a defendant in a criminal trial will enter one of two pleas: guilty or not guilty.

5. T **F** The victim has a constitutional right to participate in plea bargaining.

6. T **F** Pretrial diversion programs are only for those charged with serious felonies.

7. **T** F In recent years, reform efforts have attempted to make plea bargaining more visible, understandable, and fair.

8. **T** F Many important decisions about what happens to a defendant are made prior to trial.

9. T **F** Diversion programs are more successful at avoiding stigma and reducing recidivism according to national evaluations.

10. **T** F Most formal trials are heard by a jury.

11.   T   (F)   Preventive detention is utilized to assure the defendant's appearance at later proceedings.

12.   (T)   F   State authorities can force a mentally unfit defendant to be treated so that the defendant can be properly tried.

13.   (T)   F   Most defendants get pretrial released at some point.

14.   (T)   F   Once a plea is made, it cannot be rescinded or withdrawn.

15.   (T)   F   The standard of proof for the grand jury and preliminary hearing is probable cause.

FILL-IN-THE-BLANK

1.   A _diversion_ program is an alternative to formal processing and trial.

2.   If the grand jury accepts the prosecutor's recommendation to indict, it issues a _true_ bill.

3.   Not allowing the release of dangerous defendants before trial is called _preventive_ detention.

4.   Most defendants appearing before the courts plead _guilty_ prior to the trial stage.

5.   The _presentment_ report of a grand jury usually contains a recommendation of indictment.

6.   Except for its use in civil cases, a plea of _nolo_ contendere is the same as not guilty.

7.   To be valid, a defendant's guilty plea must be _voluntary_ and without pressure.

8.   At the end of the rebuttal, the defense may be allowed _surrebuttal_-presenting witnesses to respond to issues raised the first time in the prosecutor's rebuttal case.

9.   Research shows that prosecutorial _discretion_ rather than defendant characteristics controls plea negotiations.

10.   The formal court hearing where the defendant is notified of the charges and asked to enter a plea is the _arraignment_ .

11. Following the prosecutor's opening statement; the defense attorney has the opportunity to make an _opening_ statement.

12. If the grand jury refuses to indict, it issues a _no_ bill.

13. A writ of _habeas corpus_ is the primary means by which state prisoners have their convictions or sentences reviewed in the federal court.

14. Delays in the trial process conflict with the _Sixth_ Amendment's guarantee of a right to a speedy trial.

15. A jury array or _venire_, generally consists of citizens who are potentially capable of being jurors.

ESSAY

1. Discuss the two functions of the grand jury. Provide examples. What is the main criticism of grand juries?

2. This chapter identified nine legal rights provided to defendants during trial. Identify and explain four of these rights.

3. This chapter identified six types of bail. Identify four and briefly explain each.

4. Discuss the pros and cons of plea bargaining and provide examples. Present and defend your position on the issue.

5. There are numerous junctures during which bail is conducted. Provide a description for the following junctures:
   a. Jail Citation Release
   b. Bail Schedule
   c. Judicial Release

CHAPTER 8 ANSWER KEY

Multiple Choice

1. d [p. 172, LO1]   2. b [p. 182, LO6]   3. b [p. 177, LO3]   4. b [p. 177, LO3]   5. c [p. 172, LO1]

6. a [p. 170, LO1]   7. a [p. 171, LO1]   8. b [p. 180, LO6]   9. d [p. 171, LO1]   10. a [p. 191, LO10]

11. a [p. 173, LO1]   12. d [p. 175, LO2]   13. c [p. 176, LO3]   14. b [p. 177, LO3]   15. b [p. 183, LO7]

16. d [p. 176, LO3]   17. c [p. 179, LO3]   18. a [p. 180, LO5]   19. a [p. 184, LO8]   20. a [p. 182, LO6]

21. a [p. 171, LO1]   22. c [p. 184, LO8]   23. c [p. 185, LO9]   24. b [p. 184, LO8]   25. b [p. 184, LO9]

26. d [p. 184, LO9]   27. c [p. 185, LO9]   28. a [p. 185, LO9]   29. a [p. 185, LO9]   30. c [p. 187, LO9]

True/False

1. F [p. 177, LO3]   2. T [p. 180, LO4]   3. F [p. 179, LO4]   4. F [p. 179, LO4]   5. F [p. 182, LO6]

6. F [p. 183, LO7]   7. T [p. 183, LO5]   8. T [p. 184, LO8]   9. F [p. 184, LO7]   10. T [p. 184, LO8]

11. F [p. 175, LO2]   12. T [p. 185, LO9]   13. T [p. 172, LO1]   14. T [p. 179, LO5]   15. T [p. 188, LO3]

Fill-in-the-Blank

1. diversion [p. 184, LO7]   2. true [p. 176, LO3]   3. preventive [p. 175, LO1]

4. guilty [p. 179, LO4]   5. presentment [p. 176, LO3]   6. nolo [p. 179, LO4]

7. voluntary [p. 181, LO5]   8. surrebuttal [p. 192, LO10]   9. discretion [p. 181, LO5]

10. arraignment [p. 179, LO3]   11. opening [p. 191, LO10]   12. no [p. 176, LO3]

13. habeas corpus [p. 195, LO9]   14. Sixth [p. 186, LO9]   15. venire [p. 190, LO10]

Essay

1.   **Discuss the two functions of the grand jury. Provide examples. What is the main criticism of grand juries?**

The grand jury has the power to act as an independent investigating body that is responsible for examining criminal activity within its jurisdiction. These investigative efforts may be directed toward general rather than individual criminal conduct—for example, organized crime or insider trading. After an investigation is completed, a report called a presentment is issued; this report contains not only information concerning the findings of the grand jury but also, usually, a recommendation of indictment.

The grand jury's second role is to act as the community's conscience in determining whether the accusation of the state (the prosecution) justifies a trial. In this role the grand jury relies on the testimony

225

of witnesses called by the prosecution through its subpoena power. After examining the evidence and the testimony of witnesses, the grand jury decides whether probable cause exists for prosecution. If it does, an indictment, or true bill, is affirmed. If the grand jury fails to find probable cause, a no bill (the indictment is ignored) is passed.

The grand jury has been criticized as being a "rubber stamp" for the prosecution, because the presentation of evidence is shaped by the prosecutor, who is not required by law to reveal information that might exonerate the accused.

[pp. 176-177, LO5]

2.   **This chapter identified nine legal rights provided to defendants during trial. Identify and explain four of these rights.**

- **The Right to an Impartial Judge.** Even though the Constitution does not say so, every criminal defendant enjoys the right to a trial by an impartial judge.

- **The Right to Be Competent at Trial.** To stand trial, a criminal defendant must be considered mentally competent to understand the nature and extent of the legal proceedings. If a defendant is considered mentally incompetent, his trial must be postponed until treatment renders him capable of participating in his own defense.

- **The Right to Confront Witnesses.** The Sixth Amendment states that "In all criminal prosecutions, the accused shall enjoy the right... to be confronted with the witnesses against him." The accused enjoys this right not just by being able to confront witnesses in person, but by being allowed to participate in his or her trial. That is, trials cannot be conducted without the accused being afforded the right to appear in person. This right can be waived or forfeited through misconduct. The confrontation clause is essential to a fair criminal trial because it restricts and controls the admissibility of hearsay evidence. Hearsay evidence is akin to secondhand evidence; rather than being told firsthand, it consists of information related by a second party (it is what one person hears and then says—hence the term "hearsay").

- **The Right to Compulsory Process.** The Sixth Amendment says, in part, that the accused shall "have compulsory process for obtaining witnesses in his favor." Compulsory process means to compel the production of witnesses via a subpoena. A subpoena is an order requiring a witness to appear in court at a specified time and place. The Supreme Court decided that compulsory process is a fundamental right in the case of *Washington v. Texas* (1967).

- **The Right to an Impartial Jury.** It is no accident that of all the rights guaranteed to the people by the Constitution, only the right to a jury trial in criminal cases appears in both the original Constitution (Article III, Section 2) and the Bill of Rights (the Sixth Amendment). Although they may have disagreed on many points, the Framers did not question the wisdom of the jury trial.

- **The Right to Counsel at Trial.** Recall from previous chapters that the defendant has a right to counsel at numerous points in the criminal justice process. Today, state courts must provide counsel at trial to indigent defendants who face even the possibility of incarceration. The threat of incarceration need not be immediate. Even if the defendant might be sentenced to probation in which a prison or jail term is suspended, or might receive any other type of sentence containing a threat of future incarceration, he is afforded the right to counsel at trial.

- **The Right to a Speedy Trial.** The tactics employed by wary defense attorneys (pretrial motions, complex plea negotiations, delay tactics during trial), along with inefficiencies in the court process (such as the frequent granting of continuances, poor scheduling procedures, and the abuse of time by court personnel), have made delay in criminal cases a serious and constitutional issue.

- **The Right to a Public Trial.** The Sixth Amendment refers to a "public trial." This simply means that all trials must be open to the public. The right to a public trial is generally unrestricted. Anyone who wants to see a criminal trial can do so.

- **The Right to Be Convicted by Proof beyond a Reasonable Doubt.** The standard required to convict a defendant charged with a crime at the adjudicatory stage of the criminal process is proof beyond a reasonable doubt. This requirement dates back to early American history and over the years has become the accepted measure of persuasion needed by the prosecutor to convince the judge or jury of the defendant's guilt.

[pp. 184-188, LO9]

3.   **This chapter identified six types of bail. Identify four and briefly explain each.**

- **Full cash bail.** The defendant pays the full bail amount out of pocket. In some jurisdictions, property can be pledged instead of cash.

- **Deposit bail.** The defendant deposits a percentage of the bail amount, typically 10 percent, with the court. When the defendant appears in court, the deposit is returned, sometimes minus an administrative fee. If the defendant fails to appear, he or she is liable for the full amount of the bail.

- **Surety bail.** The defendant pays a percentage of the bond, usually 10 percent, to a bonding agent who posts the full bail. The fee paid to the bonding agent is not returned to the defendant if he or she appears in court. The bonding agent is liable for the full amount of the bond should the defendant fail to appear. Bonding agents often require posting collateral to cover the full bail amount. This is the most common form of bail.

- **Conditional bail.** The defendant is released after promising to obey some specified conditions in lieu of cash, such as attending a treatment program before trial.

- **Unsecured bond.** The defendant is released with no immediate requirement of payment. However, if the defendant fails to appear, he or she is liable for the full amount.

- **Release on recognizance.** According to the release on recognizance (ROR) concept, eligible defendants are released without bail upon their promise to return for trial.

[pp. 172-173, LO2]

4.   **Discuss the pros and cons of plea bargaining and provide examples. Present and defend your position on the issue.**

Proponents contend that plea bargaining actually benefits both the state and the defendant. Those who favor plea bargaining believe it is appropriate to enter into plea discussions when the interests of the state in the effective administration of justice will be served. Some arguments in favor of plea bargaining includes:

- Overall costs of the criminal prosecution are reduced
- Administrative efficiency of the courts is greatly improved
- Prosecution can devote more time to more serious cases
- Defendant avoids possible detention and an extended trial and may receive a reduced sentence
- Resources can be devoted more efficiently to cases that need greater attention. The ability to divert a case (consider the case of a first time offender or non-violent crime) away from the full array of criminal justice services makes room for cases that need these services

Opponents of the plea bargaining process believe that the negotiated plea should be eliminated for the following reasons:

- It encourages defendants to waive their constitutional right to trial
- Plea bargains allow dangerous offenders to receive lenient sentences. An example includes; the case where a previously convicted sex offender, was given a 10-year plea-bargained sentence for child rape, upon his release, he raped and killed a seven-year-old
- Plea bargaining also raises the danger that an innocent person will be convicted of a crime if he or she is convinced that the lighter treatment ensured by a guilty plea is preferable to the risk of conviction and a harsher sentence following a formal trial

[pp. 180-181, LO6]

5. **There are numerous junctures during which bail is conducted. Provide a description for the following junctures:**
   a. Jail Citation Release
   b. Bail Schedule
   c. Judicial Release

Jail Citation Release: The determination of an arrestee's eligibility and suitability for citation release (release with a violation or "ticket") and the actual release of the arrestee are deferred until after he or she has been delivered by the arresting department to a jail or other pretrial detention facility for screening, booking, and admission.

Bail Schedule: An arrestee can post bail at the station house or jail according to amounts specified in a bail schedule. The schedule is a list of all bailable charges / crimes and a corresponding dollar amount for each. Schedules vary widely from jurisdiction to jurisdiction.

Judicial Release: In some cases (usually felonies) the judge will consider bail at a court hearing conducted shortly after a person has been taken into custody. At the hearing, such issues as type of crime, flight risk, and dangerousness are considered before a bail amount is set. In some jurisdictions, court staff often interview arrestees detained at the jail before the first hearing, verify their background information, and present recommendations to the court at arraignment. This information is utilized by the judge in determining bail eligibility.

[p. 172, LO2]

CHAPTER 9
Punishment and Sentencing

After studying this chapter, students will:

1. Outline the historical development of punishment
2. List the major goals of contemporary sentencing
3. Distinguish among general and specific deterrence, incapacitation, and retribution
4. Compare rehabilitation with just deserts
5. Identify various sentencing models
6. Explain how sentences are imposed
7. Summarize factors associated with sentencing decisions
8. List the arguments for and against capital punishment.
9. Be familiar with the legal issues associated with capital punishment

KEY TERMS AND CONCEPTS

penitentiary (p. 203) A state or federal correctional institution for incarceration of felony offenders for terms of one year or more.

general deterrence (p. 203) A crime control policy that depends on the fear of criminal penalties. General deterrence measures, such as long prison sentences for violent crimes, are aimed at convincing the potential law violator that the pains associated with paying for the crime outweigh the benefits.

specific deterrence (p. 203) A crime control policy suggesting that punishment should be severe enough to convince convicted offenders never to repeat their criminal activity.

incapacitation (p. 204) The policy of keeping dangerous criminals in confinement to eliminate the risk of their repeating their offense in society.

blameworthy (p. 205) Culpable or guilty of participating in a particular criminal offense.

just desert (p. 205) The philosophy of justice asserting that those who violate the rights of others deserve to be punished. The severity of punishment should be commensurate with the seriousness of the crime.

rehabilitation (p. 205) The strategy of applying proper treatment so an offender will present no further threat to society.

equity (p. 205) The action or practice of awarding each person what is due him or her; sanctions based on equity seek to compensate individual victims and the general society for their losses due to crime.

indeterminate sentence (p. 206) A term of incarceration with a stated minimum and maximum length, such as a sentence to prison for a period of from 3 to 10 years. The prisoner would be eligible for parole after the minimum sentence has been served. Based on the belief that sentences should fit the criminal, indeterminate sentences allow individualized sentences and provide for sentencing flexibility. Judges can set a high minimum to override the purpose of the indeterminate sentence.

determinate sentence (p. 207) A fixed term of incarceration, such as 3 years' imprisonment. Many people consider determinate sentences too restrictive for rehabilitative purposes; the advantage is that offenders know how much time they have to serve—that is, when they will be released.

sentencing guidelines (p. 207) A set of standards that define parameters for trial judges to follow in their sentencing decisions.

mandatory sentence (p. 208) A statutory requirement that a certain penalty shall be set and carried out in all cases upon conviction for a specified offense or series of offenses.

concurrent sentences (p. 210) Prison sentences for two or more criminal acts, served simultaneously and run together.

consecutive sentences (p. 210) Prison sentences for two or more criminal acts, served one after the other.

chivalry hypothesis (p. 213) The view that the low rates of female crime and delinquency are a reflection of the leniency with which police and judges treat female offenders.

victim impact statement (p. 214) A postconviction statement by the victim of crime that may be used to guide sentencing decisions.

brutalization effect (p. 220) An outcome of capital punishment that enhances, rather than deters, the level of violence in society. The death penalty reinforces the view that violence is an appropriate response to provocation.

CHAPTER OUTLINE

I. **THE HISTORY OF PUNISHMENT**
    1. The punishment and correction of criminals has changed considerably through the ages reflecting:
        a. Custom
        b. Economic conditions

    c. Religious and political ideals

A. From Exile to Fines, Torture to Forfeiture

1. In early Greece and Rome, the most common state-administered punishment was banishment or exile
2. Only slaves were subjected to harsh treatment
3. During the Middle Ages (5th to 15th centuries), there was little law or governmental control
4. Offenses were settled with blood feuds carried out by families of the injured parties
5. When possible, the Roman custom of settling disputes with fines or exchange of property was adopted as means of resolving conflict in the Middle Ages
6. After the eleventh century, forfeiture of land and property was common punishments for persons who violated law and custom
7. The word felony had its origins in the twelfth century and stems from felonia (breach of faith with one's feudal lord)
8. The emphasis on criminal law and punishment was on maintaining public order
9. Freemen would pronounce punishment, in some cases a fine, known as *wergild*
   a. The purpose of the fine was to pacify the injured party to prevent a blood feud from developing
   b. Inability of the peasantry to pay a fine led to the use of corporal punishment, such as whipping or branding, as a substitute penalty
10. The common law developed in the eleventh century; it brought standardization to penal practices
11. Corrections remained an amalgam of fines and brutal physical punishments
12. Punishment was applied differently to the wealthy and the poor
    a. Execution, banishment, mutilation, branding, and flogging were used on a whole range of offenders, from murderers and robbers to vagrants and Gypsies
13. Punishments became unmatched in their cruelty featuring a variety of physical tortures, suggests that retribution, sadism, and spectacle were more important than any presumed deterrent effect

B. Public Work and Transportation to Colonies

1. By the end of the sixteenth century, the rise of the city and overseas colonization provided tremendous markets for manufactured goods and spurned a need for labor
2. Many offenders were sentenced to labor
3. Labor shortages in Europe prompted convicts to be transported overseas as labor
4. Transporting convicts became popular, cost little, and was profitable for the government. Transported prisoners endured significant hardships
5. The American Revolution ended the transportation of felons to North America, but continued in Australia and New Zealand

C. The Rise of the Prison

1. Between 1776 and the first decade of the nineteenth century, the European and American populations increased rapidly

2. Transportation to North America was no longer an option
3. The gulf between poor workers and wealthy landowners and merchants widened
4. The crime rate rose significantly, prompting a return to physical punishment and the death penalty
5. During the later part of the eighteenth century, 350 crimes were punishable by death in England
6. Use of the death penalty was common at this time
7. Abandoned ships anchored in rivers and harbors in England were used as prisons and to house prisoners
8. By the 1820s, long periods of incarceration in walled institutions began to replace physical punishment in the United States and England known as:
   a. Reformatories
   b. Penitentiaries
9. In contemporary society, prison as a method of punishment has been supplemented by a sentence to community supervision for less serious offenders
   a. Death penalty reserved for the most serious and dangerous

II. **THE GOALS OF MODERN SENTENCING**
   1. Sentiments may be at work when sentences are formulated
   2. The objectives of sentencing can be grouped into five general areas:
      a. Deterrence (general and specific), incapacitation, retribution/just desert, rehabilitation, and equity/restitution
   A. Deterrence
      1. According to general deterrence, people will be afraid to break the law if they believe they will be caught and punished severely
      2. The more certain and severe the punishment, the greater the deterrence
      3. Some justice experts believe the decline in the crime rate is a result of increasing penalties
      4. Once arrested, people have a greater chance of being convicted today than in the past, this is known as expect punishment
      5. Expected punishment rates are still low because:
         a. Crime clearance rates remain well under 50 percent
         b. Many cases are dropped at the pretrial and trial stages
         c. About 1/3 of convicted felons are given probationary rather than prison
      6. Because the justice system is still inefficient, the general deterrent effect of punishment is less than desired
      7. The percentage of convicted offenders who now receive a prison sentence has declined during the past decade
         a. Estimated average prison sentence received by violent felony offenders in state courts decreased from nearly 10 years in 1994 to 7.5 years in 2004
         b. The actual time served has increased however
      8. Specific Deterrence is intended to convince offenders that the pains of punishment are greater than the benefits of crime
         a. They will not repeat their criminal offending

9. Claims for specific deterrence are weakened by data showing most inmates released from prison have prior convictions and a great majority will reoffend soon after their release

10. Despite the sketchy results, it remains a fundamental part of sentencing

B. Incapacitation

1. Because criminals will be unable to repeat their criminal acts while under state control, incapacitation of criminals is another goal of sentencing

2. The evidence is mixed as to whether incapacitating criminals reduces the crime rate

   a. Statistics reveal that during different periods, the results are mixed:
      i. Higher incarceration and lower crime rate
      ii. Higher incarceration and higher crime rate

3. We now have 1.4 million people behind bars

4. Incarceration trends may influence crime rates but that reductions in crime may also be related to other factors:

   a. Population makeup
   b. Police effectiveness
   c. Declining drug use
   d. Economy

5. Incarceration effects diminish as more people are incarcerated

C. Retribution/Just Desert

1. According to the goal retributive sentencing, the essential purpose of the criminal process is to punish offenders – fairly and justly – in a manner that is proportionate to the gravity of their crimes

2. Offenders are punished simply and solely because they deserve to be disciplined for what they have done; the punishment should fit the crime

3. According to this view, punishments must be equally and fairly distributed to all people who commit similar illegal acts

4. Punishment should be no more or less than the offender's action deserve:

   a. It must be based on how blameworthy the person is
      i. Concept of just desert

5. Determining just punishments can be difficult because there is generally little consensus about the treatment of criminals, the seriousness of crimes, and the proper response to criminal acts

D. Rehabilitation

1. Some sentences are based on the need to treat and/or rehabilitate offenders

2. The idea is that society has failed them, and they have been forced to grow up in disorganized neighborhoods that have been the target of biased police officers. There is also a belief that they are disadvantaged at home, at school, and in the job market

   a. To compensate for these deprivations, the justice system is obligated to help these unfortunate people and not simply punish them

3. Advocates believe that if proper treatment is applied, an offender will present no further threat to society

E. Equity/Restitution

1. Because criminals gain from their misdeeds, it seems both fair and just to demand they reimburse society for its loss caused by their crimes
2. The equity goal of punishment means that convicted criminals must pay back their victims for their loss, the justice system for the costs of processing the case, and society for the disruption the offender has caused
   a. Convicted offenders might be required to:
      i. Pay a fine
      ii. Forfeit the property they acquired through illegal gain
      iii. Do community service work
      iv. Make financial restitution to their victim
      v. Reimburse the state for the costs of the criminal process

III. **SENTENCING MODELS**
1. When an offender is sentenced to prison, the statutes of the jurisdiction in which the crime was committed determine the penalties that may be imposed by the court. Sentences include indeterminate sentences, determinate sentences, and mandatory sentences
   A. Indeterminate Sentences
   1. In the 1870s, prison reformers Enoch Wines and Zebulon Brockway called for the creation of indeterminate sentences, tailored to fit individual needs
   2. The argument was that offenders should be placed in confinement until rehabilitated and released on parole
   3. The indeterminate sentence is still the most widely used sentence in the United States
   4. Sentences range from minimum to maximum terms for each offender. The outer boundary can be adjusted by the correctional agency and the judge
   5. The basic purpose of indeterminate sentences is to individualize each sentence in the interests of rehabilitating the offender
   6. Most jurisdictions that use indeterminate sentencing allow judicial officials to fix the actual sentence within the limits
      a. Typical minimum sentence is at least for one year, a few states require at least a two year minimum sentence for felons
   B. Determinate Sentences
   1. Dissatisfaction with the disparity and uncertainty of indeterminate sentences has prompted some states and the federal government to abandon it in favor of determinate sentencing
   2. Determinate sentencing is aimed at curbing judicial discretion
   3. Determinate sentences offer a fixed term of years, the maximum set in law
   4. Most jurisdictions that employ these sentences have developed methods and structure to control the sentencing process to make it more rational
      a. To accomplish this, sentencing guidelines have been implemented by determinate sentencing states and the federal government
      b. Guidelines give judges a recommended sentence based on:
         i. The seriousness of the offense
         ii. The background of the offender

      c. Guidelines are designed to reduce racial and gender disparity by eliminating judicial discretion

  5. The Future of Guidelines

      a. About eighteen states use some form of structured sentencing

      b. Sentencing guidelines that are in use

         i. Voluntary/advisory guidelines — suggest rather than mandate sentences

         ii. Presumptive sentencing guidelines — require judges to use the guidelines to shape sentencing decisions

      c. Supreme Court cases have recently put a moratorium on the use of presumptive guidelines and placed their future in doubt:

         i. *Blakely v. Washington* – Court found that Washington State's sentencing guidelines were a violation of the defendant's Sixth Amendment rights because they allow a judge to consider aggravating factors that would enhance the sentence

         ii. *United States v. Booker* – Court ruled that the federal guidelines were unconstitutional, allowing that judges should consider the guideline ranges but must also be permitted the right to alter sentences in consideration of other factors

      d. Presumptive guidelines have been criticized as being

         i. Rigid

         ii. Harsh

         iii. Overly complex

         iv. Disliked by the judiciary

      e. Since the Supreme Court cases guidelines are now advisory rather than mandatory

C. Mandatory Sentences

  1. Another effort to limit judicial discretion, and at the same time get tough on crime, has been the development of mandatory sentences

  2. Some states have passed legislation prohibiting people convicted of certain offenses, such as violent crimes or drug trafficking, from being placed on probation

  3. Mandatory sentencing usually limits judges' discretionary power to impose any disposition but that authorized by legislature

  4. Mandatory sentencing laws give prosecutors considerable power

  5. Have helped increase the size of correctional populations to record levels

  6. Mandatory sentences have also failed to eliminate racial disparity from the sentencing process

D. Three Strike Laws

  1. These laws provide lengthy terms for any person convicted of three felony offenses, even if the third crime is relatively trivial

  2. California's three-strike laws are aimed at getting habitual offenders off the street, any third felony can result in life in prison

  3. Three-strike laws have undeniable political appeal to legislators being pressured by their constituents to "do something about crime"

  4. Opponents of three strike laws argue:

      a. Many "three-time losers' are on the brink of aging out of crime

       b. Current sentences for chronic violent offenders are already severe

       c. Criminals typically underestimate the risk of apprehension, while overestimating the rewards of crime

    5. Vast majority of studies reveal three strike laws have little or no effect on crime

    6. Have been challenged and upheld constitutionally

E. Truth in Sentencing

    1. These laws require an inmate serve a substantial portion of their sentence behind bars

    2. Parole eligibility and good-time credits are restricted or eliminated

    3. These laws were part of the government's 1994 crime act

    4. The act requires an offender serve at least 85 percent of the prison sentence in order to qualify for funding

    5. Act is already having an effect:

       a. 1996 – offenders released from prison served slightly more than half their prison sentence or 45 months

       b. Today, average inmate will serve an average of 88 months

IV.   **IMPOSING THE SENTENCE**

    1. In most felony cases, except where the law provides for mandatory prison systems, sentencing is usually based on a variety of information available to the judge

    2. Most judges consider pre-sentence investigation reports by the probation department

       a. This report is a social and personal history, as well as an evaluation of the defendant's chances for rehabilitation within the community

A. Concurrent vs. Consecutive Sentences

    1. In some instances, when an accused is convicted of two or more charges, the judge must decide whether to impose consecutive or concurrent sentences

    2. Concurrent sentences begin the same day and end on the last day of the longest sentence

    3. Consecutive sentences mean that upon completion of the sentence for one crime the offender begins serving the second crime's sentence

B. The Effect of Good Time

    1. When judges sentence offenders, they consider the effect that the amount of time off for good behavior will also have

    2. The concept of good time was first used in 1817 in New York and was quickly adopted into most other jurisdictions

    3. Good time is still in use today, inmates can accrue standard good time at a rate ranging from 10-15 days per month

    4. Good time can also be earned for inmates who participate in treatment programs

    5. Good time allows inmates to calculate their release date at the time they enter prison by subtracting expected good time from their sentence

    6. Good time can be lost if an inmate breaks the rules, gets into fights, or disobeys correctional officers

      a. Former inmates can be returned to prison for failing to conform to conditions set down for their release

V. **HOW PEOPLE ARE SENTENCED**
1. The federal government conducts surveys on sentencing practices in state and federal courts
2. The most recent survey found that one million adults are convicted of felonies each year
3. 70 percent of all felons convicted in state courts are sentenced to a period of confinement
    a. 40 percent to state prisons
    b. 30 percent to local jails
    c. Remaining sentenced to probation with no jail or prison
4. Felons sentenced to state prison had an average sentence of 4 ½ years, but were only likely to serve half that
5. About one third of convicted felons also ordered to:
    a. Pay a fine
    b. Pay victim restitution
    c. Receive treatment
    d. Perform community service
    e. Comply with some other penalty
6. Number of convicted offenders being sent to prison today is lower than a decade ago
    a. Illustrates the popularity of cost-effective community sentencing
7. Because of tough sentencing laws though, average time service has not decreased substantially

A. What factors affect sentencing?
    a. The crime's seriousness and the offender's record are considered in sentencing
    b. State sentence codes that usually detail what factors can be legitimately considered in determining a sentence:
        i. Severity of the crime
        ii. Offender's prior record
        iii. Offender used violence
        iv. Whether the offender used a weapon
        v. Whether the crime was committed for money
    c. Research shows a correlation between these legal variables and the type of sentence received
    d. Judges sentence more severely for more serious crimes
    e. Sentencing experts suspect that judges may also be influenced by the defendant's
        i. Social class
        ii. Gender
        iii. Age
        iv. Race
        v. Victim characteristics

1. Social Class
   e. Evidence supports an association between social class and sentencing outcomes
      i. Members of lower class may expect to get longer prison sentences than more affluent defendants
      ii. Affluent defendants are more likely than the indigent to receive lenient sentences
2. Gender
   a. Some theorists believe gender influences sentencing with favorable treatment to women
   b. Some favorable treatment is attributed to the fact that the criminal justice system is dominated by men, and they have a paternalistic view toward women (chivalry hypothesis)
   c. Research indicates that women receive increased favorable treatment the further they go in the system
   d. Gender favoritism crosses racial and ethnic lines
   e. Mandatory and structured sentences, designed to limit bias and discretion, have resulted in harsher sentences for women
3. Age
   a. Age is another extralegal factor that may play a role in sentencing
   b. This association is not necessarily linear
4. Race
   a. A key issue in sentencing is the suspicion that race as a personal factor has an influence on sentencing
   b. Racial disparity in sentencing has been suspected because of the disproportionate number of African American inmates in state prison or on death row
   c. Minorities seem to receive longer sentences than Caucasians, especially those that are indigent or unemployed
   d. Research indicates that it is the victim's race, rather than the offender's that structures sentencing outcomes
      i. Minority defendants are sanctioned more severely if their victim is white than if their target is a fellow minority member
5. Victim Characteristics
   a. Victim characteristics may also influence sentencing
   b. Victims may be asked or allowed to make a victim impact statement before the sentencing judge. This gives the victim an opportunity to tell their experiences and describe their ordeal
   c. A victim's personal characteristics may influence sentencing
      i. Sentences may be reduced when victims have "negative" personal characteristics or qualities:
         a) Prostitute
         b) Drug abuser

VI. **CAPITAL PUNISHMENT**
1. The most severe sentence in the United States is capital punishment, or execution
2. More than 14,500 confirmed executions have been carried out in the United States under civil authority
   a. Most for murder and rape
   b. Federal, state, and military laws have conferred the death penalty for other crimes including:
      i. Robbery
      ii. Kidnapping
      iii. Treason
      iv. Espionage
      v. Desertion from military service
3. In recent years, the Supreme Court has limited the death penalty to first-degree murder, and only then when there are aggravating circumstances
4. The federal government still has provisions of the death penalty for members of the armed forces for espionage, treason, and killing during a criminal conspiracy
5. This is the most emotional and controversial issue in the criminal justice
6. The death penalty has long been one of the most controversial aspects of the criminal justice system

A. Arguments for the Death Penalty:
1. Deterrence
   a. Proponents of capital punishment argue that executions serve as a strong deterrent for serious crimes
   b. Proponents argue that the deterrent effect of an execution can produce a substantial decline in the murder rate
   c. The death penalty scares would-be criminals, homicide rates drop after a well-publicized execution
2. Morally Correct
   a. This argument contends that the death penalty is morally correct; it has roots in the Bible and other religious works
   b. The death penalty is morally correct because it provides the greatest justice for the victim and helps alleviate the psychic pain of the victim's family and friends
3. Proportional to the Crime
   a. Putting dangerous criminals to death also conforms to the requirement that the punishment must be proportional to the seriousness of the crime
4. Reflects Public Opinion
   a. This argument states that the death penalty is justified because it represents the will of the people
   b. Public approval rests on the belief that the death penalty is an important instrument of social control
      i. Can deter crime
      ii. Less costly than maintaining a murderer in prison for life
5. Unlikely Chances of Error

       a. The number of legal controls and appeals make it almost impossible for an innocent person to be executed

       b. Federal courts closely scrutinize all death penalty cases and rule for the defendant is an estimated 60-70% of the appeals

B. Arguments against the Death Penalty

       a. Arguments for the death penalty are matched by those who support its abolition

1. Possibility of Error

       a. Critics of the death penalty believe capital punishment has no place in a mature democratic society

       b. A report revealed 42 exonerations of death row inmates occurred each year between 1989-2003.

          i. Recent attention to exonerations has both prompted and been influenced by an "innocence movement"

             a) Today more than 50 innocent projects exist, collectively they:

                1. Screen claims of innocence

                2. Work to exonerate the factually innocent

                3. Promote policies to reduce errors of justice

                4. Provide support to exonerees

       c. Several reasons for errors:

          i. As many as 25 percent of all eyewitness identifications may be wrong, many of these errors are caused by suggestive police lineups

          ii. Police are not required to include exculpatory evidence in investigative reports

       d. Because of the chance for error, a number of states have placed a moratorium on the death penalty

2. Unfair Use of Discretion

       a. Critics frown on the tremendous discretion used in seeking the death penalty and the arbitrary manner in which it is imposed

          i. Of the approximately 10,000 persons convicted each year on homicide charges, only 250-300 are sentenced to death, an equal number receive a sentence of probation or community supervision only

       b. Some escape death by cooperating or giving testimony against their partners in crime

3. Misplaced Vengeance

       a. Critics acknowledge that the general public approves of the death penalty

       b. Critics maintain that prevailing attitudes reflect primitive desire for revenge and not 'just desert'

       c. At least thirty states now have a sentence of life in prison without parole, and this can more than make-up for execution

       d. Being locked up may be more punishment that painless death

4. Weak Public Support

       a. Politicians favor the death penalty in the mistaken belief that the public favors such harsh treatment

       b. Well-publicized, wrongful convictions contribute to weakened public support

      c. While the majority of the public still support the death penalty, substantial portions lack confidence in its use

      d. There is support for halting the death penalty until it is foolproof

      e. Personal characteristics of the offender may influence public opinion:

         i. Juveniles

         ii. Mentally challenged

         iii. Mentally ill

5. Little Deterrent Effect

      a. Three methods have been used to determine if death more effective deterrent than life imprisonment:

         i. Immediate-impact studies

           a) Calculate the effect of a well publicized execution on short term murder rate

         ii. Time-series analysis

           a) Compares long-term trends in murder and capital punishment rates

         iii. Contiguous-state analysis

           a) Compares murder rates in states that have death penalty with similar states that have abolished capital punishment

      b. Using these methods over 60-year period, most researchers have failed to show any deterrent effect of capital punishment

      c. Murder is a crime of passion involving people who know each other

         i. Many murders committed by people under influence of drugs and alcohol

           a) More than 50% of all people arrested for murder test positive for drug use

      d. Many people still hold the efficacy of the death penalty as a crime deterrent, recent U.S. Supreme Court decisions seem to justify its use

6. No Hope of Rehabilitation

      a. The death penalty rules out offender rehabilitation

      b. There is evidence that convicted killers make good parole risks and are often model prisoners

      c. It is possible that the juries overestimate the dangerousness of people who commit murder

      d. Those given life sentence for capital murder have less than a 1% chance of committing another homicide over a 40-year term, the risk of their committing an assault is about 16 percent

7. Race Gender and Other Bias

      a. Capital punishment may be tarnished by gender, racial, ethnic, and other biases

      b. The death penalty is used more often in nations where there is a large minority population

      c. This is called minority group-threat hypothesis

      d. Certain crime scenarios are more likely to receive the death penalty as opposed to the inverse scenario

         i. Male homicide offender with female victim

         ii. Homicides involving strangers

          iii. Offender kills a white victim

    e. Since the death penalty was first used in the United States, disproportionate numbers of minorities have been executed

    f. This has been especially true in rape cases

    g. Today, about 40 percent of the inmates on death row are African American, disproportionate to the minority representation in the population

8. Causes More Crime Than It Deters

    a. Critics fear that the introduction of capital punishment will encourage criminals to escalate their violence

    b. A suspect may be inclined to kill during a botched robbery rather than surrender

    c. Research suggests that the greater number of inmates on death row, the greater number of police officer murders

    d. May produce more violence than it prevents, brutalization effect

          i. Executions may increase murder rates because they raise the general violence level in society and because violence-prone people actually identify with the executioner, not with the target of the death penalty

9. It Is Cruel and Inhuman

    a. Abolitionists believe that executions are unnecessarily cruel and inhuman and come at a high moral and social cost

    b. Even lethal injection is believed to impart more pain that readily received

    c. Execution has been described as a form of torture that includes psychological torture

    d. Suicides are a constant problem among those on death row

10. Most Developed Countries Have Abandoned it

    a. Over half the countries in the world have abolished the death penalty in law or practice

11. It is Expensive

    a. Some complain of having to provide inmate support thirty years

    b. The costs are compounded by the number of appeals

    c. In California, the time between conviction and execution averaged fourteen years, and the state spends more than $5 million per year on death row appeals

12. Morally Wrong

    a. The death penalty is brutal and demeaning

    b. Even with public support for it, abolitionists counter that it is primitive revenge that stands in the way of moral progress

    c. Early religious leaders accepted the death penalty, but today, the Catholic Church condemns it

    d. While the debate continues, it is clear that support for the death penalty has weakened

C. Legal Issues in Capital Punishment

    1. The Supreme Court has ruled that the discretionary application of the death penalty violated the Eighth and Fourteenth Amendments as cruel and unusual punishment

        a. 1972 — *Furman v. Georgia*

b. The Supreme Court did not completely rule out its use as a penalty, rather it objected to arbitrary and capricious application

2. In 1976 Supreme Court ruled on five state death penalty statutes:
   a. *Gregg v. Georgia*
      i. Found valid statute holding that a finding by the jury of at least 1 aggravating circumstance out of 10
         a) Jury imposed the death penalty after finding beyond a reasonable doubt two aggravating circumstances:
            1. The offender was engaged in the commission of two other capital felonies
            2. The offender committed the offense of murder for the purpose of receiving money and other financial gains
      ii. Signaled the return of capital punishment as a sentencing option

3. Although the court has generally supported the death penalty, it has placed limits on its use
   a. *Ring v. Arizona*
      i. Juries not judges must make the critical findings that send convicted killers to death row
   b. Limited the crimes where it can be applied
      i. Impermissible in cases of rape
      ii. Cannot be applied to mentally ill
         a) 2002 case of *Adkins v. Virginia*
      iii. Restricted age to a minimum of eighteen
         a) 2005 case of *Roper v. Simmons*

CHAPTER SUMMARY

Historically, people who violated the law were considered morally corrupt and in need of strong discipline. The common conception was that if the punishment was harsh enough, they would never repeat their mistakes. The punishment and correction of criminals has changed considerably through the ages, reflecting custom, economic conditions, and religious and political ideals.

The objectives of criminal sentencing can be grouped into five areas: deterrence (general and specific), incapacitation, retribution/just desert, rehabilitation, and equity/restitution. In most felony cases, except where the law provides for mandatory prison terms, sentencing is usually based on a variety of information available to the judge. The judge must decide whether to impose consecutive or concurrent sentences. Concurrent sentences begin the same day and are completed when the longest term has been served. A consecutive sentence means that on completion of the sentence for one crime, the offender begins serving time for the second.

Over the years, a variety of sentencing structures have been used in the United States. They include indeterminate sentences, determinate sentences, and mandatory sentences. About eighteen states use some form of structured sentencing. One effort to limit judicial discretion has been the development of the mandatory sentence. Mandatory sentencing generally limits the judge's discretionary power to impose any disposition but that authorized by the legislature. Three-strike laws provide lengthy terms for any person convicted of three felony offenses, even if the third crime is relatively trivial. Truth-in-sentencing laws require offenders to serve a substantial portion of their prison sentence behind bars.

More than one million adults are convicted of felonies in a single year. Besides being sentenced to incarceration or probation, felons were also ordered to pay a fine, victim restitution, receive treatment, perform community service, or comply with some other penalty. State sentencing codes include various factors that can influence the length of prison sentences, including the severity of the offense, the offender's criminal record, use of violence or weapons, or whether the crime was committed for money. Besides these factors, sentencing experts suspect that judges may also be influenced by the defendant's social class, gender, age, race, and victim characteristics.

The most severe sentence used is capital punishment. More than 14,500 confirmed executions have been carried out in America under civil authority. Opponents and proponents have formulated a number of powerful arguments in support of their positions. Proponents of the death penalty argue that is has an incapacitation effect, it is a deterrence, it is morally correct, it is proportional to the crime, it reflects public opinion, and there is an unlikely chance of error. Opponents argue that there is the possibility of error, there is unfair use of discretion, there is misplaced vengeance, it has weak public support, it shows little deterrent effect, there is no hope of rehabilitation, there is a race, gender, or other bias, it causes more crime than it deters, it is cruel and inhuman, it is expensive, and it is morally wrong.

The Supreme Court has supported the death penalty, but it has also placed some limitations on it. The Court has limited the crimes for which the death penalty can be employed by ruling that it is not permissible to punish rapists with death, that only people who commit intentional or felony murder may be executed, that people who are mentally ill may not be executed, and that those sentenced to death must be at least eighteen years old.

The key issue in the capital punishment debate is whether it can actually lower the murder rate and save lives. Considerable empirical research has been carried out on the effectiveness of capital punishment as a deterrent. Three methods have been used: immediate-impact studies, time-series analysis, and contiguous-state analysis.

DISCUSSION QUESTIONS

1. Discuss the sentencing dispositions in your jurisdiction. What are the pros and cons of each?
2. Compare the various types of incarceration sentences. What are the similarities and differences? Why are many jurisdictions considering the passage of mandatory sentencing laws?
3. Discuss the issue of capital punishment. In your opinion, does it serve as a deterrent? What new rulings has the Supreme Court made on the legality of the death penalty?

4.   Why does the problem of sentencing disparity exist? Do programs exist that can reduce the disparity of sentences? If so, what are they? Should all people who commit the same crime receive the same sentence? Explain.

5.   Should convicted criminals be released from prison when correctional authorities are convinced they are rehabilitated? Why or why not?

MEDIA TOOLS

A considerable portion of this chapter is related to sentencing, its goals, models, and factors that affect sentencing are covered. For one view of proponents that are trying to reform the current sentencing model visit the website of The Sentencing Project. This website addresses issues such as policy, gender disparity, and racial disparity. The website of The Sentencing Project can be found at: http://www.sentencingproject.org/template/index.cfm

To learn more about federal sentencing guidelines visit the United States Sentencing Commission website. When you visit this website you can view the actual Federal Sentencing Guidelines Manual and how individuals make determinations regarding sentencing. Visit the United States Sentencing Commission website at: http://www.ussc.gov/index.cfm

Frontline, a production of the Public Broadcasting System has compiled a fairly comprehensive examination into the story of and execution of Clifford Boggess. There are many resources and interesting stories in this project. The Execution can be found at: http://www.pbs.org/wgbh/pages/frontline/shows/execution

The Death Penalty Information Center is a comprehensive site that has many resources about the death penalty that address many of the topics mentioned in this chapter. According to the Death Penalty Information Center: "The Death Penalty Information Center is a non-profit organization serving the media and the public with analysis and information on issues concerning capital punishment. The Center was founded in 1990 and prepares in-depth reports, issues press releases, conducts briefings for journalists, and serves as a resource to those working on this issue. The Center is widely quoted and consulted by all those concerned with the death penalty." The website can be found at: http://www.deathpenaltyinfo.org/home

As discussed briefly in this chapter, innocence projects have flourished throughout the country. Collectively, innocence projects screen claims of innocence, work to exonerate the innocent based upon facts, promote polices to reduce errors of justice, and provide support for those who have been exonerated. Visit the website of the Innocence Project to learn more and read through some of the stories and projects. The website of the Innocence Project can be found at: http://www.innocenceproject.org

PRACTICE TEST BANK

MULTIPLE CHOICE

1. The number of days in prison a typical criminal can expect to serve per crime is known as
    a. a sentence.
    b. time served.
    c. expected punishment.
    d. truth in sentencing.

2. In ancient Greece and Rome, the most common form of state punishment for citizens was
    a. execution.
    b. slavery.
    c. torture.
    d. banishment or exile.

3. Which term best describes the circumstances where an offender completes one sentence and then begins another sentence for a different crime?
    a. Competent sentence
    b. Concurrent sentence
    c. Consecutive sentence
    d. Commissioned sentence

4. What laws require an offender to serve out a substantial portion of his or her prison sentence?
    a. Concurrent Sentencing
    b. Three-Strike Sentencing
    c. Progressive Sentencing
    d. Truth-in-Sentencing

5. Near 1820, what began to replace physical punishments for serious crimes in the U.S. and England?
    a. Transportation
    b. Penitentiaries
    c. Fines
    d. Banishment

6. Proportionality between sentence and harm is most consistent with
    a. rehabilitation.
    b. deterrence.
    c. just desert.
    d. incapacitation.

7. Under which sentencing theory are people most likely to see criminals as unfortunate victims of society?
    a. General deterrence
    b. Specific deterrence
    c. Incapacitation
    d. Rehabilitation

8. Which theory assumes that persons should be imprisoned as long as they pose a significant threat to society?
    a. Incapacitation
    b. Deterrence
    c. Just desert
    d. Equity/restitution

9. Which sentencing goal is most consistent with indeterminate sentencing schemes?
    a. Incapacitation
    b. Rehabilitation
    c. Just desert
    d. Deterrence

10. Using incapacitation to reduce crime rates always yields
    a. diminishing returns.
    b. lower crime rates.
    c. less recidivism.
    d. prison overcrowding.

11. Determining punishments can be difficult, because there is generally little consensus on all of the listed except
    a. the treatment of criminals.
    b. the treatment of victims.
    c. the seriousness of crimes.
    d. the proper response to criminal acts.

12. Which of the following is not a legitimate factor in the sentencing decision?
    a. Race
    b. Prior record
    c. Severity of the offense
    d. Use of weapons during crime

13. Most research indicates that women who go further in the criminal justice system receive
    a. a disproportionate number of death sentences.
    b. more favorable outcomes than males.
    c. longer prison sentences than males.
    d. a disproportionate number of denials of parole.

14. Research on race and sentencing has shown
    a. a clear and strong pattern of discrimination against minorities.
    b. that whites receive tougher sentences than any other group.
    c. some race-specific crimes are punished more harshly than others.
    d. that Asian Americans are disproportionately sentence to death.

15. The death penalty is least consistent with which sentencing goal/theory?
    a. Incapacitation
    b. General deterrence
    c. Specific deterrence
    d. Rehabilitation

16. Victims can have an impact on the perpetrators sentence through the use of
    a. victim harm statements.
    b. victim input statements.
    c. victim fault statements.
    d. victim impact statements.

17. Expected punishment rates are still quite low for a number of reasons except
    a. crime clearance rates remain well under 50%.
    b. many cases are dropped at the pretrial and trial stages.
    c. about 1/3 of convicted felons are given probation instead of prison.
    d. prison overcrowding.

18. Some theorists believe that women benefit from sentence disparity because the criminal justice system is dominated by men who have a paternalistic or protective attitude toward women. This is referred to as
    a. the chauvinistic hypothesis.
    b. paternalism.
    c. the chivalry hypothesis.
    d. the protectionist theory.

19. The goal of which sentencing philosophy is that the essential purpose of the criminal process is to punish offenders fairly and justly, in a manner proportionate to the gravity of their crimes?
    a. Rehabilitation
    b. Retribution
    c. Incapacitation
    d. Deterrence

20. Which one of the listed sentencing structures is tailored to fit individual offender needs?
    a. Determinate
    b. Indeterminate
    c. Incapacitation
    d. Equity

21. Legal issues related to capital punishment include all of the following except
    a. juries must make the finding that sends a convicted person to death row.
    b. the assignment of the death penalty in an arbitrary and capricious manner.
    c. limiting the crimes for which a person can receive the death penalty.
    d. the death penalty causes more crimes than it deters.

22. Arguments against the death penalty include all of the following except
    a. unfair use of discretion.
    b. it serves as a deterrent to crime.
    c. the possibility for error.
    d. misplaced vengeance.

23. The U.S. Supreme Court has limited the death penalty to cases involving
    a. first-degree murder.
    b. first-degree murder with aggravating circumstances.
    c. first-degree murder where a child was the victim.
    d. first-degree murder involving treason.

24. What concept is best described as "people will be afraid to break the law if they believe that they will be caught and punished severely"?
    a. General deterrence
    b. Incapacitation
    c. Specific deterrence
    d. Rehabilitation

25. Which punishment goal requires convicted criminals to pay back their victims for their loss, the justice system for the costs of processing their case, and society for any disruption they may have caused?
    a. Benign
    b. Theoretical
    c. Empirical
    d. Equity

26. Which of the listed factors considered by a judge in her sentencing decision would be a violation of the defendant's due process and equal protection rights?
    a. Severity of the offense
    b. Prior criminal record
    c. Defendant's use of violence
    d. Defendant's gender

27. Good time allows inmates to calculate their _____ at the time they enter prison by subtracting the expected good time from their sentence.
    a. trustee time
    b. work release time
    c. release date
    d. infirmary time

28. The federal government can grant the death penalty for all of the following crimes except
     a.   espionage by a member of the armed forces.
     b.   piracy on the high seas.
     c.   treason.
     d.   killing during a conspiracy.

29. What punishment goal supports applying proper treatment to offenders to eliminate an offender's threat to society?
     a.   Restitution
     b.   Incapacitation
     c.   Rehabilitation
     d.   Deterrence

30. All of the listed were methods of studies to try and determine whether the death sentence serves a more effective deterrent than life imprisonment for capital crimes except
     a.   immediate impact studies
     b.   longitude studies
     c.   time-series analysis
     d.   contiguous-state analysis

TRUE/FALSE

1. T   F   Compared to indeterminate sentencing, guidelines generally restrict judicial discretion.

2. T   F   Three-strike laws are generally inconsistent with the goal of rehabilitation.

3. T   F   The U.S. Supreme Court has held that three-strike laws are unconstitutional.

4. T   F   The brutalization effect is an argument in favor of capital punishment.

5. T   F   Some states have passed legislation prohibiting people convicted of certain crimes from being placed on probation.

6. T   F   Using incapacitation to reduce crime rates always yields diminishing returns.

7. T   F   People with prior felony convictions are less likely to receive prison time than those previously convicted of misdemeanors.

8. T   F   Deterrence assumes people make choices about committing crimes.

9. T   F   Victim impact statements are used at trials to determine guilt.

10. (T)   F   Truth-in-sentencing laws require an offender to serve a substantial portion of their prison sentence behind bars.

11. (T)   F   The percentage of convicted offenders who now receive a prison sentence has declined during the past decade.

12. (T)   F   Just desert theory is the same as or similar to the theory of retribution.

13. T   (F)   The U.S. Supreme Court ruled that juveniles/persons under the age of fifteen (at the time the crime was committed) cannot be executed.

14. (T)   F   Between 1990 and 2009, the prison population more than doubled.

15. (T)   F   More than 50% of all people arrested for murder test positive for drug use.

FILL-IN-THE-BLANK

1. Sentences that are served one after another are called _consecutive_.

2. The federal government and determinate sentencing states have implemented sentencing _guidelines_ to structure and control the sentencing process.

3. Specific _deterrence_ is aimed at deterring recidivism by the offender.

4. The theory of just _desert_ focuses on the blameworthiness of the offender.

5. A(n) _indeterminate_ sentence has both a minimum and maximum term.

6. A prisoner's sentence will be reduced for _good_ time if he/she behaves well in prison.

7. As many as _25_ percent of all witness identifications may be wrong.

8. The _death_ sentence rules out any hope of offender rehabilitation.

9. The U.S. Supreme Court held that no person under the age of _eighteen_ at the time of the crime can be executed.

10. The U.S. Supreme Court has held that executing the mentally retarded violates the _Eighth_ Amendment.

11. Only people who commit intentional or felony _murder_ may be executed.

12. Sentencing experts suspect that judges may be influenced by a defendant's gender, _race_ and social class.

13. Sentences which are _concurrent_ begin on the same day and run together.

14. The death penalty may also produce more violence than it prevents; the so-called _____ _brutalization_ effect.

15. More people are sentenced to death, and the death penalty is used more often, in nations with a large minority population. This is known as the _minority group threat._ hypothesis.

ESSAY

1. Summarize the legal restrictions limiting the use of the death penalty.

2. Define, compare, and contrast the five goals of modern sentencing. Which do you think should be the dominant goal? Explain your position.

3. List four factors that can legitimately affect sentencing decisions and three factors that are in direct violation of due process and equal protection.

4. Discuss the arguments for and against the death penalty in the U.S. Present and explain your position on the issue.

5. Discuss the arguments for and against three-strike type laws. Present and explain your position on the issue.

CHAPTER 9 ANSWER KEY

Multiple Choice

1. c [p. 203, LO3]	2. d [p. 201, LO1]	3. c [p. 210, LO6]	4. d [p. 209, LO5]	5. b [p. 203, LO1]
6. c [p. 205, LO2]	7. d [p. 205, LO3]	8. a [p. 204, LO3]	9. a [p. 204, LO5]	10. a [p. 205, LO3]
11. b [p. 205, LO3]	12. a [p. 212, LO6]	13. b [p. 213, LO6]	14. c [p. 214, LO6]	15. d [p. 215, LO8]
16. d [p. 214, LO7]	17. d [p. 204, LO3]	18. c [p. 213, LO7]	19. b [p. 205, LO3]	20. b [p. 206, LO5]
21. d [p. 223, LO9]	22. b [p. 218, LO8]	23. b [p. 215, LO9]	24. a [p. 203, LO3]	25. d [p. 205, LO2]
26. c [p. 212, LO7]	27. c [p. 210, LO6]	28. b [p. 215, LO9]	29. c [p. 205, LO2]	30. b [p. 219, LO8]

True/False

1. T [p. 207, LO5]	2. T [p. 208, LO6]	3. F [p. 209, LO6]	4. F [p. 220, LO8]	5. T [p. 208, LO6]
6. T [p. 205, LO3]	7. F [p. 212, LO7]	8. T [p. 203, LO2]	9. F [p. 214, LO7]	10. T [p. 209, LO6]
11. T [p. 204, LO3]	12. T [p. 205, LO4]	13. F [p. 223, LO9]	14. T [p. 204, LO3]	15. T [p. 219, LO9]

Fill-in-the-Blank

1. consecutive [p. 210, LO6]	2. guidelines [p. 207, LO6]	3. deterrence [p. 204, LO3]
4. desert [p. 205, LO4]	5. indeterminate [p. 207, LO6]	6. good [p. 210, LO6]
7. 25 [p. 217, LO8]	8. death [p. 220, LO8]	9. eighteen [p. 223, LO8]
10. Eighth [p. 223, LO8]	11. murder [p. 223, LO9]	12. race [p. 212, LO7]
13. concurrent [p. 210, LO6]	14. brutalization [p. 220, LO1]	15. minority-group-threat [p. 220, LO7]

Essay

1. **Summarize the legal restrictions limiting the use of the death penalty.**

   - *Ring v. Arizona*, the Court found that juries, not judges, must make the critical findings that send convicted killers to death row. The Court reasoned that the Sixth Amendment's right to a jury trial would be "senselessly diminished" if it did not allow jurors to decide whether a person deserves the death penalty.
   - The Court has limited the crimes for which the death penalty can be employed by ruling that it is not permissible to punish rapists, even those who rape children, with death. Only people who commit intentional or felony murder may be executed.

- The mentally ill may not be executed. In a 2002 case, *Atkins v. Virginia*, the Court also ruled that execution of mentally challenged criminals is "cruel and unusual punishment" prohibited by the Eighth Amendment.
- In *Roper v. Simmons* (2005), the Court set a limit of 18 years as the age of defendants who could be sentenced to death. The Court said that executing young teens violates "the evolving standards of decency that mark the progress of a maturing society" and that American society regards juveniles as less responsible than adult criminals.

[pp. 222-223, LO 9]

2. **Define, compare, and contrast the five goals of modern sentencing. Which do you think should be the dominant goal? Explain your position.**

The goals of sentencing include general deterrence, incapacitation, specific deterrence, retribution (just desert), rehabilitation, and equity restitution.

- **General Deterrence:** In order to deter criminal behavior; people will be too afraid to break the law if they believe that they will be caught and punished severely.
- **Specific Deterrence:** In order to deter criminal behavior; convince offenders that the pains of punishment are greater than the potential benefits of crime.
- **Incapacitation:** Incarcerate criminals because criminals will not be able to repeat their criminal acts while they are under state secure control and confinement.
- **Retribution:** Offenders should be punished and the punishment should be fair and just in a manner that is proportionate to the gravity of their crimes.
- **Rehabilitation:** Because society has failed them, many offenders have been forced to grow up in disorganized neighborhoods, have been the target of biased police officers, and are disadvantaged at home, at school, and in the job market. To compensate for these deprivations, the justice system is obligated to help these unfortunate people and not simply punish them for their misdeeds.
- **Equity Restitution**: Because criminals gain from their misdeeds, it seems both fair and just to demand that they reimburse society for the losses their crimes have caused. Convicted criminals should pay back their victims for their loss, the justice system for the costs of processing their case, and society for any disruption they may have caused.

[pp. 203-205, LO 2]

3. **List four factors that can legitimately affect sentencing decisions and three factors that are in direct violation of due process and equal protection.**

- Various factors that can legitimately influence the length of prison sentences, including the following:
  - The severity of the offense
  - The offender's prior criminal record
  - Whether the offender used violence
  - Whether the offender used weapons
  - Whether the crime was committed for money

- Judges may also be influenced by the defendant's social class, gender, age, and race—and even by victim characteristics. Consideration of such variables would be a direct violation of constitutional due process and equal protection, as well as of federal statutes, such as the Civil Rights Act.

[pp. 212-214, LO7]

4.   **Discuss the arguments for and against the death penalty in the U.S. Present and explain your position on the issue.**

The most severe sentence used in the United States is capital punishment, or execution. More than 14,500 confirmed executions have been carried out in America. Most of these executions have been for murder and rape. However, federal, state, and military laws have conferred the death penalty for other crimes, including robbery, and kidnapping. The federal government still has provisions for imposing the death penalty for certain crimes (e.g., espionage by a member of the armed forces, military desertion, acts of treason).

<u>In Support</u>

- Supporters argue that death is the "ultimate incapacitation" and the only one that can ensure that convicted killers can never be pardoned, be paroled, or escape.
- Proponents of capital punishment argue that executions serve as a strong deterrent for serious crimes.
- Putting dangerous criminals to death also conforms to the requirement that the punishment be proportional to the seriousness of the crime.
- The death penalty is justified because it represents the will of the people.
- The many legal controls and appeals currently in use make it almost impossible for an innocent person to be executed or for the death penalty to be used in a racist or capricious manner.
- Politicians favor the death penalty in the mistaken belief that the public overwhelmingly favors such harsh punishment for criminal offenders.

<u>Opposition</u>

- Critics of the death penalty believe capital punishment has no place in a mature democratic society.
- Because of the chances of error, a number of states have placed a moratorium on executions until the issue of errors in the process can be adequately addressed.
- The pressure to ensure convictions in homicide cases may lead to a higher rate of wrongful convictions in murder cases.
- Some argue it is morally wrong.
- Critics frown on the tremendous discretion used in seeking the death penalty and on the arbitrary manner in which it is imposed.
- Capital punishment may be tarnished by gender, racial, and ethnic and other biases.
- Abolitionists believe that executions are unnecessarily cruel and inhuman and come at a high moral and social cost.

[pp. 215-221, LO8]

5.   **Discuss the arguments for and against three-strike type laws. Present and explain your position on the issue.**

Overview: of Laws: Three-Strike type laws provide lengthy terms for any person convicted of three felony offenses, even if the third crime is relatively trivial. Generally these laws provide lengthy prison terms, usually 25 years to life, for any person convicted of three felony offenses. Approximately half the states have three-strike laws, but nearly all of them require that the third felony be a serious one. In California, however, any third felony can result in life in prison.

In Support

- Three-strike laws have also been challenged on constitutional grounds. Convictions have been upheld. In one case a man was sentenced to 50 years in prison for a third offense, where the third offense involved a petty crime (stealing $153 worth of videotapes). The Court ruled that the challenged sentences were not so grossly disproportionate as to violate the Eighth Amendment's prohibition against cruel and unusual punishment.
- Political appeal; these cases appeal to legislators being pressured by their constituents to "do something about crime."
- Three-strike laws satisfy the public's desire for retribution. Not only are they "just-desert" but criminals have been duly warned of the penalty enhancements if they keep offending.

Opposition

- Many "three-time criminals" are on the brink of aging out of crime; locking them up for life should have little effect on the crime rate. This theory argues that as a person ages their criminality is greatly reduced. Therefore these laws are errant as they tend to impact older criminals.
- These laws prompt questions and studies) seeking to determine whether they deter crime. Although a handful of studies report a deterrent effect, the vast majority show that three-strike laws have little or no effect on crime. The authors of two studies even found that there is more homicide in three-strike states, which suggests that those who face life in prison have a powerful incentive not to go down without a fight.
- Three-strike laws have also been challenged on constitutional grounds. For example, on March 6, 2003, the Supreme Court upheld the three-strike sentence of Leandro Andrade, a man sentenced to prison in California for 50 years for stealing $153 worth of videotapes.32 It also upheld the conviction of Gary Ewing, who appealed a prior 25-year sentence for stealing a set of golf clubs. In both cases the Court ruled that the challenged sentences were not so grossly disproportionate as to violate the Eighth Amendment's prohibition against cruel and unusual punishment.

[pp. 208-209, LO6]

CHAPTER 10

Community Sentences:
Probation, Intermediate Sanctions, and Restorative Justice

After studying this chapter, students will:

1. Be familiar with concept of community sentencing
2. Know the history of community sentences
3. Recognize the different types of probation sentences
4. Be familiar with the rules of probation
5. Know about the organization and administration of probation services
6. List and discuss the elements of a probation department's duties"
7. Be familiar with the legal rights of probationers
8. Debate the effectiveness of probation
9. Know what is meant by intermediate sanctions
10. Define restorative justice and discuss its merits

KEY TERMS AND CONCEPTS

probation (p. 230) A sentence entailing the conditional release of a convicted offender into the community under the supervision of the court (in the person of a probation officer), subject to certain conditions for a specified time.

judicial reprieve (p. 230) The common-law practice that allowed judges to suspend punishment so that convicted offenders could seek a pardon, gather new evidence, or demonstrate that they had reformed their behavior.

recognizance (p. 230) The medieval practice of allowing convicted offenders to go unpunished if they agreed to refrain from any further criminal behavior.

sureties (p. 230) In the Middle Ages, people responsible for the behavior of an offender released before trial.

probation rules (p. 231) Conditions or restrictions mandated by the court that must be obeyed by a probationer.

revocation (p. 231) An administrative act performed by a parole authority that removes a person from parole, or a judicial order by a court removing a person from parole or probation in response to a violation on the part of the parolee or probationer.

suspended sentence (p. 231) A prison term that is delayed while the defendant undergoes a period of community treatment. If the treatment is successful, the prison sentence is terminated.

pre-sentence investigation (p. 233) An investigation performed by a probation officer attached to a trial court after the conviction of a defendant.

intake (p. 233) The process in which a probation officer settles cases at the initial appearance before the onset of formal criminal proceedings; also, the process in which a juvenile referral is received and a decision is made to file a petition in the juvenile court, release the juvenile, or refer the juvenile elsewhere.

risk classification (p. 235) Classifying probationers so that they may receive an appropriate level of treatment and control.

motivational interviewing (p. 236) A technique that increases the probationer's awareness of his potential problems by asking him to visualize a better future and learn strategies to reach his goals.

day fees (p. 240) A program requiring probationers to pay some of the costs of their treatment.

intermediate sanctions (p. 241) Punishments that fall between probation and prison ("probation plus"). Community-based sanctions, including house arrest and intensive supervision, serve as alternatives to incarceration.

fine (p. 242) A money payment levied on offenders to compensate society for their misdeeds.

day fine (p. 242) A fine geared to the average daily income of the convicted offender in an effort to bring equity to the sentencing process.

forfeiture (p. 243) The seizure of personal property by the state as a civil or criminal penalty.

zero tolerance (p. 243) The practice of seizing all instrumentalities of a crime, including homes, boats, and cars. It is an extreme example of the law of forfeiture.

restitution (p. 243) A condition of probation in which the offender repays society or the victim of crime for the trouble and expense the offender caused.

monetary restitution (p. 243) A sanction requiring that convicted offenders compensate crime victims by reimbursing them for out-of-pocket losses caused by the crime. Losses can include property damage, lost wages, and medical costs.

community service restitution (p. 243) An alternative sanction that requires an offender to work in the community at such tasks as cleaning public parks or working with disabled children in lieu of an incarceration sentence.

shock probation (p. 244) A sentence in which offenders serve a short prison term before they begin probation, to impress them with the pains of imprisonment.

split sentence (p. 244) A practice that requires convicted criminals to spend a portion of their sentence behind bars and the remainder in the community.

intensive probation supervision (IPS) (p. 245) A type of intermediate sanction involving small probation caseloads and strict monitoring on a daily or weekly basis.

house arrest (p. 246) A form of intermediate sanction that requires the convicted offender spend a designated amount of time per week in his or her own home—such as from 5 p.m. Friday until 8 a.m. Monday.

electronic monitoring (EM) (p. 246) Requiring a convicted offender to wear a monitoring device as part of their community sentence. Typically part of a house arrest order, this enables the probation department to ensure that offenders are complying with court-ordered limitations on their freedom.

residential community corrections (RCC) (p. 247) A nonsecure facility, located in the community, that houses probationers who need a more secure environment. Typically, residents are free during the day to go to work, school, or treatment, and they return in the evening for counseling sessions and meals.

day reporting center (DRC) (p. 248) A nonresidential community-based treatment program.

restorative justice (p. 248) A view of criminal justice that focuses on crime as an act against the community rather than the state. Justice should involve all parties who are affected by crime—victims, criminals, law enforcement, and the community.

sentencing circles (p. 250) A type of sentencing in which victims, family members, community members, and the offender participate in an effort to devise fair and reasonable sanctions that are ultimately aimed at reintegrating the offender back into the community.

CHAPTER OUTLINE

I. **INTRODUCTION**
   1. Probation:
      a. A criminal sentence that suspends or delays a correctional term in a prison or jail so that, instead of being incarcerated, offenders are returned to the community for a period in which they must:
         i. Abide by certain conditions set forth by the court
         ii. Be supervised by a probation officer
      b. It is the most commonly used means of dispensing correctional treatment to convicted offenders
      c. Probation is a cost-effective alternative to incarceration

II. THE HISTORY OF PROBATION AND COMMUNITY SENTENCING

1. The common-law practices of judicial reprieve allowed judges to suspend punishment so that convicted offenders could seek pardon, gather new evidence, or demonstrate they reformed their behavior
2. Recognizance enabled convicted offenders to go unpunished if they agreed to refrain from further criminal behavior
3. Sometimes sureties were required:
   a. People who made themselves responsible for the behavior of an offender after he was released

A. John Augustus and the Creation of Probation

3. John Augustus of Boston is credited with originating community sentencing
   a. For over eighteen years, Augustus supervised close to 2000 convicted offenders and helped them get jobs and establish themselves in the community
   b. In 1878, Augustus's work inspired the Massachusetts's legislature to pass a law appointing a probation officer for Boston
   c. The probation concept soon became the most widely used correctional mechanism in the United States

III. PROBATION TODAY

1. There are approximately 2000 adult probation agencies in the United States
   a. Slightly more than half are associated with a state-level agency
   b. Remainder are at the county or municipal level
   c. About 30 states combine probation and parole into a single agency
2. Adult probation population grew about two percent per year between 1995-2008 until more than four million were on probation
   a. In 2009 the number slowly began to decline

A. Awarding Probation

1. Most probation orders involve a contract between the court and the offender in which a prison term or jail term is suspended
2. The probationer promises to obey probation rules
3. Revocation of probation means the community sentence is terminated and the original sentence is reinstated
4. Probationary sentences may be granted by federal and state courts
   a. In some cases, a jury may recommend probation
   b. Judges usually have the final say on the probationary sentence
5. More than one-half of all cases involve a direct sentence to probation
6. In about 1/4 of the cases, a judge will impose a jail sentence but immediately suspend it for probation
7. Probation is usually a defined period of time but can be as long as the sentence
8. About 10 percent receive some form of split sentence in which they must first serve a jail term before being released on probation
9. For misdemeanors, probation usually extends for the entire period of the jail sentence
   a. Felonies are more likely to warrant probationary periods that are actually shorter than the suspended prison sentences

        b. Typical felony probation is a little more than three years

B. Probation Eligibility
1. Today, probation is a means of offering a second chance and a way of reducing overcrowding in the correctional system
2. Many serious criminal offenders are given probation
    a. More than 30% of first-time felons are sentenced to probation
    b. About 15% of repeat felony offenders are given community sentences
    c. About 20% of all people convicted of violent felonies receive probation
3. There are two sides of probation:
    a. Treatment and rehabilitation of nondangerous offenders
    b. Supervision and control of criminals who might otherwise be incarcerated

C. Conditions of Probation
1. When granting probation, the court sets down certain conditions or rules of behavior which the probationer is bound to obey
2. Probation officers are given some latitude to set terms and conditions but the key conditions must be set by the judicial authority
3. Sometimes the rules and conditions reflect the circumstances of the crime
4. Capricious or cruel conditions and rules may not be set
5. Probationers may have their community supervision revoked if they violate the rules and conditions

D. Administration of Probation Services
1. Probation services are organized in various ways by the states that administer them
2. Some states have statewide services but each court controls its own services
3. Thirty-five states combine probation and parole services
4. Probation departments work closely with the courts they serve
5. A Chief Probation Officer (CPO) usually runs the probation office:
    a. Sets policy
    b. Supervises hiring
    c. Determines training needs
    d. May personally discuss with or recommend sentencing to the judge
6. Probation officers (PO) are the line staff and serve under the CPO
    a. An officers working style is influenced by both personal values and the department's general policies and orientation toward the goals of probation
7. Some probation officers view themselves as social workers
    a. Maintain a treatment orientation
    b. Goal is to help offenders adjust in the community
8. Others view themselves as law enforcers
    a. Concerned with:
        i. Supervision
        ii. Control
        iii. Public safety
9. Some officers are armed

E. Elements of Probation
1. Probation departments engage in five primary tasks:
    a. Investigation

    b. Intake

    c. Diagnosis/risk classification

    d. Supervision

    e. Treatments

2. Presentence Investigation — The supervising probation officer accumulates important information on the background of the offender

    a. A pre-sentence investigation serves as the basis for sentencing

    b. At the conclusion of most pre-sentence investigations, a recommendation is made to the presiding judge that reflects the department's sentencing posture

       i. This is a critical aspects of the report because the judge follows the recommendations in most cases

3. Intake — POs who conduct intake interviews may be looking to settle the case without court hearings

    a. The PO works with police, the offender, the victim, and others to develop an equitable resolution to the case

    b. If no resolution, the case is sent for a hearing

4. Diagnosis/Risk Classification — POs analyze the client's:

       i. Character

      ii. Attitudes

     iii. Behavior

    a. Most risk classification approaches employ such objective measures as the offender's:

       a) Age

       b) Employment status

       c) Drug abuse history

       d) Prior felony convictions

       e) Number of address changes in the year prior to sentencing

    b. Some departments are using standardized tests to predict failure and assign treatment such as the Level of Service Inventory – Revised (LSI-R)

    c. The emergence of standardized diagnostic tools and test has diminished the PO's individual role in diagnosis

5. Supervision — An important part of the probation officer's duties is monitoring clients in the community:

    a. Making sure they obey their probation orders

    b. Helping them to stay out of trouble

    c. This can mean

       i. Giving random drug test

      ii. Monitoring the family situation

     iii. Keeping in touch with employers

    d. Some officers have a control orientation:

       i. Believe in strict supervision

      ii. Quick to sanction offenders who violate rules

    e. Others are more treatment oriented

       i. Question the effectiveness of punitive sanctions and strict supervision

       f. New breed of younger probation officers more inclined to control and punish rule violators than their older counterparts.
          i. One reason for closer and more punitive supervision is the threat of litigation
         ii. Failure to supervise probationers can result in the officer and department being held legally liable for civil damages
       g. Several newly developed technologies are being used to aid supervision:
          i. Sleep pattern analysis technology
         ii. Ankle bracelets
    6. Treatment – Probation staff are assigned to carry a program of therapy designed to help the client deal with the problems that are suspected of being the cause of antisocial behavior
       a. Large caseloads limit opportunities for hands-on treatment
       b. Most probation efforts rely on community resources
       c. A number of innovative techniques are now being used
          i. Motivational interviewing
         ii. Cognitive behavioral therapy
  F. Legal Rights of Probationers
       a. A number of important legal issues surround probation
    1. Civil Rights: The Supreme Court has ruled that probationers have a unique status and are entitled to fewer constitutional protections. The following court cases are applicable here
       a. *Minnesota v. Murphy (1984)*
          i. Probation officer-client relationship is not confidential
       b. *Griffin v. Wisconsin (1987)*
          i. Probationer's home may be search with a warrant
       c. *United States v. Knights (2001)*
          i. Warrantless search of a probationer's home for the purposes of gathering criminal evidence is legal under some circumstances:
             a) Search based on reasonable suspicion that he committed another crime while on probation
             b) Submitting to searches was part of probation order
    2. Revocation Rights: A violation of the rules and conditions of probation can result in the revocation of the probation at which time the offender is placed in confinement
    3. Revocation will cause a hearing
    4. Due process is afforded to the offender
    5. Supreme Court cases applicable to due process for probationer:
       a. *Mempa v. Rhay (1967)*
          i. Probationer is constitutionally entitled to counsel in a revocation-of-probation proceeding
       b. *Morrissey v. Brewer (1972)*
          i. Informal inquiry be held to determine whether there was probable cause that a parolee had violated the conditions of parole
       c. *Gagnon v. Scarpelli (1973)*

        i. Probationers and parolees have a constitutionally limited right to legal counsel in revocation proceedings

    d. *Beardon v. Georgia (1983)*

        i. Judge cannot revoke a defendant's probation for failure to pay a fine and/or make restitution

    e. *United States v. Granderson (1994)*

        i. Helped clarify what can happen to a probationer whose community sentence is revoked

       ii. Unfair to force probationer to serve more time in prison than he would have served if originally incarcerated

G. How Successful is Probation?

    1. Probation is the most commonly used sentence

       a. Probation is considered humane and cost effective

          i. Incarceration costs $25,000 per year

          ii. Probation costs $2000 per year

    2. National data suggests that 60 percent of probationers successfully complete their probation, while 40 percent rearrested

    3. Most revocations occur for technical reasons during the first three months of probation

    4. Federal probationers show even better results, 30 percent failure rate

H. How Successful is Felony Probation?

    1. The RAND Corporation (a think tank) tracked the outcome of felony probation

       a. Traced 1,672 men convicted of felonies in California

       b. Found 65 percent were rearrested

       c. Found probation was the most common sentencing alternative to prison

       d. Felt that even with a high recidivism rate for probationers, the rate of recidivism was lower than if they had been incarcerated

I. Who Fails on Probation and Who Succeeds?

    1. Clients who have a history of criminal behavior, prior probation, and previous incarceration are the most likely to fail

    2. Probationers who are married with children, have lived in the area for two or more years, and are adequately employed are the most likely to be successful on probation

    3. Female probationers with stable marriages, are better educated and are employed full or part time do better on probation than male or female probationer who are single, less educated, and unemployed

J. The Future of Probation

    1. A number of initiatives are now ongoing or being suggested that may help shape the future of probation:

       a. Making probationers pay

          i. A fee is imposed to defray costs of probation

          ii. Massachusetts initiated day fees

             a)   Based on probationer's wages

       b. Making probation more effective

          i. Legislatures are instituting policies rewarding the most effective and efficient local departments

      c. Hot spot probation
         i. Police and community members form a supervision team that evaluates the client
      d. Area needs
         i. Organize caseloads around needs of the area and not the client
      e. Specialized probation
         i. Teams of probation officers take on clients convicted of one specific type of crime
      f. Private probation
         i. Contracting with companies that for a fee, engage in many typical probation activities
      g. Swift and sure punishment
         i. Punishment that is somewhat less than a full revocation may help reduce rule violations
  2. In many jurisdictions, traditional probation being supplemented by intermediate sanctions:
      a. Penalties that fall between traditional community supervision and confinement in jail or prison

IV.   INTERMEDIATE SANCTIONS

  1. Probation plus programs add restrictive penalties and conditions to traditional community service orders
      a. Feature treatment and rehabilitation over control and restraint
  2. These newer forms of community sentences have the potential to become reasonable alternatives to many of the economic and social problems faced by correctional administrators
  3. Advantages of intermediate sanctions:
      a. Less costly than jail or prison sentences
      b. Help the offender maintain family and community ties
      c. Can be structured to maximize security and maintain public safety
      d. Can be scaled in severity to correspond to the seriousness of the crime
      e. Can feature restoration and reintegration rather than punishment and ostracism
      f. May reduce need for future jail and prison construction
      g. Meet the need for developing community sentences that are fair, equitable, and proportional
      h. Can be designed to increase control over offenders whose serious or repeat crimes make a straight probation sentence inappropriate
      i. Serve as 'halfway back' strategies for offenders who violate conditions of their community release
  4. Intermediate sanctions are administered by probation departments and include:
      a. Intensive probation supervision
      b. House arrest
      c. Electronic monitoring
      d. Restitution orders
      e. Shock probation or split sentences

          f.   Residential corrections

     5. Intermediate sanctions also involve sentences administered independently of probation:

          a. Fines and forfeiture

          b. Pretrial programs

          c. Pretrial/post-trial residential programs

A. Fines

     3. Fines are monetary payments imposed on offenders as intermediate punishment

     4. Fines are an off-shoot of the common-law practice of requiring that compensation be paid to the victim and the state (*wergild*) for criminal acts

     5. In the United States, fines are most commonly applied in misdemeanor cases and lesser offenses

     6. Fines may be sole sanction but are usually combined with other punishments such as probation.

     7. Supreme Court in *Tate v. Short* (1971) recognized that incarcerating a person who is financially unable to pay a fine discriminates against the poor

     8. Day fines — A program geared to impose fines based on the offender's daily net income

B. Forfeiture

     1. Forfeiture is an intermediate sanction with a financial basis (civil and criminal)

     2. It involves the seizure of money and goods related to the crime

     3. Origins in the Middle Ages

          a. Forfeiture of estate was a mandatory result of most felony convictions

     4. Forfeiture was reintroduced to the United States with the passage of the Racketeer Influenced and Corrupt Organization (RICO) Act and the Continuing Criminal Enterprise Act

          a. Allow the seizure of any property derived from illegal conspiracies or enterprises

     5. Originally designed to apply to ongoing criminal conspiracies such as drug or pornography rings, now being applied to a far-ranging series of criminal acts

          a. More than 100 federal statures use forfeiture of property as punishment

     6. Forfeiture has been criticized for its overzealous application by government (seizing a yacht for a small amount of marijuana), this is known as zero tolerance

C. Restitution

     1. Intermediate sanction that requires offenders to pay back victims:

          a. Monetary restitution (victims)

          b. Community service restitution (serving community)

     2. Can offer offenders alternative to jail

     3. Restitution also gives the community something of value without asking it to foot the bill

     4. Victim's loss is determined, and restitution is based upon loss

     5. Community service performed in:

          a. Public nursing homes

          b. Drug treatment unit

      c. Shelter

      d. Works program

      e. Hospital

   6. Financial restitution is:

      a. Inexpensive to administer

      b. Helps avoid stigma

      c. Provides compensation for victims of crime

   7. Restitution is viewed as a successful offender program

D. Shock Probation and Split Sentencing

   1. Split sentencing

      a. Alternative sanction where offender samples prison and community service

      b. Approximately 10 percent given split sentencing

   2. Shock probation

      a. Resentencing an offender to probation after a short prison stay

      b. Shock comes because the offender originally received a long maximum sentence but is then eligible for release to community supervision at the discretion of the judge (usually within 90 days of incarceration)

   3. Some states have linked short prison stay with a boot camp experience, shock incarceration

   4. Programs have been praised as ways to limit prison time but criticized as defeating the purpose of probation (avoiding incarceration)

E. Intensive Probation Supervision

      a. In use in about forty states with about one hundred thousand clients; also called IPS programs

      b. Probation officers monitor clients under close supervision, small case loads – 15-40 clients

      c. IPS programs have three goals:

         i. Decarceration

         ii. Control

         iii. Reintegration

      d. Probation officer has a great deal of contact with client to achieve goals

   1. Evaluations of IPS

      a. IPS programs are a mixed bag

         i. They are more serious criminals who might otherwise have been incarcerated

      b. Higher arrest rate than probationers

      c. Evidence shows that IPS clients have better records than similar offenders who are incarcerated

      d. Those with good employment records seem to do better than underemployed or unemployed

      e. Younger offenders who commit petty crimes are the most likely to fail

      f. Might be more effective if combined with particular treatment modalities such as:

         i. Cognitive-behavioral treatment which stresses life skills:

            a) Problem solving

            b) Social skills

	c)	Negotiation skills
	d)	Management of emotion
	e)	Values enhancement

F. House Arrest
 1. Requires convicted offenders to spend extended time in their own home while being monitored
 2. Programs vary by jurisdiction
 3. No conclusive data available as to success/failure of program. Data is mixed
 4. Advantages:
  a. Reducing costs
  b. Reducing overcrowding in the correctional system

G. Electronic Monitoring
 1. Electronic Monitoring (EM) devices are used to monitor and manage obedience
  a. Some utilize continuous signaling devices
  b. Newer electronic monitoring systems now feature automatic tracking devices that limit offender's movement to acceptable areas
  c. Some rely on global positions satellite technology
  d. Some utilize victim notification systems to alert victim if offender is close
  e. Field monitoring device or "drive-by" units
 2. Supporters claim EM has benefits of relatively low cost and high security, helps offender avoid pains of imprisonment in overcrowded dangerous state facilities
 3. Critics claim that the evidence EM can lower recidivism rate is thin, and may not work as a standalone program
  a. May be more effective if combined with:
   i. Social interventions and counseling

H. Residential Community Corrections (RCC)
   i. Considered the most secure intermediate sanction
  a. A freestanding nonsecure building that is not part of a prison or jail and houses pretrial and adjudicated adults
  b. Residents regularly depart:
   i. To work
   ii. To attend school
   iii. Participate in treatment activities and programs
  c. Today, the community correctional facility is a vehicle to provide intermediate sanctions as well as a prerelease center for those about to be paroled
  d. RCC can be used as a condition of probation
  e. Probation departments run RCC programs. More than 2000 public and 2,500 private, nonprofit programs exist
 1. Day reporting centers (DRCs)
  a. Provide a single location to which a variety of clients can report for supervision and treatment
  b. Used as a step up in security for probationers who have failed in the community and as a step down for jail or prison inmates

      c. Evaluations show DRCs can be successful at reducing recidivism

      d. Seem to work better with older more experienced offenders

      e. Younger offenders and those with alcohol problems, criminal companions, and poor living situations are likely to fail

V. RESTORATIVE JUSTICE PROGRAMS

1. Some experts believe that the new intermediate sanctions add a punitive aspect to community sentencing that can hinder rehabilitation efforts

2. Restorative justice advocates suggest a policy based on restoring the damage caused by crime and creating a system of justice that includes all the parties harmed by the criminal act:

      a. Victim

      b. Offender

      c. Community

      d. Society

3. Expert John Braithwaite calls for reintegrative shaming, which shames the offender's *deeds* not the offender

4. Critical element of reintegrative shaming occurs when the offenders themselves begin to understand and recognize their wrongdoing and shame

5. To be reintegrative, shaming must be:

      a. Brief and controlled

      b. Followed by ceremonies of:

         i. Forgiveness

         ii. Apology

         iii. Repentance

A. The Concept of Restoration

1. Traditional justice system, little is done to involve the community in the justice process

      a. Relies on:

         i. Punishment

         ii. Stigma

         iii. Disgrace

2. Needed is a justice policy that repairs the harm caused by crime and includes all parties that have suffered from that harm

3. Important aspect is that offenders accept accountability for actions and responsibility for the harm caused

4. Restoration involves turning the justice system into a healing process

5. The effectiveness of justice ultimately depends on the stake a person has in the community

B. Restoration Programs

1. Programs try to involve all parties involved in criminal act

2. Program generally includes:

      a. Recognition that offender caused injury

      b. Restitution and apology

      c. Community support

3. Repair the victim's injury and reintegrate the offender, using the community to help
4. Program tools include:
   a. Mediation
   b. Negotiation
   c. Consensus building
   d. Peacemaking
5. In some Native American communities, people accused of breaking the law meet with community members, victims, village elders and agents of the justice system in a sentencing circle
   a. All members express their feelings about the act that was committed and raise questions or concerns
   b. Accused can express regret
   c. People may suggest ways offender can make things up to the community
C. Restoration in Practice
   1. Restorative policies are being adopted around the world and embraced on many levels in the justice system:
      a. Schools:
         i. Some schools have employed restorative justice practices in order to deal with students who are involved in drug and alcohol abuse
      b. Police Programs:
         i. Restorative justice also has been implemented when crime is first encountered by police
         ii. It relies on criminal justice policy makers incorporating restorative principles
      c. Pre trial Programs
         i. Conferencing:
            a) Aim to divert offenders from the justice system by offering them the opportunity to attend a conference to discuss and resolve the offense instead of being charged and appearing in court
            b) Lasts 1 to 2 hours
            c) Attended by:
               1. Victims and supporters
               2. Offenders and supporters
               3. Other relevant parties
      d. Court Programs
         i. The courts utilize restorative justice by diverting the formal court process
            a) Encourage meeting and reconciliation
            b) Crime victims and offender come together
            c) Facilitate financial compensation
   2. Restorative justice has found a niche all over the world
D. The Challenge of Restorative Justice
   1. Although it has promise, there are concerns
      a. Do programs reach all community members?

      b.   Programs must be aware of cultural and social differences. What may be considered restorative in one subculture may be considered insulting and damaging in another

      c.   Greatest challenge is difficult task of balancing needs of offenders and victims

  2. Programs risk focusing on offender and turning off the victim and the victim's advocates and conversely when focusing on victim's needs

  3. Program still faces a number of obstacles but it has promise

CHAPTER SUMMARY

Probation is a criminal sentence that suspends or delays a correctional term. The offender on probation has been convicted of a crime. Instead of being incarcerated, the offender is returned to the community to abide to certain conditions set forth by the court under the supervision of a probation officer. The roots of probation can be traced back to English common law. The practice of judicial reprieve allowed judges to suspend punishment so that convicted offenders could seek a pardon, gather new evidence, or demonstrate that they had reformed. John Augustus is credited with originating the modern community corrections concept.

On probation, the offender is subject to certain rules and conditions. Most probation orders involve a contract between the court and the offender. If the rules are violated, probation may be revoked. Revocation means that the community sentence is terminated and the original sentence of incarceration is enforced. Some offenders receive some form of split sentence in which they must first serve a jail term before probation. There are two distinct sides to probation, the treatment and rehabilitation of non-dangerous offenders deserving of a second chance; and supervision and control of criminals who might otherwise be incarcerated.

The typical probation department performs the following major functions: supervise or monitor cases, attempt to rehabilitate, investigate the lives of convicted offenders, collect fines due the court, and interview complainants and defendants. They are also charged with five primary tasks: investigation, intake, diagnosis, treatment supervision, and risk classification.

Probation is undergoing dramatic changes. Traditional probation is being supplemented by intermediate sanctions. Intermediate sanctions include programs that are usually administered by probation departments: intensive probation supervision, house arrest, electronic monitoring, restitution orders, shock probation, split sentences, and residential community corrections. Advocates point that intermediate sanctions offer effective alternatives to prisons and jails, have the potential to save money, may reduce the need for future prison and jail construction, and also help meet the need for developing community sentences that are fair, equitable, and proportional. Other forms of intermediate sanctions include fines, restitution, shock probation, and split sentences.

Intensive probation supervision (IPS) or intensive supervision programs have been implemented in some form in about forty states and today include about one hundred thousand clients. IPS programs involve small caseloads of fifteen to forty clients kept under close watch by probation officers. IPS programs typically have three primary goals: decarceration, control, and reintegration. IPS initiatives include house arrest, electronic monitoring devices, and residential community corrections which include day reporting centers.

Some crime experts believe that rather than reducing crime and recidivism, policies based on getting tough on crime, even intermediate sanctions, cause crime rates to fluctuate higher and offenders to commit more crime. Restorative justice advocates suggest a policy based on restoring the damage caused by crime and creating a system of justice that includes all the parties harmed by the criminal act. An important aspect of achieving these goals is that offenders accept accountability for their actions and responsibility for the harm their actions caused. Only then can they be restored as productive members of their community. Restoration involves turning the justice system into a healing process rather than a distributor of retribution and revenge. Restorative justice is being embraced on many levels in the justice system such as schools, police, and courts. Possibly the greatest challenge to restorative justice is the difficult task of balancing the needs of offenders with those of their victims.

DISCUSSION QUESTIONS

1. What is the purpose of probation? Identify some conditions of probation and discuss the responsibilities of the probation officer.

2. Discuss the procedures involved in probation revocation. What are the rights of the probationer? Is probation a privilege or a right?

3. Should a convicted criminal make restitution to the victim? When is restitution inappropriate? Could it be considered a "bribe"?

4. Should offenders be fined on the basis of the seriousness of what they did or in terms of to their ability to pay? Is it fair to base day fines on wages? Should offenders be punished more severely because they are financially successful? Does house arrest involve a violation of personal freedom? Does wearing an ankle bracelet smack of "Big Brother"? Would you want the government monitoring your daily activities? Do you agree that criminals can be restored through community interaction? Considering the fact that recidivism rates are so high, are traditional sanctions a waste of time and restorative ones the wave of the future?

MEDIA TOOLS

Partnerships in community corrections involve policing agencies and correctional agencies. The International Association of Chiefs of Police (IACP) has produced a video that shows three partnerships in targeting criminality. View "Targeting Criminality: Successful Police-Corrections Partnerships provided by the IACP. View the video at: http://www.theiacp.org/PublicationsGuides/ResearchCenter/Projects/ViolenceReductionStrategies/TargetingCriminalityVideo/tabid/254/Default.aspx

To learn more about intermediate sanctions and research several intermediate sanctions programs visit the United States Department of Justice, Office of Justice Programs, Office of Juvenile

Justice and Delinquency Prevention's website on intermediate sanctions. The website can be found at: http://www.ojjdp.gov/mpg/intermediate_sanctions.aspx

The Bureau of Justice Statistics website on probation provides a wealth of data regarding individuals on probation and has a frequently asked questions section regarding probation. A good starting point if you are interested in probation research. The website can be found at: http://bjs.ojp.usdoj.gov/index.cfm?ty=tp&tid=151

PRACTICE TEST BANK

MULTIPLE CHOICE

1. What term best describes the process where "a community sentence is terminated and restored to the original sentence"?
    a. Restoration
    b. Revocation
    c. Reversion
    d. Reconciliation

2. What duty of a probation officer involves the officer analyzing the offender's character, attitude, and behavior?
    a. Intake
    b. Pre-sentence investigation
    c. Diagnosis/Risk classification
    d. Supervision

3. Probationers with the listed characteristics are most likely to fail except for probationers who
    a. have grown up in troubled households.
    b. have lived part of their lives in foster homes.
    c. have a history of instability.
    d. are married with children.

4. Who is generally responsible for administering policy, managing, and directing a probation department?
    a. First Supervision Officer
    b. Chief Probation Officer
    c. Captain of Probation
    d. Head Probation Manager

5. Which probation initiative uses teams of probation officers to take on clients convicted of one specific type of crime, such as drug offenses or domestic violence?
    a. Hot Spot probation
    b. Swift and Sure probation
    c. Private probation
    d. Specialized probation

6. Risk classification is the practice of classifying probationers so that they may receive an appropriate level of treatment and
    a. control.
    b. personal problems.
    c. severity of offense.
    d. prior record.

7. Which of the listed sanctions involves the seizure of goods and instrumentalities related to the commission or outcome of a criminal act?
    a. Fine
    b. Wergild
    c. Forfeiture
    d. No tolerance

8. A condition of probation that actually involves a jail term is known as
    a. boot camp.
    b. shock probation.
    c. split probation.
    d. split sentence.

9. Intermediate sanctions are the group of sanctions between
    a. jail and prison.
    b. prison and parole.
    c. juvenile court and transfer to adult court.
    d. probation and prison.

10. Who is generally responsible for carrying out the actual monitoring and treatment of probationers?
    a. Judge
    b. Chief probation officer
    c. Probation officer
    d. Victim advocate

11. A fine geared to the average daily income of the offender is known as a
    a. net fine.
    b. per diem fine.
    c. relative fine.
    d. day fine.

12. Which of the following is not considered a goal of Intensive Probation Supervision?
    a. Decarceration
    b. Control
    c. Incarceration
    d. Reintegration

13. Requiring an offender to give money to the victim as reimbursement for costs associated with the crime is called
    a. monetary day fine.
    b. monetary restitution.
    c. monetary levying.
    d. monetary tariff.

14. Picking up trash, helping out in a nursing home, and removing graffiti are examples of
    a.   financial restitution.
    b.   day laboring.
    c.   parole.
    d.   community service restitution.

15. Probation with a greater degree of supervision and assistance is referred to as
    a.   strict probation.
    b.   supervised surveillance probation.
    c.   aggressive supervised probation.
    d.   intensive probation supervision.

16. In order to better manage offender obedience during home confinement, the confinement is often combined with
    a.   electronic monitoring.
    b.   residential community corrections placement.
    c.   halfway house treatment.
    d.   split sentences.

17. All of the following are primary tasks associated with probation case administration except
    a.   risk classification.
    b.   intake.
    c.   treatment.
    d.   deliberations.

18. When compared to otherwise free citizens, the U.S. Supreme Court has ruled that probationers are entitled to
    a.   more Constitutional protections than free citizens.
    b.   the same amount of Constitutional protections as free citizens.
    c.   less Constitutional protections than free citizens.
    d.   no Constitution protections—based upon their unique criminally adjudicated status.

19. Who is credited with originating the modern concept of probation in America?
    a.   Alexander Maconochie
    b.   Zebulon Brockway
    c.   Michael Tonry
    d.   John Augustus

20. Which one of the listed clients to day reporting centers seems to be the most successful?
    a.   Clients with alcohol problems
    b.   Clients with criminal companions
    c.   Clients with poor living situations
    d.   Clients who receive counseling

21. According to restorative justice proponents, the traditional model of justice relies on many aspects except
    a.   punishment.
    b.   stigma.
    c.   disgrace.
    d.   repentance.

22. Restorative programs typically involve all of the parties affected by an offender's act. These parties include all of the listed except
    a.   the victim.
    b.   the presiding judge.
    c.   the offender.
    d.   the community.

23. Many levels of the criminal justice system are embracing restorative justice. There are restorative justice programs in all of the listed levels except
    a.   schools.
    b.   police programs.
    c.   parole programs.
    d.   pretrial programs.

24. What serves as the basis for sentencing to determine whether a convicted offender will be granted community release or be sentenced to secure confinement?
    a.   Offender screening investigation
    b.   Pre-sentence investigation
    c.   Parole offender investigation
    d.   Offender rehabilitation investigation

25. Intermediate sanctions offer effective alternatives to
    a.   parole.
    b.   prisons and jails.
    c.   pre-trial diversion.
    d.   pardon.

26. What concept requires convicted offenders to spend extended periods of time in their own home as an alternative to an incarceration sentence?
    a.   Residential confinement center
    b.   Home therapy
    c.   House arrest
    d.   Electronic monitoring

27. A sentence where an offender serves a short prison term before being released to probation is known as
    a.   pardon.
    b.   shock probation.
    c.   probation incarceration.
    d.   tethering.

28. What U.S. Supreme Court case upheld the legality of a warrantless search of a probationer's home for the purposes of gathering criminal evidence?
    a. *United States v. Knights*
    b. *United States v. Brooks*
    c. *United States v. Duane*
    d. *United States v. Raider*

29. With regard to revocation proceedings, in *Gagnon v. Scarpelli*, the U.S. Supreme Court held that both probationers and parolees have a constitutionally limited right to
    a. appeal.
    b. challenge.
    c. legal counsel.
    d. initiate a peremptory challenge.

30. Which of the listed individuals is most likely to fail Intensive Probation Supervision?
    a. Offenders with good employment records
    b. Older offenders
    c. Unemployed offenders
    d. Young offenders who commit petty crimes

TRUE/FALSE

1. T F Probationers, not parolees have a constitutionally limited right to legal counsel in revocation proceedings.

2. T F A probation officer's working style is influenced by personal values, but not by the probation department's general policies.

3. T F Due process protections do not apply to the probation revocation process.

4. T F Pre-sentence investigations are completed to assist the jury as they formulate a convicted offender's sentence.

5. T F Probation is a noncriminal sanction.

6. T F The new breed of younger probation officers are more inclined to control and punish rule violations than their older counterparts.

7. T F Probationers have the same Fourth Amendment rights as ordinary citizens.

8. T F As part of each client's entry into a probation program, an assessment is made about the "risk level" that the client poses to the community and to themselves.

9.   T   F   A probationer's home may not be searched unless the probation officer establishes probable cause and obtains a search warrant that has been approved by a judge.

10.   T   F   The probation officer-client relationship is confidential, in the same manner that attorney-client and physician-patient relationships are confidential.

11.   T   F   Most probation revocations occur for "technical" violations during the first three months of the probation sentence.

12.   T   F   National data indicate that approximately 85% of probationers successfully complete their probation sentence.

13.   T   F   Intensive probation supervision clients have a high failure rate because they are more serious criminals who might otherwise be incarcerated.

14.   T   F   One of the larger challenges to restorative justice programs is the difficult task of balancing the needs of the court with the needs of the offender.

15.   T   F   No single definition of restorative justice has been determined.

FILL-IN-THE-BLANK

1.   The most secure form of intermediate sanctions is _____ community corrections.

2.   _____ is a criminal sentence that suspends or delays a correctional term in a prison or jail.

3.   Community sentences enable offenders to be closely supervised in the _____ by trained personnel who can help reestablish good behavior.

4.   The practice of _____ allowed judges to suspend punishment so that convicted offenders could seek a pardon or gather new evidence to demonstrate they had reformed.

5.   A _____ investigation serves as the basis for sentencing and controls whether the convicted offender will be granted community release or be sentenced to secure confinement.

6.   Probationers typically receive a _____ that assigns them to a level and type of supervision on the basis of their individual case and personal needs.

7. During the course of a probation term, a violation of the rules or terms of the probation sentence can result in a _____ of the probation sentence.

8. Most revocations occur for technical violations during the first _____ months of the probation sentence.

9. In a typical probation department the _____ probation officer sets policy, supervises hiring, determines training needs, and may personally discuss with or recommend sentence to a judge.

10. By definition, intermediate sanctions are a group of punishments that fall between _____ and prison.

11. Restitution can take the form of _____restitution, where the offender is responsible to pay back the victim.

12. Split sentences are closely associated to _____incarceration.

13. The restoration portion of restorative justice involves turning the justice system into a ___ _____ process rather than a distribution of retribution and revenge.

14. Electronic monitoring is frequently combined with_____ arrest.

15. Advocates of _____ justice suggest a policy based on restoring the damage caused by crime and creating a system of justice that includes the victim, offender, community, and society.

ESSAY

1. Explain and discuss the restorative justice approach. What are some the criticisms that victims might have about this approach? What is your opinion on restorative justice? Explain your position.

2. What are the characteristics that distinguish those who fail and those who succeed on probation? What could be done to better assist the failure-prone?

3. Define intermediate sanctions and provide examples. What are the arguments in favor of using such sanctions instead of imprisoning the offender?

4. Probation officers engage in five primary tasks. Identify and explain three.

5. Three United States Supreme Court cases are presented in this chapter that found probationers have a unique status and therefore are entitled to fewer constitutional protections. Explain the findings of two of the cases.

CHAPTER 10 ANSWER KEY

Multiple Choice

1. b [p. 231, LO4]   2. c [p. 233, LO6]   3. d [p. 239, LO8]   4. b [p. 233, LO5]   5. d [p. 240, LO8]

6. a [p. 235, LO6]   7. c [p. 243, LO9]   8. d [p. 244, LO9]   9. d [p. 241, LO9]   10. c [p. 235, LO5]

11. d [p. 242, LO3]   12. c [p. 245, LO9]   13. b [p. 243, LO9]   14. d [p. 244, LO9]   15. d [p. 245, LO3]

16. a [p. 246, LO3]   17. d [p. 233, LO5]   18. c [p. 236, LO7]   19. d [p. 230, LO2]   20. d [p. 248, LO8]

21. d [p. 249, LO10]   22. b [p. 250, LO10]   23. c [p. 250, LO10]   24. b [p. 233, LO5]   25. b [p. 241, LO9]

26. c [p. 246, LO9]   27. b [p. 244, LO9]   28. a [p. 236, LO7]   29. c [p. 238, LO7]   30. d [p. 246, LO8]

True/False

1. F [p. 238, LO7]   2. F [p. 233, LO5]   3. F [p. 238, LO7]   4. F [p. 233, LO5]   5. F [p. 229, LO2]

6. T [p. 235, LO6]   7. F [p. 236, LO7]   8. T [p. 235, LO6]   9. F [p. 236, LO7]   10. F [p. 236, LO7]

11. T [p. 238, LO8]   12. F [p. 238, LO8]   13. T [p. 245, LO8]   14. F [p. 252, LO10]   15. T [p. 252, LO10]

Fill-in-the-Blank

1. residential [p. 247, LO9]   2. Probation [p. 230, LO1]   3. community [p. 230, LO1]

4. judicial reprieve [p. 230, LO2]   5. pre-sentence [p. 233, LO5]   6. risk classification [p. 235, LO6]

7. revocation [p. 237, LO7]   8. three [p. 238, LO7]   9. chief [p. 233, LO5]

10. probation [p. 241, LO9]   11. monetary [p. 243, LO9]   12. shock [p. 244, LO9]

13. healing [p. 249, LO10]   14. house [p. 246, LO9 , LO 3]   15.restorative [p. 248, LO10]

Essay

1.   **Explain and discuss the restorative justice approach. What are some the criticisms that victims might have about this approach? What is your opinion on restorative justice? Explain your position.**

Restorative justice is based on restoring the damage caused by crime and creating a system of justice that includes all the parties harmed by the criminal act: the victim, the offender, the community, and society.

Restorative justice models try to remove the stigma associated with being a criminal offender---a stigma that sets the offender apart from normative society and undermines their potential for change. The idea is to reintegrate the offender by making them realize that although their actions have caused harm, they are still valuable people—people who can be reaccepted by society. A critical element includes the point when the offenders themselves begin to understand and recognize their wrongdoing and shame. The traditional justice system has done little to involve the community in the justice process. What has developed is a system of coercive punishments administered by bureaucrats that is inherently harmful to offenders and reduces the likelihood that they will ever again become productive members of society. The intended result of the process is to repair injuries suffered by the victim and the community, while ensuring reintegration of the offender. Negotiation, mediation, consensus building, and peacemaking have been part of the dispute resolution process in European and Asian communities for centuries.

Restorative programs face criticisms from victim advocates including questions on the program's focus. Programs focusing on the offender may turn off victims and their advocates. Some believe that victims' rights are threatened by features of the restorative justice process, such as respectful listening to the offender's story and consensual dispositions. These features seem affronts to a victim's claim of the right to be seen as a victim, to insist on the offender being branded a criminal, to blame the offender, and not to be "victimized all over again by the process." Many victims do want apology, if it is heartfelt and easy to get. But some victims desire to put the traumatic incident behind them, to retrieve stolen property being held for use at trial, and to be assured that the offender will receive treatment he is thought to need if he is not to victimize someone else. For victims such as these, restorative justice processes can seem unnecessary at best

[pp. 248-252, LO10]

2.   **What are the characteristics that distinguish those who fail and those who succeed on probation? What could be done to better assist the failure-prone?**

Many probationers have grown up in troubled households in which family members are or have been incarcerated and/or are drug abusers. Others have lived part of their lives in foster homes or state institutions and have suffered high rates of physical and sexual abuse. This sort of deprived background often makes it difficult for probationers to comply with the rules of probation and forgo criminal activity. Surveys indicate that almost 20 percent of probationers suffer from mental illness and that those with a history of instability are most likely to be rearrested. Prior record is also related to probation success; clients who have a history of criminal behavior, prior probation, and previous incarceration are the most likely to fail. Also as probation sentences have become more common, caseloads now contain significant numbers of serious repeat offenders, a group that is difficult to treat and control.

In contrast, probationers who are married with children, have lived in the area for two or more years, and are adequately employed are the most likely to be successful on probation. Among female probationers, those who have stable marriages, are better educated, and are employed are more likely to complete probation orders successfully than male or female probationers who are single, less educated, and unemployed.

A number of initiatives that are now ongoing or being suggested may help shape the future of probation:

- *Making Probationers Pay:* At least 25 states now impose some form of fee on probationers to defray the cost of community corrections.
- *Making Probation More Effective:* Legislatures are instituting policies that reward the most effective and efficient local departments. In 2008, the Arizona legislature established an incentive system that rewards departments with up to 40 percent of any cost savings in each county resulting from a reduction in probation revocations. The money can then be used to fund substance abuse treatment, community supervision services, and victim services.
- *Hotspot Probation:* These probation initiatives involve police officers, probation agents, neighbors, and social service professionals in community supervision teams. Using a team approach, they

provide increased monitoring of offenders through home visits and drug testing. They also work with the offenders to ease reentry through offender creation of work crews that participate in community cleanups, work on vacant houses, and participate in other projects.

- *Area Needs*: Some experts suggest that probation caseloads be organized around area needs rather than client needs.
- *Specialized Probation:* Special probation, in which teams of probation officers take on clients convicted of one specific type of crime, such as drug offenses or domestic violence, rather than treating a mixed bag of offenders. Focusing on specialized caseloads enables probation officers to develop specific treatment and control skills.
- *Private Probation:* Private probation involves contracting traditional probation services (e.g., supervision, breathalyzer tests) to a private entity. By utilizing private probation for low-risk offenders, state probation departments can commit more resources to high-risk offenders.

[p. 239, LO8]

3.   **Define intermediate sanctions and provide examples. What are the arguments in favor of using such sanctions instead of imprisoning the offender?**

Intermediate sanctions are penalties that fall between traditional community supervision and confinement in jail or prison. These programs add extra sanctions featuring rehabilitation and treatment as supplements to traditional probation sentences. Examples of these programs include fines, day fines, asset forfeiture, shock probation, split sentencing, house arrest and intensive supervision.

Arguments for intermediate sanctions include:

- They are less costly than jail or prison sentences
- They help the offender maintain family and community ties
- They can be structured to maximize security and maintain public safety
- They can be scaled in severity to correspond to the seriousness of the crime
- They can feature restoration and reintegration rather than punishment and ostracism
- By siphoning off offenders from the secure correctional system, they reduce the need for future prison and jail construction
- Intermediate sanctions help meet the need to develop community sentences that are fair, equitable, and proportional
- They can be designed to increase control over probationers whose serious or repeat crimes make a straight probation sentence inappropriate, yet for whom a prison sentence would be unduly harsh and counterproductive
- Intermediate sanctions can potentially be used as halfway-back strategies for offenders who violate the conditions of their community release. Rule violators can be placed under increasingly more intensive supervision before actual incarceration is required

[pp. 241-248, LO9]

4.   **Probation officers engage in five primary tasks. Identify and explain three.**

Pre-Sentence Investigation. In the investigative stage, the supervising probation officer accumulates important information on the background and activities of the offender being considered for probation. This pre-sentence investigation serves as the basis for sentencing and controls whether the convicted defendant will be granted community release or sentenced to secure confinement. In the event that the offender is placed on probation, the investigation becomes useful as a tool to shape treatment and supervision efforts.

The style and content of pre-sentence investigations may vary among jurisdictions and also among individual POs within the same jurisdiction. Some departments require voluminous reports covering every aspect of the defendant's life. Other departments require that officers stick to the basic facts, such as the defendant's age, race, sex, and previous offense record.

At the conclusion of most pre-sentence investigations, a recommendation is made to the presiding judge that reflects the department's sentencing posture on the case at hand. This is a crucial aspect of the report, because the sentencing judge usually follows the probation department's recommendation. Numerous factors may contribute to a recommendation of community treatment; among the most critical are the investigator's conclusion that the defendant is someone whom probation officers can work with and effectively treat. Equally important is the belief that the perspective probationer will be able to abide by both legal and institutional rules.

Intake. Probation officers who conduct intake interviews may be looking to settle the case without the necessity of a court hearing. The probation officer will work with all parties involved in the case— offender, victim, police officer, and so on—to design an equitable resolution of the case. If the intake process is successful, the probation officer may settle the case without further court action, recommend restitution or other compensation, or recommend unofficial or informal probation. If an equitable solution cannot be found, the case would be filed for a court hearing.

Diagnosis/Risk Classification. In order to select appropriate treatment modes, probation officers analyze the client's character, attitudes, and behavior. An effective diagnosis integrates all that has been learned about the individual, organized in such a way as to facilitate the establishment of future treatment goals. Based on the risk level diagnosis, some clients may receive frequent (intensive) supervision in which they are contacted by their supervising probation officer almost every day, whereas those considered low risk are assigned to minimum monitoring. A number of risk assessment classification approaches are now used, but most employ such objective measures as the offender's age, employment status, drug abuse history, prior felony convictions, and number of address changes in the year prior to sentencing.

Supervision. An important part of the probation officer's duties is monitoring clients in the community, making sure they obey their probation orders, and helping them to stay out of trouble. In some cases this can mean giving random drug tests, monitoring the family situation, and keeping in touch with employers. Some officers have a control orientation, believe in strict supervision and are quick to sanction offenders who violate rules. Others are more treatment oriented and question the effectiveness of punitive sanctions and strict supervision.

Treatment. Probation staff are assigned to carry, a program of therapy designed to help the client deal with the problems that are suspected of being the cause of her or his antisocial behavior. In years past, the probation staff had primary responsibility for supervision and treatment, but today's large caseloads limit opportunities for hands-on treatment; most probation treatment efforts rely on community resources. Treatment protocols may vary according to client needs. Some of those who have a drinking problem may be asked to participate in a community-based 12-step program; others might spend time in a residential detoxification center. A spousal abuser may be required to enroll in an anger management program. A probation officer may work with teachers and other school officials to develop a program designed to help a young probationer reduce his or her truancy and avoid becoming a "dropout."

[pp. 233-236, LO6]

5.   **Three United States Supreme Court cases are presented in this chapter that found probationers have a unique status and therefore are entitled to fewer constitutional protections. Explain the findings of two of the cases.**

Minnesota v. Murphy (1984). The probation officer–client relationship is not confidential, as are physician–patient and or attorney–client relationships. If a probationer admits to committing a crime to his or her probation supervisor, the information can be passed on to the police or district attorney. The *Murphy* decision held that a probation officer could even use trickery or psychological pressure to get information and turn it over to the police.

Griffin v. Wisconsin (1987). *Griffin* held that a probationer's home may be searched without a warrant because probation departments "have in mind the welfare of the probationer" and must "respond quickly to evidence of misconduct."

United States v. Knights (2001). The warrantless search of a probationer's home for the purposes of gathering criminal evidence is legal under some circumstances—for example if (a) the search was based on a reasonable suspicion that the probationer had committed another crime while on probation and (b) submitting to searches was part of the probation order. The government's interest in preventing crime, combined with Knights' diminished expectation of privacy, required only a *reasonable suspicion* to make the search fit within the protections of the Fourth Amendment.

[pp. 236-237, LO 7]

CHAPTER 11

Corrections:
History, Institutions, and Populations

LEARNING OBJECTIVES

After studying this chapter, students will:

1. Understand the meaning of the term "the new penology"
2. Be able to explain how the first penal institutions developed in Europe
3. Explain how William Penn revolutionized corrections
4. Compare the New York and Pennsylvania prison models
5. Chart the development of penal reform
6. Know how parole developed
7. List the purposes of jails and be familiar with the makeup of jail populations
8. Be familiar with the term "new-generation jail"
9. Classify the different types of federal and state penal institutions
10. Discuss prison population trends

KEY TERMS AND CONCEPTS

prison (p. 256) A state or federal correctional institution for incarceration of felony offenders for terms of one year or more.

jail (p. 256) A place to detain people awaiting trial, to serve as a lockup for drunks and disorderly individuals, and to confine convicted misdemeanants serving sentences of less than one year.

hulks (p. 257) Abandoned ships, anchored in harbors and used in eighteenth-century England to house prisoners.

Walnut Street Jail (p. 258) An eighteenth-century institution that housed convicted criminals in Philadelphia.

penitentiary house (p. 258) Term used for early prisons, so named because inmates were supposed to do penitence for their sins.

congregate system (p. 259) Prison system first used in New York that allowed inmates to engage in group activities such as work, meals, and recreation.

Pennsylvania system (p. 260) The correctional model used in Pennsylvania that isolated inmates from one another to prevent them from planning escapes, make them easy to manage and give them time to do penitence.

contract system (p. 261) Practice of correctional officials selling the labor of inmates to private businesses.

convict-lease system (p. 261) The practice of leasing inmates to a business for a fixed annual fee.

medical model (p. 264) A correctional philosophy based on the belief that inmates are sick people who need treatment rather than punishment to help them reform.

maximum-security prison (p. 267) A correctional institution that houses dangerous felons and maintains strict security measures, high walls, and limited contact with the outside world.

super-maximum-security prison (p. 267) The newest form of a maximum-security prison that uses high-level security measures to incapacitate the nation's most dangerous criminals. Most inmates are in lockdown 23 hours a day.

medium-security prison (p. 269) A less secure institution that houses nonviolent offenders and provides more opportunities for contact with the outside world.

minimum-security prison (p. 269) The least secure institution, which houses white-collar and nonviolent offenders, maintains few security measures, and has liberal furlough and visitation policies.

boot camp (p. 270) A short-term militaristic correctional facility in which inmates undergo intensive physical conditioning and discipline.

shock incarceration (p. 270) A short prison sentence served in boot camp-type facilities.

halfway house (p. 271) A community-based correctional facility that houses inmates before their outright release so that they can become gradually acclimated to conventional society.

CHAPTER OUTLINE

I. **INTRODUCTION**
   1. Correctional system has branches in the federal, state, and county levels of government
   2. Felons may be placed in state of federal penitentiaries, which are usually isolated, high-security structures
   3. Misdemeanants are housed in local county jails, reformatories, or houses of correction
   4. Juvenile offenders have their own institutions called schools, camps, ranches, or homes

       a. Usually nonsecure facilities that provide both confinement and rehabilitation

       b. Some juveniles who commit serious crimes can be transferred to the adult court and serve sentence in adult prison

5. One of the greatest tragedies is that "correctional" institutions do not seem to "correct"

6. Estimated that more than half of all inmates will be back in prison within six years of their release

7. Debate over true role of secure corrections:

       a. Prisons and jails should be used to keep dangerous offenders apart from society, dispensing "just deserts"

            i. Correctional effectiveness measured in terms of:

                a) Physical security

                b) Length of incapacitation

                c) Inmates who return to society fearing criminal sanctions

       b. Purpose of corrections is treatment and successful offender rehabilitation

8. Today, the desert/incapacitation model (new penology) holds sway

II. THE HISTORY OF CORRECTIONAL INSTITUTIONS

1. Original legal punishments were typically

       a. Banishment or slavery

       b. Restitution

       c. Corporal punishment

       d. Execution

2. Penal institutions were constructed in England during the tenth century to hold pretrial detainees and those awaiting sentence

3. Le Stinche in Italy was used to punish offenders as early as 1301

       a. Prisoners were enclosed in separate cells, classified on basis of:

            i. Gender

            ii. Age

            iii. Mental state

            iv. Seriousness of their crime

       b. For the first time, a period of incarceration replaced corporal punishment for some offenses

4. From 1776 to 1785, a growing inmate population forced the English to house prisoners on hulks (abandoned ships anchored in the harbor)

       a. The hulks were abandoned in 1858

5. The writings of John Howard drew attention to the squalid conditions in British penal institutions

       a. Book was *The State of Prisons* (1777)

       b. Resulted in the Penitentiary Act

            i. Parliament established a more orderly penal system

                a) Periodic inspections

                b) Elimination of the fee system

                c) Greater consideration for inmates

A. The Origin of Corrections in the United States

1. Although Europe had jails and a variety of other penal institutions, it was in the United States that correctional reform was instituted
2. The first jail was built in James City, Virginia
3. The modern American correctional system actually started in Pennsylvania under the leadership of William Penn
    a. Penn revised Pennsylvania's criminal code to forbid:
        i. Torture
        ii. Capricious use of mutilation and physical punishment
    b. Replaced with
        i. Imprisonment at hard labor
        ii. Moderate flogging
        iii. Fines
        iv. Forfeiture of property
    c. Penn ordered each county to build a house of corrections
        i. Similar to today's jails
4. Two of the first American penal institutions were
    a. Newgate Prison in Connecticut in 1773
    b. Castle Island Prison in Massachusetts in 1785
B. The Development of Prisons
    1. William Penn's code for prisons was adopted, and a group of Quakers formed the Philadelphia Society for Alleviating the Miseries of Public Prisons
        a. The aim of the Society was to bring some degree of humane and orderly treatment to the growing penal system
    2. The only models of custodial institutions at that time were the local county jails that Penn had established
    3. In 1790, under pressure from the Quakers, the Pennsylvania legislature called for renovation of the prisoner system. A new wing of the Walnut Street Jail was installed
        a. To house convicted felons
        b. Prisoners placed in solitary cells
    4. Quarters that contained the solitary cells were called the penitentiary house
C. The New York and Pennsylvania Systems
    1. Both New York and Pennsylvania were experiencing difficulties maintaining the ever-increasing number of convicted criminals
    2. In 1816, New York built a new prison at Auburn, hoping to alleviate overcrowding at Newgate
        a. The Auburn prison design became known as the congregate system because most prisoners ate and worked in groups
            i. Three classes of prisoners created:
                a) One group remained in solitary confinement as a result of breaches of prison discipline
                b) Second group allowed labor as an occasional form of recreation
                c) Third and largest worked together during the day and was separated only at night
        b. The philosophy of the Auburn system was crime prevention through fear of punishment and silent confinement

     i. Silence was seen as key; since it kept convicts from talking to formulate escapes

     ii. The practice was abolished in 1823

   c. The combination of silence and solitude as a method of punishment was not abandoned easily

   d. Prison officials sought to overcome the side effects of total isolation while maintaining a penitentiary system

   e. The solution allowed for isolation at night but allowed inmates to work together during the day

  3. In 1818 Pennsylvania took the radical step of establishing a prison that placed each inmate in a single cell for the duration of his sentence

  4. The new Pennsylvania State Prison opened in 1826 and was called the Western Penitentiary

   a. It was built in a semicircle with the cells positioned along its circumference

   b. Its inmates were housed in solitary confinement being allowed out about one hour per day

  5. Supporters of the Pennsylvania System believed the penitentiary was truly a place to experience penitence

  6. Solitary confinement was used as a means of making work programs look attractive, and it was believed that the inmate would be well suited to resume a productive existence in society

  7. The Pennsylvania system eliminated the need for large numbers of guards or disciplinary measures

  8. Advocates of the Auburn system believed theirs was the cheapest and most productive

   a. The Pennsylvania system was criticized as cruel and inhumane

  9. New York's congregate model eventually prevailed and spread throughout the United States

   a. Many features are still in use today

 D. Corrections in the Nineteenth Century

  1. The prison of the late nineteenth century was remarkably similar to that of today

  2. The congregate system was adopted in all states but Pennsylvania

  3. Prisons were overcrowded and the single cell principle was often ignored

  4. The prison industry developed and became a prominent theme around which prisons were organized

   a. Some prisons used the contract system

     i. Officials sold the labor of inmates to private businesses

   b. Some used the convict lease system

     i. The state leased its prisoners to a business for a fixed annual fee

   c. Some institutions had prisoners produce goods for the prison's own use

  5. The development of the prison system quickly led to abuse of inmates, who were forced to work for almost no wages

 E. Reform Efforts

  1. The National Congress Penitentiary and Reformatory Discipline, held in Cincinnati in 1870, heralded a new era of prison reform

        a.   Organized by penologists Enoch Wines and Theodore Dwight

        b.   The warden of Elmira Reformatory in New York, Zebulon Brockway advocated individualized treatment, indeterminate sentences, and parole

        c.   The warden instituted elementary education for illiterates

F.   The Development of Parole

    1.   In the early seventeenth century, English judges began to spare the lives of offenders by banishing them to the newly formed overseas colonies.

    2.   In 1717, the British Parliament passed legislation embodying the concept of property in service:

        a.   Transferred control of prisoners to a contractor or shipmaster until the expiration of their sentences

        b.   Abandoned in America after the Revolution

            i.   Australia became the destination for most transported felons

    3.   The English Penal Servitude Act of 1853 ended the transportation and substituted imprisonment as a punishment

        a.   Part of this act made it possible to grant a ticket-of-leave to those who had served a sufficient portion of their prison sentence

    4.   Concept of parole spread to the United States

        a.   In the 1870s Zebulon Brockway selected rehabilitate offenders for early release under the supervision of citizen volunteers known as guardians

        b.   Parole concept spread rapidly

            i.   Ohio created the first parole agency in 1884

    5.   Parole has become institutionalized as the primary method of release for prison inmates

        a.   Half of all inmates released in the United States were paroled

G. Prisons in the Twentieth Century

    1.   The twentieth century was the time of contrasts for U.S. prisons

        a.   Some groups advocated reform, desiring humane and better treatment for inmates, while others supported conservative prison administration with stern disciplinary measures to control dangerous inmates

        b.   In time, more of the rigid prison rules gave way to liberal reforms

    2.   By the mid 1930s, inmates were wearing non-descript uniforms instead of the bold striped uniforms

    3.   Prisoners were allowed freedom of the yard and allowed to mingle and exercise

        a.   Visiting and mail policies were liberalized

    4.   Also emerging were specialized prisons to treat specialized offenders such as hardcore offenders and the criminally insane

    5.   Prison industry also evolved

        a.   Opposition from organized labor put an end to convict-lease forced inmate labor

        b.   Sumners-Ashurst Act (1940):

            i.   Made it a federal offense to transport interstate commerce goods made in prison for private use

        c.   Restrictions severely curtailed prison industry for 40 years

6. Despite some changes, the prison system in the mid-twentieth century remained a destructive penal institution
   a. Some aspects of humane treatment emerged but severe discipline and harsh rules were the way of life

H. Contemporary Correctional Institutions
1. The modern era has been a period of change and turmoil
2. Three trends stand out:
   a. Between 1960 and 1980 - Prisoners' rights movement
      i. Hands-off doctrine
      ii. State and federal courts ruled that institutionalized inmates had rights to:
         a) Freedom of religion and speech
         b) Medical care
         c) Procedural due process
         d) Proper living conditions
      iii. Since 1980 an increasingly conservative judiciary has curtailed the growth of inmate rights
   b. Second, violence within the correctional system became a national concern
      i. Riots at New York's Attica Prison and the New Mexico State Penitentiary drew attention to the potential for death and destruction that lurks in every prison
      ii. Prison rapes and killings have become commonplace
      iii. Locus of control shifted from the correctional staff to violent inmate gangs
         a) In reaction some administrators tried to improve conditions and provide programs that gave inmates a voice in running the institution
         b) Another reaction has been to tighten discipline and build new super-maximum-security prisons
   c. Third, the view that traditional correctional rehabilitation efforts have failed prompted many penologists to reconsider the purpose of incarcerating criminals
      i. The role of prisons (between 1960 and 1980) changed to the medical model
         a) Inmates were viewed as sick people in need of treatment
         b) Sickness prevented them from adjusting to society
      ii. In the 1970s, efforts were made to help offenders become reintegrated into society by providing career opportunities
         a) Including work release programs
         b) Work release suffered when a release program inmate raped a woman
         c) Work release program policies were toughened as a result of the rape incident
3. Prisons have come to be viewed as places of:
   a. Control
   b. Incapacitation

        c. Punishment rather than sites of rehabilitation and reform
4. A no frills policy (penal harm) advocated that a punishing experience would encourage inmates to go straight
5. Failure of correctional treatment, coupled with increasing costs, prompted the development of alternatives to incarceration such as
        a. Intensive probation
        b. Electronic monitoring
        c. House arrest
6. What has developed is a dual correctional policy:
        a. Keep as many nonviolent offenders out of the correctional system by means of community-based programs
        b. Incarcerate dangerous, violent offender for long periods of time
7. Despite the development of alternatives, the number of people under lock and key has skyrocketed

III.   JAILS

1. Jails have five main purposes:
        a. Detain pre-trial offenders who cannot have or make bail
        b. Hold convicted offenders awaiting sentence
        c. Serve as secure confinement for convicted misdemeanor offenders
        d. Hold probation and parole violators awaiting hearing
        e. House felons when prison is overcrowded
2. A number of formats are used to jail offenders. About 15,000 municipal and local police agencies operate short term lock-ups

A. Jail Population and Trends
1. Number of people being held in jail began to decline in 2009 and by 2010 there were about 750,000 jail inmates
        a. 242 inmates for every 100,000 U.S. residents
2. Almost nine out of ten inmates are adult males
3. Although Whites make up more than 40% of the jail population, a disproportionate number of jail inmates are minority group members
        a. Been in jail, African Americans are
            i.   Nearly five times more likely than whites
            ii. Nearly three times more likely than Hispanics
           iii. Over nine times more likely than persons of other races
        b. May be responsible in part for race based disparity in the ability to obtain bail
4. Pretrial detainees tend to get longer prison sentences and more likely to be incarcerated
5. Number of juveniles held in adult jails has been in decline since 1995
        a. Result of ongoing government initiatives to remove them from adult facilities
        b. About 7500 minors still being held in adult jails each day

B. Jail Conditions
1. Jails are usually a low priority in the criminal justice system
2. Jails are usually administered at the county level

3. Jails in some counties are physically deteriorated, holding inmates that have serious emotional problems
4. Jails are considered a revolving door of the justice system

C. New Generation Jails
1. A jail building boom is underway to alleviate overcrowding and improve effectiveness
2. New generation jails allow for continuous observation of inmates, something old facilities lacked
3. Traditional jails constructed in a linear/surveillance model
    a. Rectangular
    b. Corridors leading to either single or multiple occupancy cells
4. Two types of jails exist— direct and indirect supervision jails
    a. Direct supervision contains a cluster of cells surrounding a living area or 'pod' The officer has visual observation of and personal contact with inmates
    b. Indirect supervision uses a similar construction, but the guard is situated in a secure room. Microphones and speakers are used to communicate with inmates

IV. **PRISONS**
1. The federal Bureau of Prisoners and every state government maintain closed correctional facilities, which are also called prisons, penitentiaries, or reformatories
2. Federal, state, and local governments spent close to 70 billion per year, increasing from 12 billion in 1986
    a. About $125 per year for every American citizen
3. The prison is the final repository for the most troubled criminal offenders. Many have troubled backgrounds and little hope

A. Types of Prisons
1. There are more than 1700 public and private adult correctional facilities housing inmates
    a. About 100 federal prisons and 400 privately run institutions
2. Prisons are classified as maximum, medium, and minimum security facilities

B. Maximum Security Prisons
1. Maximum facilities house the most notorious offenders and are often fortress like
2. A typical facility is surrounded by walls and guard towers. Walls may be 25 feet high
3. Inmates live in interior, metal-barred cells with plumbing facilities and electronic locking doors
4. Maximum security stresses security

C. Super-Maximum-Security-Prisons
1. Also called supermax facilities
2. These house the most predatory offenders
3. Inmates are locked up for 22 to 24 hours per day, never allowing them out without shackles

4. Experts have given supermax prisons mixed reviews
    a. Although they can achieve benefits by enhancing security and quality of life
    b. Can infringe on the right of inmates to due process
    c. A stay in a supermax prison inhibits reintegration into other prisons, communities, and families

D. Medium Security Prisons
1. The conditions are less vigilant and less tense than maximum security facilities. The two facilities physically resemble each other
2. Medium security facilities promote treatment efforts and have a more relaxed atmosphere

E. Minimum-Security Prisons
1. Usually these facilities operate without armed guards and walls
2. They house the most trustworthy and least violent offenders
3. These facilities have dormitories or small private rooms for inmates
4. They have been criticized for being too "country club like"

V. ALTERNATIVE CORRECTIONAL INSTITUTIONS
1. In addition to prisons and jails, a number of other correctional facilities are opening within the United States

A. Prison Camps and Farms
1. Prison farms and camps are used to detain offenders
2. These facilities are found mostly in the South and the West
    a. About 40 farms
    b. 40 forest camps
    c. 80 road camps
    d. More than 60 similar facilities
3. Labor tasks include farming, ranching, forestry, and dairy production

B. Shock Incarceration in Boot Camps
1. These institutions gained popularity in the 1980s and 1990s
2. The boot camp involves youthful, first time offenders in military discipline and training
3. Some programs also include educational and training components, counseling sessions, and treatment for special needs inmates
4. Is shock incarceration a correctional panacea or another fad doomed to fail?
    a. It is portrayed as a lower cost alternative to prisons
    b. Both inmates and staff say they receive benefits from the program
    c. Some boot camp studies have revealed disappointing results
5. The future of boot camp is uncertain
6. Federal government announced the closing of its boot camp program

C. Community Correctional Facilities
1. One of the goals of correctional treatment is to reintegrate the offender back into society
2. The community treatment concept began to take off in the 1960s
    a. Correctional systems created community-based models as an alternative to closed institutions

        b. Halfway houses were included

    3. Community treatment may also be used as an intermediate sanction and sole mode of treatment

    4. Halfway houses and community correctional facilities can look like residential homes

        a. Despite the encouraging philosophical concept presented in the halfway house, evaluation of specific programs has not led to definite endorsement of the program

        b. The continued promise and low cost have kept them alive as available options

D. Private Prisons

    1. Correctional facilities are now being run by private firms and business enterprises

        a. More than 400 are now in operation

    2. In 1986, U.S. Corrections Corporation opened the first private prison in Kentucky

    3. Private prison now plays a significant role in the management of inmates

        a. Now hold almost 130,000 people

        b. Play an important correctional role in the U.S., Australia, and the U.K.

E. Do Private Prisons Work?

        a. Studies reveal there is little difference in recidivism rates between inmates released from private and public prisons

        b. Some evidence suggests inmates released from private prisons may reoffend by committing less serious offenses

        c. Some evaluators question whether private prisons can be evaluated effectively because negative evaluations may lead to the loss of a client contract for the private institution

        d. Private institutions also run into opposition from existing state correctional staff and management

        e. Some are concerned that private institutions cut corners to save on costs

VI. **INMATE POPULATIONS**

    1. The vast correctional system now with more than 2000 public and private institutions, contains over 1.6 million inmates

        a. One in 31 or 3.2% of all adults are under the control of the correctional system in the U.S.

        b. One day in prison costs more than:

            i. 10 days on parole

            ii. 22 days on probation

    2. Prison inmates are disproportionately young, male, minority, and poor

        a. One in 87 working-aged White men is in prison or jail

        b. One in 36 Hispanic men

        c. One in 12 African American men

        d. More young (20-34) African American men without a high school diploma or GED are currently behind bars than employed

        3. Inmates suffer from social problems, emotional problems, and psychological problems

  A. Growth Trends

        1. The prison population skyrocketed between 1980-2006 when it finally began to stabilize

             a. There has been a slight decline in the number of prisoners, today there are about 500 inmates for every 100,000 citizens

        2. The prison population has risen even though the crime rate has fallen, number of reasons for trend:

             a. Many people who are released from prison soon return

                 i. About 250,000 or 1/3 of the people now entering prison are parole violators

             b. Tougher sentencing requirements remove flexibility in sentencing and early release

             c. Amount of time served has increased due to truth-in-sentencing laws

                 i. Require inmates serve at least 85% of their sentences behind bars

             d. Significant association among drug use, drug arrests, and prison overcrowding

        3. About 5% of the current population or more than 13 million people will serve a prison sentence sometime during their lives

        4. The nation's prison population may be maxing out

        5. Cutbacks and belt tightening may halt prison construction

        6. As costs skyrocket, some states are spending more on corrections than on education

CHAPTER SUMMARY

The use of incarceration as a criminal punishment began in the late eighteenth to early nineteenth centuries. Penal institutions were constructed in England during the tenth century to hold pretrial detainees and those waiting for their sentence. During the twelfth century, a series of county jails were built to hold thieves and vagrants prior to their sentence. A growing inmate population forced the English to house prisoners on abandoned ships. Efforts to create humane standards in the British penal system resulted in the Penitentiary Act, which established a more orderly penal system, with periodic inspections, elimination of the fee system, and greater consideration for inmates.

The modern American correctional system has its origins in Pennsylvania. A new type of institution was built to replace the public forms of punishment— stocks, pillories, gallows, and branding irons. In 1787, a group of Quakers formed a society to bring humane and orderly treatment to the penal system. The Pennsylvania state legislature called for the renovation of the prison system. The result was the creation of a separate wing of Philadelphia's Walnut Street Jail. This legislation created a state penitentiary house.

In 1816, New York built a new prison at Auburn, hoping to alleviate overcrowding. This design became known as the congregate system because cells were built vertically. Three classes of prisoners were created: one group remained continually in solitary confinement; the second group was allowed labor as an occasional form of recreation; and the third and largest class worked and ate together during the day and were separated only at night. The philosophy was crime prevention through fear of punishment and silent confinement. Pennsylvania established a prison that placed each inmate in a single cell for the duration of his sentence. Classifications were abolished. The Auburn system eventually prevailed and spread; many of its features are still used today.

Jails have five primary purposes— detain accused offenders who cannot make bail, hold convicted offenders awaiting sentence, serve as the secure confinement for offenders convicted of misdemeanors, hold probationers and parolees picked up for violations and waiting for a hearing, and house felons when state prisons are overcrowded. The numbers of people being held in jails today has been rising for more than a decade. As prisons become more overcrowded, officials use local jails to house inmates. Jail populations also respond to the efforts being made to control particular crime problems, such as, substance abuse, spousal abuse, and driving while intoxicated.

The federal Bureau of Prisons and every state government maintain closed correctional facilities, also called prisons, penitentiaries, or reformatories. The prison is the final repository for the most troubled criminal offenders. Prisons are classified on three levels—maximum, medium, and minimum security. A number of other correctional institutions are operating, including prison farms and camps, shock incarceration, and community correctional facilities.

Correctional facilities are now run by private firms as business enterprises. In some instances, a private corporation will finance and build an institution and then contract with correctional authorities to provide services for convicted criminals. Another common method of private involvement is with specific service contracts, such as managing the prison health-care system, food services, or staff training.

The inmate population has -finally stabilized. One reason for the large number of inmates despite the nation's crime drop is that tough new criminal legislation, including mandatory sentencing laws, increases the chances that a convicted offender will be incarcerated and limits the availability for early release via parole.

DISCUSSION QUESTIONS

1. Would you allow a community correctional center to be built in your neighborhood?
2. Should pretrial detainees and convicted offenders be kept in the same institution?
3. What can be done to reduce overcrowding in correctional facilities?
4. Should private companies be allowed to run correctional institutions?
5. What are the drawbacks to shock incarceration?

MEDIA TOOLS

Justice Concepts Inc. is a correctional consulting firm that serves units of government helping decision makers determine the needs of their agency. The website provides a wealth of information regarding many topics covered in this chapter. Make sure that you visit the section on "Deciding on a New Jail Design." This section provides some photographs of the new generation jail design. Website provided by Justice Concepts Inc. The website can be found at: http://www.justiceconcepts.com

Make sure to visit the website of the Federal Bureau of Prisons. There is quite a bit of interesting information concerning inmates and especially the wide variety of prison locations and design. Check to see which federal prisons are near you, you might be surprised. Information is provided for each site, for example visitation rules. Visit the Federal Bureau of Prison website at: http://www.bop.gov

The Bureau of Justice Statistics website on prison population counts provides a wealth of data regarding prison population counts and trends. The latest reporting year available is 2009. A good starting point if you are interested in prison population and trends research. The website can be found at: http://bjs.ojp.usdoj.gov/index.cfm?ty=tp&tid=131

Visit the website of The Pennsylvania Prison Society. According to the website the Society, "Founded in 1787, the Pennsylvania Prison Society is a social justice organization advocating on behalf of prisoners, their families, and formerly incarcerated individuals. Headquartered in Philadelphia, the Prison Society offers direct services and official prison visitation through a network of statewide chapters." For an interesting history lesson, click on the "about" button and select "history." The website of The Pennsylvania Prison Society can be found at: http://www.prisonsociety.org

PRACTICE TEST BANK

MULTIPLE CHOICE

1. In which state did the American correctional system originate?
    a. Texas
    b. Massachusetts
    c. New York
    d. Pennsylvania

2. The Quakers influence on the legislature resulted in limiting the death penalty to cases involving all of the following except
    a. treason.
    b. murder.
    c. arson.
    d. theft.

3. According to the text, all of the following were problems associated with early jail systems except
    a. growing inmate population.
    b. lack of educated engineers and contractors to design and build new facilities.
    c. deplorable facility conditions.
    d. jails were catchall institutions holding criminals, vagabonds, and debtors.

4. Who is credited with the Penitentiary Act which established a more humane and orderly penal system for English inmates?
    a. Zebulon Brockway
    b. Cesar Beccaria
    c. William Penn
    d. John Howard

5. Who is credited with revising Pennsylvania's criminal code to forbid torture, physical punishment and capricious use of mutilations as inmate punishments?
    a. Zebulon Brockway
    b. Cesar Beccaria
    c. William Penn
    d. John Howard

6. Under pressure from which group did the Pennsylvania legislature call for reform of the prison system?
    a. American Civil Liberties
    b. American bar association
    c. Pennsylvania Dutch
    d. Quakers

7.   In 1790 a separate wing of Philadelphia's Walnut Street Jail was designed to house
     a.   convicted felons.
     b.   female prisoners.
     c.   male prisoners.
     d.   diseased prisoners.

8.   The congregate system provided
     a.   early release for inmates.
     b.   prisoners to work and eat in groups.
     c.   religious observation.
     d.   separate living quarters for elderly inmates.

9.   Under which philosophy did the Auburn prison operate?
     a.   Crime prevention and silent confinement
     b.   Crime prevention and work release
     c.   Crime prevention and mental rehabilitation
     d.   Crime prevention and hard labor

10. Correctional reform was first instituted in
     a.   Europe.
     b.   Asia.
     c.   the United States.
     d.   Australia.

11. The congregate system is credited with all of the following innovations except
     a.   solitary confinement.
     b.   military regimentation.
     c.   discipline.
     d.   work release.

12. As exploited cheap labor, during the Civil War prison inmates were major manufacturers of all of the following except
     a.   shoes.
     b.   clothes.
     c.   ammunition.
     d.   furniture.

13. The term penitentiary house was used for early prisons because
     a.   inmates were supposed to do penitence for their sins.
     b.   they were developed by William Penn.
     c.   the primary workhouse products were quill pens.
     d.   they were located primarily in Pennsylvania.

14. The National Congress of Penitentiary and Reformatory Discipline provided corrections experts a forum to call for
    a. inmate training and treatment.
    b. inmate early release.
    c. inmate civil liberties.
    d. inmate trade unions.

15. In the early nineteenth century, Pennsylvania and New York prison systems were having trouble keeping up with the increasing prison population. Administrators instituted a number of methods to compensate for the increase except for
    a. increasing pardons.
    b. relaxing prison discipline.
    c. increasing executions.
    d. limiting supervision.

16. Which Act ended transportation (property in service) as a sentence for convicted offenders and substituted imprisonment in its place?
    a. English Penal Servitude Act
    b. New York Servitude Act
    c. Elmira Servitude Act
    d. New Haven Servitude Act

17. An early form of parole enacted by the English Penal Servitude Act of 1853 which allowed prisoners to be released from prison after serving a sufficient portion of their sentence was known as
    a. property-in-service.
    b. the contract system.
    c. transfer-to-hulk.
    d. ticket-of-leave.

18. Which early prison system was characterized by single cells in a semicircle, isolated living conditions, in-cell activities, and the use of silence and harsh punishment as discipline?
    a. Auburn
    b. Congregate
    c. Pennsylvania
    d. New York

19. Jails as institutions, serve all of the following primary purposes except
    a. detaining accused offenders.
    b. holding probationers pending violation hearings.
    c. housing convicted misdemeanor offenders.
    d. housing pardoned offenders.

20. Rehabilitated offenders from Elmira Reformatory were released early under the supervision of volunteers known as
    a. parole officers.
    b. gate keepers.
    c. guardians.
    d. Quakers.

21. New generation jails incorporate improved designs to improve efficiency; new generation jails are often described as
    a. direct supervision jails.
    b. enforcement jails.
    c. linear jails.
    d. intermittent jails.

22. Which term best describes the new generation jail design where visibility is a key component and a cluster of cells is generally surrounded by a common living area?
    a. Bean
    b. Pod
    c. Oracle
    d. Globe

23. In which capacity did traditional jails, by virtue of their design, limit correctional officers' abilities?
    a. Concrete surfaces exacerbated worker injuries---resulting from fights or disorderly inmates
    b. Concrete surfaces impeded acoustics---making it difficult to hear inmates
    c. Visibility of inmates was greatly restricted
    d. Concrete surfaces made public safety radio communication inaudible

24. Under this model, inmates were viewed as sick people who were suffering from some social malady that prevented them from adjusting to society?
    a. Hands-off
    b. Liberal
    c. Medical
    d. Societal

25. All of the following are official prison classifications except
    a. moderate.
    b. maximum.
    c. medium.
    d. minimum.

26.	A maximum security facility is generally described as a(n)
	a.	open campus style facility where inmates have limited personal interaction.
	b.	fortress-like surrounded by high stone walls and guard towers.
	c.	lockdown facility where inmates are confined to solitary confinement and have little or no personal interaction.
	d.	facility surrounded by walls where inmates allowed frequent personal contact and in some cases work release.

27.	Minimum security prisons would most likely house
	a.	violent offenders.
	b.	white collar criminals.
	c.	death row inmates.
	d.	misdemeanor offenders.

28.	Minimum security prisons are associated with all of the following except
	a.	work furloughs.
	b.	a great deal of personal freedom.
	c.	tennis courts.
	d.	guard towers.

29.	In 1986, which company was the first to open a privately managed correctional facility in the United States?
	a.	U.S. Corrections Corporation
	b.	Pinkerton Correction Systems
	c.	UniCorp Corrections Masters
	d.	Corrections Corporation of America

30.	What correctional facility is designed to hold inmates that are transferred from a prison to just before their release into the community?
	a.	Halfway house
	b.	Boot camp
	c.	Minimum security
	d.	Jail

TRUE/FALSE

1.	T	F	One of the greatest tragedies is that "correctional" institutions do not seem to "correct."

2.	T	F	One day in prison costs more than 10 days on parole or 22 days on probation.

3.	T	F	A vast majority of the people now entering prison are parole violators.

4.	T	F	The medical model focuses on rehabilitation and treating prisoners.

5.   T   F   The "modern" American correctional system had its origins in Pennsylvania under the leadership of William Penn.

6.   T   F   About 15,000 local jurisdictions maintain short-term police or municipal lock-ups that house offenders for no more than 48 hours before a bail hearing can be held.

7.   T   F   Minimum security facilities are sometimes criticized for being like country clubs.

8.   T   F   Some prisons used the contract system, where prison officials sold the labor of inmates to private businesses.

9.   T   F   The term "parole" comes from the French word for "permissible."

10.   T   F   The Pennsylvania system eliminated the need for large numbers of guards or disciplinary measures.

11.   T   F   Many of New York's congregate model features are still in use today.

12.   T   F   Super-maximum prisons house the most predatory criminals.

13.   T   F   Maximum security prisons are often fortress like and they are associated with high level and plentiful security features.

14.   T   F   Boot camps were designed to bring militaristic structured training to repeat offenders.

15.   T   F   The drug epidemic in the 1980s and 1990s helped swell prison populations.

FILL-IN-THE-BLANK

1. Prisoners or parolees may be housed in a _____ house to facilitate their return to society.

2. The desert/incapacitation model of corrections is sometimes called the new _____ _____.

3. According to the _____ model, prisoners are sick and need treatment.

4. In the late 1700s, overcrowded facilities resulted in English prisoners being housed in abandoned ships called _____.

305

5. Under the _____ system, inmates were under the total control of private companies.

6. Under the _____ system, inmates worked in the prison for a private company.

7. In the nineteenth century the congregate system was adopted in all states except _____ _____.

8. _____-security prisons typically operate without armed guards or walls.

9. _____ serve as the principal institution of secure confinement for offenders convicted of misdemeanors.

10. New _____ jails are designed with improved security allowing for better inmate control.

11. The _____ system of prisons stressed isolation and penitence.

12. Prison inmates suffer from _____problems; they tend to be undereducated, underemployed, and come from abusive homes.

13. Traditional jails generally use the _____surveillance model of building design.

14. In 1717, the British Parliament passed legislation embodying the concept of _____ _____, which transferred control of prisoners to a contractor until the expiration of their sentence.

15. _____ incarceration is a short prison sentence served in boot camp-style facilities.

ESSAY

1. Define, compare, and contrast the Pennsylvania and New York systems of prisons.

2. Discuss three trends that had a large impact on prisons between 1960 and 1980.

3. Define and explain the term, "the new Penology."

4. Discuss the history of prison industry in the U.S.

5. Identify and explain the different types of federal and state penal institutions.

CHAPTER 11 ANSWER KEY

Multiple Choice

1. d [p. 258, LO1]   2. d [p. 258, LO2]   3. b [p. 256, LO2]   4. d [p. 257, LO3]   5. c [p. 258, LO4]

6. d [p. 258, LO5/4]   7. a [p. 258, LO4]   8. b [p. 259, LO4]   9. a [p. 259, LO5]   10. c [p. 258, LO2]

11. d [p. 260, LO5]   12. c [p. 261, LO6]   13. a [p. 258, LO5]   14. a [p. 262, LO6]   15. c [p. 259, LO4]

16. a [p. 262, LO6]   17. d [p. 262, LO6]   18. c [p. 260, LO4]   19. d [p. 265, LO7]   20. c [p. 262, LO6]

21. a [p. 266, LO8]   22. b [p. 266, LO8]   23. c [p. 266, LO8]   24. c [p. 264, LO6]   25. a [p. 267, LO9]

26. b [p. 267, LO9]   27. b [p. 269, LO9]   28. d [p. 269, LO9]   29. a [p. 272, LO9]   30. a [p. 271, LO9]

True/False

1. T [p. 255, LO1]   2. T [p. 272, LO10]   3. F [p. 273, LO10]   4. T [p. 264, LO6]   5. T [p. 258, LO3]

6. T [p. 265, LO7]   7. T [p. 269, LO9]   8. T [p. 261, LO6]   9. F [p. 262, LO6]   10. T [p. 260, LO5]

11. T [p. 260, LO5]   12. T [p. 267, LO9]   13. T [p. 267, LO9]   14. F [p. 270, LO9]   15. T [p. 274, LO10]

Fill-in-the-Blank

1. halfway [p. 271, LO9]   2. penology [p. 256, LO1]   3. medical [p. 264, LO6]

4. hulks [p. 257, LO3]   5. convict-lease [p. 261, LO5]   6. contract [p. 261, LO5]

7. Pennsylvania [p. 261, LO5   ]   8. minimum [p. 269, LO9]   9. Jails [p. 265, LO7]

10. generation [p. 266, LO8]   11. Pennsylvania [p. 260, LO5]   12. social [p. 273, LO10]

13. linear/intermittent [p. 266, LO8]   14. property-in-service [p. 262, LO6]   15. Shock [p. 270, LO9]

Essay

1.   **Define, compare, and contrast the Pennsylvania and New York systems of prisons.**

In 1816, New York built a new prison at Auburn. It was referred to as the *congregate* system, because most prisoners ate and worked in groups. In 1819, this prison started construction of a wing of solitary cells to house unruly prisoners. Prisoners were divided into three classes; solitary confinement for breaches of prison discipline, labor as recreation, and the last group worked together during the day and was separated only at night. The prison's philosophy was crime prevention through fear of punishment and silent confinement. When discipline was breached in the Auburn system, punishment was applied in the form of a rawhide whip on the inmate's back. The worst felons were kept in solitary confinement which ultimately led to medical issues and mental health problems and was abolished in 1823. The solution adopted at Auburn was to keep convicts in separate cells at night but allow them to work together during the day under enforced silence. Convict life was regimented and structured. The prison became known for the "lockstep shuffle" in which it used to move prisoners from place.

In 1818, Pennsylvania took the radical step of establishing a prison that placed each inmate in a single cell for the duration of the sentence. Prisoner classes were abolished because each cell was intended as a miniature prison that would prevent the inmates from contaminating one another. Isolation was the critical component. The penitentiary was viewed as a place to do penance. By removing the sinner from society and allowing the prisoner a period of isolation in which to consider the evils of crime, the Pennsylvania system reflected the influence of religion and religious philosophy on corrections. Some of the facilities established under this system utilized new designs where cells were built in a semicircle, with the cells positioned along its circumference. The Pennsylvania system eliminated the need for large numbers of guards or disciplinary measures. Isolated from one another, inmates could not plan escapes or collectively break rules. Since prisoners were isolated from one another, inmates could not plan escapes or collectively break rules. When discipline was a problem, however, the whip and the iron gag were used.

[pp. 259-260, LO4]

2.   Discuss three trends that had a large impact on prisons between 1960 and 1980.

The period has been characterized as the prisoners' rights movement. The period prior to 1960 was labeled as the "hands-off doctrine" era (where correctional facilities were given the control and authority to make decisions about inmate treatment instead of decision from court intervention) had come to an end. The state and federal courts ruled in case after case that institutionalized inmates had rights to freedom of religion and speech, medical care, procedural due process, and proper living conditions. Inmates won rights unheard of in the nineteenth and early twentieth centuries.

Between 1960 and 1980, it was common for correctional administrators to cling to the medical model, which viewed inmates as sick people who were suffering from some social malady that prevented them from adjusting to society. Correctional treatment could help cure them and enable them to live productive lives once they returned to the community. In the 1970s, efforts were also made to help offenders become reintegrated into society by providing them with new career opportunities that relied on work-release programs. Inmates were allowed to work outside the institution during the day and return in the evening.

Violence in the correctional system became a national concern. Riots at New York's Attica Prison and the New Mexico State Penitentiary drew attention to the potential for death and destruction that lurks in every prison. Prison rapes and killings have become commonplace. The focus became violent groups of inmates known as "gangs." New facilities emerged on the scene; new super-maximum-security prisons to control the most dangerous offenders were opened. Prison overcrowding also became an issue.

[pp. 263-265, LO10]

3.   Define and explain the term, "the new Penology."

Today the desert/incapacitation model, sometimes called the *new penology*, holds sway. Rather than administer individualized treatment, decision makers rely of actuarial tables and tests to make decisions; indeed, they seem more concerned with security and "managing" large inmate populations than with treating individual offenders. Critics charge that this policy has resulted in a rapidly increasing prison population that is bereft of the human touch; defenders counter that it is effective because the crime rate has declined as the number of people under lock and key has risen. The connection between a declining crime rate and a rising prison population is not lost on politicians who are eager to energize their political campaigns by advocating a "get tough" policy toward crime. Nonetheless, even though the new penology dominates, correctional rehabilitation is still an important element of the justice system.

[p. 256, LO1]

4.   Discuss the history of prison industry in the U.S.

In 1816, New York built a new prison at Auburn. This prison utilized a congregate system (inmates ate and worked together) and established solitary cells to house unruly prisoners. Prisoners were grouped into classes with the most unruly prisoners being isolated in solitary confinement. Inmate life was structured and regimented in a militaristic fashion. Outside of unruly inmates, other inmates were separated only at night to sleep. The philosophy was crime prevention through fear of punishment and silent confinement. In 1818, Pennsylvania took the radical step of establishing a prison that placed each inmate in a single cell for the duration of his sentence. Its inmates were kept in solitary confinement almost constantly, being allowed out for about an hour a day for exercise.

Prison programs came on scene in the 1870s. Individualized treatment, the indeterminate sentence, and parole were advocated for inmates. Prison programs included elementary education for illiterates, designated library hours, lectures by faculty members of the local college and a group of vocational training shops.

In the early 1900s, the prison industry evolved as opposition from organized labor helped and the faltering economy helped end or limit inmate labor. Despite some changes and reforms, the prison in the mid-twentieth century remained a destructive total institution. Although some aspects of inmate life improved, severe discipline, harsh rules, and solitary confinement were the way of life in prison.

Between 1960 and 1980 state and federal courts ruled in case after case that institutionalized inmates had rights to freedom of religion and speech, medical care, procedural due process, and proper living conditions. In the 1970s, efforts were also made to help offenders become reintegrated into society by providing them with new career opportunities that relied on work-release programs. Inmates were allowed to work outside the institution during the day and return in the evening.

In the 1970s violence emerged as a national concern. Riots drew attention to the potential for death and destruction that lurks in every prison. Prison rapes and killings have become commonplace. In the late 1980s and 1990s prison gangs emerged on the scene. New facilities were constructed; these facilities were designed to house specific types of inmates such as maximum-security prisons and super-max facilities for the most dangerous offenders. Medium and minimum security facilities were used to house less serious offenders.

Prison overcrowding and soaring costs have emerged in recent years as an issue. Prisons still exist to control inmates. But the idea of control has shifted toward keeping as many nonviolent offenders out of the correctional system as possible by means of community-based programs; incarcerate dangerous, violent offenders for long periods of time. Today private prisons have also entered the marketplace and are being used to house inmates. These institutions are run by private companies not the government.

[p. 261, LOs 3 & 4]

5.   Identify and explain the different types of federal and state penal institutions.

- **Maximum-Security Prisons.** Housing the most notorious criminals, and often the subject of films and stories, maximum-security prisons are probably the institutions most familiar to the public. Famous "max prisons" have included Sing Sing, Joliet, Attica, Walpole, and the most fearsome prison of all, the now-closed federal facility on Alcatraz Island known as The Rock. A typical maximum-security facility is fortress-like, surrounded by stone walls with guard towers at strategic places. These walls may be 25 feet high, and sometimes inner and outer walls divide the prison into courtyards. Barbed wire or electrified fences are used to discourage escape. High security, armed guards, and stone walls give the inmate the sense that the facility is impregnable and reassure the citizens outside that convicts will be completely incapacitated. Because they fear that violence may flair up at any minute, prison administrators have been quick to adapt the latest high-tech security measures.

- **Super-Maximum-Security Prisons.** Some states have constructed super-maximum-security prisons (supermax prisons) to house the most predatory criminals. These high-security institutions can be independent correctional centers or locked wings of existing prisons. Some supermax prisons lock inmates in their cells 22 to 24 hours a day, never allowing them out unless they are shackled. A number of experts have given supermax prisons mixed reviews. Although they can achieve correctional benefits by enhancing security and quality of life, critics believe that they infringe directly on the right of inmates to due process because they deprive them of such basic rights such as human contact; they also eliminate any opportunity for rehabilitation.

- **Medium-Security Prisons.** Although they are similar in appearance to maximum-security prisons, in medium-security prisons the security and atmosphere are neither so tense nor so vigilant. Medium-security prisons are also surrounded by walls, but there may be fewer guard towers or other security precautions; visitations with personal contact may be allowed. Although most prisoners are housed in cells, individual honor rooms in medium-security prisons are used to reward those who make exemplary rehabilitation efforts. Finally, medium-security prisons promote greater treatment efforts, and the relaxed atmosphere allows freedom of movement for rehabilitation workers and other therapeutic personnel.

- **Minimum-Security Prisons.** Operating without armed guards or perimeter walls, minimum-security prisons usually house the most trustworthy and least violent offenders; white-collar criminals may be their most common occupants. Inmates are allowed a great deal of personal freedom. Instead of being marched to activities by guards, they are summoned by bells or loudspeaker announcements, and they assemble on their own. Work furloughs and educational releases are encouraged, and vocational training is of the highest level. Dress codes are lax, and inmates are allowed to grow beards or mustaches and to demonstrate other individual characteristics. Minimum-security facilities may have dormitories or small private rooms for inmates. Prisoners are allowed to own personal possessions that might be deemed dangerous in a maximum-security prison, such as radios. Minimum-security prisons have been criticized for being like "country clubs"; some federal facilities for white-collar criminals even have tennis courts and pools (they are derisively called "Club Fed"). Yet they remain prisons, and the isolation and loneliness of prison life deeply affect the inmates.

[pp. 267-269, LO9]

CHAPTER 12
Prison Life: Living in and Leaving Prison

LEARNING OBJECTIVES

After studying this chapter, students will:

1. Discuss the problems of the adult correctional system
2. Know what is meant by the term "total institution"
3. Be familiar with the problem of sexual coercion in prison and what is being done to help.
4. Chart the prisonization process and the development of the inmate social code
5. Compare the lives and cultures of male and female inmates
6. Be familiar with the different forms of correctional treatment
7. Discuss the world of correctional officers
8. Understand the causes of prison violence
9. Know what is meant by prisoners' rights, and discuss some key privileges that have been granted to inmates
10. Be knowledgeable about the parole process and the problems of prisoner reentry

KEY TERMS AND CONCEPTS

total institution (p. 278) A regimented, dehumanizing institution such as a prison, in which inmates are kept in social isolation, cut off from the world at large.

inmate subculture (p. 280) The loosely defined culture that pervades prisons and has its own norms, rules, and language.

inmate social code (p. 280) An unwritten code of behavior, passed from older inmates to younger ones, that serves as a guideline for appropriate inmate behavior within the correctional institution.

prisonization (p. 281) Assimilation into the separate culture in the prison that has its own set of rewards and behaviors, as well as its own norms, rules, and language. The traditional prison culture is now being replaced by a violent gang culture.

make-believe family (p. 284) In female institutions, the substitute family group – including faux father, mother, and siblings – created by some inmates.

therapeutic communities (p. 285) Institutions that rely on positive peer pressure within a highly structured social environment to create positive inmate change.

work release (p. 287) A prison treatment program that allows inmates to be released during the day to work in the community and returned to prison at night.

furlough (p. 287) A correctional policy that allows inmates to leave the institution for vocational or educational training, for employment, or to maintain family ties.

hands-off doctrine (p. 293) The legal practice of allowing prison administrators a free hand to run the institution, even if correctional practices violate inmates' constitutional rights; ended with the onset of the prisoners' rights movement in the 1960s.

substantive rights (p. 294) A number of civil rights that the courts, through a slow process of legal review, have established for inmates, including the rights to receive mail and medical benefits and to practice their religion.

jailhouse lawyer (p. 294) An inmate trained in law or otherwise educated who helps other inmates prepare legal briefs and appeals.

cruel and unusual punishment (p. 295) Physical punishment or punishment that is far in excess of that given to people under similar circumstances and is therefore banned by the Eighth Amendment. The death penalty has so far not been considered cruel and unusual if it is administered in a fair and nondiscriminatory fashion.

parole (p. 296) The early release of a prisoner from imprisonment subject to conditions set by a parole board.

CHAPTER OUTLINE

I. **INTRODUCTION**
1. As the prison population has increased in size, corrections officials have responded by constructing new facilities at a record pace
   a. During the past 25 years, the number of state facilities has increased from just under 600 to over 1000
   b. Facilities take on a variety of forms:
      i. Prisons
      ii. Prison hospitals
      iii. Prison farms
      iv. Boot camps
      v. Centers for reception
      vi. Classification
      vii. Alcohol and drug treatment centers
      viii. Work release centers
2. More than half of all inmates are held in large, fortress-like maximum-security institutions
3. Prison overcrowding is a significant problem

312

4. The typical prison has been described as a "school for crime" in which young offenders are taught by older cons to become sophisticated criminals

II.   MEN IMPRISONED

1. Prisons in the United States are total institutions
   a. Inmates are locked within walls and segregated from the outside world
   b. Kept under constant surveillance
   c. Inmates must obey strict rules
2. Inmates quickly learn what a total institution means
   a. Strip searches
   b. Assigned living quarters; assignments can be based on seriousness of offense
   c. Inmates are assigned a classification
   d. Personal privacy and dignity are soon forgotten
   e. Inmates learn not to trust anyone and endure deprivation of freedoms and liberties
   f. Inmates learn to protect themselves
3. Inmates find themselves cut off from families, friends, and associates
4. Various communicable diseases are commonly found:
   a. Hepatitis C virus
   b. HIV
   c. Syphilis
5. Personal losses include:
   a. Deprivation of liberty
   b. Goods and services
   c. Heterosexual relationships
   d. Autonomy
   e. Security
6. Overcrowded prisons are filled with young, aggressive men who are responsible for the majority of inmate-on-inmate assaults
7. The most vulnerable become the target of a charismatic leader who seeks to recruit them to some cause or group

A. Coping in Prison
1. Despite hardships, many inmates learn to adapt to the prison routine
   a. Each has their own method of coping:
      i. Staying alone
      ii. Become friends with another inmate
      iii. Join a group
      iv. Seek the advice of treatment personnel
2. Older, more experienced men are better able to cope with the prison experience, younger inmates, especially juveniles sent to adult prisons, are more likely to participate in violent episodes
3. Survival in prison depends on one's ability to identify trouble inmates and avoid contact

B. Sexual Coercion

      1. Younger inmates, gay men, and bisexual men are selected most often to be targets of sexual assault
         a. Weaker inmates called "punks" and put at the bottom of the inmate sexual hierarchy
         b. "Queens", inmates who look and act as women, get more respect than punks because they chose their lifestyle, not forced on them

C. How Common is Prison Rape?
      1. Unclear how much rape and sexually violent activity occurs in prison
         a. Most go unreported because:
            i. Victims are either too embarrassed to tell anyone
            ii. May fear harassment by other inmates and further retaliation by their attackers
      2. Rape is far less common than previously believed
      3. Congress enacted the Prison Rape Reduction Act of 2003, which established three programs in the Department of Justice:
         a. A program dedicated to collecting national prison rape statistics, data, and conducting research
         b. A program dedicated to the dissemination of information and procedures for combating prison rape
         c. A program to assist in funding state programs

D. The Inmate Social Code
      1. Experts believe that for years, inmates formed their own set of norms and rules known as the inmate subculture
      2. A significant aspect of the inmate subculture is the inmate social code
      3. Inmate social code includes unwritten guidelines that express values and attitudes
         a. The unwritten guidelines are demanded by older inmates of younger inmates
      4. Donald Clemmer's classic book *The Prison Community* presented a detailed sociological study of inmate life
            i. Clemmer's most important contribution was his identification of the prisonization process
              a)   The process is an inmate's assimilation into the existing culture
            ii. Clemmer's work motivated others to explore more fully the various roles in the prison community
         b. The 'right guy' is the inmate who follows the inmate social code as a behavior guide
            i. The 'right guy' does not go looking for trouble
      5. The effects of prisonization may be long term and destructive
         a. Inmates become hostile to the legal system
         b. Some inmates use violence to solve problems

E. The New Inmate Culture
      1. The importation of outside values into inmate culture has had a dramatic effect on prison life
      2. While the 'old' inmate subculture may have been harmful, it did manage to curb some violence

3. People who violated the code were sanctioned by peers
4. The 'old' system may be almost extinct in most institutions
   a. The change seems to have been precipitated by the black power movement of the 1960s and the 1970s
   b. Black inmates were no longer content to play a subservient role and challenged power
5. In the 'new' system, Black and Latino inmates are much more cohesively organized than Whites
   a. They form groups out of religious and/or political affiliations such as:
      i. Black Muslims
      ii. La Nuestra Familia
      iii. Vice Lords
      iv. Gangster Disciples
      v. Crips
      vi. Aryan Brotherhood

III. WOMEN IMPRISONED

1. Female inmates were looked at as morally depraved people who flouted conventional rules of female behavior
2. Treatment of White and African American women differed significantly in some states:
   a. White women were placed in female-only reformatories
   b. Black women were placed in male prisons, put on chain gangs, subject to beatings

A. Female Institutions
   1. Tend to be smaller than male institutions
      a. Majority are nonsecure institutions similar to college dormitories and froup homes
   2. Like male prisons, women's prisons suffer from lack of:
      a. Adequate training
      b. Health, treatment, and educational facilities
   3. Job training opportunities are also a problem
   4. Prison does little to prepare women to reenter the workforce

B. Female Inmates
   1. Female inmates are young, minority group members, unmarried and undereducated and either underemployed or unemployed
   2. Typical woman inmate is a poor, unskilled woman of color with small children:
      a. Has health problems
      b. Has a history of abuse
      c. Incarcerated for low-level drug or property offenses
   3. High suicide rate
   4. Incarcerated women tend to have a troubled family life
   5. Significant numbers are the product of broken homes
   6. A significant number of inmates have substance abuse problems
   7. The picture of female inmates is troubling

   a. A lifetime of trouble, under-funded, and ill prepared prisons do not provide adequate turnaround to at risk women

  C. Sexual Violence in Women's Prisons

   1. There are a significant number of female inmates being sexually abused and exploited by male correctional workers

   2. Incidents often go unreported

   3. More than 40 states have legislated laws criminalizing staff sexual misconduct

  D. Adapting to the Female Institution

   1. Daily prison life for women varies from that of male inmates

    a. Female inmates do not usually present an immediate physical danger to staff and fellow inmates

   2. The rigid, anti-authority inmate social code found in male institutions does not exist in female institutions

   3. Confinement may produce anxiety and anger

   4. Another form of adaptation to prison used by women is the make-believe family

    a. Group has male and female figures acting as fathers, mothers, and children

    b. The relationships substitute for otherwise unobtainable relationships

IV. **CORRECTIONAL TREATMENT**

   1. Almost every prison facility uses some mode of treatment for inmates

   2. This can be individual therapy, group therapy, or educational or vocational training

  A. Individual and Group Treatment

   a. Prison inmates typically suffer from a variety of cognitive and psychosocial deficits:

    i. Poor emotional control

    ii. Poor social skills

    iii. Poor interpersonal problem solving

   b. These deficits are often linked to long-term substance abuse

   c. Modern counseling programs help them to:

    i. Control emotions

    ii. Communicate with others

    iii. Deal with legal concerns

    iv. Manage general life issues

    v. Develop and maintain social relationships

   d. To achieve these goals, correctional systems use a variety of intensive individual and group techniques such as:

    i. Behavior modification

    ii. Aversive therapy

    iii. Milieu therapy

    iv. Reality therapy

    v. Transactional analysis

    vi. Responsibility therapy

1. Anger Management
    a. May be the most frequent form of group therapy offered within prison settings
    b. Cognitive-behavioral approaches are often used as a means of helping inmates to find ways to control their anger
2. Faith Based Programs
    a. Research shows that inmates involved in religious programs and education do better following release that those in comparison groups but differences quickly erode
    b. Faith based programs seem to work better with some inmates that others and that those who enter the programs with feelings of self-worth are more likely to complete the course than those with less confidence
3. Drug Treatment
    a. Most prisons have programs to help inmates from alcohol and substance abuse issues
        i. One method is to provide abusers with methadone as a substitute for heroin
    b. Because substance abuse is prevalent among correctional clients, some correctional facilities have been reformulated into therapeutic communities:
        i. Use a psychosocial, experimental learning process and rely on positive peer pressure within a highly structured social environment
        ii. Encourages personal disclosure rather than the isolation of the general prison culture
4. HIV/AIDS-Treatment
    a. The AIDS infected inmate has been the subject of great concern
    b. Intravenous drug users are at high risk for HIV, as are males in same sex relationships. Both are common in prison
    c. The rate of HIV infection among state and federal prisoners is around 2 percent, there are about 25,000 HIV-infected inmates
    d. Correctional administrators have found it difficult to arrive at effective policies to confront AIDS
    e. Most correctional systems are now training staff about AIDS
B. Educational Programs
    1. Inmate rehabilitation is pursued through vocational and educational training
    2. The first prison treatment programs were educational
        a. A prison school was opened in 1784 at the Walnut Street Jail
        b. Other systems followed in the same manner
    3. Today, most institutions provide some type of educational program
    4. The number of hours devoted to educational programs and the quality and intensity of these efforts vary greatly:
        a. Some are part-time programs and some are full-time programs
        b. Some bring in volunteers from the community to tutor
    5. Most research indicates that participation in correctional education is related to lower recidivism rates upon release

C. Vocational Programs
    a. Every state correctional system also has some job-related services for inmates
    b. Vocational programs are a path to helping inmates obtain parole
  1. Vocational Training
    a. Most institutions provide vocational training programs, including technical courses
    b. On federal level, Federal Prison Industries, known as UNICOR teaches inmates to produce goods and services such as:
      i. Clothing and textiles
      ii. Industrial products
      iii. Office furniture
    c. Despite the promising aspects of such programs, they have also been criticized
  2. Work Release
    a. More than 40 states offer work release programs as a supplement to in-house job training
      i. Also called furlough programs
    b. Inmates in work release may live in the institution at night while working in the community during the day
    c. Work release has its good points and bad points:
      i. Inmates are sometimes reluctantly received
      ii. Some areas of employment are closed to inmates
      iii. On the other hand, inmates gain benefits from work release
      iv. Ability to maintain work skills
      v. Ability to maintain work ties
      vi. Ability to make transition from prison to community easier
  3. Private Prison Enterprise
    a. Private industry ventured into prisons when the federal government approved the Free Venture Program in 1976
    b. Today, private prisons use a number of models
      i. State use model — Correctional system is a supplier of goods and services that serves state-run institutions
      ii. Free enterprise model — Private companies set up manufacturing units on prison grounds or purchase goods made by inmates
  4. Post Release Programs
    a. A final element of job-related programming involves helping inmates obtain jobs before they are released
    b. A number of correctional departments have set up employment services to ease the transition between institution and community
D. Can Rehabilitation Work?
  1. Questions still remain about whether rehabilitation works
  2. Robert Martinson and his associates found that many treatment programs were failures
  3. Considerable debate has persisted over the effectiveness of treatment
  4. Some of the most carefully crafted treatment efforts have failed to show a positive impact on inmates returning to the community

V.   **GUARDING THE INSTITUTION**
1.   Control of a prison is a complex task
     a.   There are issues with balancing high security and being too liberal
2.   For years, prisons guards were viewed as ruthless people who enjoyed their positions of power
     a.   Guards were viewed as racist and anti-rehabilitation, and had a "lock psychosis" developed from years of counting, numbering, and checking inmates
3.   Correctional officers are now viewed as public servants
4.   Most guards are in favor of rehabilitation and do not hold any particular animosity toward inmates
5.   The greatest problem faced by correctional officers is the duality of their role:
     a.   Maintain order and security
     b.   Advocate humane treatment and rehabilitation
6.   Correctional officers may have an impact on prisoner recidivism rates
A.   Female Correctional Officers
6.   Women now work side by side with male guards in almost every state, performing the same duties
7.   Research has indicated that discipline has not suffered because of the inclusion of women in the guard force
8.   Some female guards feel that working in a male institution can boost their career

VI.   **PRISON VIOLENCE**
1.   Conflict, violence, and brutality are sad but ever-present facts of institutional life
2.   Violence can involve individual conflict:
     a.   Inmate v. inmate
     b.   Inmate v. staff
     c.   Staff v. inmate
3.   While often downplayed, sexual assault is a common threat
4.   Violence can also involve large groups of inmates such as the Attica Riot of 1971
     a.   More than 300 riots have occurred since 1774, 90 percent of them since 1952
A.   What Causes Violence?
1.   Individual Violence
     a.   History of prior violence – before they were incarcerated indicates inmates were prone to violence
     b.   Age – younger inmates, those with a record of prior incarceration, and who have suffered pre-arrest drug use are the ones most likely to engage in disruptive behavior in prison
     c.   Psychological factors – many inmates suffer from personality disorders
     d.   Prison conditions – prison experience itself can cause people to become violent:
          i.   Inhumane conditions

319

    ii. Overcrowding
    iii. Depersonalization
    iv. Threat of sexual assault
   e. Lack of dispute resolution – many prisons lack mechanisms that enable inmate's grievances against either prison officials or other inmates to be resolved
   f. Basic survival – inmates resort to violence to survive
  2. Collective Violence
   a. Inmate-balance theory – riots and other forms of collective violence occur when prison officials make an abrupt effort to control the prison and limit freedom
   b. Administrative-control theory – collective violence is caused by prison mismanagement

VII. PRISONERS' RIGHTS

  1. Before the early 1960s, it was accepted that on conviction an individual forfeited all rights expressly granted by statutory law or correctional policy
   a. One reason inmates lacked rights was that the state and federal courts were reluctant to intervene in the administration of prisons unless there was a serious breach of the Eighth Amendment. This policy was called the hands-off doctrine
   b. As the 1960s drew to a close, the hands-off doctrine ended
  2. In the 1960s, activists groups began to search for legal vehicles to bring inmate complaints to the courts. The most widely used device was Civil Rights Act, 42 U.S.C. 1983
   a. The legal argument — prison inmates could sue state officials when their rights were violated
   b. The subsequent prisoners' rights crusade from 1964 to 1980 paralleled women's movements and civil rights movements
  3. To slow prison litigation, Congress passed the Prison Litigation Reform Act in 1996
   a. Most important provision:
    i. Requires prisoners to exhaust all internal administrative grievance procedures before they can file a civil rights case in federal court
    ii. Bars litigation if a prisoner has not suffered a physical injury in addition to a violation of constitutional rights
  4. Supreme Court has upheld the provisions in two cases:
   a. *Booth v. Churner* (2001)
   b. *Porter v. Nussle* (2002)
    i. Constitutional to require that an inmate exhaust all administrative processes before a case can be brought to the courts
 A. Substantive Rights
   a. The courts have granted inmates a number of substantive rights that have influenced the correctional system
  1. Access to Courts, Legal Services, and Materials
    i. Courts have held that inmates are entitled to legal materials

  ii. Inmates who help others are called jailhouse lawyers
- b. Freedom of the Press and of Expression
  - i. Correctional administrators traditionally placed severe restrictions on inmate speech and expression
  - ii. Courts have ruled that corrections administrators must justify restrictions on free speech
- c. Freedom of Religion
  - i. In general, the courts have ruled that inmates have the right to assemble and pray in the religion of their choice
  - ii. Administration can draw the line if religious freedom becomes cumbersome or impossible to carry out
- d. Medical Rights
  - i. In early prisons, medical treatment was restricted under the 'exceptional circumstances doctrine'
  - ii. Using this policy, the courts would only hear those cases in which human dignity was disregarded
  - iii. To gain their rights, inmates have resorted to class action suits:
    - a) 1972: *Newman v. Alabama* – entire Alabama prison system's medical facilities were declared inadequate
    - b) 1976: *Estelle v. Gamble*— the Supreme Court mandated a prisoner's rights to have medical care
- e. Cruel and Unusual Punishment
  - i. The concept is founded in the Eighth Amendment
  - ii. The term has not been specifically defined, but circumstances have been identified that constitute cruel and unusual punishment, such as:
    - a) Degrades dignity of human beings
    - b) Is more severe than the offense
    - c) Shocks the general conscience and is fundamentally unfair
    - d) Punishes people because of their status:
      1. Race
      2. Religion
      3. Mental state
    - e) Is in flagrant disregard of due process of law, such as punishment that is capriciously applied
  - iii. Courts have placed limits on disciplinary methods that may be considered inhumane
  - iv. Corporal punishment all but ended after being condemned in *Jackson v. Bishop*, 1968
- f. Racial Segregation
  - i. *Johnson v. California* (2005)
    - a) Segregation of prison inmates based on race, in their cells or anywhere on prison grounds, is an inappropriate form of racial classification
    - b) Standard of Strict scrutiny

1. Segregation should only be allowed if a prison administrator could prove that it served a compelling interest to promote prison safety

   g. Overall Prison Conditions

      i. Prisoners have long had the right to have minimal conditions for survival:

        a) Shelter

        b) Food

        c) Medical care

        d) Clothing

      ii. A number of attempts have been made to articulate standards of care

      iii. *Farmer v. Brennen*, 1994, court ruled that prison officials are legally liable if, knowing that inmate faces a serious risk of harm, they disregard the risk

      iv. If there is a legitimate purpose for the use of government restriction, the restriction may be considered constitutional:

        a) Strip searches

        b) Prohibit mail

        c) Restrict reading material

VIII. LEAVING PRISON

1. At the end of their term, most inmates return to society and try to resume their lives

2. For some inmates, reintegration to society comes by parole. Parole equates to supervised release while in the community

   a. Once on parole, former inmates have to live by a strict set of rules that mandate they

      i. Stay out of trouble

      ii. Stay drug and alcohol free

      iii. Be employed and attend counseling

3. In some states, parole is determined by a parole board, men and women who review inmate cases and determine rehabilitative level. This is called discretionary parole

   a. Board also dictates:

      i. Parole rules parolees must obey

4. Most parole authorities are independent agencies that consist of members appointed by the governor

   a. Rest affiliated with the department of corrections

5. In a number of jurisdictions, discretionary parole has been abandoned, amount of time a person must remain in prison is a predetermined percentage of the sentence

   a. Mandatory parole release

6. Inmates can be released for a variety of reasons:

   a. Expiration of term

   b. Commutation of sentence

   c. Court orders to relieve overcrowding

7. Discretionary parole use in steep decline
8. There are more than 800,000 people currently on parole
   a. Each year about 500,000 inmates are released on parole

A. Parole Effectiveness
   1. Despite all of the efforts to treat released offenders, many return to prison shortly after release
   2. Persons released from prison face a multitude of difficulties:
      a. Largely uneducated
      b. Unskilled
      c. Lack solid family support systems
   3. Rearrests are most common in the first six months
   4. Most successful return rates based on use of strategies that:
      a. Employed programs that target motivated offenders to stay crime and drug free through a combination of:
         i. Swift and certain sanctions for prison violations
         ii. Rewards for obeying correctional rules

B. The Problem of Reentry
   1. Parole failure is still a significant problem
      a. One reason may be the very nature of the prison experience
   2. The psychological and economic problems that lead offenders to recidivism are rarely addressed
   3. Some clients return to society in the same destructive neighborhood and social groups that prompted the original law-violating behavior
   4. Parole failure may also be ties to the client's own lifelong personal deficits
   5. Once on the outside, problems do not easily subside; some inmates feel a need to show prison has not changed them

C. Why Do People Fail on Parole?
   a. A number of social, economic and personal factors interfere with re-entry success:
      i. Legal changes in how people are released from prison
      ii. Many inmates not assigned to supervision caseloads once they are back in community
         a) About 200,000 released inmates go unsupervised each year
         b) Flood of newly released inmates present the community with the risks of:
            1. Increases in child abuse
            2. Family violence
            3. Spread of infectious diseases
            4. Homelessness
            5. Community disorganization
   1. Economic Problems
      a. Most people leave prison with:
         i. No savings
         ii. No immediate entitlement to unemployment benefits
         iii. Few employment prospects
   2. Family Problems

a. Inmates with strong social support and close family ties have a better chance of making it on the outside
b. May no longer be welcome in subsidized public housing
  i. One strike and you're out
    a) All members of a household are evicted if one member is involved in crime
c. Children of inmates are affected:
  i. Educationally
    a) Significantly more likely to be expelled or suspended
  ii. Socially
    a) May suffer:
      1. Confusion
      2. Sadness
      3. Social stigma
  iii. Are more than five times more likely to serve time in prison than children whose parents are not incarcerated

D. Community Problems
1. When inmate release numbers were lower, the impact on the community was not that significant. As numbers have increased, communities face challenges
2. Condition of community inmate returns to has an effect on their success

E. Legal Problems
1. Inmates sometimes find that 'going straight' is an economic impossibility
2. Many employers are reluctant to hire people who have served time
3. Ex inmates face many legal restrictions
  a. Prohibitions on certain kinds of employment
  b. Limits on obtaining licenses
  c. Restrictions on freedom of movement

F. Improving Chances on Reentry
1. Federal and state governments have devoted energy to improve re-entry success
2. On April 9, 2008 Second Chance Act signed into law:
  a. Authorized various grants to government agencies and nonprofit groups to provide a variety of services including:
    i. Employment assistance
    ii. Substance abuse treatment
    iii. Family programming
3. State correctional agencies have made an effort to help inmates take advantage of these services

CHAPTER SUMMARY

Prisons in the United States are total institutions. This means that inmates locked within their walls are segregated from the outside world, kept under constant scrutiny and surveillance, and forced to obey strict official rules to avoid facing formal sanctions. Despite these hardships, many inmates learn to adapt to the prison routine. Each prisoner has his own method of coping.

He may stay alone, become friends with another inmate, join a group, or seek the advice of treatment personnel.

Before 1960, few women were in prison. Women's prisons were relatively rare and were usually an outgrowth of male institutions. Female inmates are young, minority, unmarried, undereducated, and either un- or underemployed.

Prison inmates suffer from poor emotional control, social skills, and interpersonal problem solving. Modern counseling programs help them to control emotions, communicate with others, deal with legal concerns, manage general life issues, and develop and maintain social relationships. To achieve these goals, correctional systems use techniques, including behavior modification, aversive therapy, milieu therapy, reality therapy, transactional analysis, and responsibility therapy.

For many years, prison guards were viewed as ruthless people who enjoyed their positions of power over inmates, fought rehabilitation efforts, were racist, and had a lock psychosis developed from years of counting, numbering, and checking on inmates. Corrections officers play a number of roles in the institution: they supervise cell houses, dining areas, shops, and other facilities as well as perch up on the walls, armed with rifles, to oversee the yard and prevent escapes.

Conflict, violence, and brutality are sad but ever-present facts of institutional life. Violence can involve individual conflict: inmate versus inmate, inmate versus staff, staff versus inmate. There is no single explanation for either collective or individual violence. Individual violence theories include history of prior violence, psychological factors, prison conditions, lack of dispute resolution mechanisms, and basic survival. Collective Violence theories include inmate-balance theory, administrative-control theory, and overcrowding.

Through a slow process of legal review, the courts have granted inmates a number of substantive rights that have influenced the correctional system. The most important of these rights are access to courts, legal services, and materials; freedom of the press and of expression; freedom of religion; medical rights; cruel and unusual punishment; and overall prison conditions.

For some inmates, their reintegration into society comes by way of parole— the planned community release and supervision of offenders before the expiration of their prison sentences. In some states, parole is granted by a parole board.

Recidivism may be a by-product of the disruptive effect a prison experience has on personal relationships. Because of America's two-decade-long imprisonment boom, more than 500,000 inmates are now being released back into the community each year. The problems of re-entry include the effect on communities, inmate's loss of rights, and attempting to improve chances of re-entry.

DISCUSSION QUESTIONS

1. Considering the dangers that men face during their prison stay, should nonviolent inmates be placed in separate institutions to protect them from harm?
2. Should women be allowed to work as guards in male prisons? What about male guards in female prisons?
3. Should prison inmates be allowed a free college education while noncriminals are forced to pay tuition?
4. Which would be more effective: telling inmates that they have to earn the right to be paroled? Or, giving inmates their parole date in advance and telling them they will lose it for misbehavior?
5. What is the role of the parole board?
6. Should a former prisoner enjoy all the civil rights afforded the average citizen?
7. Should former inmates lose their right to vote?

MEDIA TOOLS

Read an interesting article of a qualitative work by David Asma. The article was an examination of an inmate's life at a county jail and what the term "total institution" really means. The article, "Welcome to Jail: Some Dramaturgical Notes on Admission to a Total Institution" is worth an examination and review. Asma's work is posted on Critcrim.org which is affiliated with the American Society of Criminology and The Academy of Criminal Justice Sciences. The article can be found at: http://critcrim.org/redfeather/journal-pomocrim/Vol-5-Dramaturgy/welcome%20to%20jail.htm

For all things related to prison including prison descriptions and stories from some individuals who were incarcerated, check out the website Inside Prison. The Inside Prison website can be found at: http://www.insideprison.com

Read an interesting article regarding prison culture, the article describes how a sugary confectionary can control so much behind bars. The article "Honey buns sweeten life for Florida prisoners" by Drew Harwell from the St. Petersburg Times. The article can be found at: http://www.tampabay.com/features/humaninterest/honey-buns-sweeten-life-for-florida-prisoners/1142687

Make sure to visit the National Criminal Justice Reference Service's area on Inmates/Offenders under the area of Corrections. Very helpful site to get research ideas. Visit the National Criminal Justice Reference Service at: https://www.ncjrs.gov/index.html

PRACTICE TEST BANK

MULTIPLE CHOICE

1. If a violent riot follows an attempt by the prison to crack down on gangs, this would be consistent with which theory of collective prison violence?
    a. Dehumanization
    b. Administrative-control
    c. Inmate-reaction
    d. Inmate-balance

2. Which of the listed is not a central focus in faith-based programs?
    a. Helping clients gain skills or training
    b. Building support networks
    c. Creating a supportive relationship between staff, volunteers, and clients
    d. Participation in religious services or rituals

3. An inmate who has been assimilated into the prison subculture is said to be
    a. accumulated.
    b. subculturized.
    c. subconforming.
    d. prisonized.

4. In response to the problem of prison rape, Congress enacted
    a. the Rape Alliance Prevention Act.
    b. laws prohibiting opposite sex guards (i.e., male guards only in male prisons).
    c. the Prison Rape Reduction Act.
    d. the Civil Rights Act U.S.C. 42, 1983.

5. Which group is described as being better able to cope with the prison experience?
    a. Older, more experienced males
    b. Young, aggressive males
    c. Punks
    d. Older, single females

6. In general, as compared to men's prisons, women's prisons have
    a. stronger subcultures.
    b. stronger inmate codes.
    c. less violence.
    d. many more programs for inmates.

7. All of the listed are targets of prison sexual violence except
    a. younger male inmates.
    b. gay men.
    c. bisexual men.
    d. older male inmates.

8. Programs that allow inmates to leave during the day for private-sector jobs outside the prison, and then return at night, are called
   a. work release.
   b. day job.
   c. day fine.
   d. employment furlough.

9. Which prison industry model of the correctional system produces supplies and services for state institutions?
   a. Agency-utilization
   b. Internal implementation
   c. State-use
   d. In-state procurement

10. Research indicates that the use of female guards in male institutions has
    a. increased violence levels.
    b. resulted in thousands of sexual assaults.
    c. greatly improved the effect of rehabilitation programs.
    d. had beneficial effects on the self-image of inmates.

11. The most violent prison riot in recent history cost 39 lives in 1971 in New York State at
    a. Newgate.
    b. Attica.
    c. Sing-Sing.
    d. Marion.

12. Prisoners fear retaliation and often feel embarrassment with regard to reporting
    a. sexual assaults or rape.
    b. theft of personal property.
    c. homosexuality.
    d. minor policy violations.

13. Because of their security and regimented operation, prisons are considered to be
    a. participatory institutions.
    b. total institutions.
    c. incapacitating institutions.
    d. conforming institutions.

14. Inmates are tested, evaluated, and classified at a classification or
    a. reception center.
    b. assessment center.
    c. intake center.
    d. drop-off center.

15. Which of the following is a nickname for male inmates who look and act as women?
    a. Punks
    b. Queens
    c. Wives
    d. Slaves

16. Another term for the unique language that prisoners use is
    a. code.
    b. slang.
    c. inmate talk.
    d. argot.

17. The 1976 case, *Estelle V. Gamble*, focused on
    a. failure to respond to exceptional medical circumstances.
    b. medical malpractice.
    c. negligence in dealing with medical problems.
    d. deliberate indifference to serious medical needs.

18. This type of inmate is always loyal to his fellow prisoners, keeps his promises, is dependable and trustworthy, and never interferes with inmates who are conniving against officials.
    a. That guy
    b. The right guy
    c. Prison slave
    d. A punk

19 In those states that have maintained discretionary parole, the authority to release inmates is usually vested in
    a. the warden.
    b. the governor.
    c. a parole board.
    d. a parole officer.

20. The greatest problem faced by corrections officers is the stress caused by
    a. the danger of their job.
    b. the duality of their role.
    c. low pay.
    d. little chance for advancement.

21. Prisons in the United States are generally classified as
    a. total rehabilitation institutions.
    b. total institutions.
    c. military institutions.
    d. illegitimate institutions.

22. In terms of future criminality, research shows that a prison may actually
    a. defer criminal offending.
    b. rehabilitate criminal offenders.
    c. reinforce criminal behavior (offending).
    d. stop criminal offending.

23. Conflict, violence, and brutality are sad but ever-present facts of institutional life. Violence can involve individual conflict between a number of groups according to the chapter, except
    a. inmate v. inmate.
    b. inmate v. staff.
    c. staff v. staff.
    d. staff v. inmate.

24. Female inmates tend to by typically young and
    a. unemployed.
    b. educated.
    c. married.
    d. White.

25. Inmates form their own world with a unique set of norms and rules known as an
    a. inmate code.
    b. inmate harmonization.
    c. inmate norms.
    d. inmate subculture.

26. Which term describes the process where values, attitudes, and behavior are transferred from older inmates to younger inmates?
    a. Inmate bylaws
    b. Inmate social code
    c. Inmate subculture
    d. Inmate argot

27. Relational violence in women's prisons occurs when inmates
    a. fight over correctional officers as the only men in their lives.
    b. fight with correctional officers as the only men in their lives.
    c. fight over family roles.
    d. fight with family when they come to visit.

28. A significant aspect of inmate subculture involves the informal
    a. inmate clan code.
    b. inmate mores code.
    c. inmate social code.
    d. inmate code of silence.

29.   Corrections officers face challenges associated with their dual role; this role includes supervising prisoners and
    a.   advocating rehabilitation and treatment.
    b.   supporting prisoner rights laws.
    c.   issuing discipline.
    d.   aggressively enforcing rules.

30.   Which element of the inmate social code cautions inmates not to make fools of themselves or support the guards or prison administration over the interest of the inmates?
    a.   Don't exploit inmates
    b.   Don't lose your head
    c.   Don't interfere with inmates interests
    d.   Don't be a sucker

TRUE/FALSE

1.   T   F   Women's prisons tend to be larger than men's prisons since there are fewer women's prisons.

2.   T   F   Female inmates receive more support from internal and external sources than male inmates.

3.   T   F   The Supreme Court has ruled that correctional officers who knowingly violate the Eighth Amendment rights of inmates can be held liable for damages.

4.   T   F   Most correctional systems provide some form of vocational training for inmates.

5.   T   F   Congress has enacted legislation that requires national data collection, analysis, and research on prison rape.

6.   T   F   Prison inmates have no substantive rights.

7.   T   F   The traditional prison culture is now being replaced by a violent gang culture.

8.   T   F   Male inmates tend to form make-believe families to adjust to prison stress.

9.   T   F   Most female inmates come from stable, drug-free environments.

10.   T   F   Where Hispanic inmates have successfully organized; it is in the form of a neo-Nazi group called the Aryan Brotherhood.

11.   T   F   The first prison treatment programs were educational.

12.   T   F   The federal program UNICOR teaches inmates to produce goods and services for sale and use by government agencies only.

13.   T   F   Surveys have revealed that prison administrators regularly downplay the number of sexually coercive and/or rape incidents in prisons.

14.   T   F   Female correctional officers find that an assignment to a male institution can impede career advancement and success.

15.   T   F   More than 300 prison riots have occurred since 1974.

FILL-IN-THE-BLANK

1.   Parole is the early release of a prisoner from imprisonment subject to conditions set by a parole _____.

2.   The typical prison has been described as a _____ for crime in which young offenders are taught by older cons to become sophisticated criminals.

3.   An inmate who has become_____ is described as having assimilated into and accepting of prison subculture.

4.   A _____ institution is one which tightly controls most aspects of a person's life through tight security, control, and regimentation.

5.   A _____ is a temporary leave from a prison for vocational or educational training or maintaining family ties.

6.   In the new prison culture African American and _____ inmates are more cohesively organized than Whites.

7.   The "_____" is someone who uses the inmate social code as his personal behavior guide.

8.   At the turn of the _____century, female inmates were viewed as morally depraved people who flouted conventional rules of female behavior.

9.   About half of all inmates return within _____ years of being released on parole.

10.   Female prisoners sometimes form make-believe _____.

11. For some inmates, their reintegration into society comes by way of _____ _____, the planned community release and supervision of incarcerated offenders before the expiration of their full prison sentence.

12. A prisoner who has some expertise in the law and helps other prisoners with their cases is called a _____ lawyer.

13. Because substance abuse is so prevalent among correctional clients, some correctional facilities have been reformulated into _____ communities.

14. The use of solitary confinement continues for disruptive inmates, its prolonged use under barbaric conditions has been held to be in violation of the _____ Amendment.

15. It was not until 1976, in *Estelle v. Gamble*, that the Supreme Court clearly mandated an inmate's right to have _____.

ESSAY

1. Discuss the concepts of the inmate social code and prisonization. What impact do these have on the prison and on the chances of rehabilitation?

2. Discuss some of the explanations for individual and collective violence in prisons. Provide examples. Which theory do you think is best? Explain your position.

3. Explain the old and new inmate culture.

4. This chapter presented five substantive rights granted to inmates. Identify and explain three.

5. Discuss the characteristics and major problems of female inmates and female prisons. How do these differ from male inmates and prison?

CHAPTER 12 ANSWER KEY

Multiple Choice

1. d [p. 292, LO8]   2. d [p. 285, LO6]   3. d [p. 281, LO4]   4. c [p. 280, LO3]   5. a [p. 279, LO1]

6. c [p. 282, LO5]   7. d [p. 280, LO3]   8. a [p. 287, LO6]   9. c [p. 288, LO6]   10. d [p. 289, LO7]

11. b [p. 291, LO8]   12. a [p. 280, LO3]   13. b [p. 278, LO2]   14. a [p. 278, LO4]   15. b [p. 280, LO3]

16. d [p. 281, LO5]   17. d [p. 295, LO9]   18. b [p. 281, LO5]   19. c [p. 297, LO10]   20. b [p. 289, LO7]

21. b [p. 278, LO2]   22. c [p. 278, LO1]   23. c [p. 291, LO8]   24. a [p. 282, LO5]   25. d [p. 280, LO4]

26. b [p. 280, LO4]   27. a [p. 283, LO5]   28. c [p. 280, LO4]   29. a [p. 289, LO7]   30. d [p. 281, LO4]

True/False

1. F [p. 282, LO5]   2. T [p. 283, LO5]   3. T [p. 294, LO9]   4. T [p. 286, LO6]   5. T [p. 294, LO3]

6. F [p. 294, LO9]   7. T [p. 281, LO8]   8. F [p. 284, LO5]   9. F [p. 283, LO5]   10. F [p. 282, LO4]

11. T [p. 286, LO6]   12. T [p. 287, LO6]   13. T [p. 280, LO3]   14. F [p. 289, LO7]   15. T [p. 291, LO8]

Fill-in-the-Blank

1. board [p. 296, LO10]   2. school [p. 278, LO1]   3. prisonized [p. 281, LO4]

4. total [p. 278, LO2]   5. Furlough [p. 287, LO6]   6. Latino [p. 281, LO8]

7. right guy [p. 281, LO4]   8. twentieth [p. 282, LO4]   9. three [p. 297, LO1]

10. families [p. 284, LO5]   11. parole [p. 296, LO6]   12. jailhouse [p. 294, LO6]

13. theraputic [p. 285, LO6]   14. Eighth [p. 295, LO9]   15. medical care [p. 295, LO9]

Essay

1.   **Discuss the concepts of the inmate social code and prisonization. What impact do these have on the prison and on the chances of rehabilitation?**

Inmates find a unique world in prison. Inmates have collectively formed their own world with a unique set of norms and rules, known as the inmate subculture. Inmate subculture incorporates a unique inmate social code comprised of unwritten guidelines that expressed the values, attitudes, and type of behavior that older inmates demanded of young ones. The social code has been passed on from one generation of inmates to another, and represents the values of interpersonal relations in the prison.

Research into the social code identified a unique language, or argot, that prisoners use. It also revealed that prisoners group themselves tend to group themselves into cliques on the basis of such personal criteria as sexual preference, political beliefs, and offense history. Prison life became defined by the inmate's assimilation into the existing prison culture through acceptance of its language, sexual code, and norms of behavior. This process became known as "prisonization." Those who become the most "prisonized" are the least likely to reform on the outside. The effects of prisonization may be long-term and destructive. Many inmates become hostile to the legal system, learning to use violence as a means of solving problems and to value criminal peers.

The social code includes "rules" such as 'be tough and don't lose your dignity' requiring an inmate to be prepared when conflict arises---maxims include "don't cop out," "don't weaken," and "be tough; be a man."
Another "rule" "don't be a sucker" cautions inmates not to make fools of themselves or support the guards or prison administration over the interest of the inmates—maxims include "be sharp." The very nature of these self-imposed "rules" inhibits an inmate's ability to rehabilitate. The idea that inmates come first before obedience to authority (guard) flies in the face of logic---especially if the inmate wishes to do his or her time and exit as smoothly as possible. Even the code's concept of the 'right-guy' is in direct contrast to inmate rehabilitation. The "right guy" is someone who uses the inmate social code as his personal behavior guide. He is always loyal to his fellow prisoners, keeps his promises, is dependable and trustworthy, and never interferes with inmates who are conniving against the officials. The right guy does not go around looking for a fight, but he never runs away from one; he acts "like a man."

[pp. 280-281, LO4]

2. **Discuss some of the explanations for individual and collective violence in prisons. Provide examples. Which theory do you think is best? Explain your position.**

Conflict, violence, and brutality are ever-present facts of institutional life. Violence can involve individual conflict: inmate versus inmate, inmate versus staff, and staff versus inmate. Nonsexual assaults may stem from an aggressor's desire to shake down the victim for money and personal favors, may be motivated by racial conflict, or may simply be used to establish power within the institution.

Violence can also involve large groups of inmates, such as the infamous riots in the 1970s. There is no single explanation for either collective or individual violence, but theories abound. However, recent research by Benjamin Steiner shows that factors related to prison administration, inmate population characteristics, and the racial makeup of inmates and staff can influence violence levels. In many instances, street gangs maintain prison branches that unite the inmate with his former violence-prone peers. Having this connection supports and protects gang members while they are in prison, and it assists in supporting gang members' families and associates outside the wall. Gang violence is a significant source of prison conflict.

Individual Violence Factors

- **Age:** Younger inmates, those with a record of prior incarceration, and those who have suffered pre-arrest drug use are the ones most likely to engage in disruptive behavior in prison, especially if they are not active participants in institutional treatment programs.
- **Psychological Factors:** Many inmates suffer from personality disorders.
- **Prison Conditions:** The prison experience itself causes people to become violent. Inhuman conditions, including overcrowding, depersonalization, and the threat of sexual assault, are violence-producing conditions.

- **Lack of Dispute Resolution Mechanisms:** Many prisons lack effective mechanisms for handling inmate grievances against either prison officials or other inmates fairly and equitably. Prisoners who complain about other inmates are viewed as "rats" or "snitches" and are marked for death by their enemies.
- **Basic Survival:** Inmates resort to violence in order to survive---or the lack of physical security.

Group Violence Factors

- **Inmate-Balance Theory:** Riots and other forms of collective violence occur when prison officials make an abrupt effort to take control of the prison and limit freedoms. Crackdowns occur when officials perceive that inmate leaders have too much power and take measures to control their illicit privileges, such as gambling or stealing food.
- **Administrative-Control Theory:** Prison mismanagement, lack of strong security, and inadequate control by prison officials contribute to violence. Poor management may inhibit conflict management and set the stage for violence. Repressive administrations give inmates the feeling that nothing will ever change, that they have nothing to lose, and that violence is the only means for change.
- **Overcrowding:** As the prison population continues to climb, unmatched by expanded capacity, prison violence may increase. Overcrowding caused by the rapid increases in the prison population has also been linked to increases in both inmate substance abuse and prison violence.

[pp. 292-293, LO8]

3.   **Explain the old and new inmate culture.**

The importation of outside values into the inmate culture has had a dramatic effect on prison life. Although the "old" inmate subculture may have been harmful because its norms and values insulated the inmate from change efforts, it also helped create order in the institution and prevented violence among the inmates. People who violated the code and victimized others were sanctioned by their peers. An understanding developed between guards and inmate leaders: The guards would let the inmates have things their own way, and the inmates would not let things get out of hand and draw the attention of the administration.

The old system may be dying or already dead in most institutions. The change seems to have been precipitated by the black power movement in the 1960s and 1970s. Black inmates were no longer content to play a subservient role and challenged the power of established white inmates. As the black power movement gained prominence, racial tension in prisons created divisions that severely altered the inmate subculture. Older, respected inmates could no longer cross racial lines to mediate disputes. Predatory inmates could victimize others without fear of retaliation. Consequently, more inmates than ever are now assigned to protective custody for their own safety.

In the new culture, African American and Latino inmates are much more cohesively organized than whites. Their groups sometimes form out of religious or political affiliations, such as the Black Muslims; out of efforts to combat discrimination in prison, such as the Latino group La Nuestra Familia; or from street gangs, such as the Vice Lords or Gangster Disciples in the Illinois prison system and the Crips in California. Where white inmates have successfully organized, it is in the form of a neo-Nazi group called the Aryan Brotherhood. Racially homogeneous gangs are so cohesive and powerful that they are able to replace the original inmate code with one of their own.

[pp. 281-282, LO5]

4.   **This chapter presented five substantive rights granted to inmates. Identify and explain three.**

- **Access to Courts, Legal Services, and Materials.** Courts have held that inmates are entitled to have legal materials available and must be provided with assistance in drawing up and filing complaints. Inmates who help others, so-called jailhouse lawyers, cannot be interfered with or harassed by prison administrators.

- **Freedom of the Press and of Expression.** Courts have consistently ruled that only when a compelling state interest exists can prisoners' First Amendment rights be modified; correctional authorities must justify the limiting of free speech by showing that granting it would threaten institutional security. If prison administrators believe that correspondence undermines prison security, the First Amendment rights of inmates can be curtailed.

- **Freedom of Religion.** In general, the courts have ruled that inmates have the right to assemble and pray in the religion of their choice but that religious symbols and practices that interfere with institutional security can be restricted. Administrators can draw the line if responding to religious needs becomes cumbersome or impossible for reasons of cost or security. Granting special privileges can also be denied on the grounds that they will cause other groups to make similar demands that cannot be met within the institution.

- **Medical Rights.** In early prisons, inmates' right to medical treatment was restricted through the "exceptional circumstances doctrine." Using this policy, the courts would hear only those cases in which the circumstances revealed utter disregard for human dignity, while denying hearings to less serious cases. The cases that were allowed access to the courts usually entailed total denial of medical care. To gain their medical rights, prisoners have resorted to class action suits (suits brought on behalf of all individuals affected by similar circumstances—in this case, poor medical attention). In the most significant case, *Newman v. Alabama* (1972), the entire Alabama prison system's medical facilities were declared inadequate. The Supreme Court cited the following factors as contributing to inadequate care: insufficient physician and nurse resources, reliance on untrained inmates for paramedical work, intentional failure in treating the sick and injured, and failure to conform to proper medical standards. The *Newman* case forced corrections departments to upgrade prison medical facilities. It was not until 1976, in *Estelle v. Gamble,* that the Supreme Court clearly affirmed inmates' right to medical care. Gamble had hurt his back in a Texas prison and filed suit because he contested the type of treatment he had received and questioned the lack of interest that prison guards had shown in his case. The Supreme Court said, "Deliberate indifference to serious medical needs of prisoners constitutes the 'unnecessary and wanton infliction of pain,' proscribed by the Eighth Amendment." The *Gamble* ruling mandated that inmate health care reflect what is available to citizens in the general community. Consequently, correctional administrators must consider access, quality, and cost of health care as part of the prison regime.

- **Cruel and Unusual Punishment.** The concept of cruel and unusual punishment is founded in the Eighth Amendment of the Constitution. The term itself has not been specifically defined by the Supreme Court, but the Court has held that treatment constitutes cruel and unusual punishment when it does the following:
  - Degrades the dignity of human beings
  - Is more severe than (is disproportional to) the offense for which it has been given
  - Shocks the general conscience and is fundamentally unfair
  - Is deliberately indifferent to a person's safety and well-being

- Punishes people because of their status, such as race, religion, and mental state
- Is in flagrant disregard of due process of law, such as punishment that is capriciously applied

[pp. 294-296, LO9]

5. **Discuss the characteristics and major problems of female inmates and female prisons. How do these differ from male inmates and prison?**

Incarcerated women have had a troubled family life. Significant numbers were at-risk children, products of broken homes and the welfare system; over half have received welfare at some time during their adult lives. Many claim to have been physically or sexually abused at some point in their lives. This pattern continued in adult life; many female inmates were victims of domestic violence and many display psychological problems. A significant number of female inmates report having substance abuse problems involving addictive drugs, such as cocaine, heroin, or PCP. Low risk offenders face a high risk of exposure to HIV and other health threats because of their prior history of drug abuse. The typical woman behind bars is a poor, unskilled woman of color with small children, has health problems, has a history of abuse, and is incarcerated for low-level drug or property offenses. Like their male counterparts, female inmates are young (most are under age 30), minority group members, unmarried, undereducated (more than half are high school dropouts), and either unemployed or underemployed.

Women cope in prison by establishing a pseudo-family. Women use a make-believe family; this group contains masculine and feminine figures acting as fathers and mothers. Some members even act as children and take on the role of brother or sister.

Lack of opportunity is present. It is not uncommon for female prisoners to be sexually abused and exploited by male correctional workers, who apply either brute force or psychological coercion to gain sexual control over inmates. Staff-on-inmate sexual misconduct covers a wide range of behaviors, from lewd remarks, to voyeurism, to assault and rape. Because male correctional officers now are commonly assigned to women's prisons, there have also been major scandals involving the sexual exploitation and rape of female inmates.

Differences in Prison Conditions

Women's prisons tend to be smaller than those housing male inmates. Although some female institutions are strictly penal, with steel bars, concrete floors, and other security measures, the majority are nonsecure institutions similar to college dormitories and group homes in the community. Women's facilities, especially those in the community, commonly offer inmates a great deal of autonomy and allow them to make decisions affecting their daily lives.

Many female inmates are parents and had custody of their children before incarceration, but little effort is made to help them develop better parenting skills. Daily life in women's prisons differs somewhat from that in male institutions; unlike male inmates, women usually do not present an immediate physical danger to staff and fellow inmates. Relatively few engage in violent behavior, and incidents of inmate-initiated sexual aggression, so common in male institutions, are rare in women's prisons. The rigid inmate social code found in many male institutions does not exist in female institutions. Confinement for women, however, may produce severe anxiety and anger because of separation from families and loved ones and the inability to function in normal female roles. Unlike men, who direct their anger outward, female prisoners may turn to more self-destructive acts to cope with their problems. Female inmates are more likely than males to mutilate their own bodies and to attempt suicide.

[pp. 282-284, LO5]

CHAPTER 13
Juvenile Justice in the Twenty-First Century

LEARNING OBJECTIVES

After studying this chapter, students will:

1. Describe the history of juvenile justice
2. Discuss the establishment of the juvenile court
3. Describe the changes in juvenile justice that began in the 1960s and continue today
4. Summarize police processing of juvenile offenders
5. Describe the juvenile court process
6. Explain the concept of waiver
7. Explain the importance of In re Gault
8. Describe the juvenile correctional process

KEY TERMS AND CONCEPTS

parens patriae (p. 308) Latin term meaning "father of his country." According to this legal philosophy, the government is the guardian of everyone who has a disability, especially children, and has a legal duty to act in their best interests until the age of majority.

poor laws (p. 308) Seventeenth-century laws in England that bound out vagrants and abandoned children as indentured servants to masters.

child savers (p. 308) Late nineteenth-century reformers in America who developed programs for troubled youths and influenced legislation creating the juvenile justice system.

Children's Aid Society (p. 310) A child-saving organization begun by Charles Loring Brace; it took children from the streets in large cities and placed them with farm families on the prairie.

juvenile court (p. 310) A court that has original jurisdiction over persons defined by statute as juveniles and alleged to be delinquents or status offenders.

juvenile delinquency (p. 312) Participation in illegal behavior by a minor who falls under a statutory age limit.

status offender (p. 312) A juvenile who engages in behavior legally forbidden to minors, such as running away, truancy, or incorrigibility.

detention (p. 317) The temporary care of a child alleged to be a delinquent or status offender who requires secure custody, pending court disposition.

waiver (juvenile) (p. 319) A practice in which the juvenile court waives its jurisdiction over a juvenile and transfers the case to adult criminal court for trial. In some states, a waiver hearing is held to determine jurisdiction, while in others, juveniles may be automatically waived if they are accused of committing a serious crime such as murder.

transfer hearing (p. 319) The hearing in which a decision is made to waive a juvenile to the criminal court. Waiver decisions are based on such criteria as the child's age, his or her prior offense history, and the nature of the offense.

initial appearance (p. 321) A juvenile's first appearance before the juvenile court judge, in which the charges are reviewed and an effort is made to settle the case without a trial. If the child does not have legal counsel, an attorney will be appointed.

disposition (p. 322) For juvenile offenders, the equivalent of sentencing for adult offenders. The theory is that disposition is more rehabilitative than retributive. Possible dispositions include dismissing the case, releasing the youth to the custody of his or her parents, placing the offender on probation, or sending him or her to a state correctional institution.

commitment (p. 322) Decision of judge ordering an adjudicated and sentenced juvenile offender to be placed in a correctional facility.

treatment (p. 322) The rehabilitative method used to effect a change of behavior in the juvenile offender, in the form of therapy, or educational or vocational programs.

CHAPTER OUTLINE

I. **INTRODUCTION**
1. Juvenile justice system is primarily responsible for dealing with juvenile and youth crimes as well as with:
   a. Incorrigible and truant children
   b. Runaways
2. Juvenile justice system was viewed as a quasi-social welfare agency that was to act as a surrogate parent in the interests of the child
   a. Parens patriae philosophy

II. **THE HISTORY OF JUVENILE JUSTICE**
1. The modern practice of separating adult and juvenile offenders can be traced back to two developments in English custom and law:
   a. Poor laws
   b. Chancery courts
2. Poor laws were passed as English statutes in 1535
   a. Laws granted overseers for destitute or neglected children
   b. Trained them in
      i. Agricultural
      ii. Trade

          iii. Domestic services
- c. Referred to as indenture
3. Chancery courts provided judicial relief to those who had no legal standing because of the corruption and inadequacy of other common-law courts
   - a. Protected the property rights and welfare of minor children who could not care for themselves
     - i. Children whose position and property were of direct concern to the monarch
- A. Care of Children in Early America
  1. Poor laws and Chancery courts were brought from England to America
     - a. Passed in Virginia 1646, followed by other states
     - b. Courts mandated care for wayward and destitute children
  2. Local jurisdictions also developed almshouses, poorhouses, and workhouses to accommodate destitute youths
     - a. Houses were crowded and unhealthy
     - b. Houses accepted the poor, insane, diseased, vagrant, and destitute
  3. Child savers — (civic leaders) began to emerge to help alleviate burdens of the poor
- B. The Child Saving Movement
  1. Child savers were responsible for creating programs for indigent youth. Supervised labor was part of the program
  2. New York House of Refuge opened in 1825 as part of this movement
     - a. Indenture agreements allowed inmates to be loaned out to private employers
     - b. Most males were farm workers and most females were domestic laborers
- C. The Refuge Movement Spreads
  1. Critics complained that the institution was run like a prison
     - a. Strict discipline
     - b. Absolute separation of sexes
  2. Programs forced children to run away due to harsh treatment
  3. The concept expanded despite criticism
  4. Child savers influenced local and state governments, and created independent correctional facilities for minors
  5. Children's Aid Society was founded in 1853 by philanthropist Charles Brace
     - a. Alternative for dealing with neglected and delinquent youths
     - b. Provided temporary shelter and care
     - c. Sought to place them in rural communities

III. ESTABLISHMENT OF THE JUVENILE COURT

1. Nation expanded and private charities and programs could not adequately care for growing number of troubled youths
2. Child savers lobbied for a state supported juvenile court
3. First juvenile court established 1899 in Illinois
   - a. Child savers fought long, hard battle to get court
   - b. The Illinois Juvenile Court Act set up an independent court to handle criminal law violations by children

          i.   This was a major event in the history of the juvenile justice movement in the U.S.

     c. Probation department were also created

     d. Provided separation for adult and juvenile offenders

A. The Development of Juvenile Justice

     a. Juvenile justice movement spread quickly across United States

     b. Concern shifted to 'best interests of the child'

          i.   Concern was not on strict adherence to legal doctrine or constitutional rights

     c. Court was paternalistic rather than adversarial

     d. Children were encouraged to admit their "guilt" in violation of Fifth Amendment rights

     e. Verdicts based on "preponderance of evidence" not "beyond a reasonable doubt"

1. Reform Schools

     a. Youngsters found delinquent could spend years in state training school

     b. Schools viewed themselves as non-punitive but believed in reform through hard work and discipline

     c. Juveniles often housed in small cabins

          i.   Cabins managed by "cottage parents"

          ii. First cottage system was in Massachusetts, second in Ohio

     d. Psychological treatment was introduced to juvenile corrections in the 1950s

     e. Group counseling became standard procedure

2. Legal Change

     a. In the 1960s and 1970s, the U.S. Supreme Court radically altered the juvenile justice system. Series of juvenile court cases were decided

     b. Series of court decisions affected system

          i.   Juveniles to receive due process of law

          ii. Courts established that juveniles have the same rights as adults

          iii. Right to confront witnesses

          iv. Receive notice of charges

          v. Right to counsel

     c. Congress passed the Juvenile Justice Delinquency Prevention Act of 1974 (JJDP)

          i.   Legislation designed to meet needs of youth

          ii. Fund programs in juvenile justice

          iii. Main goal to separate wayward non-dangerous youths and fund programs

          iv. Minority overrepresentation addressed in 1988 amendment to act

          v. In 1996, act was amended again to make it easier to hold delinquents in adult penal institutions

IV.   **JUVENILE JUSTICE TODAY**

A. Today, the juvenile justice system has jurisdiction over two categories of offenders

    1. Delinquents

    2. Status offenders

B. Juvenile Delinquency refers to children who fall under a jurisdictional age limit and who commit an act in violation of penal code
C. Status offenders commit acts forbidden to minors, and include:
1. Truancy
2. Habitual disobedience
3. Ungovernable child
D. Status offenders were barred from being placed in secure facilities that held juvenile delinquents, in order to lessen the stigma from the system
E. Status offenses required different treatment for offenders:
1. Allowed for probation
2. Most instances barred from being placed in secure facilities that hold delinquent offenders
F. Juvenile courts generally have jurisdiction over situations involving conduct directed at juveniles
1. Parental neglect
2. Deprivation
3. Abandonment
4. Abuse
G. States set maximum ages below which children fall under the jurisdiction of the juvenile court.
H. Family courts were also created to handle child-related issues
1. Designed to provide more individualized, client-focused treatment than traditional juvenile courts and to bring a holistic approach to helping kids and their families rather than focusing on punishing and/or controlling delinquency
I. The juvenile justice system is responsible for processing and treating almost 2 million cases or youthful misbehavior annually
J. Each state's system is unique

V. **POLICE PROCESSING OF THE JUVENILE OFFENDER**
1. According to the Uniform Crime Reports, police arrest more than one million juveniles under 18 years of age each year
2. Larger police agencies have separate juvenile detective bureaus to handle the case load
3. Most states do not have specific statutory provisions distinguishing the arrest process for children from adults
4. Police may arrest youths for behavior considered legal for adults, including:
a. Running away
b. Curfew violations
c. Possession of alcohol
A. Use of Discretion
4. Police agencies are charged with the decision to charge or release a juvenile offender
5. Because of the state's interest in a child, police generally have more discretion with a juvenile than with an adult offender
6. The decision to release or detain the juvenile (at time of arrest) is based on:
a. Nature of offense

      b. Police attitudes

      c. Seriousness of child's offense

      d. Parental assistance

      e. Past contact

      f. Degree of cooperation from offender and parents and their demeanor, attitude, and personal characteristics

      g. Whether the child denies the allegations in the petition and insists on a court hearing

B. Legal Rights

    1. Once in custody; the child has the same right to be free from unreasonable searches and seizures as an adult

    2. Children can be detained, interrogated, and placed in line-ups

    3. *Miranda* Rights apply, but police must ensure that juveniles understand their constitutional rights

    4. Police interrogation tactics with juveniles are quite similar to their questioning of adults

VI. THE JUVENILE COURT PROCESS

    1. If a case is decided to need further attention, it is sent over to the prosecutor's office

    2. The prosecutor channels case through juvenile court

    3. Juvenile court plays a major role in controlling juvenile behavior and delivering social services to children in need

    4. The court case load is four times larger today than in 1960

      a. Now processes an estimated 1.6 million delinquency cases each year.

A. The Intake Process

    1. Juveniles, after processing, are remanded to the local juvenile court's intake division

    2. The child is screened to determine the best manner for handling the child offender

      a. Handle the case formally

      b. Handle the case less formally

    3. Intake process also is critically important because more than half of the referrals to the juvenile courts never go beyond this stage

B. The Detention Process

    1. The prosecutor usually makes a decision about detention— home with family or detain in a secure facility

    2. Detention has always been a controversial area of juvenile justice

    3. The Juvenile Justice Act of 1974 placed emphasis on reducing the number of children placed in inappropriate detention facilities

      a. The Act was successful and the practice continues

    4. Pretrial detention does exist for juvenile offenders and is often misapplied

    5. Seventy percent of youths in detention are held for nonviolent charges

      a. More than 2/3 are charged with:

        i. Property offenses

        ii. Public order offenses

        iii. Technical probation violations

        iv. Status offenses

C. Legal Issues

   1. Most states require a hearing on the appropriateness of detention

   2. Child has the right to counsel at hearing, also enjoys constitutional protections such as right against self-incrimination and the right to confront and cross examine witnesses

   3. Criteria for detention decision include:

      a. Does child present danger to public

      b. Need to protect the child

      c. The likelihood the child will return to court for adjudication

   4. The case of *Schall v. Martin* (1984) upheld the rights of states to detain a child before trial to protect welfare and public safety

D. Reforming Detention

   1. This has been an on-going effort

   2. Focus on removing status offenders from lock-ups containing delinquents

   3. Most states now have laws requiring non-secure shelters, rather than secure detention facilities

      a. This reduces contact with more dangerous youths

   4. Also of concern is the detention of juveniles in adult facilities:

      a. Common in rural areas

      b. Millions in aid has been given to resolve problems

      c. Juveniles in adult facilities continues to be a large problem

   5. At the last jail census:

      a. More than 7,000 persons under age 18 housed in adult jails

E. Bail

   1. Only a few states allow juvenile release on money bail

   2. This has not been ruled on by federal courts

      a. Some fear money bail imposes family hardship

      b. Most courts have ruled that juveniles do not have a right to bail

F. Plea Bargaining

   1. Before trial, prosecutors may attempt to negotiate a settlement in the case

   2. If a bargain can be reached, the child will be asked to admit in open court that he committed the act

      a. Using terminology such as:

         i. Agree to a finding

         ii. Accept the petition

   3. Procedural safeguards are ensured:

      a. The child knows of the right to a trial

      b. The plea of admission is made voluntarily

      c. Child understands the charges and consequences of the plea

G. Waiver of Jurisdiction

   1. Prior to the first juvenile court, juveniles were tried for violations of the law in criminal courts

   2. Consequences were devastating:

      a. Children were treated as criminal offenders

b. Legislation creating juvenile courts has eliminated problems
3. Juveniles can still be tried as adults in adult court
   a. This process is usually governed by statute and is called waiver
4. The decision to waive a juvenile into adult court involves a transfer hearing:
   a. Hearing determines if case should be transferred to adult court
   b. Nature of offense and child's age are key considerations
   c. Some states have minimum age requirements for waiver

H. Legal Controls
1. The U.S. Supreme Court has imposed procedural protections for juveniles in the waiver process
2. In *Kent v. United States* (1966), the Court held that the waiver proceeding is a critically important stage in the juvenile justice process and that juveniles must be afforded minimum requirements of due process of law at such proceedings:
   a. Juveniles have a right to counsel
3. Double jeopardy protections apply, *Breed v. Jones* (1975)

I. Youth in Adult Courts
1. Today, all states allow juveniles to be tried as adults in criminal courts in one of four ways:
   a. Direct file waiver:
      i. Prosecutor has the discretion of filing charges for certain legislatively designated offenses in either juvenile or criminal court
   b. Excluded offense waiver:
      i. State laws exclude from juvenile court jurisdiction certain offenses that are either very minor or very serious
   c. Judicial waiver:
      i. After formal hearing, juvenile court judge may decide to waive jurisdiction and transfer the case to criminal court
   d. Reverse waiver:
      i. State laws mandate that certain offenses be tried in adult court
2. Every state has provisions for handling juveniles that have been waived into adult criminal court

J. The Effect of the Waiver
1. The problem of youths processed in adult courts is a serious one
2. About 8000 cases are transferred annually
3. Cases involving injury with a weapon or where the offender has a record are more likely to be transferred
4. Some believe youths will be victimized if sent to adult prisons:
   a. Youths held in adult prisons and jails are five times more likely to be victims of attempted sexual attacks or rapes than those held in juvenile institutions
   b. The suicide rate for juveniles in adult prisons and jails in nearly eight times higher than that for juveniles in youth detention centers
5. Transfer decisions are not always carried out fairly or equitably
6. Some evidence suggests minorities are over represented in waivers to adult courts

  a. About 40 percent of all waived youths are African Americans, even though they represent less than 31 percent of the juvenile court population

K. The Adjudication

 1. There are usually two hearings in the juvenile process:

  a. Initial appearance

   i. The initial appearance is where the juvenile is advised of the charges, attorneys are appointed, and bail is reviewed, often followed by a community sentence

  b. Adjudicatory hearing

   a) Often called fact-finding

   b) Court hears evidence on the allegations stated in the delinquency petition

   ii. The Supreme Court case in 1967 *In re Gault* radically altered the juvenile justice system

   iii. Court ruled fundamental fairness applied to juvenile delinquency proceedings

   iv. The court granted critical rights to juveniles:

    a) Right to counsel

    b) Right to confront and cross examine witnesses

    c) Notice of charges

    d) Protection from self-incrimination

    e) Right to have a transcript of trial record

   v. The right to counsel, the privilege against self-incrimination, the right to treatment in detention and correctional facilities, and other constitutional protections are applied at all stages of the juvenile process

   vi. Gualt ushered in an era of legal rights for juveniles.

 2. Upon adjudication, the court is required to make a judgment against the child

 3. Following the judgment, the court can begin its determination of possible dispositions for the child

L. Disposition and Treatment

 1. At the dispositional hearing, the judge imposes a sentence on the offender

 2. Sentence is based on the:

  a. Juvenile's history

  b. The offense

  c. Family background

 3. The sentence can range from dismissal to institutional commitment

  a. This postadjudicative process is the most important stage in the juvenile court system because it represents the last opportunity for the court to influence the child and control behavior

  b. Most jurisdictions require a separate hearing to formulate an appropriate disposition

  c. In theory, the court seeks a disposition that represents individual treatment

  d. Decision is normally based on:

   i. Pre-sentence investigation of the probation department

   ii. Reports from social agencies

       iii. Possibly a psychiatric evaluation
     e. Sentences can include:
       i. Probation
       ii. Suspended judgment
       iii. Community treatment
       iv. Commitment to state agency
       v. Place the child with parents or relatives
       vi. Dispositional arrangements with private youth-serving agencies
       vii.   Commitment to a mental institution

M. Dispositions Outcome
1. Juvenile court judges must determine the most appropriate sanction
2. Choices of disposition include:
  a. Commitment to an institution or another residential facility
  b. Probation
  c. Referral to an outside agency or treatment program
  d. Community service
  e. Fines
  f. Restitution
3. The number of adjudicated delinquency cases resulting in residential placement has increased significantly during the past decade
  a. 10 percent of all cases petitioned to juvenile court get some form of residential treatment
  b. Additional 400,000 kids are put on probation each year

N. Juvenile Sentencing Reform
1. The public has taken note of the serious juvenile crime rate and violent acts committed by children
2. Another reform has been concerned with the effort to remove status offenders from the juvenile justice system and restrict entry into institutional programs
3. A third reform has been to standardize dispositions in juvenile court

VII. **THE JUVENILE CORRECTIONAL PROCESS**
1. After disposition, delinquent offenders may be placed in some form of correctional treatment
2. More than 100,000 are now in secure facilities

A. Probation
1. Probation is the most commonly used formal sentence
2. Probation places the juvenile under the supervision of the probation department
  a. Alternative sanctions such as community service or monetary restitution may be ordered
3. Juvenile probation is an important component of the juvenile justice system and is the most widely used disposition

B. Institutionalization
1. The most severe disposition involves confinement of the child to an institution
  a. Usually minimum-security facilities with small populations and an emphasis on treatment and education

348

2. States vary when determining the length of a confinement sentence
3. To better handle juvenile offenders, some states have created intermediate juvenile courts to handle juveniles charged with violent felonies
   a. These courts handle 14 to 17 year old offenders
   b. Juveniles are treated as adults if convicted
   c. Sentenced to new intermediate prisons
   d. Separated from both adult and regular juvenile offenders
   e. For terms of 2-5 years
4. Today, more than 100,000 juveniles being held in either privately run or publicly managed juvenile correctional facilities:
   a. About 35 percent held for person-oriented offenses
   b. 25 percent for property offenses
   c. 9 percent for drug offenses
   d. 11 percent for public order offenses
   e. 16 percent for technical violations
   f. 5 percent for status offenses
5. Typical resident of a juvenile facility is a 15-16-year old white male incarcerated for an average stay of 5 months in public facility and 6 months in a private facility
6. Private facilities tend to house younger youths
7. Public facilities provide custodial care for older youths, including a small percentage of youths between 18 and 21 years of age

C. Deinstitutionalization
   1. Some experts in delinquency question the policy of institutionalizing juvenile offenders
      a. They recommend treatment over incarceration
   2. The public shows support for community-based treatment programs

D. Aftercare
   1. Aftercare marks the final stage of formal juvenile justice process
      a. Its purpose is to help juveniles transition back to the community
   2. Most juvenile aftercare involves parole, in which a parole officer is assigned to the case
   3. Juveniles who violate the terms of parole can have their parole revoked and be returned to the institution

E. Preventing Delinquency
   1. Efforts are now underway to prevent delinquency before it occurs
      a. This is called delinquency prevention
      b. Community programs assist with the effort
   2. Comprehensive community-based programs are taking a systematic approach to preventative interventions
      a. Includes:
         i. Analyzing the delinquency problem
         ii. Identifying resources available in community
         iii. Prioritizing delinquency problems
         iv. Identifying successful programs in other communities

VIII. PROBLEMS OF JUVENILE JUSTICE

1. Crime control advocates want to reduce the juvenile court's jurisdiction over juveniles charged with serious crimes and liberalize the prosecutor's ability to waive juveniles to adult court
2. Opponents feel that the traditional parens patriae philosophy of juvenile justice ought to prevail

A. Minority Overrepresentation in Juvenile Justice

1. Another enduring problem in juvenile justice is minority over representation in the system and disparaging treatment
2. Minority youths are less likely to be diverted than white youths
3. The minority representation is a reflection of racial disparity in the system
4. Recent 2007 report by the National Council on Crime and Delinquency describes how minority youths receive differential treatment as every stage:
    a. African American youths are 16 percent of the adolescent population but are 38 percent of the youths confined in local detention and correctional systems
    b. Youths of color make up the majority of young people held in both public private facilities
    c. Latino youths are a much larger proportion of the young in public facilities than in private facilities
    d. Representing 34 percent of the U.S. population, youths of color were 62 percent of young people in detention
        i. 66 percent in public facilities
        ii. 55 percent in private facilities
    e. Youths of color were overrepresented in the detained population at 3.1 times the rate of white youths
        i. Public facilities – 2.9 times the rate of white youths
        ii. Private facilities – 2.0 times the rate of white youths
    f. Overall, custody rates were 4 times greater for African American youths than for white youths
        i. Custody rates for Latino and Native American youths were 1.8 and 2.6 times the custody rate of white youths respectively

CHAPTER SUMMARY

The modern practice of legally separating adult and juvenile offenders can be traced back to two developments in English custom and law that occurred centuries ago— the development of Elizabethan-era poor laws and the creation of the English chancery court. Poor laws were passed in America and continued in force until the early nineteenth century. They mandated care for wayward and destitute children.

The first comprehensive juvenile court developed in Illinois in 1899. The main concern was the best interests of the child, not due process of law. The court was paternalistic, rather than adversarial. In the 1960s and 1970s, the Supreme Court radically altered the juvenile justice system when it established the right of juveniles to receive due process of law. Congress passed the Juvenile Justice and Delinquency Prevention Act and established the federal Office of Juvenile Justice and Delinquency Prevention. Its main goal was to separate wayward, non-dangerous youths and adolescents from institutions housing adult offenders.

Today, the juvenile justice system has jurisdiction over two categories of offenders: delinquents and status offenders. Delinquents are children who fall under a certain age limit, which varies, and who commit an act in violation of the penal code. Status offenders commit acts forbidden to minors including truancy and being a habitually disobedient child.

Today, the juvenile justice system is responsible for processing and treating almost two million cases annually. Police officers arrest more than one million juveniles under age eighteen each year, including almost 500,000 under age fifteen. Larger police departments have separate, juvenile detectives who handle delinquency cases and focus their attention on the problems of youth.

After police processing, the juvenile offender is usually remanded to the local juvenile court's intake division. Court intake officers or probation personnel review and initially screen the child and the family. The prosecutor then usually makes a decision to release the child to the parent or guardian or to detain the child in a secure shelter pending trial. Most state statutes ordinarily require a hearing on the appropriateness of detention. At this hearing, the child has a right to counsel and may be given other procedural due process safeguards. Most state juvenile courts provide criteria to support a decision to detain the child. These include the need to protect the child, whether or not the child presents a serious danger to the public, and the likelihood that the juvenile will return to court. Most states allow juveniles to be tried as adults in one of four ways: direct file waiver, excluded offense waiver, judicial waiver, or reverse waiver.

There are usually two judicial hearings in the juvenile court process. The first, called an initial appearance, is similar to the arraignment in the adult system. If the case cannot be settled at this initial stage, it is bound over for trial. The juvenile trial process became a target of criticism because judges were handing out punishments to children without affording them legal rights. This changed with the Supreme Court's *In re Gault* decision. In Gault, the Court ruled that the concept of fundamental fairness is applicable to juvenile delinquency proceedings. Typical juvenile court dispositions are: suspended judgment, probation, placement in a community treatment program, or commitment to a state agency. The court may also place the child with parents or relatives, make dispositional arrangements with private youth-serving agencies, or order the child committed to a mental institution.

Probation is the most commonly used formal sentence for juvenile offenders, and many states require that a youth fail on probation before being sent to an institution. The most severe of the statutory dispositions involves commitment to an institution. The committed child may be sent to a state training school or private residential treatment facility. These are usually minimum-security facilities with an emphasis on treatment and education. Aftercare marks the final stage of the formal juvenile justice process. Examples of programs include electronic monitoring, counseling, treatment and community service referrals, education, work training, and intensive parole supervision.

Delinquency prevention refers to intervening in young people's lives prior to their engaging in delinquency. Comprehensive community-based delinquency prevention programs are taking a systematic approach to develop preventive interventions. This includes an analysis of the delinquency problem, an identification of available resources in the community, development of priority delinquency problems, the identification of successful programs in other communities, and tailoring them to local conditions and needs.

DISCUSSION QUESTIONS

1. Should status offenders be treated by the juvenile court? Explain. Should they be placed in confinement for such acts as running away or cutting school? Why or why not?
2. Should a juvenile ever be waived to adult court with the possible risk that the child will be incarcerated with adult felons? Why or why not?
3. Do you support the death penalty for children? Explain.
4. Should juveniles be given mandatory incarceration sentences for serious crimes, as adults are? Explain.
5. Is it fair to deny juveniles a jury trial? Why or why not?
6. Do you think the trend toward treating juveniles like adult offenders is desirable? Explain.

MEDIA TOOLS

Frontline, produced by the Public Broadcasting Service has presented a series titled "Juvenile Justice." In this series they follow the cases of four juveniles, two were charged as juveniles, two were charged as adults. To view this interesting program visit the Frontline Juvenile Justice website at: http://www.pbs.org/wgbh/pages/frontline/shows/juvenile

Review the fact sheet on juvenile delinquency provided by the U.S. Department of Health and Human Services. This is a concise document that provides many interesting facts and figures. The fact sheet is in a PDF format and can be found at: http://aspe.hhs.gov/hsp/08/boys/FactSheets/jd/report.pdf

The United States Department of Justice, Office of Justice Programs, Office of Juvenile Justice and Delinquency Prevention provide a comprehensive clearinghouse of juvenile justice statistics and documents. Great starting point for further research regarding they juvenile justice system: http://www.ojjdp.gov/ojstatbb/structure_process/index.html

Listen to the oral arguments made by attorneys arguing the In re Gault case. This recording and material related to the case is provided by the Oyez Project, Illinois Institute of Technology, Chicago-Kent College of Law. Listen to the oral arguments at: http://www.oyez.org/cases/1960-1969/1966/1966_116

PRACTICE TEST BANK

MULTIPLE CHOICE

1.   The modern practice of separating adult criminals and juvenile offenders can be traced
        back to
        a.   English custom and law.
        b.   Parens patriae.
        c.   Norman Law.
        d.   Edwardian Law.

2.   Acts that are forbidden to minors exclusively are known as
        a.   Juvenile offenses.
        b.   Status offenses.
        c.   PIN offenses.
        d.   Delinquent offenses.

3.   The first comprehensive juvenile court was established in which state in 1899?
        a.   New York
        b.   Massachusetts
        c.   Illinois
        d.   California

4.   In the 1960s and 1970s, the U.S. Supreme Court altered the nature of juvenile justice by
        holding that juveniles
        a.   were entitled to due process.
        b.   were covered by equal protection.
        c.   could not be placed in jails with adults.
        d   could not be transferred to adult courts.

5.   The juvenile justice system was conceived in the twentieth century to deal with youth
        crime and it was viewed as a
        a.   mental health care system.
        b.   quasi-social welfare agency.
        c.   foster care program.
        d.   youth advocacy system.

6.   Most juvenile aftercare involves
        a.   parole.
        b.   rehabilitation.
        c.   restitution.
        d.   probation.

7.   After the police determine that a juvenile case warrants further attention they refer it to the
     a.   parents.
     b.   court.
     c.   prosecutor's office.
     d.   truant officer.

8.   Which was the U.S. Supreme Court's landmark decision that radically altered the juvenile justice system?
     a.   *Kent v. United States*
     b.   *Breed v. Jones*
     c.   *In re Gault*
     d.   *In re Winship*

9.   Poor laws and chancery courts were brought to America from
     a.   Europe.
     b.   Africa.
     c.   Australia.
     d.   Asia.

10. Before trial, prosecutors in the juvenile courts may attempt to negotiate a settlement in the case, this practice is known as
     a.   sentencing.
     b.   plea bargaining.
     c.   settlement hearing.
     d.   transfer bargaining.

11. A transfer hearing is held to determine if the juvenile should be transferred to
     a.   a detention facility.
     b.   juvenile court.
     c.   adult court.
     d.   an institution from probation.

12. Previously, juveniles were encouraged to admit their guilt in open court. The Supreme Court in the case of *in re Gault* changed this by ruling that self-incrimination and the protections provided under which Amendment applied?
     a.   Fourteenth
     b.   Eighth
     c.   Sixth
     d.   Fifth

13. State laws mandating that juveniles be tried as adults for certain offenses are classified as
     a.   limit waivers.
     b.   reverse waivers.
     c.   mandatory waivers.
     d.   adult waivers.

14.   Truancy, running away, and incorrigibility are examples of
       a.   juvenile crimes.
       b.   corruption of the morals of a minor.
       c.   status offenses.
       d.   minor crimes.

15.   Which term best describes a prosecutor's discretion in filing charges for certain
       legislatively designated offenses in either juvenile or adult criminal court?
       a.   Direct file waiver
       b.   Prosecution waiver
       c.   Waiver of justice
       d.   Waiver of law

16.   The Gault decision centers on
       a.   constitutional protections for juvenile offenders.
       b.   early release for juvenile offenders.
       c.   secure confinement for juvenile offenders.
       d.   sentencing reform for juvenile offenders.

17.   The case of *Schall v. Martin* focused on the issue of
       a.   bail.
       b.   detention.
       c.   due process.
       d.   waiver to adult court.

18.   Juvenile trials are called
       a.   refinement hearings.
       b.   adjudicatory hearings.
       c.   further hearings.
       d.   indentured hearings.

19.   In theory, the juvenile court seeks to provide a disposition that represents an individual
       a.   incarceration plan.
       b.   behavioral modification plan.
       c.   training plan.
       d.   treatment plan.

20   The case of *Kent v. United States* focused on the issue of
       a.   bail.
       b.   detention.
       c.   due process.
       d.   waiver to adult court.

21. After disposition in juvenile court, delinquent offenders may be placed in some form of correctional treatment including
    a. probation.
    b. institutionalization.
    c. parole.
    d. all of the above.

22. Which early courts provided judicial relief to those who had no legal standing or those who could not expect relief due to corruption in common law courts?
    a. Chancery
    b. Juvenile
    c. Probate
    d. Delinquency

23. At the dispositional hearing, the judge imposes a sentence based on all of the following except
    a. prior record.
    b. race.
    c. family background.
    d. the offense.

24. The child savers were responsible for creating a number of programs for indigent youths including
    a. New York House of Reforms.
    b. New York House of Refuge.
    c. Boston House of Impoverished.
    d. Boston Child Movement.

25. The child savers were influential on state and local governments---they pushed government to create
    a. only minimum security facilities to house juveniles.
    b. independent correctional institutions to house juveniles.
    c. mental health facilities for juveniles.
    d. better health care facilities for juveniles.

26. Which U.S. Supreme Court case held that juveniles who commit murder before they turn age 18 cannot be sentenced to death?
    a. *Roper v. Simmons*
    b. *Radcliff v. Turnberry*
    c. *Schall v. Martin*
    d. *Fore v. Michael*

27. What act was passed in 1974 to identify the needs of youths and provide funding for juvenile programs?
   a. Juvenile Funding
   b. Juvenile Justice
   c. Juvenile Justice and Delinquency
   d. Child Savers

28. Typical juvenile court dispositions include
   a. suspended judgment.
   b. Probation.
   c. community treatment programs.
   d. all of the above.

29. In 1853, Charles Loring Brace helped to create
   a. foster care programs.
   b. barrack style housing for juveniles.
   c. the Children's Aid Society.
   d. Aid to Women and Dependent Children.

30. The In re Gault decision changed the juvenile trial process but it is technically limited to which stage?
   a. Arrest stage
   b. Prosecutorial stage
   c. Closing stage
   d. Adjudicatory stage

TRUE/FALSE

1. T F Juveniles taken into custody do not have the same Fifth Amendment rights as an adult does.

2. T F All juvenile offenders fall under the jurisdiction of the adult court once they attain age 18.

3. T F The U.S. Supreme Court's ruling in the case of *in re Gault* provided for fundamental fairness in juvenile adjudication proceedings.

4. T F Most states do not have specific statutory provisions distinguishing the arrest process for children from that for adults.

5. T F Juveniles are not entitled to double-jeopardy protection.

6. T F Pre-hearing detention of juveniles violates the Eighth Amendment ban on excessive bail.

7.   T   F   Some states exclude certain offenses, such as rape, from the juvenile justice system.

8.   T   F   A juvenile court cannot sentence juveniles to county jails or state prisons because these facilities are reserved exclusively for adult offenders.

9.   T   F   There is no plea bargaining in the juvenile justice system.

10.   T   F   A juvenile can be transferred to adult court if the juvenile court waives its jurisdiction.

11.   T   F   The first formal judicial hearing in the juvenile justice process is usually initial appearance.

12.   T   F   The term "delinquent child" is synonymous with the term "criminal" as it is applied to adult offenders.

13.   T   F   Police generally have more discretion in the investigatory and arrest stages of the juvenile process than they do when dealing with adult offenders.

14.   T   F   U.S. Supreme Court rulings in the 1960s and 1970s radically altered juvenile justice.

15.   T   F   Juveniles are not protected by the Fourth Amendment.

FILL-IN-THE-BLANK

1.   Because of the state's interest in the child, the police generally have more _____ in the investigatory and arrest stages of the juvenile process than they do with the adult process.

2.   Most states require a _____ on the appropriateness of detention if the initial decision is to keep a child offender in custody.

3.   In England, in the 1500s, the _____ laws were used to deal with abandoned children.

4.   The court concluded that _____ attaches when the juvenile court begins to hear evidence at the hearing.

5.   Beginning in the late 1800s, the _____, persons from the middle class and professionals, began advocating reforms in juvenile justice.

6.   The first comprehensive juvenile court was created in the state of _____ in 1899.

7.   _____ refers to children who fall under a jurisdictional age limit, which varies from state to state, and who commit an act in violation of the penal code.

8.   The decision about whether to move a juvenile to adult court is made after a _____ hearing.

9.   A juvenile who has been taken into custody and is a threat to the community or to flee may be held in _____.

10.   Beginning in the 1820s, many jurisdictions opened Houses of _____ for juveniles.

11.   In 1967, juveniles were granted basic due process rights at adjudication hearings by the U.S. Supreme Court in the case of _____.

12.   English chancery courts protected the _____ rights and welfare of minor children who could not care for themselves.

13.   After police processing, the juvenile is remanded to the local juvenile court's _____process.

14.   Offenses such as truancy and incorrigibility are classified as _____ offenses.

15.   The bifurcated hearing process ensures that the adjudicatory hearing is used solely to determine the merits of the allegations; whereas the _____ hearing determines whether the child is in need of rehabilitation.

ESSAY

1.   The chapter presented eleven important juvenile justice cases as decided by the United States Supreme Court. Identify five and explain the findings.

2.   Discuss the role of the child-saving movement and its impact on the juvenile justice system.

3.   Discuss the impact of the *Gault* decision on the juvenile trial process.

4.   Discuss juvenile sentencing reform that has occurred over the last two decades. Provide examples of each.

5.   All states allow juveniles to be tried as adults in criminal courts in one of four ways. Identify and explain two.

CHAPTER 13 ANSWER KEY

Multiple Choice

1. a [p. 308, LO1]   2. b [p. 312, LO3]   3. c [p. 310, LO1]   4. a [p. 310, LO3]   5. b [p. 310, LO2]

6. a [p. 326, LO8]   7. c [p. 316, LO5]   8. c [p. 322, LO3]   9. a [p. 308, LO1]   10. b [p. 319, LO5]

11. c [p. 319, LO6]   12. d [p. 322, LO3]   13. c [p. 319, LO6]   14. c [p. 312, LO3]   15. a [p. 320, LO6]

16. a [p. 322, LO7]   17. b [p. 317, LO5]   18. b [p. 322, LO6/7]   19. d [p. 322, LO5]   20. d [p. 320, LO6]

21. d [p. 323, LO8]   22. a [p. 308, LO1]   23. b [p. 322, LO8]   24. b [p. 308, LO2]   25. b [p. 308, LO2]

26. a [p. 311, LO5]   27. c [p. 311, LO5]   28. d [p. 323, LO8]   29. c [p. 310, LO2]   30. d [p. 322, LO7]

True/False

1. F [p. 310, LO4]   2. F [p. 312, LO2/3]   3. T [p. 322, LO3]   4. T [p. 313, LO4]   5. F [p. 320, LO5]

6. F [p, 317, LO5]   7. T [p. 312, LO2]   8. T [p. 314, LO3]   9. F [p. 319, LO5]   10. T [p. 319, LO6]

11. T [p. 321, LO5]   12. T [p. 314, LO3]   13. T [p. 313, LO4]   14. T [p. 310, LO3]   15. F [p. 311, LO4]

Fill-in-the-Blank

1. discretion [p. 313, LO4]   2. hearing [p. 317, LO2]   3. poor [p. 308, LO1]

4. jeopardy [p. 320, LO3]   5. child savers [p. 308, LO2]   6. Illinois [p. 310, LO2]

7. juvenile delinquency [p. 312, LO4]   8. transfer [p. 319, LO6]   9. detention [p. 314, LO4]

10. refuge [p. 309, LO1]   11. *In re Gault* [p. 322, LO7]   12. property [p. 308, LO1]

13. intake [p. 316, LO5]   14. status [p. 312, LO3]   15. dispositional [p. 322, LO5]

Essay

1.   **The chapter presented eleven important juvenile justice cases as decided by the United States Supreme Court. Identify five and explain the findings.**

Important Juvenile Justice Cases
- *Kent v. United States* (1966) determined that a child has the right to an attorney at any hearing to decide whether his or her case should be transferred to juvenile court (waiver hearings).
- *In re Gault* (1967) ruled that a minor has basic due process rights at trial, including: (1) notice of the charges, (2) right to counsel, (3) right to confront and cross-examine

witnesses, (4) privilege against self-incrimination, and (5) the right to a transcript of the trial record.

- *In re Winship* (1970) determined that the level of evidence for a finding of "juvenile delinquency" is proof beyond a reasonable doubt.
- *McKeiver v. Pennsylvania* (1971) held that trial by jury in a juvenile court's adjudicative stage is not a constitutional requirement.
- *Breed v. Jones* (1975) ruled that a child has the protection of the double-jeopardy clause of the Fifth Amendment and cannot be tried twice for the same crime.
- *Fare v. Michael C.* (1979) held that a child has the protection of the *Miranda* decision: the right to remain silent during a police interrogation and to request that a lawyer be provided to protect his or her interests.
- *Schall v. Martin* (1984) allowed for the placement of children in preventive detention before their adjudication.
- *New Jersey v. T.L.O.* (1985) determined that although the Fourth Amendment protection against unreasonable search and seizure applies to children, school officials can legally 0search kids who violate school rules (e.g., smoking on campus), even when there is no evidence that the student violated the law.
- *Vernonia School District v. Acton* (1995) held that the Fourth Amendment's guarantee against unreasonable searches is not violated by drug testing all students choosing to participate in interscholastic athletics.
- *Roper v. Simmons* (2005) determined that juveniles who commit murder before they turn 18 cannot be sentenced to death.
- *Graham v. Florida* (2010) prohibited life imprisonment for juveniles convicted for non-homicide offenses.

[p. 311, LO3]

2.   Discuss the role of the child-saving movement and its impact on the juvenile justice system.

Juveniles had been sheltered in workhouses and other similar facilities that were often crowded and unhealthy. These shelters accepted the poor, the insane, the diseased, and vagrant and destitute children. Civic leaders came call themselves *child savers,* as they began to develop organizations and groups to help alleviate the burdens of the poor and immigrants by sponsoring shelter care for youths, educational and social activities, and the development of settlement houses. The child savers were responsible for creating a number of programs for indigent youths, including the New York House of Refuge, which began operations in 1825. Its charter was to protect indigent youths who were at risk of crime by taking them off the streets and reforming them in a family-like environment.
A resident's daily schedule was devoted for the most part to supervised labor which was regarded as beneficial to education and discipline. Male inmates worked in shops and female sewed and performed domestic work. Critics complained that the institution was run like a prison, with strict discipline and absolute separation of the sexes. The program's harshness drove many children to run away, and it was forced to take a more lenient approach.

The child savers also influenced state and local governments to create independent correctional institutions to house minors. The first of these reform schools opened in Westboro, Massachusetts, in 1848 and in Rochester, New York, in 1849. Children lived in congregate conditions and spent their days working at institutional jobs, learning a trade and receiving basic education.

[p. 309, LO1]

3.   Discuss the impact of the *Gault* decision on the juvenile trial process.

The Supreme Court's landmark *in re Gault* decision radically altered the juvenile justice system because it ruled that the concept of fundamental fairness is applicable to juvenile delinquency proceedings. The Court granted critical rights to juvenile defendants, most important among them the notice of the charges, the right to counsel, the right to confront and cross-examine witnesses, the privilege against self-incrimination, and the right to a transcript of the trial record. Instead of dealing with children in a benign and paternalistic fashion, the courts were forced to process juvenile offenders within the framework of appropriate constitutional procedures. *Gault* was technically limited to the adjudicatory stage but it spurred further legal reform throughout the juvenile system. Today, the right to counsel, the privilege against self-incrimination, the right to treatment in detention and correctional facilities, and other constitutional protections are applied at all stages of the juvenile process, from investigation through adjudication to parole. *Gault* ushered in an era of legal rights for juveniles.

[pp. 321-322, LO7]

4.   Discuss juvenile sentencing reform that has occurred over the last two decades. Provide examples of each.

As a first reform, legislators and officials wanted to deal with the serious juvenile crime rate; they wanted to take a more serious stand with dangerous juvenile offenders. In response, state legislatures toughened juvenile codes. Some jurisdictions passed mandatory/determinate incarceration sentences for juveniles convicted of serious felonies. Not all jurisdictions abandoned rehabilitation as a primary dispositional goal---some still hold to the philosophy that placements should be based on the least detrimental alternative.

A second reform effort removed status offenders from the juvenile justice system and restricted their entry into institutional programs. Diversion programs moved children involved in truancy and incorrigible behavior (who ordinarily would have been sent to a closed institution) into community programs. The result of which is fewer status offenders in detention / institutions.

A third reform worked to standardize juvenile court dispositions. As early as 1977, Washington passed one of the first determinate sentencing laws for juvenile offenders, resulting in other states adopting similar statutes. All children found to be delinquent are evaluated on a point system based on their age, prior juvenile record, and type of crime committed. Minor offenses are handled in the community while more serious offenses are placed on probation. Children who commit the most serious offenses are subject to standardized institutional penalties. As a result, juvenile offenders who commit such crimes as rape or armed robbery are being sentenced to institutionalization for a number of years. This approach is different from the indeterminate sentencing, under which children who have committed a serious crime might be released from institutions in less than a year if correctional authorities believe they have been rehabilitated.

[p. 324, LO3]

5.   All states allow juveniles to be tried as adults in criminal courts in one of four ways. Identify and explain two.

1. *Direct file waiver.* The prosecutor has the discretion of filing charges for certain legislatively designated offenses in either juvenile or criminal court. About 15 states have this provision.

2. *Excluded offense waiver.* State laws exclude from juvenile court jurisdiction certain offenses that are either very minor, such as traffic or fishing violations, or very serious, such as murder. About 29 states now have such laws for certain crimes.

3. *Judicial waiver.* After a formal hearing at which both prosecutor and defense attorney present evidence, a juvenile court judge may decide to waive jurisdiction and transfer the case to criminal court. This procedure is also known as "binding over" or "certifying" juvenile cases to criminal court.

4. *Reverse waiver.* State laws mandate that certain offenses be tried in adult court. Once the case is heard in the adult court, the trial judge may decide that the offender would be better served by the juvenile court and order a reverse waiver. About 25 states have this provision for certain circumstances.

[p. 320, LO6]

CHAPTER 14
Criminal Justice in the New Millennium

After studying this chapter, students will:

1. Discuss the impact of criminal enterprise crime
2. Describe a Ponzi scheme
3. Be familiar with the mortgage fraud scandal
4. Be familiar with the various forms of green crime
5. Discuss the various forms of cyber crime
6. Know what is being done to thwart cyber criminals
7. Be familiar with the influence of globalization on crime
8. Understand the concept of transnational crime
9. Be familiar with some of the most important transnational crime groups
10. Tell how law enforcement is taking on transnational criminal syndicates

KEY TERMS AND CONCEPTS

corporate enterprise crime (p. 332) Conspiracies that involve bending the rules of legitimate business and commerce to make illegal profits in the marketplace. Enterprise crimes involve the violation of law in the course of an otherwise legitimate occupation.

Ponzi scheme (p. 332) A Ponzi scheme is an investment fraud that involves the payment of purported returns to existing investors from funds contributed by new investors.

securitization (p. 334) The process in which vendors take individual subprime loans and bundle them into large pools and sell them as securities.

green crime (p. 336) Criminal activity that involves violation of rules and laws designed to protect the environment, including illegal dumping, polluting, fishing, logging and so on.

cyber crime (p. 339) The theft and/or destruction of information, resources, or funds via computers, computer networks, or the Internet.

cyber theft (p. 339) The use of computer networks for criminal profits. Illegal copyright infringement, identity theft, and Internet securities fraud are examples of cyber theft.

cyber vandalism (p. 339) Malicious attacks aimed at disrupting, defacing, and destroying technology.

cyber war (p. 340) Politically motivated attacks designed to compromise the electronic infrastructure of the enemy and to disrupt its economy.

denial-of-service attack (p. 341) Extorting money from an Internet service user by threatening to prevent the user having access to the service.

warez (p. 341) Copyrighted software illegally downloaded and sold by organized groups without license to do so.

identity theft (p. 342) Using the Internet to steal someone's identity and/or impersonate the victim in order to conduct illicit transactions, such as committing fraud using the victim's name and identity.

phishing (p. 342) Also known as carding and spoofing, phishing consists of illegally acquiring personal information, such as bank passwords and credit card numbers, by masquerading as a trustworthy person or business in what appears to be an official electronic communication, such as an email or an instant message. The term "phishing" comes from the lures used to "fish" for financial information and passwords.

etailing fraud (p. 342) Using the Internet to illegally buy or sell merchandise.

cyber stalking (p. 343) Using the Internet, email, or other electronic communications devices to stalk or harass another person.

globalization (p. 346) The process of creating a global economy through transnational markets and political and legal systems.

Transnational organized crime (p. 346) Use of illegal tactics to gain profit in the global marketplace, typically involving the cross border sale and distribution of illegal commodities.

Racketeer Influenced and Corrupt Organization Act (RICO) (p. 350) Federal legislation that enables prosecutors to bring additional criminal or civil charges against people engaged in two or more acts prohibited by 24 existing federal and 8 state laws. RICO features monetary penalties that allow the government to confiscate all profits derived from criminal activities. Originally intended to be used against organized criminals, RICO has also been used against white-collar criminals.

CHAPTER OUTLINE

I. **INTRODUCTION**
1. The technological revolution has provided new tools to
    a. Misappropriate funds

      b. Damage property

      c. Sell illicit material

      d. Conduct warfare, espionage and terror

II.   CORPORATE ENTERPRISE CRIME

    1. One new crime trend is multi-billion dollar corporate enterprise crimes

      a. Amount to the hundreds of billions of dollars

      b. FBI currently pursuing more than 500 corporate fraud cases

      c. Billion dollar financial crimes have involved:

        i. Subprime lending institutions

        ii. Brokerage houses

        iii. Home-building firms

        iv. Hedge funds

        v. Financial institutions

B. Fraud on Wall Street

    1. Creation of global capital markets has created unprecedented opportunities for U.S. business to access capital and investors to diversify their portfolios.

    2. Large scale growth has provided the opportunity for misconduct and crime

      a. Perhaps the greatest committed by Bernard Madoff

      b. Madoff essentially operating a Ponzi scheme

      c. Estimated to cost clients an estimated $65 billion

        i. Maybe the largest criminal conspiracy in history

      d. Madoff sentenced to 150 years in prison, a life sentence

C. The Subprime Mortgage Scandal

    1. Subprime mortgage is a home loan given to borrowers who, because of their income, would not ordinarily qualify for bank loans.

    2. Once subprime loans issued, vendors typically bundle them into large pools and sell them as securities:

      a. Known as securitization

      b. Typically pay a higher interest rate than normal securities

    3. Those involved in mortgage lending

      a. Mortgage brokers

      b. Lenders

      c. Appraisers

      d. Underwriters

      e. Accountants

      f. Real estate agents

      g. Settlement attorneys

      h. Land developers

      i. Investors

      j. Builders

      k. Bank account representatives

      l. Trust account representatives

      m. Investment banks

      n. Credit rating agencies

4. Lenders made risky loans assuming that real estate values would always increase.
   a. When sales slowed down in housing market, loan defaults increased and securities lost value
      i. Mortgage companies experienced financial distress and bankruptcy
5. Some subprime lenders, to hold off regulators, engaged in false accounting entries and fraudulently inflated assets and revenues.

D. Billion Dollar Management Fraud
   1. Some executives in large corporations take advantage of their position to engage in management frauds
      a. Typically involve falsifying financial information for their own financial benefit
      b. May engage in:
         i. False transactions and accounting entries
         ii. Bogus trades
         iii. Insider trading
         iv. Kickbacks
         v. Backdating of executive stock options
         vi. Misuse of misappropriation of company property
         vii. Retaining one's position within the company by manipulating accounts and concealing unacceptable performance

E. Criminalizing Corporate Enterprise Crime
   a. Government is willing to punish high profile corporate criminals with long prison sentences
   b. Both justice system and general public now consider corporate crime more serious offenses than common-law theft
   c. Some say government may be going overboard
   1. Corporate Crime Law Enforcement
      a. Enforcement in the hands of:
         i. Securities and Exchange Commission (SEC)
            a) Oversees the nation's capital markets
            b) Assigned task of
               1. Protecting investors
               2. Maintaining fair, orderly, efficient markets
               3. Facilitating capital information
            c) May decide to bring case in federal court or before an administrative law judge
            d) May ask judge to issue court order, called an injunction
               1. Prohibiting any further acts or practices that violate the law or Commission rules
               2. Can require audits and accounting for fraud
               3. Can bar or suspend individuals from serving as a corporate officer or director
               4. Can seek civil monetary penalties
               5. Return of illegal profits (disgorgement)
      b. Other federal agencies with investigative arms

    i. Environmental Protection Agency
    ii. U.S. Postal Service
  2. State Level Enforcement
    a. Number of states have created special task forces and prosecution teams
    b. State legislatures have passed new laws aimed at easing prosecution

III. GREEN CRIME
  1. Violations of existing criminal laws designed to protect people and the environment.
  2. Can include crimes against:
    a. Occupational health and safety
 A. Forms of Green Crime
  1. Illegal Logging
    a. Involves harvesting, processing, and transporting timber or wood products in violation of existing laws and treaties
     i. Taking trees in protected areas
     ii. Going over legally prescribed logging quotas
     iii. Processing logs without license
     iv. Exporting logs without paying export duties
    b. Estimated at least ½ of trees cut are done illegally
    c. Illegal logging:
     i. Exhausts forests
     ii. Destroys wildlife
     iii. Damages its habitats
  2. Illegal Fishing
    a. Illegal fishers operate outside their countries rules or boundaries
    b. Illegal fishing:
     i. Reduces the number of new adults that can replace those lost from fishing
     ii. Diminishes the ability of fish population to replenish themselves
  3. Illegal Dumping
    a. Rather than pay expensive processing fees, secretly dispose of hazardous wastes
    b. One of the largest problems is obsolete high-tech electronics – e-waste:
     i. Televisions
     ii. Computers and monitors
     iii. Laptops
     iv. VCRs
  4. Illegal Polluting
    a. Intentional or negligent discharge of toxic or contaminating substance into the biosystem
    b. Can involve the ground release of
     i. Kepone
     ii. Vinyl chloride
     iii. Mercury
     iv. PCBs

          v. Asbestos
     c. Air pollutants
     d. Water pollution
          i. Dumping of a substance that degrades or alters the quality of waters to an extent that is detrimental to their use by humans or by an animal or plant that is useful to humans
  B. Enforcing Environmental Laws
     1. U.S. Environmental laws enforced by the Environmental Protection Agency:
       a. *Clean Water Act* (1972)
          i. Establishes and maintains goals and standards for U.S. water quality and purity
       b. *Emergency Planning and Community Right-to-Know Act* (1986)
          i. Requires companies to disclose information about toxic chemicals they release into the air and water and dispose of on land
       c. *Endangered Species Act* (1973)
          i. Designed to protect and recover endangered and threatened species of fish, wildlife, and plants in the U.S. and beyond
       d. *Oil Pollution Act* (1990)
          i. Streamlines federal response to oil spills by requiring oil storage facilities and vessels to prepare spill-response plans and provide for their rapid implementation

IV.   CYBERCRIME
     1. Involves the theft and/or destruction of information, resources, or funds utilizing computers, networks, or Internet
     2. Cybercrime is challenging because:
       a. It is rapidly evolving with new schemes being created daily
       b. It is difficult to detect through traditional law enforcement channels
       c. Its control demands that agents of the justice system develop technical skills which match those of the perpetrators
     3. Three forms of cybercrime:
       a. Cyber theft
          i. Illegal copyright infringement
          ii. Using technology to commit traditional theft-based offenses
            a)   Larceny
            b)   Fraud
       b. Cyber vandalism
          i. Malicious attacks aimed at disrupting, defacing, and destroying technology
       c. Cyber war
          i. Acts aimed at undermining the social. economic, and political system of an enemy nation by destroying its electronic infrastructure and disrupting its economy
            a)   Cyber espionage
  A. Cyber theft: Cyber Crimes for Profit

    a. Technology revolution has opened worldwide novel methods for cyber theft

    b. Crimes range from unlawful distribution of computer software to Internet security fraud

    c. Cyberthieves conspire to use cyberspace to either distribute illegal goods and services or to defraud people for quick profits using some common methods:

1. Computer Fraud
   a. Not a unique offense but essentially a common law crime committed using contemporary technology
   b. Not all computer related crimes are common law, stolen property may be intangible. Crimes include:
      i. *Theft of information*
         a) Obtaining unauthorized information from a computer, including software
      ii. *The "Salami slice" fraud*
         a) Perpetrator skims small sums from the balances of a large number of accounts
      iii. *Software theft*
         a) Making copies of computer software

2. Internet Pornography
   a. Internet ideal venue for selling and distributing adult material
   b. Because of vast number of users, it is difficult to estimate the numbers
   c. Pornography web pages now number over one million containing 250 pages of erotic content
   d. Revenue comes from a number of sources:
      i. Paid subscriptions
      ii. Advertisements for other port sites
      iii. Fees for diverting web traffic
      iv. Sale of sex-related products
      v. Providing auxiliary services such as age verification

3. Denial of Service Attack
   a. Characterized as an attempt to extort money from internet service users by threatening to disable their system by using tactics such as flooding a computer network

4. Copyright Infringement
   a. Groups of individuals who download and sell copyrighted software in violation of its license
      i. This is called warez
   b. Some have been prosecuted using:
      i. Computer Fraud and Abuse Act
      ii. Digital Millennium Copyright Act

5. Internet Securities Fraud
   a. Using the internet to intentionally manipulate the securities marketplace for profit
   b. Three types are common today:

        i.   Market manipulation

          a)   An individual tries to control the price of a stock by interfering with the natural forces of supply and demand

          b)   Two types include:

             1. Pump and dump – Erroneous and deceptive information posted online to get unsuspecting investors to become interested and inflate the price

             2. Cyber smear – Reverse pump and dump. Spreading negative information about a certain stock to deflate the price

       ii. Fraudulent offerings of securities

          a)   False websites to fraudulently sell securities

          b)   Offerings are made attractive by utilizing false information such as assets, expected returns, and risks

       iii. Illegal touting

          a)   Individuals make security recommendations and fail to disclose they are being paid to disseminate their favorable information

6. Identity Theft

   a. Using the internet to steal someone's identity and/or impersonate a victim in order to conduct illicit transactions such as committing fraud using the victim's name and identity

   b. Some cases involve phishing

       i.   Illegally acquiring personal information, such as bank passwords and credit card numbers, by masquerading as a trustworthy person or business in what appears to be an official electronic communication, such as an email or an instant message

       ii. Comes from the process of fishing for financial information and passwords

7. Etailing Fraud

   a. Using the internet to illegally buy or sell merchandise on the net

8. Illegal Drug Distribution

   a. Hundreds of website advertising or offering controlled prescription drugs for sale

B. Cyber vandalism: Cyber Crime with Malicious Intent

   a. Motivation is for revenge and destruction, not necessarily greed or profit

   b. Ranges from sending destructive viruses and worms— motivated by malice:

       i.   Target computers and networks seeking revenge for some perceived wrong

       ii. Wish to exhibit superior technical prowess and superiority

      iii. Want to highlight vulnerability of computer security systems

      iv. Desire to spy on other's financial or personal information

       v. Destroy computer security because they believe network should be open to all

1. What Forms of Cyber Vandalism Currently Exist?

   a. Viruses and Worms:

       i.   One type of malicious software that disrupts existing programs and networks (malware)

    b. Trojan Horses
       i. Appears as a harmless program however, it normally contains illicit codes which can damage a system's operations
    c. Web Defacement
       i. A computer hacker intrudes on another person's web by inserting or substituting codes which exposes visitors to the site to misleading information
    d. Cyberstalking
       i. Use of Internet, e-mail, or other electronic communication devices to stalk another person
    e. Cyberbullying
       i. Willful and repeated harm inflicted through the medium of electronic text. Bullies can send harassing emails, instant messages, or use online bulletin boards
    f. Cyber War
       i. The premeditated, politically motivated attack against
         a) Information
         b) Computer systems
         c) Computer programs
         d) Data which result in violence against noncombatant targets by sub-national or clandestine agents
       ii. Terrorist organizations are now adapting IT into their arsenal
       iii. Cyber espionage
         a) Hacking secure computer networks at the enemy's most sensitive military bases, defense contractors, and aerospace companies in order to steal important data or to assess their defenses
         b) Infrastructure attacks can be aimed at:
           1. Water treatment plants
           2. Electric plants
           3. Dams
           4. Oil refineries
           5. Nuclear power plants
C. Controlling Cyber Crime
  1. Proliferation of cybercrimes has created the need for new laws and enforcement processes
  2. There are new legislative initiatives designed to limit or control cybercrime:
    a. Software Piracy
       i. Government has actively pursued charges against software pirates using the Computer Fraud and Abuse Act and the Digital Millennium Copyright Act
    b. Copyright Infringement
       i. U.S. Code provides penalties for illegal copyright offender of five years' incarceration and a fine of $250,000
    c. Identity Theft — Under the Identity Theft and Assumption Deterrence Act of 1998, it is a federal crime to:

        i. Knowingly transfer or use, without lawful authority, a means of identification of another person with intent to commit, or to aid or abet, any unlawful activity that constitutes a violation of federal law, or that constitutes a felony under any applicable state or local law

       ii. Investigated by FBI, Secret Service, U.S. Postal Service

     iii. In 2004, Identity Theft Penalty Enhancement Act increased existing penalties

         a)   Individuals committing identify fraud receive a mandatory sentence of five years for those engaged in crimes associated with terrorism:

            1. Aircraft destruction

            2. Airport violence

            3. Kidnapping top government officials

  d. Internet Pornography

        i. Child Online Protection Act:

         a)   Bans web postings of material deemed harmful to minors

  e. Computer Crimes

        i. Counterfeit Access Device and Computer Fraud and Abuse Law in 1984

         a)   Protected classified defense and foreign relations information, financial institution, consumer reporting agency files, and access to computers operated for the government

         b)   Supplemented by 1996 National Information Infrastructure Protection Act

D. Enforcing Cyber Laws

  1. Interagency Telemarketing and Internet Fraud Working Group brings together representatives of numerous U.S. Attorney's offices, the FBI, the Secret Service, the Postal Inspection Service, the Federal Trade Commission, the Securities and Exchange Commission, and other law enforcement and regulatory agencies to share information about trends and patterns in Internet Fraud Schemes

V.   TRANSNATIONAL CRIME

  1. Globalization refers to the process of creating transnational markets and political and legal systems and has shifted the focus of crime from a local to a world perspective

    a. Began when large companies decided to establish themselves in foreign markets by adapting their products or services to the local culture

    b. Can improve standard of living but also be a device for criminal cartels to avoid prosecution and regulation

A. Types of Transnational Crimes

    a. Distribution of pornography

    b. Cyber crime

    c. Human trafficking

    d. Migrant smuggling

    e. Drug smuggling

    f. Arms dealing

g. Maritime piracy
h. Trafficking in environmental resources
i. Counterfeit goods
1. Profits from transnational criminal enterprise can be immense
   a. United Nations estimates immigrant smugglers earn about seven billion per year smuggling an estimated 3 million people
   b. There are between 170-250 million drug users in the world
      i. Illegal drug trade brings in about $350 billion per year
B. Transnational Crime Groups
   1. Asian Gangs
      a. Yakuza
         i. Japanese criminal group. Often involved in multinational criminal activities, including human trafficking, gambling, prostitution, and undermining licit businesses
      b. Fuk Ching
         i. Chinese organized criminal group in the United States. They have been involved in smuggling, street violence, and human trafficking
      c. Triads
         i. Underground criminal societies based in Hong Kong. They control secret markets and bus routes and are often involved in money laundering and drug trafficking
      d. Heijin
         i. Taiwanese gangsters who are often executives in large corporations. They are often involved in white collar crimes, such as illegal stock trading and bribery, and sometimes run for public office
      e. Jao Pho
         i. Organized crime group in Thailand. They are often involved in illegal political and business activity.
      f. Red Wa
         i. Gangsters from Thailand. They are involved in manufacturing and trafficking methamphetamine.
   2. Russian Transnational Crime Groups
      a. Make extensive use of the state governmental apparatus to protect and promote illegal activities
      b. Most Russian businesses must operate with the protection of a krysha (roof)
         i. Protection provided by police or security officials employed outside their official capacities
      c. In the U.S., Russian criminal groups are extensively engaged in a broad array of frauds and scams:
         i. Health care fraud
         ii. Insurance scams
         iii. Stock frauds
         iv. Antiquities swindles
         v. Forgery
         vi. Fuel tax evasion schemes

    d. Russians are believed to be the main purveyors of credit card fraud in the U.S.

  3. Mexican Drug Cartels

    a. Have become large scale suppliers of narcotics, marijuana, and methamphetamines to the U.S.

      i. Ninety percent of cocaine entering the U.S. transits Mexico

    b. Leading wholesale launderers of drug money from the U.S.

C. Controlling Transnational Crime

  1. One approach to controlling transnational crime is to form international working groups:

    a. Eurasian Organized Crime Working Group

      i. Established in 1994

      ii. Meets to discuss and jointly address the transnational aspects of Eurasian organized crime

      iii. Member countries are:

        a) Canada

        b) Great Britain

        c) Germany

        d) France

        e) Italy

        f) Japan

        g) U.S.

        h) Russia

    b. Central European Working Group

      i. Brought together FBI and Central European law enforcement agencies

        a) To discuss cooperative investigative matters

        b) Works on practical interaction to

          1. Establish lines of communication

          2. Working relationships

          3. Develop strategies and tactics to address transnational organized crime matters

          4. Identify potential common targets

    c. Southeast European Cooperative Initiative

      i. Intended to coordinate police and customs regional actions for preventing and combating trans-border crime

        a) Headquartered in Bucharest, Romania

        b) 12 member countries

        c) Has task forces for countering trans-border crime:

          1. Trafficking of people, drugs, and cars

          2. Smuggling

          3. Financial crimes

          4. Terrorism

  2. Anti Organized Crime Laws

    a. Congress has passed a number of laws which have made it easier for agencies to bring transnational gangs to justice

      i. Travel Act

        a)   Prohibits travel in interstate commerce or use of interstate facilities with the intent to promote, manage, establish, carry on, of facilitate unlawful activity

        b)   Prohibits the actual or attempted involvement in these activities

    b. 1970, Racketeer Influenced and Corrupt Organization Act (RICO)

      i. Designed to limit patterns of organized criminal activity by prohibiting involvement in acts intended to

        a)   Derive income from racketeering or the unlawful collection of debts and use or investment of such income

        b)   Acquire through racketeering an interest in or control over any enterprise engaged in interstate or foreign commerce

        c)   Conduct business through a pattern of racketeering

        d)   Conspire to use racketeering as a means of making income, collecting loans, or conducting business

      ii. An individual convicted under RICO is subject to 20 years in prison and a $25,000 fine

D. Why is it so difficult to Eradicate Global Crime?

    1. Gangs are ready to use violence and well equipped to carry out threats

    2. Drug trade is an important source of foreign revenue

    3. War and terrorism also make gang control strategies problematic

CHAPTER SUMMARY

The crimes of the e rich powerful have the most significant impact on society. Experts place the total monetary value in the hundreds of billions of dollars, far outstripping the expense of any other type of crime. Large-scale investment growth, has led to significant growth in the amount of fraud and misconduct seen in on Wall Street. Investment firms have engaged in deceptive securities sales that have cost investors billions. A Ponzi scheme is an investment fraud that involves the payment of purported returns to existing investors from funds contributed by new investors. Fraudsters focus on attracting new money to make promised payments to earlier-stage investors and to use for personal expenses, instead of engaging in any legitimate investment activity. Borrowers have provided false information to the mortgage broker and/or lender, enabling them to get loans for which they were not qualified. Those involved in mortgage lending, got involved in criminal fraud schemes including false accounting entries and fraudulently inflated assets and revenues.

Green crimes involve the environment. They include such activities as illegal fishing, pollution, dumping, forestry and the like. In some instances, environmental criminals conduct activities overseas to avoid legal controls and enforcement.

Cyber crime typically involves the theft and/or destruction of information, resources, or funds via computers, computer networks, and the Internet. Cyber theft is the use of computer networks for criminal profits. Illegal copyright infringement, identity theft, and Internet securities fraud are examples of cyber theft. Cyber vandalism, or technological destruction, involves malicious attacks aimed at disrupting, defacing, and destroying technology. Cyberwar consists of politically motivated attacks designed to compromise the electronic infrastructure of the enemy and to disrupt its economy

Numerous organizations have been set up to provide training and support for law enforcement agents. In addition, new federal and state laws have been enacted to help discourage particular types of high-tech crimes. In the future, technological prowess may make it possible to identify cyber criminals and bring them to justice before they can carry out their attacks. Globalization has shifted the focus of crime from a local to a world perspective. With money and power to spare, criminal enterprise groups can recruit new members, bribe government officials, and even fund private armies.

Transnational organized crime involves ongoing international criminal enterprise groups whose purpose is personal economic gain through illegitimate means. Transnational gangs are involved in money laundering; human smuggling; cyber crime; and trafficking of humans, drugs, weapons, body parts, or nuclear material. There is also a troubling overseas trade in prostitution. Transnational gangs export women from third world nations for the purposes of prostitution. Some may be kidnapped or forced into prostitution against their will through violence and threats. Eastern gangs, especially the Russian Mob, trace their origin to countries spanning the Baltics, the Balkans, Central/Eastern Europe, Russia, the Caucacus, and Central Asia. Russian organized crime is active in Europe, Africa, Asia, and North and South America. Asian gangs include the Yakuza Japanese criminal group. Often involved in multinational criminal activities, including human trafficking, gambling, prostitution, and undermining licit businesses. Chinese groups are also involved in human trafficking—bringing large numbers of Chinese migrants to North America and essentially enslaving them for profit. There are a number of powerful Mexican drug cartels that now dominate the cross boarder drug trade into the United States

Efforts to combat transnational organized crime is typically in the hands of Federal agencies. One approach is for them to form international working groups to collect intelligence, share information, and plot unified strategies among member nations. U.S. law enforcement agencies have cooperated in cross boarder operations to eradicate gang activity.

DISCUSSION QUESTIONS

1. Should people who illegally download movies or music be prosecuted for theft?
2. How can internet pornography be controlled considering that a great deal of adult content is available on foreign websites?
3. Considering the threat of transnational drug trafficking, should drugs be legalized and controlled by the government?
4. Should the Internet be more closely monitored and controlled to prevent the threat of cyberwar?
5. Is there any point to placing economic sanctions on billion dollar corporations? Should corporate executives be put in prison? Put another way, what is the purpose of incarcerating someone like 72 year old Bernard Madoff? Is he really a threat to society?

MEDIA TOOLS

For an overview of the efforts by the International community to combat transnational crimes visit the United Nations Office on Drugs and Crime. At this site you can view such topics as human trafficking and migrant smuggling, money laundering, and organized crime. The site is available at: http://www.unodc.org

For an excellent overview of Ponzi schemes and enforcement actions, including an overview of the Bernard Madoff case, visit the United States Security and Exchange Commission's Frequently asked Questions on Ponzi schemes including a video about Ponzi schemes produced by the FBI. The site can be found at: http://www.sec.gov/answers/ponzi.htm

The Federal Bureau of Investigation provides a robust listing of cyber crime related material including an overview of cyber threats and scams, how to protect yourself, initiatives, and information regarding cases that were solved by the FBI. Visit the FBIs site on Cyber Crime at: http://www.fbi.gov/about-us/investigate/cyber/cyber

Carnegie Mellon University is leading the education community in the investigation of cyber crimes and related attacks. With the site "MySecureCyberspace" Carnegie Mellon provides a resource to empower individuals to secure their part of the cyber space. Visit the Carnegie Mellon University MySecureCyberspace website at: https://www.mysecurecyberspace.com

The FBI just released the 2010 Mortgage Fraud Report. According to the FBI, "The purpose of this study is to provide insight into the breadth and depth of mortgage fraud crimes perpetrated against the United States and its citizens during 2010." Take a look at the report to understand the breadth and depth of mortgage fraud during 2010. The report can be found at: http://www.fbi.gov/stats-services/publications/mortgage-fraud-2010/2010-mortgage-fraud-report

PRACTICE TEST BANK

MULTIPLE CHOICE

1. One new trend, responsible for multi-billion losses and frauds, facing the justice system today is multi-billion dollar
    a. transnational crime.
    b. corporate enterprise crime.
    c. white-collar crime.
    d. green crime.

2. Bernard Madoff pled guilty to crimes involving
    a. investment fraud schemes.
    b. capital murder.
    c. kidnapping.
    d. counterfeiting.

3. Which term best describes risky loans in which lenders assumed real estate values would always increase?
    a. Modified loans
    b. Government backed loans
    c. Subprime loans
    d. Transitional loans

4. The Securities and Exchange Commission has been given the responsibility for overseeing the nation's
    a. real estate.
    b. capital markets.
    c. hedge fund markets.
    d. stock markets.

5. The Ponzi scheme was named after Charles Ponzi committed
    a. crimes involving a postage speculation scheme.
    b. crimes involving welfare fraud.
    c. crimes involving wall street stock trades.
    d. crimes involving counterfeit food stamps.

6. Once subprime loans have been issued, the vendors typically bundle them into large pools and sell them as
    a. deeds.
    b. securities.
    c. bonds.
    d. certificates.

7. Bernie Madoff's criminal activity can best be described as an elaborate
   a.   fraud scheme.
   b.   pigeon scheme.
   c.   Ponzi Scheme.
   d.   RICO Scheme.

8. What type of scheme tends to collapse when it becomes difficult to attract new investors?
   a.   Security Fraud
   b.   Pigeon Fraud
   c.   Pyramid Scheme
   d.   Ponzi Scheme

9. The Securities and Exchange Commission can seek the return of illegal profits or
   a.   incarceration.
   b.   licensing revocation.
   c.   civil monetary penalties.
   d.   criminal penalties.

10. As a result of the mortgage crisis the state of Florida has created
   a.   a mortgage ban.
   b.   a mortgage moratorium.
   c.   mortgage fraud task force.
   d.   mortgage deregulation.

11. The scale of illegal logging is difficult to estimated but it is believed that more than half of all logging activities involve the most vulnerable forest regions in
   a.   Southeast Asia.
   b.   Central Africa.
   c.   South America.
   d.   All of the above

12. Illegal fishing
   a.   is a billion dollar crime.
   b.   involves large scale commercial ships.
   c.   impacts fish species populations.
   d.   All of the above

13. Which term best describes the intentional or negligent discharge of toxic or contaminating substances into the bio-system that is known to have an adverse effect on the natural environment or life?
   a.   Green crime
   b.   Illegal polluting
   c.   Bio-crime
   d.   Environmental crime

14. Which of the following are considered to be green crimes?
    a. Illegal logging
    b. Illegal fishing
    c. Illegal dumping
    d. All of the above

15. Which fraud involves small amounts of money being skimmed from balances of large number of to avoid or bypass internal controls?
    a. Salami slice fraud
    b. Spoke fraud
    c. Particle fraud
    d. Pizza slice fraud

16. A computer virus is a type of
    a. network.
    b. malware.
    c. encryption.
    d. identity theft.

17. Congress has treated computer-related crimes as distinct federal offenses since the passage of which act?
    a. Counterfeit Access Device and Computer Abuse Law in 1984
    b. Counterfeit Identity Theft Prevention Law in 1984
    c. Congressional Computer Abuse Law in 1984
    d. Combating Fraud and Computer Abuse Law in 1984

18. The use of cyber space to either distribute illegal goods and services or defraud people for quick profits is known as
    a. cyber vandalism.
    b. cyber theft.
    c. cyber fraud.
    d. cyber war.

19. The use of cyber space for revenge, destruction, or to achieve malicious ends is known as
    a. cyber vandalism.
    b. cyber theft.
    c. cyber fraud.
    d. cyber war.

20. The use of cyber space where an enemy disrupts the intersection where the virtual electronic reality of computers meets the physical world is known as
    a. cyber vandalism.
    b. cyber theft.
    c. cyber fraud.
    d. cyber war.

21. Illegally acquiring personal information by masquerading as a trustworthy business or person in what appears to be an official electronic communication, such as an email, is known as
    a.   cyber bullying.
    b.   cyber theft.
    c.   phishing.
    d.   security fraud.

22. Which term best describes the process of creating transnational markets and political and legal systems where the focus of crime has shifted from local to global?
    a.   Phishing
    b.   Capital markets
    c.   Consumerism
    d.   Globalization

23. Globalization has reduced the
    a.   overall cost of crime.
    b.   risk of apprehension and punishment.
    c.   amount of cross border movement.
    d.   focus on transnational crime.

24. The new global economy is challenging for law enforcement agents because it
    a.   expands the reach of criminal organizations.
    b.   creates new opportunities for criminal conspiracies.
    c.   makes it easier for criminal organizations to avoid prosecution.
    d.   All of the above

25. Transnational crime groups have exploited a new freedom to travel to regions where
    a.   laundering money is easier.
    b.   extradition is difficult or impossible.
    c.   bank secrecy is lawful.
    d.   All of the above

26. Women primarily from Southeast Asia and Eastern Europe are lured by the promise of good jobs and often find themselves forced into brothels or
    a.   labor camps.
    b.   sexual exploitation.
    c.   slavery.
    d.   All of the above

27. Trafficking gangs are primarily located in Eastern European area of
    a.   France.
    b.   Spain.
    c.   Russia.
    d.   Germany.

28. In the United States, Russian criminal groups are engaged heavily in
    a.   drug trafficking.
    b.   slave trading.
    c.   fraud type schemes.
    d.   weapon sales and trading.

29. In the United States, efforts to combat transnational organized crime is typically in the hands of
    a.   local law enforcement agencies.
    b.   state law enforcement agencies.
    c.   federal law enforcement agencies.
    d.   Interpol.

30. The Racketeer Influenced and Corrupt Organization Act (RICO) is part of
    a.   USA Patriot Act of 2001
    b.   Organized Crime Control Act of 1970
    c.   Southwest Cooperative Crime Control Act of 1974
    d.   Federal Crime Control Act of 1996

TRUE/FALSE

1.   T   F   The technological revolution has broadened the scope of crime and increased the demands of the criminal justice system.

2.   T   F   Cyber crimes include copyright infringement, computer fraud, internet pornography and denial-of-service attacks.

3.   T   F   The creation of global capital markets has eliminated opportunities for business to access legitimate capital for investors to diversify their portfolios.

4.   T   F   Cyber vandalism schemes range from illegally copying material under copyright protection to larceny and fraud.

5.   T   F   The major enforcement arm against environmental crimes is the Federal Bureau of Investigation.

6.   T   F   Illegal fishing and illegal polluting are examples of green crime.

7.   T   F   Mortgage fraud involved lenders, mortgage brokers, appraisers, underwriters, real estate agents and land developers.

8.   T   F   The Clean Water Act and the Endangered Species Act are examples of laws to fight green crimes.

9. T   F   The globalization of crime involves only the distribution of pornography.

10. T   F   Globally, Russian criminal groups are involved in a range of crimes including drug trafficking and arms trading

11. T   F   The Eurasian Organized crime group was disbanded in 1994 after failing to successfully prosecute its transnational crime groups in Europe.

12. T   F   The Travel Act prohibits travel in interstate commerce or use of interstate facilities with the intent to promote unlawful activity.

13. T   F   Because many "porn" sites are located in foreign lands enforcement has proven difficult.

14. T   F   One mechanism to combat transnational crime syndicates is to form international groups who share a unified purpose and collect and share intelligence information.

15. T   F   An individual convicted under the RICO Act is subject to 5 years in prison and a $25,000 fine.

FILL-IN-THE-BLANK

1. A _____ scheme is an investment fraud that involves the payment of purported returns to existing investors from funds contributed by new investors.

2. Some _____ lenders engaged in false accounting entries and inflated assets and revenues.

3. Management fraud involves _____ in large corporations who take advantage of their position to commitment large scale financial frauds.

4. Executives in the _____ Company (an oil and gas trading company) engaged in massive fraud that caused the company to go bankrupt.

5. A number of states have started creating specialty _____ forces and prosecution teams to crack down on fraudulent schemes and bring perpetrators to justice.

6. Criminal environmental pollution is defined as intentional or negligent discharge of a toxic or contaminating substance into the bio-system that is known to have an adverse effect on the _____ or life.

7. Cyber stalking is the use of the _____, email or other communications devices to stalk another person.

8. Extorting money from an Internet service user by threatening to prevent the user from having access to the services is known as a _____ attack.

9. Stock market manipulation occurs when an individual tries to control the price of a _____ _____ by interfering with the natural forces of supply and demand.

10. The unauthorized obtaining of information from a computer is also commonly called ____ _____.

11. One reason that it is so tough to for law enforcement to combat the drug cartels is that they employ _____ gangs to protect them and eradicate enemies.

12. The _____ Copyright Act makes it a crime to circumvent antipiracy measures built into most commercial software.

13. Global trafficking gangs use force, fraud, or _____ to exploit a person for profit.

14. Traditional slavery, _____ labor and holding people are all forms of labor exploitation human trafficking.

15. The Central _____ Working Group is part of a project that brings together the FBI and Central European law enforcement agencies to discuss cooperative investigations.

ESSAY

1. Describe a Ponzi scheme.

2. This chapter presented four forms of green crime, identify and explain two.

3. Describe the various forms of cybercrime.

4. As outlined in this chapter, identify and describe the three most important transnational crime groups. Provide examples of their activity.

5. Explain how law enforcement is taking on transnational criminal syndicates. Identify and describe one international working group.

CHAPTER 14 ANSWER KEY

Multiple Choice

1. b [p. 332, LO1]   2. a [p. 332, LO1/2]   3. c [p. 333, LO3]   4. b [p. 335, LO3]   5. a [p. 333, LO2]

6. b [p. 334, LO3]   7. c [p. 332, LO2]   8. d [p. 333, LO2]   9. c [p. 335, LO6]   10. c [p. 335, LO3]

11. d [p. 337, LO4]   12. d [p. 337, LO4]   13. d [p. 338, LO4]   14. d [p. 337, LO4]   15. a [p. 340, LO5]

16. b [p. 342, LO5]   17. a [p. 345, LO6]   18. b [p. 340, LO5]   19. a [p. 340, LO5]   20. d [p. 340, LO5]

21. c [p. 342, LO5]   22. d [p. 346, LO6]   23. b [p. 346, LO7]   24. d [p. 346, LO7]   25. d [p. 346, LO8]

26. d [p. 348, LO9]   27. c [p. 348, LO9]   28. c [p. 349, LO8]   29. c [p. 349, LO10]   30. b [p. 350, LO10]

True/False

1. T [p. 331, LO1]   2. T [p. 339, LO5]   3. F [p. 332, LO1]   4. F [p. 339, LO5]   5. F [p. 339, LO4]

6. T [p. 337, LO4]   7. T [p. 334, LO3]   8. T [p. 339, LO4]   9. F [p. 346, LO8]   10. T [p. 348, LO9]

11. F [p. 349, LO10]   12. T [p. 350, LO10]   13. T [p. 341, LO5]   14. T [p. 349, LO10]   15. F [p. 350, LO9]

Fill-in-the-Blank

1. Ponzi [p. 333, LO2]   2. subprime [p. 334, LO3]   3. executives [p. 334, LO2]

4. Enron [p. 334, LO1/2]   5. task [p. 335, LO1/3]   6. environment [p. 338, LO4]

7. Internet [p. 343, LO5]   8. denial-of-service [p. 341, LO5]   9. stock [p. 341, LO5]

10. hacking [p. 340, LO5]   11. enforcer [p. 350, LO10]   12. Digital Millennium [p. 344, LO6]

13. coercion [p. 348, LO8]   14. Forced [p. 348, LO8]   15. European [p. 349, LO10]

Essay

1.   **Describe a Ponzi scheme.**

A Ponzi scheme is an investment fraud that involves the payment of purported returns to existing investors from funds contributed by new investors. Ponzi scheme organizers often solicit new investors by promising to invest funds in opportunities claimed to generate high returns with little or no risk. In many Ponzi schemes, the fraudsters focus on attracting new money to make promised payments to earlier-stage investors and to use for personal expenses, instead of engaging in any legitimate investment activity. With little or no legitimate earnings, the schemes require a consistent flow of money from new investors to continue. Ponzi schemes tend to collapse when it becomes difficult to recruit new investors or when a large number of investors ask to cash out.

Why are they called "Ponzi Schemes?" The term comes from one Charles Ponzi, who duped thousands of New England residents into investing in a postage stamp speculation scheme back in the 1920s. At a time when the annual interest rate for bank accounts was five percent, Ponzi promised investors that he could provide a 50% return in just 90 days. Ponzi initially bought a small number of international mail coupons in support of his scheme, but quickly switched to using incoming funds to pay off earlier investors.

[p. 333, LO2]

2.   This chapter presented four forms of green crime, identify and explain two.

Illegal Logging Illegal logging involves harvesting, processing, and transporting timber or wood products in violation of existing laws and treaties. It is a universal phenomenon, occurring in major timber-producing countries, especially in the third-world where enforcement is lax. Logging violations include taking trees in protected areas such as national parks, going over legally prescribed logging quotas, processing logs without acquiring licenses, and exporting logs without paying export duties. By sidestepping the law, loggers can create greater profits than those generated through legal methods. As a result, in five of the top ten most-forested countries on the planet, it is estimated that at least half of the trees cut are done so illegally. The situation is serious because illegal logging can have severe environmental and social impact: Illegal logging exhausts forests, destroys wildlife, and damages its habitats. It causes ruinous damage to the forests, including deforestation and forest degradation worldwide. The destruction of forest cover can cause flash floods and landslides that have killed thousands of people.

Illegal Fishing Unlicensed and illegal fishing practices is another billion-dollar green crime. It can take on many forms and involve highly different parties, ranging from huge factory ships operating on the high seas that catch thousands of tons of fish on each voyage, to smaller, locally operating ships that confine themselves to national waters. Illegal fishing occurs when these ships sign on to their home nation's rules but then choose to ignore their scope and boundary, or operate in a country's waters without permission or on the high seas without a flag. Because catches remain clandestine and are not reported, their illegal fishing can have a detrimental effect on species because government regulators have no idea how many are being caught. As a result, stocks become depleted and species endangered. Because of the relatively long time it takes fish to mature, illegal fishing means that many are caught before they have a chance to reproduce. Illegal fishing reduces the number of new adults that can replace those lost from fishing, and the ability of populations to replenish themselves is quickly lost.

Illegal Dumping Some green-collar criminals want to skirt local, state, and federal restrictions on dumping dangerous substances in the environment. Rather than pay expensive processing fees, they may secretly dispose of hazardous wastes in illegal dump sites. Illegally dumped wastes can either be hazardous or nonhazardous materials that are discarded in an effort to avoid either disposal fees or the time and effort required for proper disposal. Materials dumped ranged from used motor oil to waste from construction sites. One of the largest and fastest growing problems is the disposal of 7 million tons of obsolete high-tech electronics, called e-waste, such as televisions, computers and computer monitors, laptops, VCRs, and so on. A considerable amount of e-waste is now being sent abroad to developing nations for recycling, often in violation of international laws restricting such commerce. All too often, the material overwhelms recycling plants and is instead dumped in local villages near people and water sources.

Illegal Polluting Criminal environmental pollution is defined as the intentional or negligent discharge of a toxic or contaminating substance into the biosystem that is known to have an adverse effect on the natural environment or life. Individuals and companies may commit this crime to save processing and dumping fees, thereby adding to profits. Illegal pollution schemes may involve the ground release of toxic chemicals such as kepone, vinyl chloride, mercury, PCBs, and asbestos. Illegal and/or controlled air pollutants include hydrochlorofluorocarbons (HCFCs), aerosols, asbestos, carbon monoxide, chlorofluorocarbons (CFCs), criteria air pollutants, lead, mercury, methane, nitrogen oxides (NOx), radon, refrigerants, and sulfur oxides (SO2). Water pollution is defined as the dumping of a substance that degrades or alters the quality of the waters to an extent that is detrimental to their use by humans or by an animal or a plant that is useful to humans. This includes the disposal into rivers, lakes, and streams of toxic chemicals.

[pp. 337-338, LO4]

3.   Describe the various forms of cybercrime.

Cyber crime typically involves the theft and/or destruction of information, resources, or funds via computer networks, and/or the Internet. This relatively new category of crimes presents a compelling challenge for the justice system and the law enforcement community because (a) it is rapidly evolving, with new schemes being created daily, (b) it is difficult to detect through traditional law enforcement channels, and (c) to control it, agents of the justice system must develop technical skills that match those of the perpetrators. It is even possible that the recent decline in crime is actually a result of cyber crime replacing traditional street crime. Instead of robbing a bank at gun point, a new group of contemporary thieves find it easier to hack into accounts and transfer funds to offshore banks. Instead of shoplifting from a bricks-and-mortar store, the contemporary cyber thief devises clever schemes to steal from etailers.

There are actually three forms of cyber crime. Some cyber criminals use modern technology to accumulate goods and services. Cyber theft schemes range from illegally copying material under copyright protection to using technology to commit traditional theft-based offenses such as larceny and fraud. Other cyber criminals are motivated less by profit and more by the urge to commit cyber vandalism, or technological destruction. They aim their malicious attacks at disrupting, defacing, and destroying technology they find offensive. Finally, cyber war consists of acts aimed at undermining the social, economic, and political system of an enemy nation by destroying its electronic infrastructure and disrupting its economy. This can range from stealing secrets from foreign nations (cyber espionage) to destroying an enemy's Web-based infrastructure.

[pp. 339-344, LO5]

4.   As outlined in this chapter, identify and describe the three most important transnational crime groups. Provide examples of their activity.

Asian Gangs Asian groups are also involved in human trafficking—bringing and enslaving large numbers of Chinese migrants to North America. Among the best known groups are also included:

- **Yakuza** Japanese criminal group. Often involved in multinational criminal activities, including human trafficking, gambling, prostitution, and undermining licit businesses.
- **Fuk Ching** Chinese organized criminal group in the United States. They have been involved in smuggling, street violence, and human trafficking.
- **Triads** Underground criminal societies based in Hong Kong. They control secret markets and bus routes and are often involved in money laundering and drug trafficking.
- **Heijin** Taiwanese gangsters who are often executives in large corporations. They are often involved in white collar crimes, such as illegal stock trading and bribery, and sometimes run for public office.

- **Jao Pho** Organized crime group in Thailand. They are often involved in illegal political and business activity.
- **Red Wa** Gangsters from Thailand. They are involved in manufacturing and trafficking methamphetamine.

Russian Transnational Crime Groups Since the collapse of the Soviet Union in 1991, criminal organizations in Russia and other former Soviet republics such as the Ukraine have engaged in a variety of crimes: drugs and arms trafficking, stolen automobiles, trafficking in women and children, and money laundering. No area of the world seems immune to this menace, especially not the United States. America is the land of opportunity for unloading criminal goods and laundering dirty money.

Russian criminals make extensive use of the state governmental apparatus to protect and promote their criminal activities. For example, most businesses in Russia—legal, quasi-legal, and illegal—must operate with the protection of a *krysha* (roof). The protection is often provided by police or security officials employed outside their "official" capacities for this purpose. In other cases, officials are "silent partners" in criminal enterprises that they, in turn, protect. The criminalization of the privatization process has resulted in the massive use of state funds for criminal gain. Valuable properties are purchased through insider deals for much less than their true value and then resold for lucrative profits. Criminals have been able to directly influence the state's domestic and foreign policy to promote the interests of organized crime, either by attaining public office themselves or by buying public officials.

In the United States, Russian criminal groups are extensively engaged in a broad array of frauds and scams, including health care fraud, insurance scams, stock frauds, antiquities swindles, forgery, and fuel tax evasion schemes. Russians are believed to be the main purveyors of credit card fraud in the United States. Legitimate businesses, such as the movie business and textile industry, have become targets of criminals from the former Soviet Union, and they are often used for money laundering and extortion.

Mexican Drug Cartels Mexican drug cartels have become large scale suppliers of narcotics, marijuana and methamphetamines to in the United and Mexico have become a drug producing and transit country. In additions, an estimated 90% of cocaine entering the United States transits Mexico. Mexican drug gangs routinely use violence and fighting for control of the border regions has affected U.S. citizens: more than 60 Americans have been kidnapped and Mexican drug cartel members have threatened to kill U.S. journalists covering drug violence in the border region. Mexican drug cartels now dominate the wholesale illicit drug market in the United States. As a result Mexican cartels are the leading wholesale launderers of drug money from the United States. Mexican and Colombian trafficking organizations annually smuggle an estimated 25 billion in drug proceeds into Mexico for laundering.

[pp. 347-349, LO9]

5. **Explain how law enforcement is taking on transnational criminal syndicates. Identify and describe one international working group.**

Efforts to combat transnational organized crime are typically in the hands of Federal agencies. One approach is to form international working groups to collect intelligence, share information, and plot unified strategies among member nations. The FBI belongs to several international working groups aimed at combating transnational gangs in various parts of the world. For example, to combat the influence and reach of Eurasian Organized Crime the FBI is involved in the following groups and activities:

- **Eurasian Organized Crime Working Group**
  Established in 1994, it meets to discuss and jointly address the transnational aspects of Eurasian organized crime that impact member countries and the international community in general. The member countries are Canada, Great Britain, Germany, France, Italy, Japan, the U.S., and Russia.

- **Central European Working Group**

  This group is part of a project that brings together the FBI and Central European law enforcement agencies to discuss cooperative investigative matters covering the broad spectrum of Eurasian organized crime. A principal concern is the growing presence of Russian and other Eurasian organized criminals in Central Europe and the U.S. The initiative works on practical interaction between the participating agencies to establish lines of communication and working relationships, to develop strategies and tactics to address transnational organized crime matters impacting the region, and to identify potential common targets.

- **Southeast European Cooperative Initiative**

  The Southeast European Cooperative Initiative is an international organization intended to coordinate police and customs regional actions for preventing and combating trans-border crime. It is headquartered in Bucharest, Romania, and has 12 fully participating member countries. The U.S. has been one of 14 countries with observer status since 1998. The initiative's center serves as a clearing house for information and intelligence sharing, allowing the quick exchange of information in a professional and trustworthy environment. The initiative also supports specialized task forces for countering trans-border crime such as the trafficking of people, drugs, and cars; smuggling; financial crimes; terrorism; and other serious trans-border crimes.

- **Anti Organized Crime Laws.** Congress has passed a number of laws which have made it easier for agencies to bring transnational gangs to justice. One of the first measures aimed directly at organized crime was the Interstate and Foreign Travel or Transportation in Aid of Racketeering Enterprises Act (Travel Act). The Travel Act prohibits travel in interstate commerce or use of interstate facilities with the intent to promote, manage, establish, carry on, or facilitate an unlawful activity; it also prohibits the actual or attempted engagement in these activities. In 1970, Congress passed the Organized Crime Control Act. Title IX of the act, probably its most effective measure, is the Racketeer Influenced and Corrupt Organization Act (RICO). RICO did not create new categories of crimes but rather new categories of offenses in racketeering activity, which it defined as involvement in two or more acts prohibited by 24 existing federal and 8 state statutes. The offenses listed in RICO include state-defined crimes, such as murder, kidnapping, gambling, arson, robbery, bribery, extortion, and narcotic violations; and federally defined crimes, such as bribery, counterfeiting, transmission of gambling information, prostitution, and mail fraud. RICO is designed to limit patterns of organized criminal activity by prohibiting involvement in acts intended to do the following:

  - Derive income from racketeering or the unlawful collection of debts and use or investment of such income
  - Acquire through racketeering an interest in or control over any enterprise engaged in interstate or foreign commerce
  - Conduct business through a pattern of racketeering
  - Conspire to use racketeering as a means of making income, collecting loans, or conducting business

An individual convicted under RICO is subject to 20 years in prison and a $25,000 fine. Additionally, the accused must forfeit to the U.S. government any interest in a business in violation of RICO.

[pp. 349-350, LO10]

CPSIA information can be obtained
at www.ICGtesting.com
Printed in the USA
FFOW030631200213
900FF